T0301315

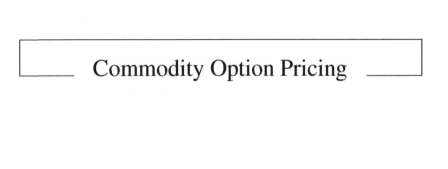

Commodity Option Pricing

For other titles in the Wiley Finance series
please see www.wiley.com/finance

Commodity Option Pricing

A Practitioner's Guide

Iain J. Clark

Library of Congress Cataloging-in-Publication Data

Clark, Iain J.
  Commodity option pricing : a practitioners guide / Iain J. Clark.
    pages cm
  Includes bibliographical references and index.
  ISBN 978-1-119-94451-5 (cloth)
 1. Commodity options.   2. Options (Finance)–Prices.   I. Clark, Iain J.   II. Title.
  HG6046.C5736 2014
  332.63′28–dc23

                                                            2013051276

A catalogue record for this book is available from the British Library.

ISBN 978-1-119-94451-5 (hbk) ISBN 978-1-444-36240-4 (ebk)
ISBN 978-1-444-36241-1 (ebk) ISBN 978-1-118-87178-2 (ebk)

Cover images reproduced by permission of Shutterstock.com

Set in 11/13pt Times by Aptara Inc., New Delhi, India
Printed in Great Britain by TJ International Ltd, Padstow, Cornwall, UK

For Elizabeth Clark (born July 2013).

Who made the completion of this book a challenge – in the nicest possible way.

Contents

Acknowledgements

Firstly, I would like to thank my wife yet again for her incredible patience and fortitude during the completion of this work, which somehow coincided with the happy arrival of our daughter Elizabeth; my efforts to finish the book in nine months were not nearly so successful. Elizabeth – Section 8.5.5 is for you. Grateful thanks are certainly due to my literary agent Isabel White for helping me navigate my latest project from conception through to completion. I am grateful to Betty, my mother-in-law, for visiting and taking good care of my wife, child and myself for the final few weeks.

I am indebted to many friends and colleagues for their encouragement and assistance in the preparation of this book. In no particular order, I should like to thank Lars Schouw, Brian Shydlo (from pnl-explained.com), Will Smith, Nina Lange, Peter Leoni, Paul Rothnie, Joe Chen, Valery Kholodnyi, Nic Narti, Arvind Hariharan, Marcelo Labre and John Crosby. I should also like to thank Laura Ballotta and Gianluca Fusai from Cass Business School, Paul Bilokon and Saeed Amen from Thalesians (www.thalesians.com), and Lorenz Schneider from EMLYON for giving me the opportunity to road-test the material on a willing audience. Many thanks are due to Bloomberg for generously providing access to their services and permitting the reproduction of various materials, similar thanks are due to the EIA. I should also like to say thank you to my father John Clark for helping me out (and letting me know when I was lapsing into jargon) with the Glossary.

Many thanks are due to Werner Coetzee, Jennie Kitchin, Viv Wickham, Tess Allen, Caroline McPherson and Lori Laker as well as the whole Wiley Finance team for all their kind assistance at all the stages from the commissioning, preparation and production of this work through to sales and marketing.

While I gratefully acknowledge the help and assistance of everyone above, responsibility for any errors and omissions rests entirely with me. Both an errata and updates to the text (market updates, new references and the like) will be made available in due course at the web page below.

WEB PAGE FOR THIS BOOK

www.commodityoptionpricing.com

Notation

$\mathbf{E}[\cdot]$ – expectation

$\mathbf{Var}[\cdot]$ – variance

r^d – domestic interest rate (assumed constant)

r_t^d – domestic short rate at time t

D_{t_1,t_2}^d – domestic discount factor from time t_1 to time t_2

D_{t_1,t_2}^f – foreign discount factor from time t_1 to time t_2

S_t – spot price at time t

$F_{t,T}$ – forward price, quoted at time t, for delivery at time T

$f_{t,T}$ – futures contract price, quoted at time t, for delivery at time T

$\mathbf{P}$ – real-world measure

W_t – Brownian motion with respect to $\mathbf{P}$

$\mathbf{P}^d$ – (domestic) risk-neutral measure

$\mathbf{P}^{d;T}$ – (domestic) T-maturity forward measure

$\mathbf{E}^d[\cdot]$ – expectation with respect to the (domestic) risk-neutral measure

$\mathbf{E}^{d;T}[\cdot]$ – expectation with respect to the T-maturity forward measure

$\mathbf{Var}^d[\cdot]$ – variance with respect to the (domestic) risk-neutral measure

$A_{t_0;\{t_1,t_n\}}^{A;f}$ – commodity swap price, quoted at t_0, for a fixed/floating swap of futures contracts at times $t_1 \dots t_n$

$A_T^{G;s}$ – continuous geometric average of spot computed over $[0, T]$

$A_T^{A;s}$ – continuous arithmetic average of spot computed over $[0, T]$

$A_{t_1,t_n}^{A;s}$ – discrete arithmetic average of spot computed over times $t_1 \dots t_n$

$A_{t_1,t_n}^{A;f}$ – discrete arithmetic average of prompt futures computed over times $t_1 \ldots t_n$

$A_{t_1;t_n}^{G;s}$ – discrete geometric average of spot computed over times $t_1 \ldots t_n$

$A_{t_1;t_n}^{G;f}$ – discrete geometric average of prompt futures computed over times $t_1 \ldots t_n$

σ_A – Asian volatility

σ_{imp} – implied volatility

T_{stl} – settlement time

List of Figures

List of Tables

1

Introduction

At the time of the writing of this book, and since about the turn of the century, commodities have experienced a continued surge in both price (as shown in Figure 1.1) and interest in a world of increasingly scarce resources and rapid population growth together with demand growth in the rapidly industrialising emerging markets. This book is a practical quantitative analyst's guide to how to get professionally involved in the world of commodities.

While the book is focused primarily on the market in commodity derivatives and the quantitative analysts (quants) who work in these markets, much commodity trading occurs through the vehicle of futures trading on organised exchanges, so I envisage this work will be of use to the traders, quant developers, structurers and finance professionals who work alongside the quants. Though this is first and foremost a practitioners' book, I have attempted to put the material into context with regard to the literature in the area, which I believe will be of tangible benefit to academics and students of financial mathematics from all areas, who are interested in learning more about the fascinating world of commodities.

Although this is a technical book, I have attempted to make it as accessible as possible on several levels. One barrier to making the transition into commodities is the necessary, and unavoidable, jargon, which I have tried to cut through for the benefit of the reader (see the Glossary at the end of the book, for example). This I hope should set the avid reader on course to apply the theory from his or her studies to build the models and systems required to add real value to a commodities desk. Content has been developed using real-world data throughout and has been written in conjunction with both industry professionals and university lecturers in commodities.

Once again, the preferred mathematical background for the derivatives elements of this book is a familiarity with option pricing at the level of Hull (2011) and, ideally, Baxter and Rennie (1996). There is necessarily some overlap with my previous FX book (Clark, 2011) but this book is a standalone work and introduces the various commodity markets

Figure 1.1   Price history of TR/J CRB Commodity Index (1994–2012, log-scale).

and develops the option pricing toolkit for commodity derivatives in a self-contained manner. This book is not purely mathematical, however; it is important to have some familiarity with the physical aspect of the various commodities also, in order to develop intuition and to have credibility when talking with traders (or in interviews). I have therefore attempted to relate the technical machinery back to the practical aspects throughout.

Producers, intermediaries and consumers are all exposed to risk. Additionally, some investors have been increasingly attracted towards speculative investment in some commodities due to the benefits of diversification and perceived underperformance in other asset classes. Finally, the durable physical aspect of some commodities (especially the metals and energy) may appeal to those who have lost money on purely financial investments during the collapse of the dot com equity bubble and the subprime financial crisis thereafter.

As well as trading the physical commodity itself, it is commonplace to trade financial contracts linked to commodities. Simple examples are futures contracts on oil and the base metals; more complicated are option contracts which provide the owner with the right but not the obligation to take profits on price moves in a particular direction. Commodity derivatives also allow participants in the financial markets to spread their risk exposure over the course of a calendar period, and to "lock-in" profits on a spread between the price of a refined product and an unrefined product.

This book shows how these derivatives are priced in the industry context. It is a practitioner's guide which introduces commodity options, describing the features of the various commodity markets and what industry professionals need to know when developing option pricing analytics for trading desks and risk departments. What sort of products might one encounter? What typical price quotes might one obtain and have to calibrate a model to? What makes oil options different from precious metal or base metal options, for example.

These questions, and more, are the concern of this book.

1.1   TRADE, COMMERCE AND COMMODITIES

The oldest financial markets are the commodity markets. By a commodity, we mean an undifferentiated physical item that satisfies an economic want or need. The oldest commodity markets are therefore the agricultural and metal markets – wheat, gold, etc. Energy (fossil fuels) is a comparatively recent commodity. Differentiation is what makes gold as a commodity different from gold as jewelry or coinage, for example, where there are particular features that may have particular appeal to the purchaser. In contrast, wheat of a particular grade is wheat, and so long as it is of the promised grade and quality, no one can be expected to care too much about anything apart from the actual physical amount available. That is what makes it a commodity.

As described in Section 7.2 of Clark, Lesourd and Thiéblemont (2001), one can categorise production systems into four various modes of production using Woodward's classification, as described in Table 1.1.

From this we see that commodities are specifically outputs of process production, in that they are standardised (within various grades, typically) and divisible. Note that this has not always been the case, agriculture historically used to be more of a craft production enterprise. Commodities are generally tradeable goods, though there are some instruments that sometimes fall under the heading of commodity derivatives which are not, e.g. freight derivatives, weather derivatives, and other instruments that more closely resemble insurance products.

Within tradeable goods, there are some specific features of commodity markets within the sector of process production. Firstly, these goods generally have a long lead time for production (electricity generation being the notable exception) and generally have a liquid supply and

Table 1.1 Woodward's categorisation of production systems.

System	Features	Examples
Mass production	Large scale production of an indivisible standardised product	Automobile manufacturing
Process production	Large scale production of a divisible standardised product	Food, chemical manufacturing
Craft production	Small scale production of a nonstandardised product	Fashion
Project production	Production of a unique product to bespoke client specifications	Infrastructure construction (e.g. airports, bridges), building construction

demand market with reference pricing – this means that an equilibrium between supply and demand can in principle be found. In times when supply and demand are greatly out of line, generally inventories and storage come into play, as physical commodities can usually be warehoused subject to storage costs (electricity once again being an exception). This does, however, have the effect of increasing volatility both in historical terms and implied volatility (see Chapter 2) for commodities.

Basically, commodities are comparatively simple tangible goods created by means of process production, differentiated purely by price and prespecified grades of quality rather than by any specific branding or differentiating factors.

Note the difference between upstream and downstream commodities – upstream means that the commodity in question is used primarily to satisfy industrial demand (e.g. crude oil) and may well be reprocessed, whereas downstream means that the commodity is marketed to endusers, such as gasoline and gold. This is based largely upon the role of the consumer, not the producer.

We can see evidence of early commodity markets. From 1698, a merchant called John Castaing published twice a week a series of pocketbooks called "The Course of the Exchange" (see Figure 1.2) tabulating the price of various stocks and commodities as gold, silver, pieces of eight and so forth, as traded at Jonathan's Coffee House in the City of London. It is worth noticing that commodity trading is linked to trade, in that most commodities are produced or extracted at a distance from where they are finally used. Markets such as Smithfield cattle market in London are an example, with cattle being driven to market from the countryside for consumption in the city. Other historical markets are

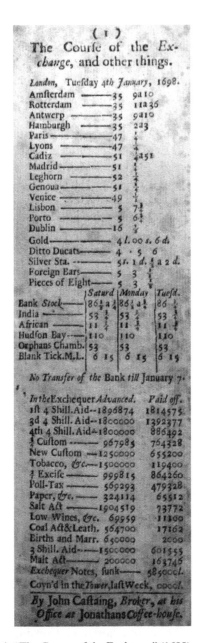

Figure 1.2   Castaing's "The Course of the Exchange" (1698).

well known, for example the Forum in Rome, the Agora in Athens and the Roman Forum in London (under the present day site of Leadenhall Market), all of which were markets for cash transactions for immediate delivery.

Obviously these ancient empires did not last, and for a while thereafter markets became more fragmented and localised. Not indefinitely, though. By the 12th century, however, medieval fairs had become increasingly popular in England and France (among other locations), where the markets were preannounced and the so-called *Pieds Poudres*[1] travelled from town to town organising the fairs. What often happened at these travelling fairs is that samples were sold for a cash price, together with a contract for later delivery of merchandise in accordance with the quality of the established sample. In such a manner, the forward market began to take hold.

As trade routes opened up, transport of commodities over greater distances became viable and quite profitable – the silk route across Central Asia, the spice trade with East India, transport of silver from the mines of South America to Spain and Portugal, etc. Other more localised examples certainly existed: the speculation in tulips in the Netherlands from 1634–37, for example. In parallel, specialised markets developed in the major cities and replaced the trade fairs, these centers being called exchanges or bourses.[2]

Relative scarcity in one region and abundance in another drives the markets to develop trade routes – a modern example being the continuing shipment of crude oil from the Middle East to Asia, Europe and the Americas. A trade route has to have a start and a finish and, at the destination end, markets developed around the construction of large city docks, warehouses and markets such as the docks in the City of London (both around London Bridge and the geographically named docks around Canary Wharf) and similarly in other cities – Paris, New York, Chicago and so on. Relatively sophisticated systems for landing bonded cargos and making payments of the various customs duties were part of this grand system of commerce, all being part of the trade in the physical commodity.

Financial markets, however, take a different view and allow participants to trade with different time horizons. Consider a bond – one can deposit a certain amount of cash and obtain the principal at some fixed

---

[1] Men of dusty feet.

[2] We can thank an 18th-century Bruge innkeeper named Van der Beurs for this name.

time in the future, together with a series of coupon payments. Separating cashflows over different time horizons is one of the features of the financial markets, and one that certainly applies to commodities.

The simplest and earliest financial instruments are the forward and futures contracts (see Chapter 2), which allow buyers and sellers to fix a price today for purchase of a commodity at some prespecified time in the future. These have been around a surprisingly long time. As well as the OTC forward transactions at medieval trade fairs, we can go back to around 1730 to see forward contracts on rice trading at the Dojima Rice Market in Osaka (cash trading in rice on that market dates back only some 30 years earlier). Interestingly, there was also trading on edible oils, cotton and precious metals in Dojima, but the volumes were completely dwarfed by those for rice.

Commodity markets in the USA date back to 1750 or so, but it was not until the early 1800s that futures trading in the USA really took off. Much of this growth can be linked to the urban growth of Chicago itself, a rapidly growing city which served as a grain terminal for the fertile lands of the Midwest. As anyone who has visited knows, transport in the region can be easily disrupted by inclement weather, and this was undoubtedly much more the case in the early 1800s. Snow and rain made transport exceedingly difficult and wagonloads of grain were often brought in on plank roads made of wooded boards. Once in Chicago, there were still problems with inadequate warehouse storage, which immediately led to the unfortunate state of affairs where gluts sometimes had to be disposed of in the street if a buyer could not be found. One problem is that harvests are generally gathered in late autumn/early winter, when the problems with transportation are getting worse – just when you need to get the goods to market (basically around Thanksgiving holiday in North America, which lines up with harvest season).

Forward contracts were first used by river merchants who received corn from farmers but had to store it themselves until spring, when the corn had dried sufficiently and the rivers and canals were free of ice to make transportation possible. The first recorded forward contract on corn was made on 13 March 1851, for 3,000 bushels of corn to be delivered to Chicago in June at a one cent discount to the March price. Wheat contracts developed subsequently, and tended to be sold for delivery forward to millers and exporters east of Chicago.

In 1848, 82 merchants founded the Chicago Board of Trade (CBOT), a centralised location for trading forward contracts on agricultural commodities. In early days, there was no standardisation with respect to quality or delivery time, and it was not infrequent that merchants and traders reneged on their commitments. In 1865, therefore, the CBOT developed futures contracts which were standardised with regard to quality, quantity and time and place of delivery for the underlying commodity. Later that year, a margining system was set up also to mitigate against the underlying counterparty risk.

The choice of months may seem arbitrary, but in fact was very much by design. March was chosen to coincide with the end of winter, when transportation became feasible again. May was a preferred delivery month due to old-crop oats and wheat, harvested in the previous summer. December was chosen for new-crop corn (harvested in the autumn) and also because it was the final month before inclement weather would make attempts at winter transportation foolhardy.

From futures it was only a small step to introducing options on futures – these were introduced in 1984 as options on soybean futures and 1985 saw the introduction of options on corn futures contracts.

The CBOT has since merged with other exchanges including the Chicago Mercantile Exchange (CME), and now encompasses the New York Mercantile Exchange (NYMEX) as part of the CME group, showing that the history of trading in financial products in commodity markets is a long and continuing one.

For those who are interested, a great deal of further historical information about the development of the commodities and futures markets can be found in CBOT (1989).

It is financial contracts such as these, based on the various commodities, together with more modern contracts, such as options, that will be the focus of this book.

1.2 ADAPTING TO COMMODITIES AS AN ASSET CLASS

Many of the readers of this book may well not have commodities as their only area of interest, it is quite possible that they will have some exposure to other asset classes such as equities, fixed income and foreign exchange. This book attempts to demonstrate how some of the techniques which are commonly seen in option pricing in those asset classes can be used for commodity option pricing.

The first thing to note is the immense variety of different types of commodities that can be encountered. We can do worse than survey the various commodity indices to get an idea of what generally falls within the realm of commodities.

Thomson Reuters/Jefferies CRB Index

The TR/J CRB index dates back to 1957, when the prices of 28 commodities were tabulated in the 1958 CRB Commodity Year Book. It is the oldest of the commodity indices.

The index currently is comprised of the prices of 19 commodities. We have already seen a historical chart of the TR/J CRB index from 1994 to mid-2012 in Figure 1.1 at the start of the book.

S&P GSCI Index

The GSCI index comprises 24 commodities from various commodity sectors – energy, industrial metals, agricultural products, livestock products and precious metals. It is the second oldest of the commodity indices, and dates back to 1992.

The GSCI is calculated on a production-weighted basis and is comprised of physical commodities that are the subject of active, liquid futures markets. The weightings are far from equal, energy makes up over 78% of the basket and precious metals slightly under 2%. In fact the top six components by weighting are easily the six commodities within the energy category, with corn, wheat, copper and aluminium making up the remaining top ten.

DJ UBS Index

The Dow Jones-UBS commodities index is composed of commodities traded on the exchanges, with the exception of aluminium, nickel and zinc, which are traded on the London Metal Exchange (copper is traded on COMEX).

RICI Index

The Rogers International Commodity Index (RICI) is a measure of the price action of commodities on a worldwide basis. It currently includes 37 commodities weighted according to their importance in international trade, from WTI crude oil (21%), Brent crude oil (14%), Corn and Wheat (4.75% each) down to Milk (0.15%).

1.2.1   Classification of Commodities into Sub-categories

One can see from Tables 1.2 to 1.5 that commodities can be broadly categorised into three major types – energy, metals and agricultural commodities – being further divisible into subtypes. We also include power (electricity) and a fifth "other" category for commodities which do not neatly fall into the groupings above, such as lumber and all the contracts to be discussed in Chapter 9. Figure 1.3 shows a useful categorisation we can use to place the various commodities we shall encounter into various subtypes.

Table 1.2   Composition of Thomson Reuters/Jefferies CRB Index.

Energy	Industrial metals	Precious metals	Softs	Grains & seeds	Livestock
WTI crude oil	Al	Au	Cocoa	Corn	Live cattle
Heating oil	Cu	Ag	Coffee	Wheat	Lean hogs
Unleaded gas	Ni		Cotton	Soybeans	
Natural gas			Orange juice		
			Sugar		

Table 1.3   Composition of S&P GSCI Index.

Energy	Industrial metals	Precious metals	Softs	Grains & seeds	Livestock
WTI crude oil	Al	Au	Cotton	Wheat	Live cattle
Brent crude oil	Cu	Ag	Sugar	Red wheat	Feeder cattle
Unleaded gas	Pb		Coffee	Corn	Lean hogs
Heating oil	Ni		Cocoa	Soybeans	
Gas oil	Zn				
Natural gas					

Table 1.4   Composition of Dow Jones–UBS Commodities Index.

Energy	Industrial metals	Precious metals	Softs	Grains & seeds	Livestock
Natural gas	Cu	Au	Coffee	Corn	Live cattle
WTI crude oil	Al	Ag	Cotton	Soybeans	Lean hogs
Brent crude oil	Zn		Sugar	Wheat	
Unleaded gasoline	Ni			Kansas wheat	
Heating oil				Soybean meal	
				Soybean oil	

Table 1.5   Composition of Rogers International Commodity Index.

Energy	Industrial metals	Precious metals	Softs	Grains & seeds	Livestock & others
WTI crude oil	Al	Au	Cotton	Corn	Live cattle
Brent crude oil	Cu	Ag	Coffee	Wheat	Lean hogs
Natural gas	Pb	Pt	Cocoa	Soybeans	Milk class III
RBOB gasoline	Zn	Pd	Sugar	Soybean oil	Lumber
Heating oil	Ni		White sugar	Kansas wheat	
Gas oil	Sn		Orange juice	Milling wheat	
			Rubber	Rapeseed	
				Rice	
				Soybean meal	
				Oats	

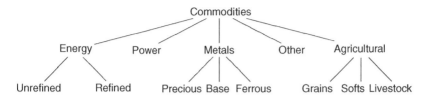

Figure 1.3   Taxonomic classification of commodities.

Energy commodities broadly can be separated into *primary* or unrefined energy products such as crude oil, coal, natural gas and nuclear fuels, which are generally obtained and traded in a standardised but unrefined form for further processing, and *secondary* or refined energy products such as residual oil, fuel oils, heating oil, diesel fuel, RBOB gasoline (US) or petrol (UK), jet kerosene and liquefied petroleum gas (LPG) which are sold to end-users. There are intermediate energy products which do not fit so neatly into this categorisation, such as ethylene and naphtha, but these are of minor importance compared to the refined and unrefined energies.

Not usually included with energy but clearly related to it is **power**, by which we mean electricity. This differs markedly from the other energy commodities in that it cannot easily be stored on an industrial scale – there is such a thing as a "barrel" of electricity, but we probably know it as a battery. This greatly affects the volatility and the pricing of electricity derivatives, as we shall discuss in Chapter 7.

Metals broadly can be separated into three major categories: (i) *precious metals* such as gold, silver and various platinum group metals; (ii) *base metals*, which are industrial non-ferrous metals such as copper, aluminium, lead, nickel, tin and zinc; and finally (iii) *ferrous*, by which we mean iron ore, iron, rolled iron, or steel or refined steel products such as rolled products, flat products, wires, bars and beams.

Additionally to these three categories, but of comparatively minor importance, we can include specialist non-ferrous metals such as chromium, molybdenum, titanium, tantalum, vanadium and the rare earth metals such as scandium, yttrium and the lanthanides. Many of these have niche applications in technology, e.g. tantalum is used in capacitors for mobile phones, and the rare earth metal neodymium is used in the rare-earth magnets found in precision guided munitions. While interesting, there are no derivatives markets on these, so we shall not need to discuss them any further in this book.

Agricultural derivatives can be similarly categorised into three major categories: (i) *softs* such as the main four: cocoa, coffee, sugar and rubber (Savaiko, 1985) but also including orange juice, tea, cotton, jute, wool, jute and hides; (ii) *grains and seeds* such as wheat, corn, soybeans and soybean products, rice and oats; and (iii) *livestock* such as live cattle, feeder cattle, lean hogs and pork bellies. It is interesting that the soft commodities are mostly of tropical or subtropical origin.

Finally, we reserve the **other** derivatives designation for those which are hard to categorise into the preceding four classes, such as lumber, milk, freight and weather derivatives, carbon emissions, bandwidth derivatives and water (potentially).

1.3   CHALLENGES IN COMMODITY MODELS

1.3.1   Futures

Readers who come to commodities from other asset classes, like equity or FX, are typically used to the concept of a spot price process, the price one pays today to take either immediate delivery or delivery at the spot date (usually two good business days later) of the investment asset. While this is true for precious metals, it is not true for most of the other commodities discussed in the book, which trade for forward delivery at agreed times in the future, in the futures markets. The reason for this is clearly evident from our discussion in Section 1.1, it relates to the uncertainty in matching supply and demand for goods that have a long lead time to produce and deliver.

What this means from a modelling perspective is that we need to regard the futures contracts as the underlying stochastic variables which need to be modelled – either individually, or as a coupled system. This of course bring us to the next complication.

1.3.2   Correlation

Looking ahead to Chapter 5, let us take WTI crude oil as an example. At any point in time, we have a sequence of futures contracts with maturity dates spaced out monthly, the one with the shortest time to maturity being known as the *prompt future*. Generally, the entire forward curve for a commodity moves in a coupled manner, so we expect a high degree of correlation between the various components, e.g. between the prompt future and the next futures contract one month further out. This is quite clearly visible both in Figure 1.4(a), where we show the historical price

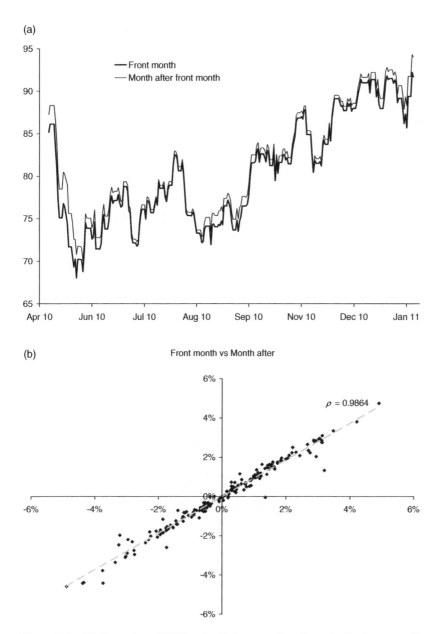

Figure 1.4   (a) Time series of WTI crude oil (front month and month after front month). (b) Correlation of logreturns on WTI crude oil (front month vs month after front month).

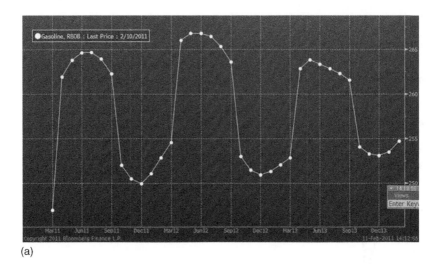

(a)

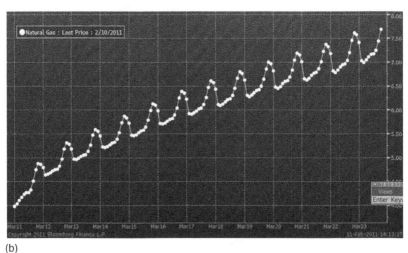

(b)

Figure 1.5 (a) Futures curve for RBOB gasoline – © 2013 Bloomberg Finance L.P. All rights reserved. Used with permission.
(b) Futures curve for natural gas – © 2013 Bloomberg Finance L.P. All rights reserved. Used with permission.

chart for the two adjacent WTI futures contracts, and in Figure 1.4(b) where the correlation between daily logreturns is graphed, revealing a historical correlation of 0.9864.

Correlations such as these are very high and certainly need to be handled accurately, as for many commodity options (e.g. spread options) the value is very sensitive to the correlation.

1.3.3   Seasonality

We can see little evidence of seasonality in the price of WTI crude oil in Figure 1.4(a) above. This is to be expected, as the overall supply and demand for crude oil is relatively constant throughout the year. The same is not true of various refined products, however. Demand for gasoline in the US peaks markedly in the so-called "driving season" from late May to early September, and demand for heating oil peaks in the winter, both of which are reflected in peaks and troughs in the futures curves for forward delivery. We can see clear visual evidence of this in Figure 1.5(a) and Figure 1.5(b).

We need to use the price information embedded in the entire futures curve in order to price options on such commodities correctly, which will depend on the nature of the model used.

1.3.4   American and Asian Features

A final complicating factor with commodity options is that many of the quoted options are either American straddles or Asian (average rate) options, which are more complicated to deal with than straightforward Europeans. Not only that, but the average rate options are generally exposed to an average of the prompt future over the course of a period, during which the prompt future rolls from one contract to the next. This will all be discussed in Chapter 2, where we attempt to build the technical foundations for commodity option pricing. In subsequent chapters, we shall relate this technical toolkit to each of the various sub-categories described in Section 1.2.1.

2
Commodity Mathematics and Products

In this chapter, we shall start with the convenient framework of one-factor models familiar to all students of mathematical finance. After revising the familiar Black–Scholes analysis for traded spot markets, I shall show how this can be extended to forwards and futures markets, such as are encountered in commodities, together with a discussion of some peculiarities of these markets. Having discussed such linear products, we can go on to options – which is what this book is about! So thereafter, I shall describe some of the typical products encountered in commodity options markets together with techniques for their valuation under these models, and the chapter will conclude with a discussion of the more advanced models which appear in the literature.

2.1 SPOT, FORWARDS AND FUTURES

One of the main aspects that differentiates many (but not all) commodities from other asset classes is the absence of a traded spot contract. Typically a spot transaction is for settlement a few good business days in the future (T+2 is customary in FX and, more relevantly, for precious and base metals; T+5 is usual in energy). Let us consider the metals. This means that if a spot trade is entered into on Monday 10 September 2012, then settlement will occur on Wednesday 12 September 2012. By settlement, we mean that the required cashflows and exchanges of commodities of value are scheduled to occur on that date. As the trade date advances forward in time, the spot date rolls forward also, subject to settlement rules and holidays. For example, a spot trade entered into on Tuesday 11 September 2012 will settle on Thursday 13 September 2012.

This is perfectly fine for financial instruments, but one can easily see that trading many physical commodities with such short notice is unrealistic. Oil needs to be shipped from location to location, base metals similarly. For this reason it is absolutely standard in the commodities markets to expect settlement and delivery to occur some time in the future. There are two ways to achieve this. One is effectively an over-the-counter (OTC) **forward contract**, where Counterparty A agrees to trade N units of a particular commodity (of a particular grade) at a known forward price K_{Fwd} with Counterparty B at some prespecified time T in the future. The other is an exchange traded **futures contract**, where a market participant is obliged – and note importantly that the obligation is now with the exchange and not directly with the other counterparty – to deliver or take delivery of (once again) N units of a particular grade of a commodity at some known time T in the future for a known futures price K_{Fut}. The contract sizes and delivery dates are generally standardised to provide sufficient liquidity. The exchange manages the obligation through the use of margin and mark-to-market; we shall discuss how in Section 2.1.3.

Should we therefore attempt to model spot, forwards or futures? Section 2.2 describes two possible ways to get started, both of which are used in practice.

The rest of this section introduces the spot, forward and futures contracts and markets; further details can be found in Carlton (1984), Williams (1986), Chapter 8 of Duffie (1996), Chapter 5 of Pilipović (1998), Pindyck (2001), and Geman (2005) and references therein.

2.1.1 Spot

A spot transaction is generally understood to be the shortest dated transaction that can be entered into in standard fashion. It comprises an agreement to trade a certain amount of a particular commodity at the spot date. For commodities, it only really used for precious metals, where the spot date is two business days after today (allowing for holidays), and for electricity.

We generally use S_t to denote the spot price at time t, a quantity which will make its appearance mathematically speaking in Section 2.2.1. Even where a spot contract does not exist *per se*, it is commonplace to take the shortest dated futures contract (also known as the "prompt future") as a proxy for spot. We shall use the notation $\vec{T}(t)$ to denote the maturity of the prompt future at time t, the arrow indicating that $\vec{T}(t)$ is the first expiry date to the right of t when viewed on a typical time axis, e.g. if we allow the expiry dates of the futures contracts to be denoted T_1, T_2, ... I attempt to show this graphically in Figure 2.1.

Figure 2.1   Futures contracts $T_1, T_2, T_3 \ldots$ as viewed from time t.

Note that the expiry dates for options on futures are different from the expiry dates of the underlying futures contracts themselves – more on this in Section 2.5.2.

2.1.2   Forwards

Consider a forward contract, entered into at time t with maturity T. In such a trade, Counterparty A has the obligation to deliver 1 unit of the commodity to Counterparty B, and to receive K units of (domestic) cash – both at time T in the future. The contract is an agreement that holds whether it is economically advantageous or disadvantageous for either party. There is no optionality. These contracts can be cash settled or physically settled (I shall assume cash settled, as we are concerned with financial valuation).

The price of such a T-forward contract at time t is denoted $F_{t,T}$. As this contract can have a negative value as well as a forward value, depending on the strike K, it is customary to solve for the value of K such that it makes the forward costless to enter into. This choice of strike K for which this is the case is denoted $F_{0,T}$.

Forward prices are rarely identical and rarely equal to the spot price (where a spot contract exists). In the case where shorter dated forward prices are less than longer dated forward prices, i.e. $F_{0,T_1} < F_{0,T_2}$ with $T_1 < T_2$, we refer to the forward curve as being in *contango*. The other case where shorter dated forward prices are greater than longer dated forward prices, i.e. $F_{0,T_1} > F_{0,T_2}$ with $T_1 < T_2$, is called *backwardation*, reflecting increased demand for contracts with shorter term delivery. More complicated shapes for the term structure of forward curves definitely exist, very possibly including seasonality.

The discrepancy between spot prices and forward prices is often rationalised by appealing to the balance to be obtained between the benefit of holding a commodity until a particular time T in the future and the storage costs required to keep it on hand until that time. Consider a commodity such as heating oil, which has a marked demand peak in the Northern hemisphere winter. Since a higher price can be attained for contracts with delivery in the winter months due to natural seasonal demand, then if storage costs were sufficiently low it would be economically advantageous to buy heating oil in the summer, store it, and deliver it in the winter months.

The fact that the forward curve is not flat indicates that the market has to price in two different effects when comparing contracts with different maturities. The first is the imputed benefit that "accrues to the owner of the physical commodity" (Geman, 2005, p. 24) and the second is the storage and maintenance costs required to keep the commodity to hand.

This is quantified as the **convenience yield** in spot commodity markets, where we refer to the instantaneous benefit (or cost) to the holder of a commodity in terms of an effective rate, which we denote r^f by analogy with the foreign risk-free rate encountered in foreign exchange. Basically this means that in the absence of any spot price movements, we still expect the economic value of a commodity to appreciate or depreciate from S_0 to $S_0 \exp(r^f \delta t)$ over the course of a small time interval δt, as described in Section 2.2 of Geman (2005).

Note that no cashflows take place with a forward contract except at maturity (and at initiation if the strike isn't chosen so that the contract is costless to enter into, which is unusual).

Note that forward contracts are almost always traded over-the-counter (OTC) directly between market participants, and consequently the creditworthiness of the participants should be taken into consideration (this will be outside the scope of this work though).

Having introduced these contracts, we shall obtain the fair price for the forward contract in Section 2.2 under the risk-neutral measure.

2.1.3 Futures

Following the notation of Musiela and Rutkowski (1997), who provide a thorough discussion of forwards and futures in the discrete time setting in Sections 2.5.1, 1.6, 3.2 and 3.3 of their book, we use $F_{t,T}$ for the forward price and $f_{t,T}$ for the futures price.

A futures contract has the same value payout at expiry as a forward contract, but differs from it in two important ways. Firstly, futures contracts are exchange traded and therefore subject to much greater standardisation in terms of which contract sizes and maturity dates are tradeable. Secondly, futures contracts are traded directly with the exchange and "marked to market", which has the benefit of removing credit counterparty risk from the purchaser of the futures contract.[1]

Generally, futures contracts corresponding to the various calendar months are exchange traded, and each month's contract (however it is defined) has a particular ticker symbol associated with it:

Jan	Feb	Mar	Apr	May	Jun	Jul	Aug	Sep	Oct	Nov	Dec
F	G	H	J	K	M	N	Q	U	V	X	Z

These ticker symbols, which seem somewhat arbitrary, are actually chosen by exclusion, as various other commodities had (and often still have) one letter trading codes, e.g. C for corn.

One needs to be careful, though, as the actual maturity date for a particular month's contract sometimes falls into the latter part of the *preceding* month, as seen in an example below. The contracts at the end of each quarter are very often the more liquid, i.e. HMUZ, and indeed out beyond a year or two one often only sees the June (M) and December (Z) contracts quoted.

For poets and quants, a small piece of doggerel may be useful to help remember the codes:

> *Fragrant garden handshake*
> *Jasmine kettle mandrake*
> *Never quite unseemly*
> *Viewing X-ray zucchini*

In addition to the character code for the contract maturity, there is usually a quote code for the particular class of commodity – for example, WTI-NYMEX is denoted CL (for Crude Light). These two, together with the final digit (sometimes final two digits) of the year, are concatenated to produce a quote code.

For example, the FEB12 WTI-NYMEX contract has the code "CL G2" and Table 2.1 shows the following dates of importance for this contract.

On occasion, for the so-called "weekly" options on the CME, it is necessary to specify the particular week on which a contract expires or matures. Taking the example of a Weekly Live Cattle option expiring on the fifth Friday in September 2011 from the CME, the product or telequote code for this is "LC5U11" – where "LC" refers to live cattle options (which expire on Friday, see Section 8.5.2) 5 indicates that the

---

[1] Except risk relating to the creditworthiness of the exchange itself!

Table 2.1   Contract dates of importance for typical WTI futures contract.

Commodity	Quote code	Futures contract	Maturity date	Settlement date
WTI-NYMEX	CL G2	FEB12	20-Jan-12	27-Jan-12

expiry is on the *fifth* Friday, "U" means September and "11" indicates 2011.

The market conventions for determining these dates vary according to the particular quoted commodity and will be described further in subsequent chapters.

The process of marking to market requires some explanation, details can be found in Exercise 2.17 of Duffie (1996), Chapter 2 of Collins and Fabozzi (1999) and Schneider (2012). Let the price at time t of a commodities future contract with maturity T be denoted by $f_{t,T}$. Corresponding to $t = 0$, the price of the same T-future contract today is denoted by $f_{0,T}$ – meaning that a T-futures contract can be entered into today with a strike of $K = f_{0,T}$ at no cost to enter (we shall discuss the pricing of this in Section 2.2 also).

An investor buys a T-futures contract at the market price $f_{0,T}$. Whereas for the equivalent forward contract no cashflows occur until T, in this case the investor must post an **initial margin** into an (interest earning) margin account. The value of the futures contract is calculated daily by the exchange in a procedure known as "marking to market" – where the change in value of the position over the course of a trading day is called the "variation margin". The margin held on deposit is used to fund changes in the variation margin. If, during the lifetime of the contract, the value is determined to be above the initial margin, then the excess funds can be withdrawn from the margin account. In contrast, if the mark-to-market (MTM) value decreases below the initial margin, then no such withdrawals are possible, and indeed if the value goes down to or below a lower level known as the **maintenance margin** then the margin account must be topped up with additional cash reserves to return the balance to the initial margin.

From this it is immediately apparent that futures contracts are subject to uncertain cashflows over the entire lifetime of the contract, unlike forward contracts. As pointed out by Jarrow and Oldfield (1981), a forward contract only has a cash flow at the expiry date T. In contrast, a futures contract has a number of cash flows throughout the interval $[0, T]$ depending on the mark-to-market of the underlying position. We shall explore this point in a worked example in Section 2.3.

In the presence of stochasticity in the domestic interest rate, the futures contract can have a different value to the equivalent forward contract – though this discrepancy vanishes if the forward contract and domestic bonds have zero correlation (see Cox, Ingersoll and Ross, 1981). Basically, if the price of a traded commodity is positively correlated with interest rates, then profits on a long futures position in that commodity can be reinvested at a higher interest rate than the interest rate used to finance losses on the position (and vice versa for negative correlation). While beyond the scope of this book, discussion of futures convexity adjustments in the context of interest rate options can be found in Flesaker (1993), Vaillant (1995), Pelsser (2000), Piterbarg and Renedo (2006) and Exercise 2.5.2 (2) in Tan (2012).

More directly related to this chapter, Pilz and Schlögl (2013) present a variation of the LIBOR market model for commodity options, wherein the convexity correction relating commodity forwards and commodity futures is discussed, as well as the dependence upon correlation.

Another potential source of discrepancy between forward and futures prices, of course, is counterparty risk, as forward contracts are clearly subject to credit risk. We shall not discuss that here, commodity forward contracts being encountered far less frequently than futures contracts, and merely refer the reader to Section 6.3 of Burger *et al.* (2007) for discussion of credit risk in the context of commodity markets.

For this book, therefore, we shall work under the assumption that futures prices and forward prices coincide, i.e.

$$f_{t,T} = F_{t,T}. \tag{2.1}$$

Note that this does *not* mean that the present value of a T-futures contract with strike K is the same as present value of a T-forward contract with the same maturity T and the same strike K – see Section 2.3 – it does however mean that if the strike K is such that the T-futures contract is costless to enter into, then the T-forward contract is costless to enter into also (and $K = f_{t,T} = F_{t,T}$).

Standard references detailing the similarities and differences between forwards and futures are Jarrow and Oldfield (1981), Cox, Ingersoll and Ross (1981) and, with special reference to commodity markets, Pindyck (2001). Appendix 3B of Sundaram and Das (2010) is also recommended.

2.2 THE BLACK–SCHOLES AND BLACK-76 MODELS

Much of this material will be familiar to the reader who has tackled Baxter and Rennie (1996), Shreve (2004) or indeed my previous book (Clark, 2011). While there are many useful references regarding risk neutrality, two which I have found particularly useful are Sundaram (1997) and Bingham and Kiesel (1998).

Suppose a rational investor has two investment opportunities open for his or her consideration. Such an investor should have no reason to favour one portfolio over another if both are riskless, as this would admit a clear arbitrage opportunity. This leads to the framework of risk-neutral pricing – if we have a risky stock, and a risky derivative on that stock, then by constructing a dynamically rebalanced portfolio which is instantaneously riskless, we can obtain a framework for pricing derivatives. One important note is that when we work through the pricing analysis, the expected drift of the spot process doesn't appear in the partial differential equation, so the drift can be set to the risk-free rate. Further, we shall see that both forward prices and futures prices are martingales.[2]

2.2.1 The Black–Scholes Model

The Black–Scholes analysis for obtaining a partial differential equation governing the price of commodities without any storage costs or imputed benefits from holding the commodity over particular time intervals, is equivalent to the pricing of equity derivatives in the absence of dividends. We therefore follow Black and Scholes (1973) and describe the spot rate by a geometric Brownian motion

$$dS_t = \mu S_t dt + \sigma S_t dW_t \qquad (2.2)$$

with the standard Black–Scholes assumptions, as in Hull (2011):

1. The spot price S_t (in domestic currency) of 1 unit of a tradeable commodity follows a lognormal process (2.2).
2. Short selling is permissible.
3. No transaction costs or taxes.

---

[2] Technical footnote: forward prices are martingales in the T-forward measure, whereas futures prices are martingales in the domestic risk-neutral measure respectively, though these coincide in the absence of stochastic interest rates.

4. The domestic currency has risk-free rate r^d constant across all maturities; the convenience yield of the commodity is denoted r^f by analogy with the foreign risk-free rate encountered in foreign exchange. Note that r^f can be either positive or negative (and so too these days can r^d).
5. No riskless arbitrage.
6. Trading is continuous between now ($t = 0$) and expiry ($t = T$).

2.2.2   The Black–Scholes Model Without Convenience Yield

Suppose that the price of a contingent claim $V(S_t, t)$, which derives its value from the performance of a tradeable asset with spot price S_t, is known. Let $V_t = V(S_t, t)$ denote the value of the contingent claim at time t, conditional on the asset spot price being S_t at that time. Applying Itô, we have

$$dV_t = \frac{\partial V}{\partial t}dt + \frac{\partial V}{\partial S}dS_t + \frac{1}{2}\frac{\partial^2 V}{\partial S^2}dS_t^2. \tag{2.3}$$

However we know from (2.2) that $dS_t^2 = \sigma^2 S_t^2 dt$ and consequently at time t, we have

$$dV_t = \left[\frac{\partial V}{\partial t} + \frac{1}{2}\sigma^2 S^2 \frac{\partial^2 V}{\partial S^2}\right]dt + \frac{\partial V}{\partial S}dS_t. \tag{2.4}$$

The term inside the square brackets above is deterministic, whereas the term appearing in front of dS_t is the only stochastic term. We remove the stochastic term by construction of a portfolio Π_t which is long one unit of the contingent claim (with value V_t) and short $\partial V/\partial S$ units of the underlying asset

$$\Pi_t = V_t - \frac{\partial V}{\partial S}S_t. \tag{2.5}$$

This has the SDE

$$d\Pi_t = dV_t - \frac{\partial V}{\partial S}dS_t \tag{2.6}$$

and from (2.4), we have

$$d\Pi_t = \left[\frac{\partial V}{\partial t} + \frac{1}{2}\sigma^2 S^2 \frac{\partial^2 V}{\partial S^2}\right]dt. \tag{2.7}$$

As the growth of Π_t is riskless, we can appeal to risk-neutrality and equate the expected growth of Π_t to that of the domestic risk-free bond B_t^d which is described by

$$dB_t^d = r^d B_t^d dt. \tag{2.8}$$

We therefore put

$$d\Pi_t = r^d \Pi_t dt \tag{2.9}$$

where r^d denotes the domestic interest rate. Equating terms in (2.7) and (2.9) we have

$$\frac{\partial V}{\partial t} + \frac{1}{2}\sigma^2 S^2 \frac{\partial^2 V}{\partial S^2} = r^d \Pi_t$$
$$= r^d \left[V_t - \frac{\partial V}{\partial S} S \right] \tag{2.10}$$

leading to the familiar Black–Scholes equation

$$\frac{\partial V}{\partial t} + \frac{1}{2}\sigma^2 S^2 \frac{\partial^2 V}{\partial S^2} + r^d S \frac{\partial V}{\partial S} - r^d V_t = 0. \tag{2.11}$$

It is standard, and important, at this point to note that the real world growth rate μ does not appear in the Black–Scholes equation in any form.

2.2.3   The Black–Scholes Model With Convenience Yield

When the commodity is assumed to have a non-zero convenience yield, it is assumed that the value of the tradeable asset is the spot rate multiplied by the returns on that commodity, i.e. $S_t B_t^f$, where

$$dB_t^f = r^f B_t^f dt \tag{2.12}$$

takes into account the convenience yield r^f. By analogy with FX, B_t^f can be thought of as a foreign commodity bond, though it more correctly refers to a continuously rolled over long spot position in a particular commodity. Let us call B_t^f foreign commodity bond for brevity.

As in Section 2.2.2 we suppose that the price of a contingent claim $V(S_t, t)$ is known, which derives its value from the performance of a spot price S_t.

Using V_t to denote the price of the contingent claim at time t, we still have

$$dV_t = \left[\frac{\partial V}{\partial t} + \frac{1}{2}\sigma^2 S^2 \frac{\partial^2 V}{\partial S^2} \right] dt + \frac{\partial V}{\partial S} dS_t \qquad (2.13)$$

but the construction of the delta-hedged portfolio is somewhat different. We cannot buy and sell units of the spot commodity without taking on exposure to the convenience yield – so the construction of the hedged portfolio Π_t is obtained by going long one unit of the contingent claim (with value V_t) and short Δ_t units of the underlying foreign commodity bond

$$\Pi_t = V_t - \Delta_t S_t B_t^f. \qquad (2.14)$$

The question is what value of Δ_t makes Π_t riskless. We have

$$
\begin{aligned}
d\Pi_t &= dV_t - \Delta_t d(S_t B_t^f) \\
&= dV_t - \Delta_t B_t^f dS_t - \Delta_t S_t dB_t^f \\
&= dV_t - \Delta_t B_t^f dS_t - \Delta_t S_t r^f B_t^f dt \\
&= dV_t - \Delta_t B_t^f \left[(r^d - r^f)S_t dt + \sigma S_t dW_t \right] - \Delta_t S_t r^f B_t^f dt \\
&= dV_t - \Delta_t B_t^f \left[r^d S_t dt + \sigma S_t dW_t \right] \\
&= \frac{\partial V}{\partial t} dt + \frac{1}{2}\sigma^2 S^2 \frac{\partial^2 V}{\partial S^2} dt + \frac{\partial V}{\partial S} dS_t - \Delta_t B_t^f \left[r^d S_t dt + \sigma S_t dW_t \right] \\
&= \frac{\partial V}{\partial t} dt + \frac{1}{2}\sigma^2 S^2 \frac{\partial^2 V}{\partial S^2} dt + \frac{\partial V}{\partial S} dS_t - \Delta_t B_t^f r^d S_t dt - \Delta_t B_t^f \sigma S_t dW_t \\
&= \left[\frac{\partial V}{\partial t} + \frac{1}{2}\sigma^2 S^2 \frac{\partial^2 V}{\partial S^2} - \Delta_t B_t^f r^d S_t \right] dt + \frac{\partial V}{\partial S} dS_t - \Delta_t B_t^f \sigma S_t dW_t \\
&= \left[\frac{\partial V}{\partial t} + \frac{1}{2}\sigma^2 S^2 \frac{\partial^2 V}{\partial S^2} - \Delta_t B_t^f r^d S_t \right] dt + \frac{\partial V}{\partial S} \left[(r^d - r^f)S_t dt + \sigma S_t dW_t \right] \\
&\quad - \Delta_t B_t^f \sigma S_t dW_t \\
&= \left[\frac{\partial V}{\partial t} + \frac{1}{2}\sigma^2 S^2 \frac{\partial^2 V}{\partial S^2} - \Delta_t B_t^f r^d S_t + \frac{\partial V}{\partial S}(r^d - r^f)S_t \right] dt \qquad (2.15) \\
&\quad + \left[\frac{\partial V}{\partial S} - \Delta_t B_t^f \right] \sigma S_t dW_t.
\end{aligned}
$$

To cancel the dW_t term, we require that Δ_t must satisfy $\Delta_t B_t^f = \partial V / \partial S$, i.e.

$$\Delta_t = \frac{1}{B_t^f} \frac{\partial V}{\partial S}. \qquad (2.16)$$

Substituting (2.16) into (2.15) we obtain

$$d\Pi_t = \left[\frac{\partial V}{\partial t} + \frac{1}{2} \sigma^2 S^2 \frac{\partial^2 V}{\partial S^2} - r^d S_t \frac{\partial V}{\partial S} + \frac{\partial V}{\partial S} (r^d - r^f) S_t \right] dt. \qquad (2.17)$$

Once again, as in Section 2.2.2, we appeal to domestic risk-neutrality and put $d\Pi_t = r^d \Pi_t dt$, where in the context with non-zero convenience yields, using (2.14) and the analysis above, it gives

$$\Pi_t = V_t - \frac{\partial V}{\partial S} S_t. \qquad (2.18)$$

We therefore have

$$\left[\frac{\partial V}{\partial t} + \frac{1}{2} \sigma^2 S^2 \frac{\partial^2 V}{\partial S^2} - r^d S_t \frac{\partial V}{\partial S} + \frac{\partial V}{\partial S} (r^d - r^f) S_t \right] dt = r^d \left[V_t - \frac{\partial V}{\partial S} S_t \right] dt$$

which reduces to

$$\frac{\partial V}{\partial t} + \frac{1}{2} \sigma^2 S^2 \frac{\partial^2 V}{\partial S^2} + (r^d - r^f) S \frac{\partial V}{\partial S} - r^d V = 0. \qquad (2.19)$$

We see the convenience yield r^f appear in the convection term (the term containing a multiple of $\frac{\partial V}{\partial S}$) but not in the forcing term (the term containing a multiple of V), and the absence of any μ term.

2.2.4   The Black-76 Model

The standard Black–Scholes analysis presumes that we can price an option that depends on a continuously traded spot rate S_t, as presented above. If, however, we model the T-forward contract $F_{t,T}$ or the T-futures contract $f_{t,T}$ (for fixed T) rather than the spot process S_t then we obtain something different.

2.2.4.1   The Black-76 Model with Respect to Futures

In Black (1976), one assumes that the T-futures price $f_{t,T}$ of a tradeable commodity follows a *driftless* lognormal process

$$df_{t,T} = \sigma f_{t,T} dW_t^d \qquad (2.20)$$

where the process should be understood to be driftless with respect to the domestic risk-neutral measure $\mathbf{P}^d$.

For simplicity, let T be fixed *a priori*, we can then use the shorthand $f_t \equiv f_{t,T}$. We then let $V_t = V(f_t, t)$ denote the value of the contingent claim at time t, conditional on the T-futures price being f_t at that time. Applying Itô, we have

$$dV_t = \frac{\partial V}{\partial t}dt + \frac{\partial V}{\partial f}df_t + \frac{1}{2}\frac{\partial^2 V}{\partial f^2}df_t^2. \tag{2.21}$$

However we know from (2.20) that $df_t^2 = \sigma^2 f_t^2 dt$ and consequently at time t, we have

$$dV_t = \left[\frac{\partial V}{\partial t} + \frac{1}{2}\sigma^2 f^2 \frac{\partial^2 V}{\partial f^2}\right]dt + \frac{\partial V}{\partial f}df_t. \tag{2.22}$$

In the same manner as Section 2.2.2 we now remove the stochastic term by constructing a portfolio Π_t which is long one unit of the contingent claim (with value V_t) and short $\partial V/\partial f$ units of the underlying T-futures contract $f_t \equiv f_{t,T}$

$$\Pi_t = V_t - \frac{\partial V}{\partial f}u_t, \tag{2.23}$$

where we suppose that such a T-futures contract is entered into at initial cost u_0, and tracks the profit/loss of f_t according to $du_t = df_t + r^d u_t dt$ – i.e. the gain on the futures position plus any interest earned or paid on the margin account.[3] While u_0 will generally be zero at initiation, an observation which can be used to explain the absence of the convection term in (2.29) compared with (2.11), this need not be assumed.

The portfolio Π_t in (2.23) then has the SDE

$$\begin{aligned} d\Pi_t &= dV_t - \frac{\partial V}{\partial f}du_t \\ &= dV_t - \frac{\partial V}{\partial f}[df_t + r^d u_t dt]. \end{aligned} \tag{2.24}$$

From the above and (2.22), we have

$$d\Pi_t = \left[\frac{\partial V}{\partial t} + \frac{1}{2}\sigma^2 f^2 \frac{\partial^2 V}{\partial f^2} - r^d u_t \frac{\partial V}{\partial f}\right]dt. \tag{2.25}$$

---

[3] While there will be a certain amount of cash in the margin account at all times, we can consider the interest on the gains or losses on the futures position on an incremental basis.

As the growth of Π_t is riskless, we can appeal to risk-neutrality and equate the expected growth of Π_t to that of the domestic risk-free bond B_t^d which is described by

$$dB_t^d = r^d B_t^d dt. \tag{2.26}$$

We therefore put

$$d\Pi_t = r^d \Pi_t dt \tag{2.27}$$

where r^d denotes the domestic interest rate. Equating terms in (2.25) and (2.27), and then using (2.23) we have

$$\frac{\partial V}{\partial t} + \frac{1}{2}\sigma^2 f^2 \frac{\partial^2 V}{\partial f^2} - r^d u_t \frac{\partial V}{\partial f} = r^d \Pi_t$$

$$= r^d \left[V_t - \frac{\partial V}{\partial f} u_t \right]. \tag{2.28}$$

We arrive at the Black-76 equation

$$\frac{\partial V}{\partial t} + \frac{1}{2}\sigma^2 f^2 \frac{\partial^2 V}{\partial f^2} - r^d V = 0. \tag{2.29}$$

2.2.4.2   The Black-76 Model with Respect to Forwards

The analysis above assumes that futures contracts earn interest on the margin, which we know not to be the case for forwards. The analysis of that case is subtly different, and worth going through. We assume that the forwards are driftless under the domestic risk-neutral measure,[4] i.e.

$$dF_{t,T} = \sigma F_{t,T} dW_t^d \tag{2.30}$$

and let $V_t = V(F_t, t)$ denote the value of the contingent claim at time t. By use of Itô we obtain

$$dV_t = \left[\frac{\partial V}{\partial t} + \frac{1}{2}\sigma^2 F^2 \frac{\partial^2 V}{\partial F^2} \right] dt + \frac{\partial V}{\partial F} dF_t. \tag{2.31}$$

Suppose that a T-forward contract is entered into at initial cost v_0, and tracks the profit/loss of $F_{t,T}$ according to $v_t = e^{-r^d(T-t)} F_{t,T}$ with no

---

[4] Strictly, we should use the T-forward measure, but unless interest rates are assumed to be stochastic, the domestic risk-neutral measure is equivalent.

interim cashflows – this is why the discounting is required, to obtain the present value at t. Note that, using the shorthand $F_t \equiv F_{t,T}$, we have

$$dv_t = d[e^{-r^d(T-t)}F_t]$$
$$= r^d e^{-r^d(T-t)}F_t dt + e^{-r^d(T-t)}dF_t.$$

We then construct a portfolio $\Pi_t = V_t - \Delta_t v_t$ and attempt to remove the random component by a suitable choice of Δ_t. We can write

$$d\Pi_t = dV_t - \Delta_t dv_t$$
$$= dV_t - \Delta_t[r^d e^{-r^d(T-t)}F_t dt + e^{-r^d(T-t)}dF_t]$$
$$= \left[\frac{\partial V}{\partial t} + \frac{1}{2}\sigma^2 F^2 \frac{\partial^2 V}{\partial F^2} - \Delta_t r^d e^{-r^d(T-t)}F_t\right]dt + \left(\frac{\partial V}{\partial F} - \Delta_t e^{-r^d(T-t)}\right)dF_t.$$

We consequently set $\Delta_t = e^{r^d(T-t)}\frac{\partial V}{\partial F}$ to remove the random term, obtaining

$$d\Pi_t = \left[\frac{\partial V}{\partial t} + \frac{1}{2}\sigma^2 F^2 \frac{\partial^2 V}{\partial F^2} - r^d \frac{\partial V}{\partial F}F_t\right]dt.$$

Being riskless, this can be equated to $r^d \Pi_t dt$, and we have

$$\frac{\partial V}{\partial t} + \frac{1}{2}\sigma^2 F^2 \frac{\partial^2 V}{\partial F^2} - r^d \frac{\partial V}{\partial F}F_t = r^d \Pi_t \qquad (2.32)$$

which can be reduced to

$$\frac{\partial V}{\partial t} + \frac{1}{2}\sigma^2 F^2 \frac{\partial^2 V}{\partial F^2} - r^d \frac{\partial V}{\partial F}F_t = r^d[V_t - \Delta_t v_t].$$

Now, $\Delta_t v_t = e^{r^d(T-t)}\frac{\partial V}{\partial F} \cdot e^{-r^d(T-t)}F_t = \frac{\partial V}{\partial F}F_t$, so we can simplify the above to

$$\frac{\partial V}{\partial t} + \frac{1}{2}\sigma^2 F^2 \frac{\partial^2 V}{\partial F^2} - r^d \frac{\partial V}{\partial F}F_t = r^d V_t - r^d \frac{\partial V}{\partial F}F_t.$$

The result follows immediately

$$\frac{\partial V}{\partial t} + \frac{1}{2}\sigma^2 F^2 \frac{\partial^2 V}{\partial F^2} - r^d V = 0. \qquad (2.33)$$

2.2.4.3   Terminal Conditions and Present Value

Black–Scholes type PDEs, such as (2.11), (2.19), (2.29) or (2.33), are able to describe the value of a derivative contract, either with or without path dependency. If path-independent, the value of the contract depends solely on the value at expiry T of the tradeable process S_T, f_{T,T^*} or F_{T,T^*} corresponding to spot, T^*-futures or T^*-forwards respectively.

Considering the case of derivatives on spot for now, at expiry T, i.e. $V_T = V_T(S_T)$, we have the terminal condition

$$V(S_T, T) = V_T(S_T).$$

Given a solution (analytical or numerical) of the PDE, the value V_0 of the derivative contract today (the "present value", or PV) can be directly read off from the $t = 0$ time slice

$$V_0 = V(S_0, 0),$$

and similarly $V_0 = V(f_{0,T^*}, 0)$ and $V_0 = V(F_{0,T^*}, 0)$ for options on futures and forwards respectively.

2.2.4.4 Feynman–Kac and Risk-Neutral Expectation

From Section 2.2, we have a backward parabolic partial differential equation, such as (2.11), (2.19), (2.29) or (2.33), which the price V of a derivative security must obey.

We make the observation that the drift μ of the underlying process for the tradeable asset does not enter into the partial differential equation.

The Feynman–Kac formula makes the connection between the solution of such a partial differential equation, and the expectation of the terminal value of the derivative under an artificial measure – i.e. *not* the real world measure. If we have a backward Kolmogorov equation of the form

$$\frac{\partial g}{\partial t} + a(x, t)\frac{\partial g}{\partial x} + \frac{1}{2}b^2(x, t)\frac{\partial^2 g}{\partial x^2} = 0 \qquad (2.34)$$

with terminal condition $g(x, T) = h(x)$, then the solution of (2.34) can be expressed as an expectation[5]

$$g(x, 0) = \mathbf{E}^d\left[h(X_T)|X_0 = x\right] \qquad (2.35)$$

where X_t is described by the diffusion

$$dX_t = a(X_t, t)dt + b(X_t, t)dW_t^d. \qquad (2.36)$$

---

[5] We use the notation $\mathbf{E}^d[\cdot]$ as we shall identify this as expectation with respect to the domestic risk-neutral measure in Section 2.2.5.1.

The Feynman–Kac result can be verified by considering the process $g_t = g(X_t, t)$ and constructing the stochastic differential for dg_t

$$dg_t = \frac{\partial g}{\partial t}dt + \frac{\partial g}{\partial x}dX_t + \frac{1}{2}\frac{\partial^2 g}{\partial x^2}dX_t^2. \tag{2.37}$$

Substituting (2.36) into (2.37), we have

$$dg_t = \left[a(X_t, t)\frac{\partial g}{\partial x} + \frac{1}{2}b^2(X_t, t)\frac{\partial^2 g}{\partial x^2} + \frac{\partial g}{\partial t}\right]dt + b(X_t, t)\frac{\partial g}{\partial x}dW_t^d. \tag{2.38}$$

The term in square brackets above vanishes due to (2.34), and so

$$dg_t = b(X_t, t)\frac{\partial g}{\partial x}dW_t^d. \tag{2.39}$$

Integrating from $t = 0$ to T, we have

$$g_T = g_0 + \int_0^T b(X_t, t)\frac{\partial g}{\partial x}dW_t^d.$$

Taking expectations, and recognising that the expectation of the Itô integral above is zero, we have

$$g_0 = \mathbf{E}^d[g_T].$$

We therefore have, as in (2.35), $g(X_0, 0) = \mathbf{E}^d\left[h(X_T)\right]$.

In the presence of a forcing term f, i.e.

$$\frac{\partial V}{\partial t} + a(x, t)\frac{\partial V}{\partial x} + \frac{1}{2}b^2(x, t)\frac{\partial^2 V}{\partial x^2} + f(x, t)V = 0, \tag{2.40}$$

the analysis above gives

$$dV_t + f(X_t, t)Vdt = b(X, t, t)\frac{\partial V}{\partial x}dW_t^d. \tag{2.41}$$

This is amenable to the stochastic integrating factor technique. Multiply the LHS and RHS of (2.41) by $\exp(\int_0^t f(X_s, s)ds)$, and put $\hat{V}_t = \exp(\int_0^t f(X_s, s)ds)V_t$. By the chain rule, we have

$$d\hat{V}_t = \exp\left(\int_0^t f(X_s, s)ds\right)dV_t + \exp\left(\int_0^t f(X_s, s)ds\right)f(X_t, t)Vdt.$$

We therefore have, from (2.41),

$$d\hat{V}_t = \exp\left(\int_0^t f(X_s, s)ds\right)b(X, t, t)\frac{\partial V}{\partial x}dW_t^d.$$

Taking expectations as before and recognising that the expectation of the Itô integral above vanishes, we have $\hat{V}_0 = \mathbf{E}^d[V_T]$, i.e.

$$V_0 = \mathbf{E}^d \left[\exp \left(\int_0^t f(X_s, s)ds \right) V_T \right].$$ (2.42)

In the case where $f(X_s, s)$ is nonstochastic, though potentially a deterministic function of time t, we can take it outside the expectation, obtaining the result $V_0 = \exp(\int_0^t f(X_s, s)ds)\mathbf{E}^d[\hat{V}_T]$.

For Black–Scholes, comparing (2.40) with (2.19), we put $a(S, t) = (r^d - r^f)S$, $b(S, t) = \sigma S$ and $f(S, t) = -r^d$, where we use S in place of x in (2.40). The process (2.36) under which we take the expectation is therefore

$$dS_t = (r^d - r^f)S_t dt + \sigma S_t dW_t^d$$ (2.43)

and the result for the present value today of a derivative on a spot contract is the discounted risk-neutral expectation under the domestic risk-neutral measure

$$V_0 = e^{-r^d T} \mathbf{E}^d \left[V_T \right].$$ (2.44)

The Black-76 case is even simpler. Compare (2.40) with (2.29) or (2.33), and put $a(x, t) = 0$, $b(x, t) = \sigma x$ and $f(S, t) = 0$, where x denotes f or F as appropriate (consider f for now). The process (2.36) under which we take the expectation is therefore

$$df_t = \sigma f_t dW_t^d$$ (2.45)

(and similarly for F_t) so the present value today of a derivative on either a futures or a forward contract is the risk-neutral expectation under the domestic risk-neutral measure, either with or without discounting:

$$V_0 = e^{-r^d T} \mathbf{E}^d \left[V_T \right], \quad \text{or}$$ (2.46a)

$$V_0 = \mathbf{E}^d \left[V_T \right].$$ (2.46b)

Whether to use (2.46a) or (2.46b) depends on whether the derivative instrument pays/receives interest rate linked cashflows between today and maturity T, or whether the derivative *only* pays a cashflow at maturity T.

For a forward contract which only pays out at time T with no other interim cash flows, we use (2.46a) as discounting must be included between the time T cashflow and today. For futures contracts which incorporate margining, since the margin earns interest and incorporates interim cashflows as necessary to fund the position, (2.46b) should be used.

Examples are given below in Sections 2.3.1 and 2.3.2. Note that one should properly use the T-forward measure for forward contracts, but if interest rates are presumed deterministic then the domestic risk-neutral measure is equivalent.

What have we obtained from this exercise? We see that the value today of a derivative written on a spot, forward or futures contract can be expressed in terms of the domestic risk-neutral expectation of the value at expiry.

Fuller discussions of the Feynman–Kac approach can be found in Section 6.2.2.1 of Grigoriu (2002), Chapter VIII of Øksendal (2010), Section 5.8 of Bingham and Kiesel (1998) and Section 4.7 of Lipton (2001).

2.2.5 Risk-Neutral Valuation

Obtaining the Black–Scholes and Black-76 equations for derivatives written on spot, forward and futures contracts, we noticed that the real-world drift term μ does not appear, indicating that all rational market participants can be assumed to price derivatives identically no matter what value of μ is assumed for the expected drift. We saw in Section 2.2.4 above that the present value can be identified as the expectation under a particular choice of measure, which we refer to as the domestic risk-neutral measure.

2.2.5.1 Domestic Risk-Neutral Measure

The domestic investor sees the foreign commodity bond B_t^f as the risky asset, which denominated in domestic currency is valued at $B_t^f S_t$. Construct the ratio of this against the domestic bond

$$
\begin{aligned}
Z_t &= S_t B_t^f / B_t^d \\
&= S_0 \exp\left(\sigma W_t + \left(\mu - \frac{1}{2}\sigma^2\right)t\right) \exp\left((r^f - r^d)t\right) \\
&= S_0 \exp\left(\sigma W_t - \frac{1}{2}\sigma^2 t\right) \exp\left((\mu + r^f - r^d)t\right).
\end{aligned}
$$

To attain the martingale property we require that

$$\mu = \mu^d \equiv r^d - r^f \qquad (2.47)$$

so under the domestic risk-neutral measure $\mathbf{P}^d$ we can write

$$S_t = S_0 \exp\left(\sigma W_t^d + \left(r^d - r^f - \frac{1}{2}\sigma^2\right)t\right), \qquad (2.48)$$
$$dS_t = (r^d - r^f)S_t dt + \sigma S_t dW_t^d.$$

The drift change required is

$$W_t^d = W_t + \frac{\mu - \mu^d}{\sigma}t \qquad (2.49)$$

which gives a Radon–Nikodym derivative at time T of

$$\frac{d\mathbf{P}^d}{d\mathbf{P}} = \exp\left(-\gamma^d W_T - \frac{1}{2}[\gamma^d]^2 T\right), \quad \text{where } \gamma^d = \frac{\mu - \mu^d}{\sigma}. \qquad (2.50)$$

2.2.5.2   *Foreign Risk-Neutral Measure*

As discussed in Clark (2011), we can also see the domestic risk-free bond as a risky investment from the viewpoint of a foreign denominated investor. Under the foreign risk-neutral measure $\mathbf{P}^f$ we have

$$S_t = S_0 \exp\left(\sigma W_t^f + \left(r^d - r^f + \frac{1}{2}\sigma^2\right)t\right), \qquad (2.51)$$
$$dS_t = (r^d - r^f + \sigma^2)S_t dt + \sigma S_t dW_t^f.$$

The applicable drift change required is

$$W_t^f = W_t + \frac{\mu - \mu^f}{\sigma}t, \qquad (2.52)$$

which gives a Radon–Nikodym derivative at time T of

$$\frac{d\mathbf{P}^f}{d\mathbf{P}} = \exp\left(-\gamma^f W_T - \frac{1}{2}[\gamma^f]^2 T\right), \quad \text{where } \gamma^f = \frac{\mu - \mu^f}{\sigma} \qquad (2.53)$$

and

$$\mu^f \equiv r^d - r^f + \sigma^2. \qquad (2.54)$$

2.2.6   Forwards

Forwards, with payout function $V_T = S_T - K$ at time T as illustrated in Figure 2.2, can have a negative value as well as a positive value,

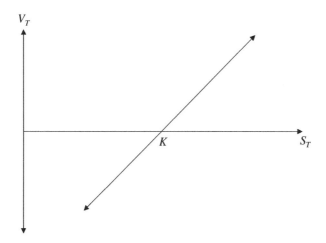

Figure 2.2 Payout function V_T for forward.

depending on the strike K. It is therefore customary to solve for the value of K that makes the forward costless to enter into. This choice of strike K for which $V_0 = e^{-r^d T} \mathbf{E}^d \left[S_T - K \right] = 0$ is denoted $F_{0,T}$, i.e. $F_{0,T} = \mathbf{E}^d \left[S_T \right]$.

By (2.48) we easily obtain

$$
\begin{aligned}
F_{0,T} &= \mathbf{E}^d \left[S_T \right] \\
&= S_0 \mathbf{E}^d \left[\exp \left(\sigma W_T^d + \left(r^d - r^f - \frac{1}{2}\sigma^2 \right) T \right) \right] \\
&= S_0 e^{(r^d - r^f)T} \mathbf{E}^d \left[\exp \left(\sigma W_T^d - \frac{1}{2}\sigma^2 T \right) \right] \\
&= S_0 e^{(r^d - r^f)T}
\end{aligned}
\tag{2.55}
$$

and more generally, taking the conditional expectation at time t we obtain

$$
F_{t,T} = S_t e^{(r^d - r^f)(T-t)}.
\tag{2.56}
$$

From this, a simple application of Itô's Lemma demonstrates that forwards are driftless under the risk-neutral measure. Write (2.56) as $F_{t,T} = h(S_t, t)$ with $h(s, t) = s \exp((r^d - r^f)(T - t)) = s \exp((r^d - r^f)T) \exp((r^f - r^d)t)$. Clearly $h_s = \exp((r^d - r^f)(T - t))$, $h_{ss} = 0$ and

$h_t = (r^f - r^d)s \exp((r^d - r^f)T)$. We then have

$$
\begin{aligned}
dF_{t,T} &= d[h(S_t, t)] \\
&= h_s dS_t + h_t dt \\
&= \exp((r^d - r^f)(T - t))dS_t + (r^f - r^d)S_t \exp((r^d - r^f)T)dt \\
&= \exp((r^d - r^f)(T - t))[(r^d - r^f)S_t dt + \sigma S_t dW_t^d] + (r^f - r^d)F_{t,T}dt \\
&= (r^d - r^f)F_{t,T}dt + \sigma F_{t,T}dW_t^d + (r^f - r^d)F_{t,T}dt \\
&= \sigma F_{t,T}dW_t^d
\end{aligned}
\tag{2.57}
$$

which verifies the earlier assumed form for the GBM given earlier in (2.20) and (2.30).

2.2.7   The Black–Scholes Term Structure Model

The Black–Scholes model of Section 2.2.1 does not allow any term structure of interest rates or volatility.

We can easily extend the model in (2.2) to

$$
dS_t = \mu_t S_t dt + \sigma_t S_t dW_t,
\tag{2.58}
$$

where both μ_t and σ_t are deterministic processes. By risk-neutrality, we obtain

$$
\mu_t = r_t^d - r_t^f.
\tag{2.59}
$$

It follows (see Clark, 2011) that the risk-neutral valuation methods of this chapter can be directly applied to valuation of commodity derivatives with expiry T, with r^d, r^f and σ replaced by effective counterparts $\bar{r}_T^d$, $\bar{r}_T^f$ and $\bar{\sigma}_T$, where

$$
\bar{r}_T^{d;f} = \frac{1}{T} \int_0^T r_s^{d;f} ds
$$

are the effective (continuously compounded) domestic rate and convenience yield respectively over the time interval $[0,T]$, and

$$
\bar{\sigma}_T = \sqrt{\frac{1}{T} \int_0^T \sigma_s^2 ds}
$$

defines the effective volatility $\bar{\sigma}_T$ applicable over the time interval $[0,T]$.

2.3   FORWARD AND FUTURES CONTRACTS

We are now in position to start introducing actual financial derivative contracts, including the pricing mechanics in the Black case. The simplest are the forward and futures contracts, which we already encountered in Section 2.1. Note, however, that what we introduced there were the forward and futures prices, which are not the same thing as the PVs of a forward or a futures contract. Some explanation is definitely in order.

2.3.1   Forwards

Consider a forward contract, with payout function $V_T = F_{T,T} - K = S_T - K$ at time T shown in Figure 2.2. As introduced in Section 2.2.6, the choice of strike K for which the forward is costless to enter into is denoted $F_{0,T}$, i.e. $F_{0,T} = \mathbf{E}^d\left[S_T\right] = S_t e^{(r^d - r^f)(T-t)}$.

If the forward was not entered into on a costless basis, or if time has passed since the original strike was set and the commodity price has moved, then the strike price K today will not be equal to $F_{0,T}$ and we need to PV it (i.e. to obtain the present value). Quite trivially we obtain

$$V_0 = e^{-r^d T} \mathbf{E}^d\left[S_T - K\right] = e^{-r^d T}[\mathbf{E}^d[S_T] - K] = e^{-r^d T}[F_{0,T} - K]. \quad (2.60)$$

In the event where the final settlement of the forward is at a later time T_{stl} than the fixing T, with $T < T_{\text{stl}}$, we have

$$V_0 = e^{-r^d T_{\text{stl}}}[F_{0,T} - K]. \qquad (2.61)$$

2.3.2   Futures

Consider now the T-futures contract, with strike price $K = f_{0,T}$. This is valued similarly to the forward contract treated in Section 2.3.1, but note that the payout function for the futures contract $V_T = f_{T,T} - K = S_T - K$ at time T neglects the interest accrued on the margin account over the lifetime of the futures contract. Consequently we need to adjust for this in obtaining the value of a futures contract today. With $f_{t,T}$ denoting the price of the T-futures contract today, we let $\hat{f}_{t,T}^{(K)}$ denote the value of a portfolio consisting of the T-futures contract with strike K together with any accrued or payable interest on the margin account (we can rebase the maintenance levels without loss of generality). Since this portfolio earns (or is liable for) interest at the instantaneous risk free rate r^d on positive or negative values of $f_{t,T} - K$ respectively, we can write

$$d\hat{f}_{t,T}^{(K)} = df_{t,T} + r^d(f_{t,T} - K)dt. \tag{2.62}$$

Because $f_{t,T}$ is a martingale under the domestic risk-neutral measure, and because r^d only applies a drift correction, we clearly have

$$\mathbf{E}^d\left[\hat{f}_{T,T}^{(K)}\right] = f_{0,T} - K + (f_{0,T} - K)(e^{r^d T} - 1) \tag{2.63a}$$

$$= (f_{0,T} - K)e^{r^d T} \tag{2.63b}$$

where the first two terms on the right hand side of (2.63a) correspond to the expected value of the futures contract at expiry, and the third term corresponds to the expected gain (or loss) due to interest accrued (or paid) on the margin account over $[0, T]$.

Discounting (2.63) appropriately, we obtain

$$V_0 = e^{-r^d T}\mathbf{E}^d\left[\hat{f}_{T,T}^{(K)}\right] = f_{0,T} - K. \tag{2.64}$$

Comparing (2.61) with (2.64), we see that the prices agree up to a discount factor – i.e. PVs for forward contracts are discounted, whereas PVs for equivalent futures contracts are not.

2.3.3   Case Study

We conclude this section with an example. Consider a WTI contract on NYMEX as the example in question. Suppose short positions in two contracts are entered into on 21 October 2010, a forward contract and a DEC10 futures contract, each to be closed out on 19 November 2010 when the futures contract matures.[6] This may seem unusual but it is standard for NYMEX futures, see Chapter 5. Suppose that the US interest rate is 0.25% and that strike $K = 85$.

With initial and variation margins of $9,788 and $7,250 respectively and a contract size of 1,000 barrels, i.e. $9.788 and $7.25 respectively per barrel, we can tabulate the cashflows on a per-barrel basis for each of these two contracts in Table 2.2, given NYMEX oil prices over that period of interest.

---

[6] Note that actual final cash settlement is five NYMEX business days later; for this example we presume that positions are closed out on the maturity date.

Table 2.2   Case Study: forward vs futures contract.

| t | $f_{t,T}$ | P/L | Margin a/c balance | | | Cashflow on | |
			c/o	+P/L	+P/L + Margin	Forward	Futures
21-Oct-10	80.36	+4.64	9.788	14.428	14.428		−9.788
22-Oct-10	81.63	−1.27	14.428	13.158	13.158		
25-Oct-10	82.52	−0.89	13.158	12.268	12.268		
26-Oct-10	82.57	−0.05	12.268	12.218	12.218		
27-Oct-10	81.91	+0.66	12.219	12.879	12.879		
28-Oct-10	82.18	−0.27	12.879	12.614	12.614		
29-Oct-10	81.45	+0.72	12.614	13.339	13.339		
1-Nov-10	82.98	−1.53	13.339	11.809	11.809		
2-Nov-10	83.91	−0.93	11.809	10.879	10.879		
3-Nov-10	84.67	−0.76	10.879	10.119	10.119		
4-Nov-10	86.47	−1.80	10.119	8.319	8.319		
5-Nov-10	86.85	−0.38	8.319	7.944	7.944		
8-Nov-10	87.02	−0.17	7.944	7.769	7.769		
9-Nov-10	86.73	+0.29	7.769	8.059	8.059		
10-Nov-10	87.80	−1.07	8.060	6.990	7.250		−0.260
11-Nov-10	87.81	−0.01	7.250	7.240	7.250		−0.010
12-Nov-10	84.91	+2.91	7.250	10.155	10.155		
15-Nov-10	84.84	+0.06	10.155	10.220	10.220		
16-Nov-10	82.34	+2.50	10.220	12.720	12.720		
17-Nov-10	80.46	+1.88	12.720	14.600	14.600		
18-Nov-10	81.87	−1.41	14.601	13.191	13.191		
19-Nov-10	81.51	+0.36	13.191	13.551	13.551	+3.490	+13.551

PV-ing these cashflows and discounting back to 21 October 2010, we obtain prices for the forward and futures contract of $3.48931 and $3.48954 per barrel respectively. Note that the futures price is slightly above the forward price.

The forward contract only has a cashflow on 19 November 2010, as one would expect. However the futures contract has the cashflow corresponding to depositing the initial margin on 21 October 2010 and two further injections of cash on 10 and 11 October 2010 into the margin account to bring the balance up to the variation margin, in addition to the final cashflow on 19 November 2010 where the balance (including profits or losses) is retrieved in full.

Given the final oil price of $81.51/bbl and a strike of 85, we would expect a short futures contract to be valued at $3.49/bbl and a short forward contract to be valued at $3.48931/bbl (including discounting at 2.5%). The PV of the forward contract is exactly in line with this, the futures contract is not so because the $3.49 estimate is purely an *expectation*. The PV for the futures contract of $3.48954/bbl in this case was obtained from a *particular* asset price trajectory ending at $81.51/bbl, other trajectories similarly ending at $81.51/bbl exist which will give PVs for the futures contract higher than $3.49/bbl and we expect the average to be $3.49/bbl.

It is not hard to see that the actual value of a futures contract must depend on the trajectory of the asset price process – for example, if the oil price shoots to $81.51/bbl immediately, that will give a different P/L for the margin account than if the oil price only goes up to $81.51/bbl in late October.

2.4 COMMODITY SWAPS

A futures contract is exposed to only one price fixing, on the expiry date of the futures itself. This may be too much fixing risk for a market participant, given the volatilities in commodity markets. For this reason it is quite common for products to be fixed against the average of a futures contract, and since a particular contract needs to be chosen, the one usually referenced is the prompt futures contract.

As discussed in Das (2005), Section 8.3.1 of Flavell (2009) and Section 2.1.3 of Burger *et al.* (2007), a commodity swap involves exchanging floating commodity prices against a fixed known commodity price K, with cash settlement either at the end of the swap or on a monthly basis. A long position in a commodity swap involves collecting the cash amount equivalent to the arithmetic difference between the (variable) fixing and the (fixed) strike K at each of the fixing dates t_i, i.e.

$$V_i = f_{t_i, \vec{T}(t_i)} - K$$

where t_i refers to the time of the i-th fixing and $\vec{T}(t_i)$ denotes[7] the expiry of the prompt future at time t_i.

Note that these values V_i are computed at each of the times t_i and the value today of the swap is equivalent to

$$V_0 = e^{-r^d T_{su}} \mathbf{E}^d \left[\frac{1}{n} \sum_{i=1}^{n} V_i \right].$$

---

[7] As introduced in Section 2.1.1, the arrow is meant to denote moving along the time axis, in the direction of increasing time, from time t_i to the first futures expiry $\vec{T}(t_i)$ after t_i.

It is customary to solve for the strike that makes the swap costless to enter into, i.e. solving for $V_0 = 0$, thereby obtaining

$$K_{\text{Swap}} = \frac{1}{n} \sum_{i=1}^{n} \mathbf{E}^d \left[f_{t_i, \bar{T}(t_i)} \right]$$

$$= \frac{1}{n} \sum_{i=1}^{n} f_{0, \bar{T}(t_i)} \tag{2.65}$$

since futures prices are martingales under the domestic risk-neutral measure. We sometimes call this the "crossing" level.

Note that this "swap price" is not the same as the PV of a swap, in the same way as the forward/futures prices are not the PVs of the equivalent forward or futures contract. In fact it is nothing more than the arithmetic average of the futures contracts computed using today's futures prices

$$A_{0;\{t_1, t_n\}}^{A;f} = \frac{1}{n} \sum_{i=1}^{n} f_{0, \bar{T}(t_i)}. \tag{2.66}$$

Note that $A_{0;\{t_1, t_n\}}^{A;f}$ is a deterministic quantity that can be computed today, being a linear combination of today's futures prices. It should not be confused with the arithmetic averages of either spot or futures prices that we can construct as stochastic processes, i.e.

$$A_{t_1, t_n}^{A,s} = \frac{1}{n} \sum_{i=1}^{n} S_{t_i} \tag{2.67a}$$

$$A_{t_1, t_n}^{A,f} = \frac{1}{n} \sum_{i=1}^{n} f_{t_i, \bar{T}(t_i)} \tag{2.67b}$$

which can only be known deterministically once all n observations have taken place. We will see more of these in Section 2.7 on Asian options.

In the event of a swap longer dated than a calendar month, with settlement each month, we can use $T_{\text{stl};i}$ to denote the settlement dates and then have

$$V_0 = \frac{1}{n} \mathbf{E}^d \left[\sum_{i=1}^{n} e^{-r^d T_{\text{stl};i}} V_i \right]. \tag{2.68}$$

Swaps for durations in excess of one calendar month can easily be decomposed into the various constituent months.

Now, since the prompt futures contract generally rolls during the course of a calendar month rather than neatly at the end, this means that a commodity swap is effectively a weighted average of the two futures contracts which comprise the prompt future over that particular month. One sometimes sees the terminology "calendar month average" (CMA) used for this.

The only troublesome aspect of pricing commodity swaps is working out the specifics of handling the roll date. It is commonplace to use Swap(1,0) and Swap(1,1) to denote two different variants, the first being the case where the prompt future rolls at the end of the expiry date, the second being where the prompt future rolls at the beginning of the expiry date.

Cash settlement for NYMEX swaps (and most other energy swaps) is usually on the 5th business day of the subsequent month, i.e. five business days after the final fixing.

A case study of commodity swap pricing with respect to oil can be found in Section 5.1.2.

2.5   EUROPEAN OPTIONS

Forward, futures and swap contracts are all directional trades, being the obligation to buy (or sell) a particular commodity at a particular time in the future, where the price is either fixed at the maturity date or by averaging the price over a number of fixing dates. As such, any of these trades can have positive or negative value to the buyer (or indeed the seller).

Potentially, however, a market participant may be happy to accept a higher price for an asset he or she is selling, but wants to avoid the possibility of lower prices. Alternatively, a purchaser of oil may be quite happy with lower prices, but wants to avoid higher prices. Both of these possibilities can be catered for with option contracts, which typically convey the right but not the obligation to buy (or sell) an asset at a prespecified strike price K at some known time in the future. Note that the option can *only* be exercised at this specific time, i.e. on the exercise date.

In spite of the fact that most commodity options are options on futures, we can equivalently consider the case of options on the forward $F_{t,T}$ given the assumption for all the models considered in this work: that futures and forwards prices coincide, or options on the spot process S_t. In order to be able to describe all of these, we shall discuss options

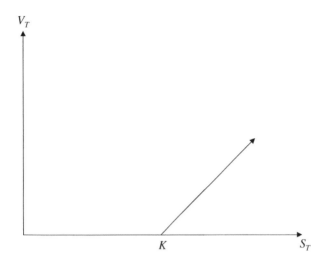

Figure 2.3 Payout function V_T for European call.

on the spot process S_t, since driftless processes for $F_{t,T}$ and $f_{t,T}$ can be handled as special cases of S_t with the convenience yield r^f set equal to the interest rate r^d, to kill the drift.

2.5.1 European Options on Spot

Consider a European call option, with payout function $V_T = \max(S_T - K, 0) = (S_T - K)^+$ at time T shown in Figure 2.3.

One can compute the price of such an option today by constructing the following risk-neutral expectation in the domestic risk-neutral measure:

$$
\begin{aligned}
V_0 &= e^{-r^d T} \mathbf{E}^d \left[(S_T - K)^+ \right] \\
&= e^{-r^d T} \mathbf{E}^d \left[(S_T - K)\mathbf{1}_{\{S_T \geq K\}} \right] \\
&= e^{-r^d T} \mathbf{E}^d \left[S_T \mathbf{1}_{\{S_T \geq K\}} - K\mathbf{1}_{\{S_T \geq K\}} \right] \\
&= e^{-r^d T} \mathbf{E}^d \left[S_T \mathbf{1}_{\{S_T \geq K\}} \right] - K e^{-r^d T} \mathbf{E}^d \left[\mathbf{1}_{\{S_T \geq K\}} \right] \\
&= e^{-r^d T} \mathbf{E}^d \left[S_T \mathbf{1}_{\{S_T \geq K\}} \right] - K e^{-r^d T} \mathbf{P}^d \left[S_T \geq K \right].
\end{aligned}
\tag{2.69}
$$

Evaluating $\mathbf{P}^d \left[S_T \geq K \right]$, which is nothing more than the domestic risk-neutral probability that $S_T \geq K$, is straightforward as we know the distribution of S_T. The second term requires a change of measure. In Section 2.2.5 we had expressions for the Radon–Nikodym derivatives relating the domestic and foreign risk-neutral measures to the real-world measure, so the Radon–Nikodym derivative relating one risk-neutral measure to the other needs to be obtained. From (2.50) and (2.53) we have

$$\frac{d\mathbf{P}^f}{d\mathbf{P}^d} = \exp\left(-\gamma^{f,d}W_T^d - \frac{1}{2}[\gamma^{f,d}]^2 T\right), \quad \text{where } \gamma^{f,d} = \frac{\mu^d - \mu^f}{\sigma}. \quad (2.70)$$

In short,

$$W_t^f = W_t^d + \frac{\mu^d - \mu^f}{\sigma}t = W_t^d - \sigma t. \quad (2.71)$$

From (2.47) and (2.54) we have $\mu^f - \mu^d = \sigma^2$ and consequently $\gamma^{f,d} = (\mu^d - \mu^f)/\sigma = -\sigma$, which gives

$$\frac{d\mathbf{P}^f}{d\mathbf{P}^d} = \exp\left(\sigma W_T^d - \frac{1}{2}\sigma^2 T\right). \quad (2.72)$$

Let us now use (2.72) to complete (2.69). The term requiring attention is $\mathbf{E}^d\left[S_T \mathbf{1}_{\{S_T \geq K\}}\right]$, which admits the following reduction

$$\begin{aligned}
\mathbf{E}^d\left[S_T \mathbf{1}_{\{S_T \geq K\}}\right] &= \mathbf{E}^d\left[S_0 \exp\left(\left(r^d - r^f - \frac{1}{2}\sigma^2\right)T + \sigma W_T^d\right)\mathbf{1}_{\{S_T \geq K\}}\right] \\
&= S_0 e^{(r^d - r^f)T}\mathbf{E}^d\left[\exp\left(\sigma W_T^d - \frac{1}{2}\sigma^2 T\right)\mathbf{1}_{\{S_T \geq K\}}\right] \\
&= S_0 e^{(r^d - r^f)T}\mathbf{E}^d\left[\frac{d\mathbf{P}^f}{d\mathbf{P}^d}\mathbf{1}_{\{S_T \geq K\}}\right] \\
&= S_0 e^{(r^d - r^f)T}\mathbf{E}^f\left[\mathbf{1}_{\{S_T \geq K\}}\right] \\
&= S_0 e^{(r^d - r^f)T}\mathbf{P}^f\left[S_T \geq K\right]. \quad (2.73)
\end{aligned}$$

This yields

$$V_0 = S_0 e^{-r^f T}\mathbf{P}^f\left[S_T \geq K\right] - Ke^{-r^d T}\mathbf{P}^d\left[S_T \geq K\right]. \quad (2.74)$$

Next, we calculate the two risk-neutral probabilities (in $\mathbf{P}^d$ and $\mathbf{P}^f$) that $S_T \geq K$. Recall from (2.48) and (2.51) that

$$S_T = S_0 \exp\left(\sigma W_T^d + \left(r^d - r^f - \frac{1}{2}\sigma^2\right)T\right), \quad (2.75a)$$

$$S_T = S_0 \exp\left(\sigma W_T^f + \left(r^d - r^f + \frac{1}{2}\sigma^2\right)T\right). \quad (2.75b)$$

To enable us to perform the computations in both measures, introduce the index i which takes values in $\{1, 2\}$ and $X(\cdot)$ defined such that $X(1) \equiv f$ and $X(2) \equiv d$. We then have

$$S_T = S_0 \exp\left(\sigma W_T^{X(i)} + \left(r^d - r^f + \left[\frac{1}{2} - (i-1)\right]\sigma^2\right)T\right). \quad (2.76)$$

The probabilities in (2.74) for domestic and foreign risk-neutral measures are obtained by computing $\mathbf{P}^{X(i)}\left[S_T \geq K\right]$ for $i = 1, 2$. We then use (2.76) to write

$$\mathbf{P}^{X(i)}\left[S_0 \exp\left(\sigma W_T^{X(i)} + \left(r^d - r^f + \left[\frac{1}{2} - (i-1)\right]\sigma^2\right)T\right) \geq K\right]$$

$$= \mathbf{P}^{X(i)}\left[\exp\left(\sigma W_T^{X(i)} + \left(r^d - r^f + \left[\frac{1}{2} - (i-1)\right]\sigma^2\right)T\right) \geq \frac{K}{S_0}\right]$$

$$= \mathbf{P}^{X(i)}\left[\sigma W_T^{X(i)} + \left(r^d - r^f + \left[\frac{1}{2} - (i-1)\right]\sigma^2\right)T \geq \ln\left(\frac{K}{S_0}\right)\right]$$

$$= \mathbf{P}^{X(i)}\left[\sigma W_T^{X(i)} \geq \ln\left(\frac{K}{S_0}\right) - \left(r^d - r^f + \left[\frac{1}{2} - (i-1)\right]\sigma^2\right)T\right]$$

$$= \mathbf{P}^{X(i)}\left[\sigma W_T^{X(i)} \leq \ln\left(\frac{S_0}{K}\right) + \left(r^d - r^f + \left[\frac{1}{2} - (i-1)\right]\sigma^2\right)T\right]$$

$$= \mathbf{P}\left[\sigma\sqrt{T}\xi \leq \ln\left(\frac{S_0}{K}\right) + \left(r^d - r^f + \left[\frac{1}{2} - (i-1)\right]\sigma^2\right)T\right]$$

$$= \mathbf{P}\left[\xi \leq \frac{\ln\left(\frac{S_0}{K}\right) + \left(r^d - r^f + \left[\frac{1}{2} - (i-1)\right]\sigma^2\right)T}{\sigma\sqrt{T}}\right]$$

where ξ is a standard $N(0, 1)$ normal distribution. Let us now define d_1 and d_2 by

$$d_i = \frac{\ln\left(\frac{S_0}{K}\right) + \left(r^d - r^f + \left[\frac{1}{2} - (i-1)\right]\sigma^2\right)T}{\sigma\sqrt{T}}, \quad (2.77)$$

which lets us write

$$\mathbf{P}^{X(i)}\left[S_T \geq K\right] = N(d_i), \quad (2.78)$$

where $N(x) = \int_{-\infty}^{x} n(u)du$ is the cumulative distribution function and

$$n(u) = (2\pi)^{-1/2} \exp\left(-\frac{1}{2}u^2\right) \qquad (2.79)$$

is the probability density function for the standard normal distribution $N(0, 1)$.

Finally, substituting (2.78) into (2.74) yields the standard Garman–Kohlhagen (Garman and Kohlhagen, 1983) formula for a European call

$$V_0^C = S_0 e^{-r^f T} N(d_1) - K e^{-r^d T} N(d_2) \qquad (2.80)$$

with

$$d_{1,2} = \frac{\ln\left(\frac{S_0}{K}\right) + \left(r^d - r^f \pm \frac{1}{2}\sigma^2\right)T}{\sigma\sqrt{T}}. \qquad (2.81)$$

The result is familiar.

The same argument applies for the European put option, with payout function $V_T = \max(K - S_T, 0) = (K - S_T)^+$ at time T shown in Figure 2.4, for which we obtain

$$V_0^P = K e^{-r^d T} N(-d_2) - S_0 e^{-r^f T} N(-d_1). \qquad (2.82)$$

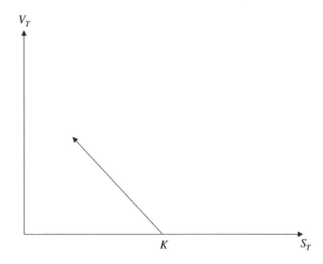

Figure 2.4   Payout function V_T for European put.

Both can be expressed more concisely by introducing a variable ω which is $+1$ for a call and -1 for a put, we then have

$$V_0^{C/P} = \omega S_0 e^{-r^f T} N(\omega d_1) - \omega K e^{-r^d T} N(\omega d_2). \qquad (2.83)$$

2.5.2 European Options on Futures

If, instead of options on spot S_T, we have options on the T^*-forward or a T^*-futures contract, then instead of dS_t as in (2.43) we have df_{t,T^*} or dF_{t,T^*} as in (2.20) or (2.30). Let's suppose without loss of generality that we are dealing with options on the T^*-forward. Supposing that the volatility σ of the T^*-forward is known, we have

$$V_0^{C/P} = \omega e^{-r^d T} [F_{0,T^*} N(\omega d_1) - K N(\omega d_2)] \qquad (2.84a)$$

with

$$d_{1,2} = \frac{\ln\left(F_{0,T^*}/K\right) \pm \frac{1}{2}\sigma^2 T}{\sigma \sqrt{T}}. \qquad (2.84b)$$

2.5.3 Settlement Adjustments

Finally, let us suppose that an option has expiry date T but actual settlement possibly later on. We shall use T_{stl} to denote the time to settlement, where $T_{\text{stl}} \geq T$. If the option is cash settled, then this just means we have some additional discounting, corresponding to the extra period we have to wait to receive the cash. If, however, the option is physically settled and it is an option on a spot process (i.e. not on a futures contract or on a forward), then we also need to adjust the strike for options on spot to take into account the expected drift of the process between T and T_{stl}. Define K' by

$$K' = \begin{cases} K \cdot D_{T,T_{\text{stl}}}^d / D_{T,T_{\text{stl}}}^f, & \text{physically settled option on } S_T \\ K, & \text{otherwise.} \end{cases}$$

As a result, in the case of European options with late settlement we merely use

$$V_0^{C/P;\text{dd}}(K, T) = D_{T,T_{\text{stl}}}^d \cdot V_0^{C/P}(K', T), \qquad (2.85)$$

where dd denotes "delayed delivery".

2.6   AMERICAN OPTIONS

While European options are easily priced in closed form, at least under a simple model such as the Black–Scholes or the Black-76 model, it is commonplace in the markets for options on futures to be exercisable continuously up to and on the exercise date. Some approximations do exist for this, such as Barone-Adesi and Whaley (1987), Bjerksund and Stensland (1993) and Bjerksund and Stensland (2002), but it is equally commonplace to use a binomial tree or PDE lattice method.

2.6.1   Barone-Adesi and Whaley (1987)

Firstly, I shall introduce the Barone-Adesi and Whaley (1987) approximation, in the special case where the drift of the stochastic process identically vanishes (such as it does in the Black-76 model). Let $V_A(F, T)$ denote the price of an American option with maturity T and $V_E(F, T)$ denote the price of an equivalent European option without the early exercise feature. We shall suppose that these are options on the forward F.

As both American and European options satisfy the same linear partial differential equation (2.33), we know by the principle of superposition that $\epsilon = V_A(F, T) - V_E(F, T)$ must also satisfy (2.33).

We therefore require

$$\frac{\partial \epsilon}{\partial t} + \frac{1}{2}\sigma^2 F^2 \frac{\partial^2 \epsilon}{\partial F^2} - r^d \epsilon = 0 \qquad (2.86)$$

or, after multiplying by $2/\sigma^2$ and denoting $M = 2r^d/\sigma^2$, we have

$$F^2 \frac{\partial^2 \epsilon}{\partial F^2} - \frac{M}{r^d} \frac{\partial \epsilon}{\partial \tau} - M\epsilon = 0 \qquad (2.87)$$

where we switch to time reversed coordinates $\tau = T - t$.

We then use a separation of variables approach and posit the following form for the early exercise premium

$$\epsilon(F, k) = k(\tau)g(F, k). \qquad (2.88)$$

Note that k above bears no relationship to strike – basically we're saying that k depends on τ and then $\epsilon(F, \tau) = \epsilon(F, k(\tau)) = k(\tau)g(F, k(\tau))$.

We have

$$\frac{\partial^2 \epsilon}{\partial F^2} = k \frac{\partial^2 g}{\partial F^2} \quad \text{and} \quad \frac{\partial \epsilon}{\partial \tau} = \frac{\partial k}{\partial \tau}g + k\frac{\partial k}{\partial \tau}\frac{\partial g}{\partial k}. \qquad (2.89)$$

Substituting (2.89) into (2.87) we get

$$F^2 \frac{\partial^2 g}{\partial F^2} - Mg \left[1 + \frac{1}{r^d k} \left(1 + \frac{k}{g} \frac{\partial g}{\partial k} \right) \frac{\partial k}{\partial \tau} \right] = 0. \qquad (2.90)$$

The Barone-Adesi and Whaley approach now puts $k(\tau) = 1 - e^{-r^d \tau}$, and so $k' = r^d e^{-r^d \tau}$. With this, we can simplify (2.90) somewhat. Let us take a fragment of the term on the right hand side and apply some simple algebra to it. We have

$$g \left[1 + \frac{1}{r^d k} \left(1 + \frac{k}{g} \frac{\partial g}{\partial k} \right) \frac{\partial k}{\partial \tau} \right] = \left(1 + \frac{1}{r^d k} \frac{\partial k}{\partial \tau} \right) g + \frac{1}{r^d} \frac{\partial k}{\partial \tau} \frac{\partial g}{\partial k}$$

$$= \left(1 + \frac{1}{r^d} \frac{k'}{k} \right) g + e^{-r^d \tau} \frac{\partial g}{\partial k}$$

$$= \left(1 + \frac{e^{-r^d \tau}}{1 - e^{-r^d \tau}} \right) g + (1 - k) \frac{\partial g}{\partial k}$$

$$= \left(\frac{1}{k} \right) g + (1 - k) \frac{\partial g}{\partial k},$$

where the final step follows from $1 + \frac{e^{-r^d \tau}}{1 - e^{-r^d \tau}} = \frac{1 - e^{-r^d \tau} + e^{-r^d \tau}}{1 - e^{-r^d \tau}} = \frac{1}{1 - e^{-r^d \tau}} = \frac{1}{k}$. Consequently we arrive at

$$F^2 \frac{\partial^2 g}{\partial F^2} - \frac{M}{k} g - M(1 - k) \frac{\partial g}{\partial k} = 0. \qquad (2.91)$$

Barone-Adesi and Whaley (1987) then make the approximation that the final $M(1 - k) \frac{\partial g}{\partial k}$ term in (2.91) can be supposed to be negligible (particularly so when τ is very small or very large), thereby arriving at

$$F^2 \frac{\partial^2 g}{\partial F^2} - \frac{M}{k} g = 0. \qquad (2.92)$$

Note that (2.91) is a partial differential equation but (2.92) is now an ordinary differential equation since $g(\cdot)$ is now a univariate function of q.

This can be solved by substituting $g(F) = F^q$ into (2.92) which reduces (as the second derivative $g''(F) = q(q - 1)F^{q-2}$ trivially) to

$$q(q - 1)F^q - \frac{M}{k} F^q = 0. \qquad (2.93)$$

This requires solution of a quadratic in q

$$q^2 - q - \frac{M}{k} = 0 \qquad (2.94)$$

which has solutions $q_1 = \frac{1}{2}(1 - \sqrt{1 + 4M/k})$, $q_2 = \frac{1}{2}(1 + \sqrt{1 + 4M/k})$. Our solution of (2.93) is

$$g(F) = a_1 F^{q_1} + a_2 F^{q_2}$$

where a_1 and a_2 are real constants and $q_1 < 0$ and $q_2 > 0$. For an American call we require $a_1 = 0$ in order that the price not explode as $F \to 0$, and for an American put we require $a_2 = 0$ so that the price is similarly well behaved for large values of F.

We know that for sufficiently in-the-money options, it is optimal to exercise immediately (so as to obtain the intrinsic value today rather than having to wait until T). What this means is that for American calls, there must exist an F^* such that the value of the American call is equal to the (positive) intrinsic value in $[F^*, \infty)$, i.e. $V_A(F, t) = F - K \ \forall \ F > F^*$. For American puts, the exercise region is $[0, F^*]$, i.e. the value of the American put $V_A(F, t) = K - F \ \forall \ F < F^*$.

The task is to find F^*. Since we are dealing with a diffusion equation, we know that the function and its first derivative must be continuous across the domain transition at F^*. For the American call we have

$$F^* - K = V_E^C(F^*, T) + ka_2(F^*)^{q_2} \qquad (2.95a)$$

$$1 = \frac{\partial}{\partial F^*} \left(V_E^C(F^*, T) \right) + ka_2 q_2 (F^*)^{q_2 - 1}$$
$$= e^{-r'T} N(d_1(F^*)) + ka_2 q_2 (F^*)^{q_2 - 1} \qquad (2.95b)$$

and for the American put

$$K - F^* = V_E^P(F^*, T) + ka_1(F^*)^{q_1} \qquad (2.96a)$$

$$-1 = \frac{\partial}{\partial F} \left(V_E^P(F^*, T) \right) + ka_1 q_1 (F^*)^{q_1 - 1}$$
$$= -e^{-r'T} N(-d_1(F^*)) + ka_1 q_1 (F^*)^{q_1 - 1}. \qquad (2.96b)$$

As Barone-Adesi and Whaley (1987) point out, either (2.95) or (2.96) constitute a system of two equations in two unknowns. Consider the American call. We can use (2.95b) to solve for a_2, obtaining

$$ka_2(F^*)^{q_2} = \frac{F^*}{q_2} \left[1 - e^{-r'T} N(d_1(F^*)) \right] \qquad (2.97)$$

which plugs directly into (2.95a), giving

$$F^* - K = V_E^C(F^*, T) + \frac{F^*}{q_2}\left[1 - e^{-r^f T}N(d_1(F^*))\right]. \qquad (2.98)$$

As (2.98) is an implicit equation in F^*, solving for the critical value F^* (above which the value of the American call is equal to its intrinsic value) requires a numerical scheme such as Newton–Raphson to be used. We refer the reader to the original paper by Barone-Adesi and Whaley (1987), Section 7.2 of Briys, Bellalah, Mai and de Varenne (1998) or Chapter 3 of Haug (2007) for further discussion.

Once F^* has been determined, the value of an American call option can then be computed directly by addition of the early exercise premium ϵ to the European call price $V_E^C(F^*, T)$ by use of (2.97). We have

$$\epsilon = kg(F) = ka_2 F^{q_2}$$
$$= \left(\frac{1}{F^*}\right)^{q_2}\frac{F^*}{q_2}\left[1 - e^{-r^f T}N(d_1(F^*))\right]F^{q_2}$$
$$= A_2\left(\frac{F}{F^*}\right)^{q_2},$$

where $A_2 = \frac{F^*}{q_2}\left[1 - e^{-r^f T}N(d_1(F^*))\right]$. The price of the American option can then be written as

$$V_A(F, T) = V_E(F, T) + A_2\left(\frac{F}{F^*}\right)^{q_2}. \qquad (2.99)$$

We make the final remark that other approximations, such as Bjerksund and Stensland (1993) and Bjerksund and Stensland (2002), are also worth investigating.

2.6.2 Lattice Methods

While fast, approximations like the above are inexact. For this reason, lattice methods, such as binomial trees or a finite difference PDEs, are often used. The formulation of these is well beyond the scope of this book and will very likely be familiar to some extent; we refer the reader to standard PDE references such as (but by no means limited to) Wilmott, Dewynne and Howison (1993) and/or Wilmott, Howison and Dewynne (1995), Tavella and Randall (2000) and Duffy (2006) as well as my previous book for discussion of the finite difference approach to option pricing.

For these methods, at each step of the backward induction, a comparison is made between the PV of the option (conditional on spot and time) and the intrinsic value of the product. For each node on the finite difference grid, if the intrinsic value is greater, then one replaces the lattice PV with the intrinsic value. The use of PDEs in option pricing is discussed in Chapter 8 of Clark (2011) with the specific condition relating to value monitoring for American options in Section 8.7.2.

For each timestep where the American option is early exercisable, we apply the following condition, where ω is 1 for a call and -1 for a put.

$$V(S, t^-) = \max(V(S, t^+) - K_C, (\omega(S_t - K)^+)). \qquad (2.100)$$

2.7 ASIAN OPTIONS

One of the features that differentiates commodities from other asset classes is the extent to which Asian options (in this context meaning average price options) are used. Part of this is because commodities tend to experience greater volatility than many other asset classes, so there is a high degree of fixing risk attached to having an option which expires on one particular day and has a payout which is only a function of the marginal distribution at that one time. Additionally, the demand for commodities is relatively continuous – market participants tend to produce or consume commodities on an ongoing basis.

There are, however, two other features attached to the Asian options encountered in commodity markets (and in industry in general): firstly, the averaging is on the arithmetic average[8] and secondly the averaging is invariably over a set of discrete fixings rather than a continuous average (integral). These two features complicate the analysis, so let's start with something simple.

2.7.1 Geometric Asian Options – Continuous Averaging

Angus (1999) provides a very clear and easy to follow introduction to mathematical option pricing theory for Asian options, purely in the case where the average is a geometric average.

---

[8] Harmonic averages are additionally encountered in FX as the spot rate can be interpreted in one of two ways depending on which currency the notional is in.

As usual, we suppose that X_t denotes the logspot, i.e. $X_t = \ln S_t$. From (2.75a) we have

$$X_t = X_0 + \sigma W_t^d + \left(r^d - r^f - \frac{1}{2}\sigma^2\right)t. \tag{2.101}$$

First we construct the logspot integral I_t^X, which is given by

$$I_t^X = \int_0^t X_u du$$

and then we use this to express the continuous geometric average $A_t^{G;s} = \exp\left(I_t^X/t\right)$. A geometric average price call option, for example, will have payout $V_T = (A_T^{G;s} - K)^+$, whereas a geometric average strike option will have payout $V_T = (S_T - A_T^{G;s})^+$. To be able to price both styles of Asian options, we need to consider the joint distribution of (S_T, I_t^X), but for average price options we need only the statistical properties of I_t^X. Since average strike features are quite rare in the commodity markets, we shall restrict ourselves to considering only average price options, which make up the vast majority of the Asian options traded.

By stochastic integration of dX_t we have

$$X_t = X_0 + \left(r^d - r^f - \frac{1}{2}\sigma^2\right)t + \sigma W_t^d$$

so we can write

$$
\begin{aligned}
I_t^X &= \int_0^t X_u du \\
&= \int_0^t \left[X_0 + \left(r^d - r^f - \frac{1}{2}\sigma^2\right)u + \sigma W_u^d\right] du \\
&= tX_0 + \frac{1}{2}\left(r^d - r^f - \frac{1}{2}\sigma^2\right)t^2 + \sigma \int_0^t W_u^d du.
\end{aligned}
$$

From this, we can compute first and second moments. The first is given by

$$\mathbf{E}^d\left[I_t^X\right] = tX_0 + \frac{1}{2}\left(r^d - r^f - \frac{1}{2}\sigma^2\right)t^2$$

since $\mathbf{E}^d\left[\int_0^t W_u^d du\right] = 0$. Let us now define $\hat{I}_t^X = I_t^X - \mathbf{E}^d\left[I_t^X\right] = \sigma \int_0^t W_u^d du$, which we will use to compute $\mathbf{Var}^d\left[I_t^X\right] = \mathbf{E}^d\left[(\hat{I}_t^X)^2\right]$.

The analysis is simple:

$$\mathbf{E}^d\left[(\hat{I}_t^X)^2\right] = \sigma^2 \mathbf{E}^d\left[\left(\int_0^t W_s^d ds\right)\left(\int_0^t W_u^d du\right)\right]$$

$$= \sigma^2 \mathbf{E}^d\left[\int_0^t\int_0^t W_s^d W_u^d ds du\right]$$

$$= \sigma^2 \int_0^t\int_0^t \mathbf{E}^d\left[W_s^d W_u^d\right] ds du$$

$$= \sigma^2 \int_0^t\int_0^t \min(s,u) ds du.$$

Note that the final line can be obtained by assuming (without loss of generality) $s \leq u$ and writing $W_u = W_s + (W_u - W_s)$, and writing $\Delta W = W_u - W_s$, where W_s and ΔW are independent. We then have $\mathbf{E}\left[W_s W_u\right] = \mathbf{E}\left[W_s(W_s + \Delta W)\right] = \mathbf{E}\left[W_s^2\right] + \mathbf{E}\left[W_s \Delta W\right] = \mathbf{E}\left[W_s^2\right] = s$. If, however, $u \leq s$, then by the same argument $\mathbf{E}\left[W_s W_u\right] = u$, so the general result $\mathbf{E}\left[W_s W_u\right] = \min(s,u)$ follows.

Now let us evaluate $\int_0^t\int_0^t \min(s,u) ds du$, using (x,y) instead of (s,u).

$$\int_0^t\int_0^t \min(x,y) dx dy = 2\int_0^t\int_0^x \min(x,y) dx dy$$

$$= 2\int_0^t\int_0^x y dy dx$$

$$= 2\int_0^t \left[\frac{1}{2}y^2\right]_0^x dx$$

$$= \int_0^t x^2 dx$$

$$= \left[\frac{1}{3}x^3\right]_0^t = \frac{1}{3}t^3.$$

The first and second moments follow:

$$\mathbf{E}^d\left[I_t^X\right] = tX_0 + \frac{1}{2}\left(r^d - r^f - \frac{1}{2}\sigma^2\right)t^2, \qquad (2.102a)$$

$$\mathbf{Var}^d\left[I_t^X\right] = \frac{1}{3}\sigma^2 t^3, \qquad (2.102b)$$

i.e. with $\ln A_T^{G;s} = I_T^X/T$ we have

$$\mathbf{E}^d\left[\ln A_T^{G;s}\right] = X_0 + \frac{1}{2}\left(r^d - r^f - \frac{1}{2}\sigma^2\right)T, \qquad (2.103a)$$

$$\mathbf{Var}^d\left[\ln A_T^{G;s}\right] = \frac{1}{3}\sigma^2 T. \qquad (2.103b)$$

We can therefore write

$$I_t^X = tX_0 + \frac{1}{2}\left(r^d - r^f - \frac{1}{2}\sigma^2\right)t^2 + \sigma\sqrt{\frac{1}{3}t^3}\cdot\xi \qquad (2.104)$$

where $\xi \sim N(0, 1)$ under the domestic risk-neutral measure.

We now have the machinery to price the continuously monitored average price call option, with payoff at expiry

$$V_T = \left(A_T^{G;s} - K\right)^+$$

where $A_T^{G;s} = \exp\left(I_T^X/T\right)$. Following the risk-neutral approach, we construct the fair price today for the option by

$$\begin{aligned}
V_0 &= e^{-r^d T}\mathbf{E}^d\left[(A_T^{G;s} - K)^+\right] \\
&= e^{-r^d T}\mathbf{E}^d\left[(A_T^{G;s} - K)\mathbf{1}_{\{A_T^{G;s}\geq K\}}\right] \\
&= e^{-r^d T}\mathbf{E}^d\left[\left(\exp\left(I_T^X/T\right) - K\right)\mathbf{1}_{\{\exp(I_T^X/T)\geq K\}}\right] \\
&= e^{-r^d T}\mathbf{E}^d\left[\left(\exp\left(I_T^X/T\right) - K\right)\mathbf{1}_{\{I_T^X\geq T\ln K\}}\right] \\
&= e^{-r^d T}\mathbf{E}^d\left[\exp\left(I_T^X/T\right)\mathbf{1}_{\{I_T^X\geq T\ln K\}}\right] - Ke^{-r^d T}\mathbf{E}^d\left[\mathbf{1}_{\{I_T^X\geq T\ln K\}}\right] \\
&= e^{-r^d T}\mathbf{E}^d\left[\exp\left(I_T^X/T\right)\mathbf{1}_{\{I_T^X\geq T\ln K\}}\right] - Ke^{-r^d T}\mathbf{P}^d\left[I_T^X \geq T\ln K\right].
\end{aligned}$$
$$(2.105)$$

We commence by calculating the domestic risk-neutral probability in the second of the terms in (2.105). Write

$$\begin{aligned}
\mathbf{P}^d\left[I_T^X \geq T\ln K\right] &= \mathbf{P}^d\left[TX_0 + \frac{1}{2}\left(r^d - r^f - \frac{1}{2}\sigma^2\right)T^2 + \sigma\sqrt{\frac{1}{3}T^3}\cdot\xi \geq T\ln K\right] \\
&= \mathbf{P}^d\left[\sigma\sqrt{\frac{1}{3}T^3}\cdot\xi \geq T\ln K - TX_0 - \frac{1}{2}\left(r^d - r^f - \frac{1}{2}\sigma^2\right)T^2\right] \\
&= \mathbf{P}^d\left[\sigma\sqrt{\frac{1}{3}T}\cdot\xi \geq \ln K - X_0 - \frac{1}{2}\left(r^d - r^f - \frac{1}{2}\sigma^2\right)T\right]
\end{aligned}$$

$$
= \mathbf{P}^d \left[\sigma \sqrt{\frac{1}{3}T} \cdot \xi \leq \ln S_0 - \ln K + \frac{1}{2} \left(r^d - r^f - \frac{1}{2}\sigma^2 \right) T \right]
$$

$$
= \mathbf{P}^d \left[\xi \leq \frac{\ln S_0 - \ln K + \frac{1}{2} \left(r^d - r^f - \frac{1}{2}\sigma^2 \right) T}{\sigma \sqrt{\frac{1}{3}T}} \right]
$$

$$
= N(d_2^G)
$$

with

$$
d_2^G = \frac{\ln(S_0/K) + \frac{1}{2} \left(r^d - r^f - \frac{1}{2}\sigma^2 \right) T}{\sigma \sqrt{\frac{1}{3}T}}.
$$

It remains to calculate the first term in (2.105) which requires a change of measure argument. We need to compute

$$
\mathbf{E}^d \left[\exp \left(I_T^X / T \right) \mathbf{1}_{\{I_T^X \geq T \ln K\}} \right]
$$

with

$$
\frac{I_T^X}{T} = X_0 + \frac{1}{2} \left(r^d - r^f - \frac{1}{2}\sigma^2 \right) T + \sqrt{\frac{1}{3}T} \cdot \sigma \xi
$$

$$
= X_0 + \frac{1}{2} \left(r^d - r^f - \frac{1}{2}\sigma^2 \right) T + \sqrt{\frac{1}{3}} \cdot \sigma \hat{W}_T^d,
$$

where $\hat{W}_t^d$ is a Brownian motion under the domestic risk-neutral measure – not to be confused with the Brownian motion W_t^d driving the logspot process. We then have

$$
\exp \left(\frac{I_T^X}{T} \right) = S_0 \exp \left(\frac{1}{2} \left(r^d - r^f - \frac{1}{2}\sigma^2 \right) T + \sqrt{\frac{1}{3}} \cdot \sigma \hat{W}_T^d \right)
$$

$$
= S_0 \exp \left(\sqrt{\frac{1}{3}} \cdot \sigma \hat{W}_T^d - \frac{1}{6}\sigma^2 T + \frac{1}{6}\sigma^2 T + \frac{1}{2} \left(r^d - r^f - \frac{1}{2}\sigma^2 \right) T \right)
$$

$$
= S_0 \exp \left(\sqrt{\frac{1}{3}} \cdot \sigma \hat{W}_T^d - \frac{1}{6}\sigma^2 T \right) \exp \left(\frac{1}{2} \left(r^d - r^f \right) T - \frac{1}{12}\sigma^2 T \right).
$$

The reason for this somewhat unusual grouping of terms is so that we can put $\alpha = \frac{1}{\sqrt{3}}\sigma$, and thereby identify the first of the two exponential terms above as a Radon–Nikodym derivative

$$\frac{d\mathbf{P}^*}{d\mathbf{P}^d} = \exp\left(\alpha \hat{W}_T^d - \frac{1}{2}\alpha^2 T\right).$$

Note that $\hat{W}_T^d$ is no longer a martingale under $\mathbf{P}^*$, but $\hat{W}_T^* = \hat{W}_T^d - \alpha t$ is most definitely a $\mathbf{P}^*$-martingale. We then have, for an event ε

$$\mathbf{E}^d\left[\exp\left(I_T^X/T\right)\mathbf{1}_\varepsilon\right] = S_0 \exp\left(\frac{1}{2}\left(r^d - r^f\right)T - \frac{1}{12}\sigma^2 T\right)\mathbf{E}^d\left[\frac{d\mathbf{P}^*}{d\mathbf{P}^d}\mathbf{1}_\varepsilon\right]$$

$$= S_0 \exp\left(\frac{1}{2}\left(r^d - r^f\right)T - \frac{1}{12}\sigma^2 T\right)\mathbf{E}^*\left[\mathbf{1}_\varepsilon\right]$$

and of course $\mathbf{E}^*\left[\mathbf{1}_\varepsilon\right] = \mathbf{P}^*\left[\varepsilon\right]$.

For an average price call option, $\varepsilon = \{I_T^X \geq T \ln K\}$, which means that we need to compute $\mathbf{P}^*\left[I_T^X/T \geq \ln K\right]$. Expressing I_T^X/T in terms of the new Brownian $\hat{W}_T^*$, we have

$$\frac{I_T^X}{T} = X_0 + \frac{1}{2}\left(r^d - r^f - \frac{1}{2}\sigma^2\right)T + \sqrt{\frac{1}{3}}\cdot\sigma[\hat{W}_T^* + \alpha T]$$

$$= X_0 + \frac{1}{2}\left(r^d - r^f\right)T - \frac{1}{4}\sigma^2 T + \frac{1}{\sqrt{3}}\sigma\hat{W}_T^* + \frac{1}{\sqrt{3}}\sigma\alpha T$$

$$= X_0 + \frac{1}{2}\left(r^d - r^f\right)T + \frac{1}{\sqrt{3}}\sigma\hat{W}_T^* + \frac{1}{12}\sigma^2 T.$$

We therefore have

$$\mathbf{P}^*\left[I_T^X/T \geq \ln K\right] = \mathbf{P}^*\left[X_0 + \frac{1}{2}\left(r^d - r^f\right)T + \frac{1}{\sqrt{3}}\sigma\hat{W}_T^* + \frac{1}{12}\sigma^2 T \geq \ln K\right]$$

$$= \mathbf{P}^*\left[\frac{1}{\sqrt{3}}\sigma\hat{W}_T^* \geq \ln\left(\frac{K}{S_0}\right) - \frac{1}{2}\left(r^d - r^f\right)T - \frac{1}{12}\sigma^2 T\right]$$

$$= \mathbf{P}^*\left[\hat{W}_T^* \geq \frac{\ln\left(\frac{K}{S_0}\right) - \frac{1}{2}\left(r^d - r^f\right)T - \frac{1}{12}\sigma^2 T}{\frac{1}{\sqrt{3}}\sigma}\right]$$

$$= \mathbf{P}^*\left[\hat{W}_T^* \leq \frac{\ln\left(\frac{S_0}{K}\right) + \frac{1}{2}\left(r^d - r^f\right)T + \frac{1}{12}\sigma^2 T}{\frac{1}{\sqrt{3}}\sigma}\right]$$

$$
= \mathbf{P} \left[\xi \leq \frac{\ln \left(\frac{S_0}{K} \right) + \frac{1}{2} \left(r^d - r^f \right) T + \frac{1}{12} \sigma^2 T}{\frac{1}{\sqrt{3}} \sigma \sqrt{T}} \right] \text{with } \xi \sim N(0, 1)
$$

$$
= N(d_1^G)
$$

where

$$
d_1^G = \frac{\ln \left(\frac{S_0}{K} \right) + \frac{1}{2} \left(r^d - r^f \right) T + \frac{1}{12} \sigma^2 T}{\frac{1}{\sqrt{3}} \sigma \sqrt{T}}.
$$

Putting this together, we have

$$
\mathbf{E}^d \left[\exp \left(I_T^X / T \right) \mathbf{1}_{\{ I_T^X \geq T \ln K \}} \right] = S_0 \exp \left(\frac{1}{2} \left(r^d - r^f \right) T - \frac{1}{12} \sigma^2 T \right) N \left(d_1^G \right)
$$

which we can substitute into (2.105) to obtain the closed form price for a continuously monitored geometric average price call option

$$
V_0^{GAC} = e^{-r^d T} \left[S_0 \exp \left(\frac{1}{2} \left(r^d - r^f \right) T - \frac{1}{12} \sigma^2 T \right) N \left(d_1^G \right) - KN \left(d_2^G \right) \right].
$$
(2.106)

Comparing this with equation (2.8) in Angus (1999) in the special case where $t = 0$, we see the result is proven.

The continuous geometric average price put is priced along the same lines, an exercise which we encourage readers to work through for themselves. The result is

$$
V_0^{GAP} = e^{-r^d T} \left[KN \left(-d_2^G \right) - S_0 \exp \left(\frac{1}{2} \left(r^d - r^f \right) T - \frac{1}{12} \sigma^2 T \right) N \left(-d_1^G \right) \right].
$$
(2.107)

Expressions for the price of partially seasoned geometric average price options and geometric average strike options can be found in Angus (1999), along with average price and average strike binary options. This is discussed also in Section 6.2 of Geman (2005).

2.7.2   Arithmetic Asian Options – Continuous Averaging

Zhang (1998) provides a solid discussion of the various types of mean that can be used for computing the payouts and prices of Asian options, using the general mean

$$M(\gamma|S) = \left(\frac{1}{n}\sum_{i=1}^{n} S_i^{\gamma}\right)^{1/\gamma}.$$

Note that $\lim_{\gamma \to 0} M(\gamma|S) = \left(\prod_{i=1}^{n} S_i\right)^{1/n}$, which is nothing more than the discrete geometric average, whereas $M(1|S) = \frac{1}{n}\sum_{i=1}^{n} S_i$ is the discrete arithmetic average and the case $\gamma = -1$, i.e. $M(-1|S) = \left(\frac{1}{n}\sum_{i=1}^{n} \frac{1}{S_i}\right)^{-1}$, corresponds to the harmonic mean. However, we're still working in the continuous time framework, so we begin by introducing the continuous arithmetic average via the spot integral I_t^S

$$I_t^S = \int_0^t S_u du.$$

With this, the continuous arithmetic average is given by $A_t^{A;s} = I_t^S/t$.

Zhang (1998) demonstrates that the arithmetic average can be approximated by the geometric average together with a correction, so in the continuous case

$$A_T^{A;s} = \kappa A_T^{G;s}$$

where

$$\kappa_c = 1 + \frac{1}{24}\left(r^d - r^f - \frac{1}{2}\sigma^2\right)^2 T^2 + \frac{1}{576}\left(r^d - r^f - \frac{1}{2}\sigma^2\right)^4 T^4,$$

the averaging period being understood to be $[0, T]$.

We arrive at

$$V_0^{AAC} = e^{-r^d T}\left[\kappa_c S_0 \exp\left(\frac{1}{2}\left(r^d - r^f\right) T - \frac{1}{12}\sigma^2 T\right) N\left(d_1^A\right) - K N\left(d_2^A\right)\right]$$

$$(2.108)$$

where

$$d_1^A = \frac{\ln(\kappa_c S_0/K) + \frac{1}{2}\left(r^d - r^f\right) T + \frac{1}{12}\sigma^2 T}{\sigma\sqrt{\frac{1}{3}T}}$$

and

$$d_2^A = \frac{\ln(\kappa_c S_0 / K) + \frac{1}{2}\left(r^d - r^f - \frac{1}{2}\sigma^2\right)T}{\sigma\sqrt{\frac{1}{3}T}}.$$

For further details, we refer the reader to Section 6.7 of Zhang (1998).

2.7.3 Geometric Average Options – Discrete Fixings – Kemna and Vorst (1990)

Section 2.7.1 demonstrates how closed form solutions can be found in the simplest case, where the averaging is continuous and performed using the geometric average. This rests on the property that the continuous geometric average of a logspot process is itself lognormally distributed. In fact, the same is true for a geometric average computed over a discrete set of time points. This was first described in the original paper by Kemna and Vorst (1990), who recognised that the continuous geometric average of a lognormal process is itself lognormal and used this feature to obtain a closed form expression for the price. A useful compendium of results for Asian options can be found in Chapters 5 to 7 of Zhang (1998) – our aim here is to cover a subset of that work.

Let us suppose a sequence of n observation times $\{t_1, \ldots, t_n\}$ is given over the interval $[0, T]$ with $0 < t_1 < t_2 < \cdots < t_n \le T$.

For the sake of exposition, though, let us suppose that the timepoints are equally spaced – purely to simplify the algebra below (the computations can easily be performed for arbitrary fixing schedules)

$$t_i = T - (n - i)h. \tag{2.109}$$

Note that depending on the magnitude of h, the period over which the averaging is performed can be a subset of $[0, T]$ or can even be a superset, i.e. extending into the past $(t < 0)$. We shall not concern ourselves with this possibility here, though.

From (2.75a) after taking logs we have

$$\ln S_{t_i} = \ln S_0 + \left(r^d - r^f - \frac{1}{2}\sigma^2\right)t_i + \sigma W_{t_i}^d. \tag{2.110}$$

We can now define the geometric average over these observations

$$
A_{t_1,t_n}^{G;s} = \left(\prod_{i=1}^{n} S_{t_i} \right)^{1/n}
$$

$$
= \exp\left(\frac{1}{n} \ln\left(\prod_{i=1}^{n} S_{t_i} \right) \right)
$$

$$
= \exp\left(\frac{1}{n} \sum_{i=1}^{n} \ln S_{t_i} \right)
$$

$$
= \exp\left(\ln S_0 + \frac{1}{n} \sum_{i=1}^{n} \left(r^d - r^f - \frac{1}{2}\sigma^2 \right) t_i + \frac{1}{n} \sum_{i=1}^{n} \sigma W_{t_i}^d \right)
$$

and by inspection we can see that $A_{t_1,t_n}^{G,s}$ is lognormally distributed.

$$
\ln A_{t_1,t_n}^{G,s} = \ln S_0 + \frac{1}{n} \sum_{i=1}^{n} \left(r^d - r^f - \frac{1}{2}\sigma^2 \right) t_i + \frac{1}{n} \sum_{i=1}^{n} \sigma W_{t_i}^d. \quad (2.111)
$$

Let us therefore try to extract the first and second moments of the distribution of $\ln A_{t_1,t_n}^{G,s}$. We use the notation of Section 5.3 of Zhang (1998) and restrict ourselves to the case where no historical fixings have taken place yet (i.e. with $j = 0$ in his notation). The first moment is trivial:

$$
\mathbf{E}^d \left[\ln A_{t_1,t_n}^{G,s} - \ln S_0 \right] = \frac{1}{n} \sum_{i=1}^{n} \left(r^d - r^f - \frac{1}{2}\sigma^2 \right) t_i
$$

$$
= \frac{1}{n} \left(r^d - r^f - \frac{1}{2}\sigma^2 \right) \sum_{i=1}^{n} [T - (n - i)h]
$$

$$
= \frac{1}{n} \left(r^d - r^f - \frac{1}{2}\sigma^2 \right) \left[nT - n^2 h + h \sum_{i=1}^{n} i \right]
$$

$$
= \frac{1}{n} \left(r^d - r^f - \frac{1}{2}\sigma^2 \right) \left[nT - n^2 h + h\frac{n(n + 1)}{2} \right]
$$

$$
= \left(r^d - r^f - \frac{1}{2}\sigma^2 \right) \left[T - \frac{1}{2}h(n - 1) \right]
$$

i.e.

$$\mathbf{E}^d \left[\ln A_{t_1,t_n}^{G,s} \right] = \ln S_0 + \left(r^d - r^f - \frac{1}{2}\sigma^2 \right) \left[T - \frac{1}{2}h(n-1) \right]. \quad (2.112)$$

The second moment is not. From (2.111) we have

$$\begin{aligned}
\mathbf{Var}^d \left[\ln A_{t_1,t_n}^{G,s} \right] &= \mathbf{Var}^d \left[\frac{1}{n} \sum_{i=1}^{n} \sigma W_{t_i}^d \right] \\
&= \frac{\sigma^2}{n^2} \mathbf{Var}^d \left[\sum_{i=1}^{n} W_{t_i}^d \right] \\
&= \frac{\sigma^2}{n^2} \mathbf{E}^d \left[\sum_{i,j=1}^{n} W_{t_i}^d W_{t_j}^d \right] \\
&= \frac{\sigma^2}{n^2} \sum_{i,j=1}^{n} \min(t_i, t_j) \\
&= \frac{\sigma^2}{n^2} \sum_{i=1}^{n} t_i[2(n-i)+1].
\end{aligned}$$

We now use the timepoint specification (2.109) to evaluate the term above.

$$\begin{aligned}
\sum_{i=1}^{n} t_i[2(n-i)+1] &= \sum_{i,j=1}^{n} [T - (n-i)h][2(n-i)+1] \\
&= n(T-nh)(2n+1) + (4nh - 2T + h)\sum_{i=1}^{n} i - 2h\sum_{i=1}^{n} i^2 \\
&= n^2 T - \frac{1}{6}nh(4n+1)(n-1)
\end{aligned}$$

via $\sum_{i=1}^{n} i = \frac{1}{2}n(n+1)$ and $\sum_{i=1}^{n} i = \frac{1}{6}n(n+1)(2n+1)$. From this we obtain

$$\mathbf{Var}^d \left[\ln A_{t_1,t_n}^{G,s} \right] = \sigma^2 T - \frac{1}{6}\frac{\sigma^2 h}{n}(4n+1)(n-1). \quad (2.113)$$

Note that this is in agreement with the terms in Theorem 5.1 of Zhang (1998) in the case where $j = 0$.

In the case where the discrete time points are equally distributed over the interval $[0, T]$, i.e. $t_1 = h$ and $t_n = T$, we have $h = T/n$ which when substituted into (2.112) and (2.113) gives

$$\mathbf{E}^d \left[\ln A_{t_1,t_n}^{G,s} \right] = \ln S_0 + \frac{1}{2} \left(r^d - r^f - \frac{1}{2}\sigma^2 \right) \left[1 + \frac{1}{n} \right] T, \qquad (2.114a)$$

$$\mathbf{Var}^d \left[\ln A_{t_1,t_n}^{G,s} \right] = \sigma^2 T \left[1 - \frac{1}{6} \frac{(4n+1)(n-1)}{n^2} \right]. \qquad (2.114b)$$

Note that in the limit as $n \to \infty$, (2.7.3) reduces to

$$\mathbf{E}^d \left[\ln A_{t_1,t_n}^{G,s} \right] = \ln S_0 + \frac{1}{2} \left(r^d - r^f - \frac{1}{2}\sigma^2 \right) T, \qquad (2.115a)$$

$$\mathbf{Var}^d \left[\ln A_{t_1,t_n}^{G,s} \right] = \frac{1}{3}\sigma^2 T, \qquad (2.115b)$$

which is entirely consistent with (2.7.1) in the limit.

Similarly to (2.104), but with different first and second moments, we can therefore write

$$\frac{I_T^X}{T} = \mathbf{E}^d \left[\ln A_{t_1,t_n}^{G,s} \right] + \sqrt{\mathbf{Var}^d \left[\ln A_{t_1,t_n}^{G,s} \right]} \cdot \xi \qquad (2.116)$$

where the first and second moments are obtained from (2.112) and (2.113) and $\xi \sim N(0, 1)$ under the domestic risk-neutral measure. From that point on, the pricing of discretely monitored geometric average price options proceeds the same way as in Section 2.7.1.

2.7.3.1 Discretely Monitored Geometric Average Options on Forwards

In reality, commodity Asian options are always specified with a schedule of fixings, and very often with each fixing being referenced against the prompt futures contract on the fixing date (just as in commodity swaps). What this means is that the drift terms corresponding to r^d and r^f are suppressed and the terms $\mathbf{E}^d \left[\ln A_{t_1,t_n}^{G,s} \right]$ and $\mathbf{Var}^d \left[\ln A_{t_1,t_n}^{G,s} \right]$ are adjusted to take into account the relevant prompt future at each of the fixing times, i.e.

$$\mathbf{E}^d \left[\ln A_{t_1,t_n}^{G,f} \right] = \frac{1}{n} \sum_{i=1}^{n} \left[\ln f_{t_i, \vec{T}(t_i)} - \frac{1}{2}[\sigma_{\text{imp}}(\vec{T}(t_i))]^2 t_i \right]. \qquad (2.117)$$

Since the time points are arbitrary, it is straightforward to handle the case where the fixings occur over a particular period some way away in the future.

Note that, similarly to commodity swaps, the roll date can be handled one of two ways – so we use Asian(1,0) and Asian(1,1) to denote two different variants, the first being the case where the prompt future (and the associated volatility) rolls at the end of the expiry date, the second being where the roll occurs at the start of the expiry date. Clearly these two possibilities for handling the roll date associated with discrete fixings can be applied to either geometric average options or arithmetic average options. We've met the former and now we introduce the latter.

2.7.4   Arithmetic Average Options – Discrete Fixings – Turnbull and Wakeman (1991)

The overwhelming majority of Asian options in actual traded markets are with arithmetic averaging not geometric averaging. Recall from (2.67) in Section 2.4 that discretely monitored arithmetic averages over the observations $\{t_1, \ldots, t_n\}$ have already been used to value commodity swaps. We shall be using the same arithmetic averages here.

We introduce the presentation in Section 10.2 of West (2009) and the similar presentation of Schneider (2012), the first being with regard to averages on spot, the second being with averages on the futures. The first will assume perfect correlation across the entire futures curve derived from the spot, the second permits some decorrelation across the futures contracts, which is more representative of actual traded commodity markets.

2.7.4.1   Turnbull–Wakeman for Spot Averages

Since $\mathbf{E}^d[S_t] = f_{0,t}$, we clearly have

$$\mathbf{E}^d\left[A_{t_1,t_n}^{A,s}\right] = \frac{1}{n}\sum_{i=1}^{n}\mathbf{E}^d[S_{t_i}] = \frac{1}{n}\sum_{i=1}^{n}f_{0,t_i} \tag{2.118}$$

which we already know to be the fair value of the commodity swap (i.e. the strike that makes it costless to enter into).

Also from (2.67a) we have

$$\left[A_{t_1,t_n}^{A,s}\right]^2 = \frac{1}{n^2}\sum_{i,j=1}^{n}S_{t_i}S_{t_j} \tag{2.119}$$

which can be expanded to give

$$\mathbf{E}^d\left[\left[A_{t_1,t_n}^{A,s}\right]^2\right] = \frac{1}{n^2}\sum_{i,j=1}^{n}\mathbf{E}^d[S_{t_i}S_{t_j}] = \frac{1}{n^2}\sum_{i=1}^{n}\mathbf{E}^d\left[S_{t_i}^2\right] + \frac{2}{n^2}\sum_{j=2}^{n}\sum_{i=1}^{j-1}\mathbf{E}^d[S_{t_i}S_{t_j}]$$

(2.120)

where $i < j$ by the choice of summation. The term $\mathbf{E}^d[S_{t_i}S_{t_j}]$ can be resolved in the following manner

$$\begin{aligned}\mathbf{E}^d[S_{t_i}S_{t_j}] &= \mathbf{E}^d\left[\mathbf{E}^d[S_{t_i}S_{t_j}|\mathcal{F}_{t_i}]\right]\\ &= \mathbf{E}^d\left[S_{t_i}\mathbf{E}^d[S_{t_j}|\mathcal{F}_{t_i}]\right]\\ &= \mathbf{E}^d\left[S_{t_i}^2\right]\exp(r^d - r^f)(t_j - t_i))]\\ &= f_{0,t_i}f_{0,t_j}\exp\left(\sigma_i^2 t_i\right)\end{aligned}$$

(2.121)

where σ_i denotes the implied volatility for time t_i.

We thereby obtain

$$\mathbf{E}^d\left[\left[A_{t_1,t_n}^{A,s}\right]^2\right] = \frac{1}{n^2}\sum_{i=1}^{n}f_{0,t_i}^2\exp\left(\sigma_i^2 t_i\right) + \frac{2}{n^2}\sum_{j=2}^{n}f_{0,t_j}\sum_{i=1}^{j-1}f_{0,t_i}\exp\left(\sigma_i^2 t_i\right).$$

(2.122)

We now apply the moment matching technique. Assume that $A_{t_1,t_n}^{A,s}$ is lognormally distributed, i.e. that $\ln A_{t_1,t_n}^{A,s} \sim N(\mu_A, \sigma_A^2 t_n)$, where by the properties of lognormal distributions we have

$$\sigma_A^2 t_n = \ln\frac{\mathbf{E}^d\left[\left[A_{t_1,t_n}^{A,s}\right]^2\right]}{\left(\mathbf{E}^d\left[[A_{t_1,t_n}^{A,s}]\right]\right)^2}$$

(2.123)

$$\mu_A = \ln\mathbf{E}^d\left[\left[A_{t_1,t_n}^{A,s}\right]^2\right] - \frac{1}{2}\sigma_A^2$$

(2.124)

which is equivalent to seeing that an arithmetic average price option can be priced using (2.84) from the Black-76 model on a synthetic asset with a volatility of σ_A given by

$$\sigma_A = \sqrt{\frac{1}{t_n} \ln \left[\frac{\mathbf{E}^d \left[\left[A^{A,s}_{t_1,t_n} \right]^2 \right]}{\left(\mathbf{E}^d \left[\left[A^{A,s}_{t_1,t_n} \right] \right] \right)^2} \right]}, \qquad (2.125)$$

an initial futures price of $\mathbf{E}^d \left[[A^{A,s}_{t_1,t_n}] \right]$, a strike of K and a settlement time T_{stl} using (2.118) and (2.122) together with the settlement adjustment described in Section 2.5.3.

Note that σ_A is referred to as the Asian volatility.

2.7.4.2   Turnbull–Wakeman for Futures Averages

Suppose instead of an average of spot price fixings we have an average of futures prices over an averaging period. This average is as defined in (2.67b), i.e.

$$A^{A,f}_{t_1,t_n} = \frac{1}{n} \sum_{i=1}^{n} f_{t_i, \vec{T}(t_i)} \qquad (2.126)$$

where $t_1 \ldots t_n$ comprise the set of fixing times and $\vec{T}(t)$ denotes the maturity time of the prompt future at each time t.

As we know from Section 2.4, the averaging of a strip of futures can be constructed in one of two ways depending on the roll date. Let us continue to use the same notation, supposing that we have a strip of futures with maturities T_k (we use capitals here to avoid confusing the futures maturity times T_i with the fixing times t_i) – each of which is described by a stochastic differential equation

$$df_{t,T_k} = \sigma_k f_{t,T_k} dW^k_t,$$

where dW^k_t is the driving Brownian motion for f_{t,T_k} and $\langle dW^k_t, dW^l_t \rangle = \rho_{kl} dt$ describes the correlation structure of the futures. Along with $\vec{T}(t)$, we introduce a maturity index $m(i)$ defined such that $T_{m(i)} = \vec{T}(t_i)$, i.e. $f_{t_i, T_{m(i)}} = f_{t_i, \vec{T}(t_i)}$. Note that the maturity index $m(\cdot)$ is a mapping from the fixing time index to the futures time index, and these are *not* the same.

For arbitrary t_i and t_j in the set of time fixings, i.e. $1 \le i \le j \le n$ (note $i \le j$) we have

$$\mathbf{E}^d \left[f_{t_i, \vec{T}(t_i)} \right] = f_{0, \vec{T}(t_i)}$$

$$\mathbf{E}^d \left[f^2_{t_i, \vec{T}(t_i)} \right] = f^2_{0, \vec{T}(t_i)} \exp \left(\int_0^{t_i} \sigma^2_{m(i)} ds \right) = f^2_{0, \vec{T}(t_i)} \exp \left(\sigma^2_{m(i)} t_i \right)$$

$$\mathbf{E}^d \left[f_{t_i, \vec{T}(t_i)} f_{t_j, \vec{T}(t_j)} \right] = f_{0, \vec{T}(t_i)} f_{0, \vec{T}(t_j)} \exp \left(\int_0^{t_i} \rho_{m(i),m(j)} \sigma_{m(i)} \sigma_{m(j)} ds \right)$$

$$= f_{0, \vec{T}(t_i)} f_{0, \vec{T}(t_j)} \exp \left(\rho_{m(i),m(j)} \sigma_{m(i)} \sigma_{m(j)} t_i \right) .$$

Note that in the case where $\rho_{m(i),m(j)} = 1$ and $\sigma_{m(i)} = \sigma$ for all i, j the equations above reduce to $\mathbf{E}^d \left[f_{t_i, \vec{T}(t_i)} \right] = f_{0, \vec{T}(t_i)}$, $\mathbf{E}^d \left[f^2_{t_i, \vec{T}(t_i)} \right] = f^2_{0, \vec{T}(t_i)} \exp \left(\sigma^2 t_i \right)$ and $\mathbf{E}^d \left[f_{t_i, \vec{T}(t_i)} f_{t_j, \vec{T}(t_j)} \right] = f_{0, \vec{T}(t_i)} f_{0, \vec{T}(t_j)} \exp \left(\sigma^2 t_i \right)$ which are very reminiscent of $\mathbf{E}^d[S_t] = f_{0,t}$ and (2.121) in the preceding section.

The first moment is immediate by taking the expectation of (2.126), i.e.

$$\mathbf{E}^d \left[A^{A,f}_{t_1, t_n} \right] = \frac{1}{n} \sum_{i=1}^{n} f_{0, \vec{T}(t_i)} \tag{2.127}$$

while the second moment is given by

$$\mathbf{E}^d \left[[A^{A,f}_{t_1, t_n}]^2 \right] = \mathbf{E}^d \left[\left(\frac{1}{n} \sum_{i=1}^{n} f_{t_i, \vec{T}(t_i)} \right) \left(\frac{1}{n} \sum_{j=1}^{n} f_{t_j, \vec{T}(t_j)} \right) \right] \tag{2.128}$$

$$= \frac{1}{n^2} \mathbf{E}^d \left[\sum_{i,j=1}^{n} f_{t_i, \vec{T}(t_i)} f_{t_j, \vec{T}(t_j)} \right]$$

$$= \frac{1}{n^2} \sum_{i,j=1}^{n} \mathbf{E}^d \left[f_{t_i, \vec{T}(t_i)} f_{t_j, \vec{T}(t_j)} \right]$$

$$= \frac{1}{n^2} \sum_{i,j=1}^{n} f_{0, \vec{T}(t_i)} f_{0, \vec{T}(t_j)} \exp \left(\rho_{m(i),m(j)} \sigma_{m(i)} \sigma_{m(j)} t_{\min(\{i,j\})} \right) .$$

From this we can use Black-76 with a volatility of

$$\sigma_A = \sqrt{\frac{1}{t_n} \ln \left[\frac{\mathbf{E}^d \left[\left[A_{t_1,t_n}^{A,f} \right]^2 \right]}{\left(\mathbf{E}^d \left[\left[A_{t_1,t_n}^{A,f} \right] \right] \right)^2} \right]}$$ (2.129)

and an initial futures price $f_{0,T} = \mathbf{E}^d \left[\left[A_{t_1,t_n}^{A,f} \right] \right] = A_{0;\{t_1,t_n\}}^{A;f}$, using (2.127) and (2.128) together with the settlement adjustment from Section 2.5.3.

Other approximations are well known, which involve matching higher order moments. The practical benefit of these is somewhat limited and the two-moment Turnbull–Wakeman (TW2) approximation is very standard in the world of commodity derivatives.

Further reading on the topic of Asian options can be found in Kwok (1998) and Zhang (1998), together with original references including – but by no means limited – to Turnbull and Wakeman (1991), Levy (1992), Carverhill and Clewlow (1990), Levy and Turnbull (1992) and Curran (1994).

2.8 COMMODITY SWAPTIONS

Järvinen and Toivonen (2004) and Larsson (2011) introduce these products, which are not covered extensively in the literature by any means, but which are relevant particularly for the coal market.

An Asian option is an option on the arithmetic average which pays the positive component of the difference at expiry between the discretely monitored arithmetic average over the fixing times $\{t_1, \ldots, t_n\}$ and strike (subject to different sign convention for calls and puts). Note that the exercise decision is made at the point in time when the last fixing is determined, and generally settlement occurs five business days later.

In contrast, a swaption is an option on a forward swap which requires the holder to elect whether to exercise the swaption *before* the swap commences (unlike an Asian option, which is more like a European option referenced against an underlying swap). An Asian option is exercised (or not) once all the fixings have been determined, whereas the decision rule for a commodity swaption necessarily has to be with respect to an underlying forward swap.

Let $t_0 = T$ denote the expiry date of the swaption, and $t_1, \ldots, t_n$ the fixing dates for the underlying commodity swap, with $t_0 < t_1 < \ldots < t_n$.

Typically, the swap will be marked against the prompt futures, so each cashflow will be of the form $V_i = f_{t_i, \bar{T}(t_i)} - K$. We shall not concern ourselves here with swaptions referenced against spot, as these are hardly ever encountered in practice.

We can thereby consider (2.68) but at time $t_0 > 0$, i.e.

$$V_{t_0} = \frac{1}{n} \mathbf{E}^d \left[\sum_{i=1}^{n} e^{-r^d(T_{\text{stl};i} - t_0)} \cdot V_i \middle| \mathcal{F}_{t_0} \right] \tag{2.130}$$

and split this into floating and fixed components, i.e.

$$V_{\text{float}}(t_0) = \frac{1}{n} \sum_{i=1}^{n} e^{-r^d(T_{\text{stl};i} - t_0)} f_{t_i, \bar{T}(t_i)}, \tag{2.131a}$$

$$V_{\text{fixed}}(t_0) = \frac{1}{n} \sum_{i=1}^{n} e^{-r^d(T_{\text{stl};i} - t_0)} K. \tag{2.131b}$$

A commodity payer swaption (or call on the underlying swap) then has value at t_0 equal to

$$V_{t_0}^C = \max(V_{\text{float}}(t_0) - V_{\text{fixed}}(t_0), 0)$$

whereas a commodity receiver swaption (or put on the underlying swap) has value at t_0 equal to

$$V_{t_0}^P = \max(V_{\text{fixed}}(t_0) - V_{\text{float}}(t_0), 0).$$

The terminology comes from the holder of the swaption having the right to pay a fixed price, or to receive a fixed price, which offsets against the floating price of the commodity in question.

This should be quite reminiscent of the Turnbull–Wakeman result in the previous section. Compare (2.131a) against (2.67b) and we see that $V_{\text{float}}(t_0)$ is the same as $A_{t_1, t_n}^{A, f}$ except with n discount factors included.

In fact, it is not unusual for settlement to be rolled up into one cashflow at one particular time in the future (generally aligned with the settlement rules for swaps and Asians with the same fixing schedule), in which case we have

$$V_{\text{float}}(t_0) = \frac{1}{n} e^{-r^d(T_{\text{stl}} - t_0)} \sum_{i=1}^{n} f_{t_0, \bar{T}(t_i)} \tag{2.132a}$$

$$V_{\text{fixed}}(t_0) = e^{-r^d(T_{\text{stl}} - t_0)} K. \tag{2.132b}$$

The value of the commodity payer swaption at time t_0 is therefore

$$V_{t_0}^C = \max(V_{\text{float}}(t_0) - V_{\text{fixed}}(t_0), 0)$$

$$= e^{-r^d(T_{\text{stl}} - t_0)} \max\left(\frac{1}{n} \sum_{i=1}^{n} f_{t_i, \bar{T}(t_i)} - K, 0\right)$$

$$= e^{-r^d(T_{\text{stl}} - t_0)} \max\left(A_{t_1, t_n}^{A, f} - K, 0\right)$$

with $A_{t_1, t_n}^{A, f}$ as defined in (2.67b).

We know from Section 2.7.4 that $A_{t_1, t_n}^{A, f}$ is approximately lognormally distributed, with mean $\mathbf{E}^d\left[[A_{t_1, t_n}^{A, f}]\right] = A_{0; \{t_1, t_n\}}^{A, f}$ and effective volatility σ_A as given in (2.129).

We then aim to price the swaption as

$$V_0^C = e^{-r^d t_0} \mathbf{E}^d\left[V_{t_0}^C\right]$$

$$= e^{-r^d t_0} \mathbf{E}^d\left[e^{-r^d(T_{\text{stl}} - t_0)} \max\left(A_{t_1, t_n}^{A, f} - K, 0\right)\right]$$

$$= e^{-r^d t_0} e^{-r^d(T_{\text{stl}} - t_0)} \mathbf{E}^d\left[\mathbf{E}^d\left[\max\left(A_{t_1, t_n}^{A; f} - K, 0\right) \middle| \mathcal{F}_{t_0}\right]\right]$$

$$= e^{-r^d T_{\text{stl}}} \mathbf{E}^d\left[\max\left(A_{t_0; \{t_1, t_n\}}^{A; f} - K, 0\right)\right].$$

From the above, we see that we need to construct the distribution of $A_{t_0; \{t_1, t_n\}}^{A; f}$ at time t_0. A useful practitioner's approximation is to use the Asian volatility σ_A as defined in (2.125) and to presume that this is applicable over the time interval $[0, t_0]$. Basically, this is saying that we use the Turnbull–Wakeman moment matching technique to estimate the mean and variance of the swap (upon which an Asian option depends), and then to presume that the instantaneous forward variance of the swap is evenly distributed over the time interval $[0, t_0]$.

An energy swaption can therefore be approximately valued under the presumption of a one-factor geometric Brownian motion as a European option, with the initial asset level equal to $A_{t_0; \{t_1, t_n\}}^{A; f}$, volatility set to σ_A, time to expiry of t_0, and delayed settlement to T_{stl}.

More complex and realistic techniques certainly exist, but are beyond the scope of this introductory discussion. We refer the reader to Järvinen and Toivonen (2004) and Larsson (2011), together with Riedhauser (2005a, 2005b) and Huang (2007).

2.9 SPREAD OPTIONS

Spread options are options which pay a certain amount according to the difference of two (or sometimes more) financial quantities. These quantities can either be futures contracts with different maturities on the same commodity, or futures contracts with the same maturity, but on different commodities. The first is known as an intra-commodity calendar spread option (often called calendar spread option, or CSO), the second is known as an inter-commodity futures spread (there are many frequently encountered flavours of these such as crack spreads, which will be introduced later in the text).

As such, the payout of a two-asset spread option at expiry is given by

$$V_T = \max\left(S_T^{(1)} - S_T^{(2)} - K, 0\right) \qquad (2.133a)$$

where $S_T^{(1)}$ and $S_T^{(2)}$ are two financial quantities observed at time T.

This can, of course, be extended to a multi-asset spread option

$$V_T = \max\left(\sum_{i=1}^{n} \omega_i S_T^{(i)} - K, 0\right) \qquad (2.133b)$$

where $\min_i\{\omega_i\} < 0$ and $\max_i\{\omega_i\} > 0$. Note that the presence of negative weights in (2.133b) is what differentiates spread options from basket options with strictly positive weights.

Note that the financial observables need not be stochastic all the way out to time T; for example, one can construct a forward starting option with the strike set at $t_1 < T$ as a special case of a calendar spread option, i.e. with $V_T = \max\left(S_T - S_{t_1} - K, 0\right)$, where clearly S_{t_1} is stochastic up to t_1 and then constant thereafter.

Further it is quite commonplace in commodities for the quantities to be arithmetic averages, for example, an Asian calendar spread option which pays the difference between two averages

$$V_T = \max\left(A_{t_1,t_{n1}}^{A,f} - A_{t_{n1+1},t_{n1+n2}}^{A,f} - K, 0\right) \qquad (2.134)$$

or an inter-commodity Asian futures spread

$$V_T = \max\left(A_{t_1,t_n}^{A,f_1} - A_{t_1,t_n}^{A,f_2} - K, 0\right). \qquad (2.135)$$

We shall restrict ourselves here to the case of two risky assets, described by the SDEs

$$dS_t^{(1)} = [r^d - r^{f;1}]S_t^{(1)}dt + \sigma^{(1)}S_t^{(1)}dW_t^{(1;d)} \qquad (2.136a)$$

$$dS_t^{(2)} = [r^d - r^{f;2}]S_t^{(2)}dt + \sigma^{(2)}S_t^{(2)}dW_t^{(2;d)} \qquad (2.136b)$$

where $W_t^{(1;d)}$ and $W_t^{(2;d)}$ are Brownian motions with respect to the domestic risk-neutral measure $\mathbf{P}^d$, subject to correlation $\langle dW_t^{(1;d)}, dW_t^{(2;d)} \rangle = \rho_{12;d}dt$.

2.9.1   Margrabe Exchange Options

The analysis is simplest in the case of two-asset spread options where $K = 0$. In this case we have the option to exchange the second asset and receive the first, with no extra payment being required. The payout at expiry, for an option to surrender the second risky asset and receive the first risky asset, is

$$V_T = \max\left(S_T^{(1)} - S_T^{(2)}, 0\right). \qquad (2.137)$$

as discussed in Margrabe (1978).

By adopting the second asset as numeraire, this can be viewed as a call on the first asset – there is a nice parallel interpretation in the context of foreign exchange, which I discuss in Chapter 10 of Clark (2011). Pricing of this instrument proceeds exactly as in Section 2.2. Rubinstein (1991) quotes the price

$$V_0^{exch} = S_0^{(1)}e^{-r^{f;1}T}N(d_1) - S_0^{(2)}e^{-r^{f;2}T}N(d_2) \qquad (2.138a)$$

where

$$d_{1;2} = \frac{\ln\left(\frac{S_0^{(1)}e^{-r^{f;1}T}}{S_0^{(2)}e^{-r^{f;2}T}}\right) \pm \frac{1}{2}[\sigma^{(1;2)}]^2T}{\sigma^{(1;2)}\sqrt{T}} \qquad (2.138b)$$

with

$$[\sigma^{(1;2)}]^2 = [\sigma^{(1)}]^2 + [\sigma^{(2)}]^2 - 2\rho_{12;d}\sigma^{(1)}\sigma^{(2)}$$

through construction of the cross $S_t^{(1;2)} = S_t^{(1)}/S_t^{(2)}$.

The same result can be found in Equation (2) of Venkatramanan and Alexander (2011).

However, for commodity options, the presumption that $K = 0$ is too restrictive. We therefore continue by introducing a common approximation used in the energy markets for two-asset spread options: the Kirk approximation.

2.9.2 The Kirk Approximation

The Margrabe approach above works nicely because we are considering the difference between two lognormal quantities, namely $S_T^{(1)} - S_T^{(2)}$. If the strike is nonzero, we have

$$V_T = \max\left(S_T^{(1)} - S_T^{(2)} - K, 0\right)$$

$$= \max\left(S_T^{(1)} - (S_T^{(2)} + K), 0\right)$$

The approximation of Kirk (1995) is that when $K \ll S_T^{(2)}$ we can regard $S_T^{(2)} + K$ as being approximately lognormal. The ratio of two lognormal processes X_t and Y_t is itself lognormal; suppose $\ln X_t \sim N(\mu_X, \sigma_X^2)$ and $\ln Y_t \sim N(\mu_Y, \sigma_Y^2)$ and $\mathbf{Cov}(\ln X_t, \ln Y_t) = \varrho \sigma_X \sigma_Y$. Note that ϱ is the terminal correlation between $\ln X_t$ and $\ln Y_t$, *not* the correlation between $S_t^{(1)}$ and $S_t^{(2)}$. We then construct the ratio $\ln(X_t/Y_t) = \ln X_t - \ln Y_t$ which gives $\ln(X_t/Y_t) \sim N(\mu_X - \mu_Y, \sigma_X^2 + \sigma_Y^2 - 2\varrho\sigma_X\sigma_Y)$.

Let us follow Venkatramanam and Alexander (2011) and define two new stochastic processes Y_t and Z_t by

$$Y_t = S_t^{(2)} + Ke^{-r^d(T-t)}, \tag{2.139a}$$

$$Z_t = S_t^{(1)}/Y_t, \tag{2.139b}$$

noting that at expiry, $Y_T = S_T^{(2)} + K$. With this, we can straightforwardly put

$$\max\left(S_T^{(1)} - (S_T^{(2)} + K), 0\right) = \max\left(S_T^{(1)} - Y_T, 0\right)$$

$$= \max\left(Y_T\left(\frac{S^{(1)}}{Y_T} - 1\right), 0\right)$$

$$= Y_T \max\left((Z_T - 1), 0\right).$$

In fact it is shown in Venkatramanam and Alexander (2011) that

$$\frac{dZ_t}{Z_t} = (r^d - \tilde{r}^d - (r^{f;1} - \tilde{r}^{f;2}))dt + \sigma_Z dW_t^*$$

where $\tilde{r}^d = r^d \frac{S_t^{(2)}}{Y_t}$, $\tilde{r}^{f;2} = r^{f;2} \frac{S_t^{(2)}}{Y_t}$, $\tilde{\sigma}^{(2)} = \sigma^{(2)} \frac{S_t^{(2)}}{Y_t}$ and

$$\sigma_Z = \sqrt{[\sigma^{(1)}]^2 + [\tilde{\sigma}^{(2)}]^2 - 2\varrho_{12;d}\sigma^{(1)}\tilde{\sigma}^{(2)}}.$$

Note that W_t^* is a Brownian motion under a different probability measure $\mathbf{P}^*$ related to $\mathbf{P}^d$ by

$$\frac{d\mathbf{P}^*}{d\mathbf{P}^d} = \exp\left(-\frac{1}{2}\left[\tilde{\sigma}^{(2)}\right]^2 T + \tilde{\sigma}^{(2)} dW_t^{(2;d)}\right).$$

We can now construct the price for a spread option with payoff $V_T = (S_T^{(1)} - S_T^{(2)} - K)^+$

$$V_0 = e^{-r^d T} \mathbf{E}^d \left[\max\left(S_T^{(1)} - S_T^{(2)} - K, 0\right)\right]$$
$$= e^{-r^d T} \mathbf{E}^d \left[Y_T \left(Z_T - 1\right)^+\right]$$
$$= e^{-r^d T} \mathbf{E}^d \left[(S_T^{(1)} - Y_T)^+\right].$$

Upon shifting to the measure corresponding to using Y_t as numeraire, which is just a portfolio of the second asset $S_T^{(2)}$ together with an amount of cash that FVs to amount K at time T, we obtain

$$V_0 = S_0^{(1)} e^{-r^{f;1} T} N\left(d_1^Z\right) - Y_0 e^{-(r^d - (\tilde{r}^d - \tilde{r}^{f;2}))T} N\left(d_2^Z\right)$$

where

$$d_2^Z = \frac{\ln Z_0 + (r^d - r^{f;1} - (\tilde{r}^d - \tilde{r}^{f;2}) - \frac{1}{2}\sigma_Z^2)T}{\sigma_Z \sqrt{T}} \qquad (2.140a)$$

$$d_1^Z = d_2^Z + \sigma_Z \sqrt{T}. \qquad (2.140b)$$

Note that if we kill the drift terms, as is standard in Black-76, we get

$$V_0 = e^{-r^d T} \left[F_{0,T}^{(1)} N\left(d_1^Z\right) - Y_0 N\left(d_2^Z\right)\right]$$

with $d_1^Z = (\ln Z_0 + \frac{1}{2}\sigma_Z^2 T)/\sigma_Z\sqrt{T}$ and $d_2^Z = (\ln Z_0 - \frac{1}{2}\sigma_Z^2 T)/\sigma_Z\sqrt{T}$. In this case $Z_0 = S_0^{(1)}/(S_0^{(2)} + K)$.

2.9.3   Calendar Spread Options

2.9.3.1   Calendar Spread Options on Spot

The analysis above presumes that we have two separate but correlated assets which are presumed to evolve stochastically over $[0, T]$, and we have payoff $V_T = (S_T^{(1)} - S_T^{(2)} - K)^+$. It is quite common in commodities to have options which depend on the asset values for a single commodity, but evaluated at two particular times, e.g.

$$V_T = (S_T - S_{t_1} - K)^+ \tag{2.141}$$

where $t_1 < T$. In the case where $K = 0$, this reduces to a forward starting option, for which a closed form expression is quoted in Equation (8.5) of Zhang (1998)

$$V_0 = S_0 \left[e^{-r^f T} N(d_1^{\text{fwd}}) - e^{-r^d(T-t_1) - r^f t_1} N\left(d_2^{\text{fwd}}\right) \right], \tag{2.142}$$

with

$$d_1^{\text{fwd}} = d_2^{\text{fwd}} + \sigma \sqrt{T - t_1} \tag{2.143a}$$

$$d_2^{\text{fwd}} = \frac{r^d - r^f - \frac{1}{2}\sigma^2}{\sigma} \sqrt{T - t_1}. \tag{2.143b}$$

Now we can identify S_T with $S_T^{(1)}$ and S_{t_1} with $S_T^{(2)}$ for a stochastic process $S_t^{(2)}$ that has volatility $\sigma^{(2)}$ for $0 \le t \le t_1$, and zero volatility and drift thereafter. Note that $S_T^{(2)}$ has total variance $[\sigma^{(2)}]^2 t_1$, which is the same as $\left[\bar{\sigma}^{(2)}\right]^2 T$ for $\bar{\sigma}^{(2)} = \sigma^{(2)} \sqrt{t_1/T}$. This means we can assume (these products not being path dependent) that (2.141) can be expressed equivalently as

$$V_T = (S_T^{(1)} - S_T^{(2)} - K)^+. \tag{2.144}$$

Now we can apply the Kirk approximation but with $\bar{\sigma}^{(2)} = \sigma^{(2)} \sqrt{t_1/T}$ used in (2.136b).

2.9.3.2   Calendar Spread Options on Futures

Of course, if we are modelling driftless futures, then in reality the futures contracts being observed at the two dates t_1 and T will be the two corresponding to whichever will be the prompt future at t_1 and T. We already have the notation $f_{t,\bar{T}(t_1)}$ and $f_{t,\bar{T}(T)}$ for these. Let us suppose that the volatilities for each of these two can be denoted by $\sigma^{(1)}$ and $\sigma^{(2)}$ respectively, in which case the Kirk approximation is still applicable, but with initial asset levels $f_{0,\bar{T}(t_1)}$ and $f_{0,\bar{T}(T)}$ instead of $S_0^{(1)}$ and $S_0^{(2)}$.

2.9.4 Asian Spread Options

In reality, in the commodities markets, calendar spread options are rarely determined according to the difference of prompt futures at only two dates. More often, the spread is computed by taking the arithmetic average over the far month, minus the arithmetic average over the near month. This, as introduced in (2.134), can be expressed as

$$V_T = \max\left(A_{t_1,t_{n_1}}^{A,f} - A_{t_{n_1+1},t_{n_1+n_2}}^{A,f} - K, 0 \right) \qquad (2.145)$$

with

$$A_{t_1,t_{n_1}}^{A,f} = \frac{1}{n_1} \sum_{i=1}^{n_1} f_{t_i,\bar{T}(t_i)}, \text{ and} \qquad (2.146a)$$

$$A_{t_{n_1+1},t_{n_1+n_2}}^{A,f} = \frac{1}{n_2} \sum_{i=n_1+1}^{n_1+n_2} f_{t_i,\bar{T}(t_i)}. \qquad (2.146b)$$

We can quite straightforwardly apply the Turnbull–Wakeman adjustment of Section 2.7.4 to (2.146a) and (2.146b), obtaining effective Asian volatilities $\sigma^{(1)}$ and $\sigma^{(2)}$. These can then be subjected to the same approach as detailed in Section 2.9.3 – noting that it is the short end volatility, i.e. $\sigma^{(1)}$ that needs to be transformed into $\bar{\sigma}^{(1)} = \sigma^{(1)}\sqrt{(t_n/T)}$.

We shall provide a case study example on WTI oil calendar spreads in Chapter 5.

For intra-commodity spread options with payoff as described in (2.135), we just use the moment matching approach without needing to adjust the near end volatility, but where the near and far end terms will be driven off different futures curves and volatilities.

See Sections 6.6 and 7.5 for how these spreads arise in practice in commodity markets.

2.10 MORE ADVANCED MODELS

The products we have presented in this chapter have, so far, all been discussed solely with reference to the standard Black-76 and Black–Scholes analysis. Our intent in this chapter has been to provide the reader with a technical introduction which he or she can use to guide the development of more complex models, under which these products (and more) can be priced. Let us sketch some directions in which work can proceed.

There are many shortcomings to the use of geometric Brownian motion for commodity option pricing. The first is the absence of volatility smile. This can be remedied for simple products by looking up the volatility σ from an implied volatility surface $\sigma_{imp}(K, T)$ – depending on the strike K and the maturity (or fixing time) T. For more complicated path-dependent products, we should properly construct a local volatility surface or engage a stochastic volatility (or local stochastic volatility) model, though this is complicated when one needs to model several futures contracts.

2.10.1   Mean Reverting Models

The second problem with pure geometric Brownian motion is the absence of mean reversion. It is well known that many commodities experience some degree of seasonality – and while it is clearly possible to avoid having to deal with this by just pricing using today's future curve (incorporating seasonal expectations) as a reference, and working with a family of futures curves $f_{t,T_1}, \ldots, f_{t,T_n}$, this requires estimation of the correlation matrix connecting the stochastic evolution of all of these tradeables.

2.10.1.1   The Schwartz (1997) One-Factor Model

Schwartz (1997) introduces a one-factor model ("Model 1" in the original paper) that incorporates mean reversion into spot price, expressed in mean reversion in logspot.[9] The process followed is

$$dS_t = \kappa(\alpha_S - \ln S_t)S_t dt + \sigma S_t dW_t \qquad (2.147a)$$

or equivalently, for $X_t = \ln S_t$

$$dX_t = \kappa(\alpha_X - X_t)dt + \sigma dW_t \qquad (2.147b)$$

with $\alpha_X = \alpha_S - \sigma^2/2\kappa$. The proof of this is a simple exercise in Itô calculus. Put $X_t = f(S_t)$ with $f(x) = \ln x$, where $f'(x) = x^{-1}$ and $f''(x) = -x^{-2}$.

---

[9] Pilipović (1998) discusses in Section 4.3.2.2 a model where the mean reversion is in terms of spot rather than logspot.

From Itô, we obtain $dX_t = f'(S_t)dS_t + \frac{1}{2}f''(S_t)dS_t^2$. But from (2.147a) we have $dS_t/S_t = \kappa(\alpha_S - X_t)dt + \sigma dW_t$ and therefore $dS_t^2/S_t^2 = \sigma^2 dt$. We thereby have $dX_t = \kappa(\alpha_S - X_t)dt + \sigma dW_t - \frac{1}{2}\sigma^2 dt$ which can be written as (2.147b) with the substitution $\alpha_X = \alpha_S - \sigma^2/2\kappa$.

Note that (2.147b) is the same SDE as encountered in the Vasicek model, in the context of interest rate modelling

$$dr_t = (\theta - \kappa r_t)dt + \sigma dW_t. \tag{2.148}$$

The intent here is to capture the general trend that when commodity spot prices rise, the futures curves tend to experience backwardation, and low spot prices more often occur together with contango markets – this basically being the observation that the short end of the futures curve fluctuates a lot more than the long end. This model pulls the spot price back to the long term level $S_\infty = \exp(\alpha_S)$.

We introduce a stochastic integrating factor $\exp(\kappa t)$, and write

$$\hat{X}_t = \exp(\kappa t)X_t$$

under which we have, by the Itô product rule,

$$
\begin{aligned}
d\hat{X}_t &= e^{\kappa t}dX_t + \kappa e^{\kappa t}X_t dt \\
&= e^{\kappa t}dX_t + \kappa \hat{X}_t dt \\
&= e^{\kappa t}(\kappa(\alpha_X - X_t)dt + \sigma dW_t) + \kappa \hat{X}_t dt \\
&= \kappa e^{\kappa t}[\alpha_X dt - X_t dt] + \sigma e^{\kappa t}dW_t + \kappa \hat{X}_t dt \\
&= \kappa e^{\kappa t}\alpha_X dt - \kappa e^{\kappa t}X_t dt + \sigma e^{\kappa t}dW_t + \kappa \hat{X}_t dt \\
&= \kappa e^{\kappa t}\alpha_X dt - \kappa \hat{X}_t dt + \sigma e^{\kappa t}dW_t + \kappa \hat{X}_t dt \\
&= \kappa e^{\kappa t}\alpha_X dt + \sigma e^{\kappa t}dW_t.
\end{aligned}
$$

This can of course be integrated. We have

$$
\begin{aligned}
\hat{X}_T &= \hat{X}_0 + \int_0^T d\hat{X}_t \\
&= \hat{X}_0 + \kappa \alpha_X \int_0^T e^{\kappa t}dt + \sigma \int_0^T e^{\kappa t}dW_t \\
&= \hat{X}_0 + \alpha_X[e^{\kappa T} - 1] + \sigma \int_0^T e^{\kappa t}dW_t.
\end{aligned}
$$

Consider now the integral $\sigma \int_0^T e^{\kappa t}dW_t$. Since Brownian motion is driftless, this integral is a martingale with expectation equal to zero. We can compute the variance of $\int_0^T e^{\kappa t}dW_t$, however, by use of the Itô isometry, namely

$$\mathbf{E}\left[\left(\int_0^T \Phi_t dW_t\right)^2\right] = \mathbf{E}\left[\int_0^T \Phi_t^2 dt\right]$$

where Φ_t is an adapted process. Putting $\Phi_t = e^{\kappa t}$, which is deterministic and therefore trivially adapted, we have no need of expectations and can simply compute

$$\int_0^T e^{2\kappa t}dt = \left[\frac{e^{2\kappa t}}{2\kappa}\right]_{t=0}^T = \frac{e^{2\kappa T} - 1}{2\kappa}.$$

We therefore have (note that $\hat{X}_0 = X_0$)

$$\mathbf{E}\left[\hat{X}_T\right] = X_0 + \alpha_X[e^{\kappa T} - 1] \qquad (2.149a)$$

$$\mathbf{Var}\left[\hat{X}_T\right] = \frac{\sigma^2}{2\kappa}\left[e^{2\kappa T} - 1\right]. \qquad (2.149b)$$

Finally, since $X_T = e^{-\kappa T}\hat{X}_T$, we have

$$\mathbf{E}\left[X_T\right] = e^{-\kappa T}\mathbf{E}\left[\hat{X}_T\right] = X_0 e^{-\kappa T} + \alpha_X[1 - e^{-\kappa T}] \qquad (2.150a)$$

and

$$\mathbf{Var}\left[X_T\right] = e^{-2\kappa T}\mathbf{Var}\left[\hat{X}_T\right] = \frac{\sigma^2}{2\kappa}\left[1 - e^{-2\kappa T}\right]. \qquad (2.150b)$$

Note that this gives rise to a lognormally distributed S_T, i.e. X_T has a lognormal distribution characterised by first and second moments which can be used in exactly the same manner as the moments arising from a standard geometric Brownian motion for option pricing. We have

$$V_0^{C/P} = \omega e^{-r^d T}[F_{0,T}N(\omega d_1) - KN(\omega d_2)] \qquad (2.151a)$$

with

$$d_{1,2} = \frac{\ln\left(F_{0,T}/K\right) \pm \frac{1}{2}\sigma_{0,T}^2 T}{\sigma_{0,T}\sqrt{T}}. \qquad (2.151b)$$

where, from (2.150b),

$$\sigma_{0,T} = \sqrt{\frac{\sigma^2}{2\kappa}\left[1 - e^{-2\kappa T}\right]}. \qquad (2.151c)$$

To match T-forward prices, i.e. to choose α_X such that $\mathbf{E}^d\left[S_T\right] = F_{0,T}$, we use the result quoted in (3.11) of Burger et al. (2007)

$$\mathbf{E}\left[S_T\right] = \exp\left(\mathbf{E}\left[X_T\right] + \frac{1}{2}\mathbf{Var}\left[X_T\right]\right). \qquad (2.152)$$

Substituting (2.150) into (2.152), we obtain

$$\mathbf{E}\left[S_T\right] = \exp\left(X_0 e^{-\kappa T} + \alpha_X[1 - e^{-\kappa T}] + \frac{\sigma^2}{4\kappa}\left[1 - e^{-2\kappa T}\right]\right). \qquad (2.153)$$

One final adjustment is required, to convert the expectation to the expectation under the risk-neutral measure. If we let λ denote the market price of risk, as in Burger *et al.* (2007), then we write $\hat{\alpha}_X = \alpha_X - \lambda/\kappa$ and then we have

$$\mathbf{E}^d\left[S_T\right] = \exp\left(X_0 e^{-\kappa T} + \hat{\alpha}_X[1 - e^{-\kappa T}] + \frac{\sigma^2}{4\kappa}\left[1 - e^{-2\kappa T}\right]\right). \qquad (2.154)$$

Taking the limit as $T \to \infty$, we have

$$\lim_{T \to \infty} F_{0,T} = \exp\left(\hat{\alpha}_X + \frac{\sigma^2}{4\kappa}\right)$$

$$= \exp\left(\alpha_S - \frac{\sigma^2}{4\kappa} - \frac{\lambda}{\kappa}\right) \qquad (2.155)$$

while for finite T we have

$$F_{0,T} = [S_0]^{e^{-\kappa T}} \cdot \exp\left(\hat{\alpha}_X[1 - e^{-\kappa T}] + \frac{\sigma^2}{4\kappa}\left[1 - e^{-2\kappa T}\right]\right) \qquad (2.156)$$

and more generally

$$F_{t,T} = [S_0]^{e^{-\kappa(T-t)}} \cdot \exp\left(\hat{\alpha}_X[1 - e^{-\kappa(T-t)}] + \frac{\sigma^2}{4\kappa}\left[1 - e^{-2\kappa(T-t)}\right]\right). \qquad (2.157)$$

If the domestic rate r^d and convenience yield r^f to time T are known, then we can write $F_{0,T} = S_0 e^{(r^d - r^f)T}$ and solve (2.156), obtaining

$$\hat{\alpha}_X = \ln S_0 + \frac{\left[(r^d - r^f)T + \frac{\sigma^2}{4\kappa}\left[e^{-2\kappa T} - 1\right]\right]}{1 - e^{-\kappa T}}. \qquad (2.158)$$

Note that $\sigma_{0,T}^2$ is the integrated variance from 0 to T. One can follow Clewlow and Strickland (2000) and Geman (2005) in differentiating (2.157) to obtain the instantaneous proportional volatility of $F_{t,T}$, i.e. that quantity $\sigma_F(t, T)$ such that $\frac{dF_{t,T}}{F_{t,T}} = \sigma_F(t, T)dW_t^F$ for a suitably chosen Brownian motion W_t^F.

Alternatively, one can recognise that $\sigma_{0,T}^2 = \int_0^T \sigma_F^2(t, T)dt$, or more generally, $\sigma_{t,T}^2 = \int_t^T \sigma_F^2(u, T)du$ with

$$\sigma_{t,T}^2 = \frac{\sigma^2}{2\kappa}\left[1 - e^{-2\kappa(T-t)}\right]. \tag{2.159}$$

Differentiating under the integral sign, we have

$$\frac{\partial}{\partial t}\int_t^T \sigma_{t,T}^2 du = -\sigma_F^2(t, T).$$

However, using (2.189) directly we have

$$\begin{aligned}
\frac{\partial}{\partial t}\int_t^T \sigma_{t,T}^2 du &= \frac{\partial}{\partial t}\left[\frac{\sigma^2}{2\kappa}\left[1 - e^{-2\kappa(T-t)}\right]\right] \\
&= \frac{\sigma^2}{2\kappa}\frac{\partial}{\partial t}\left[1 - e^{-2\kappa(T-t)}\right] \\
&= -\frac{\sigma^2}{2\kappa}e^{-2\kappa T}\frac{\partial}{\partial t}\left[e^{2\kappa t}\right] \\
&= -\frac{\sigma^2}{2\kappa}e^{-2\kappa T}2\kappa e^{2\kappa t} \\
&= -\sigma^2 e^{-2\kappa(T-t)}.
\end{aligned}$$

Equating, we have $\sigma_F^2(t, T) = \sigma^2 e^{-2\kappa(T-t)}$, from which the result follows

$$\sigma_F(t, T) = \sigma e^{-\kappa(T-t)}. \tag{2.160}$$

Note that this is consistent with the Samuelson effect, where forward contracts of greater maturity are often observed to have smaller volatilities than shorter dated forward contracts.

2.10.1.2 *Mean Reverting One-Factor Models with Term Structure*

Mean reverting models are also discussed in Section 33.4 of Hull (2011), where the mean reversion level is allowed to have a term structure, i.e.

$$dX_t = (\theta_t - \kappa X_t)dt + \sigma dW_t \tag{2.161}$$

This is analogous to the Hull–White model in interest rate modelling, and similar techniques can be used to fit θ_t to the term structure of observed futures prices. This can be done on trees, as discussed in Hull and White (1996) in the context of interest rate derivatives, and is also discussed in the commodities context in Section 33.4 of Hull (2011), where the logspot process is modelled as the sum of a process mean reverting around zero, plus a time-dependent drift.

This approach is often known as the "deterministic shift decomposition," and is described in Ludkovski and Carmona (2004) in the context of adding term structure to the mean reversion level of the Gibson–Schwartz model. For the Schwartz (1997) one-factor model, a term structure of mean reversion level is handled by integrating (2.161). This proceeds using the same stochastic integrating factor technique. Write $\hat{X}_t = \exp(\kappa t)X_t$ and employ $d\hat{X}_t = e^{\kappa t}dX_t + \kappa e^{\kappa t}X_t dt$. Using (2.161) we obtain

$$d\hat{X}_t = e^{\kappa t}\theta_t dt + \sigma e^{\kappa t}dW_t.$$

Integrating from 0 to T we have

$$\hat{X}_T = \hat{X}_0 + \int_0^T e^{\kappa t}\theta_t dt + \int_0^T \sigma e^{\kappa t}dW_t.$$

Multiplying by $e^{-\kappa T}$ we obtain

$$X_T = X_0 e^{-\kappa T} + \int_0^T e^{-\kappa(T-t)}\theta_t dt + \sigma \int_0^T e^{-\kappa(T-t)}dW_t. \qquad (2.162)$$

The Itô integral $\int_0^T e^{-\kappa(T-t)}dW_t$ is once again a martingale, from which we have

$$\mathbf{E}\left[X_T\right] = X_0 e^{-\kappa T} + \int_0^T e^{-\kappa(T-t)}\theta_t dt. \qquad (2.163a)$$

Since no term structure for κ nor σ is supposed at this stage, we still have, from (2.150b),

$$\mathbf{Var}\left[X_T\right] = \frac{\sigma^2}{2\kappa}\left[1 - e^{-2\kappa T}\right]. \qquad (2.163b)$$

Alternatively, let us now define A_t by

$$dA_t = -\kappa A_t dt + \sigma dW_t, \qquad (2.164)$$

with $A_0 = 0$, and let us attempt to decompose X_t into the sum $X_t = A_t + \alpha_t$. We have $\alpha_t = X_t - A_t$, so

$$\begin{aligned} d\alpha_t &= dX_t - dA_t \\ &= (\theta_t - \kappa X_t)dt + \sigma dW_t + \kappa A_t dt - \sigma dW_t \\ &= (\theta_t - \kappa(X_t - A_t))dt \\ &= (\theta_t - \kappa\alpha_t)dt \end{aligned} \qquad (2.165)$$

which is clearly nonstochastic. Introduce an integrating factor $e^{\kappa t}$ and write $\hat{\alpha}_t = \alpha_t e^{\kappa t}$, as a result of which we have $d\hat{\alpha}_t = e^{\kappa t}d\alpha_t + \kappa e^{\kappa t}\alpha_t dt = e^{\kappa t}[d\alpha_t + \kappa\alpha_t dt]$. From (2.165) we know $d\alpha_t + \kappa\alpha_t dt = \theta_t dt$, so we need only solve $d\hat{\alpha}_t = e^{\kappa t}\theta_t dt$. Integration of this is simple, we have

$$\hat{\alpha}_t = \hat{\alpha}_0 + \int_0^t e^{\kappa s}\theta_s ds$$

or, since $\alpha_t = \hat{\alpha}_t e^{-\kappa t}$ and $\alpha_0 = X_0$,

$$\alpha_t = X_0 e^{-\kappa t} + \int_0^t e^{-\kappa(t-s)}\theta_s ds. \tag{2.166}$$

Since $\mathbf{E}[A_t] = 0$, we have $\mathbf{E}[X_t] = \alpha_t$, which is consistent with (2.163a).

We can now use (2.152) together with (2.163) to compute $\mathbf{E}^d[S_T]$ and infer suitable values for θ_t in order to solve $\mathbf{E}^d[S_T] = F_{0,T}$ and thereby recover correct forward prices $F_{0,T}$.

2.10.1.3   The Clewlow–Strickland (1999) One-Factor Model for Forwards

There are two approaches, basically, to modelling commodities, as we already know. One is to model an underlying spot price process[10] and then to infer the dynamics of the forwards. The second approach is to model the forward curve directly. This is the approach introduced in Clewlow and Strickland (1999a), who proposed a one-factor model to describe the stochastic evolution of the forward curve. A general form of the one-factor model can be written as

$$\frac{dF_{t,T}}{F_{t,T}} = \sigma_F(t, T)dW_t. \tag{2.167}$$

What the authors recognised was that, if the instantaneous proportional volatility of $F_{t,T}$ under the one-factor Schwartz (1997) model is known to be (2.160), then the same volatility specification can be used to build a forward curve based model, but where the initial forward curve can be specified exogenously rather than needing to be determined using today's spot and model parameters.

---

[10] Whether it exists or not is another story.

Under this specific model, we have

$$\frac{dF_{t,T}}{F_{t,T}} = \sigma_F(t, T)dW_t = \sigma e^{-\kappa(T-t)}dW_t. \qquad (2.168)$$

Note that, unlike the one-factor Schwartz (1997) model, the only required parameters are the short term volatility σ and the mean reversion rate κ. One important observation: the mean reversion parameter κ is *embedded* in the volatility function, there is no actual stochastic mean reversion term in (2.168).

We follow Section 8.5 of Clewlow and Strickland (2000) and integrate (2.167). Squaring this gives

$$\frac{dF_{t,T}^2}{F_{t,T}^2} = \sigma_F^2(t, T)dt. \qquad (2.169)$$

Simple application of Itô's lemma to $\ln F_{t,T} = f(F_{t,T})$ with $f(x) = \ln x$ gives

$$d\ln F_{t,T} = \frac{dF_{t,T}}{F_{t,T}} - \frac{1}{2}\frac{dF_{t,T}^2}{F_{t,T}^2}$$

$$= \sigma_F(t, T)dW_t - \frac{1}{2}\sigma_F^2(t, T)dt.$$

We integrate this expression, obtaining

$$\ln F_{t,T} = \ln F_{0,T} - \frac{1}{2}\int_0^t \sigma_F^2(s, T)ds + \int_0^t \sigma_F(s, T)dW_s. \qquad (2.170)$$

If one sets $T = t$ then (2.170) reduces to

$$\ln S_t = \ln F_{t,t} = \ln F_{0,t} - \frac{1}{2}\int_0^t \sigma_F^2(s, t)ds + \int_0^t \sigma_F(s, t)dW_s. \qquad (2.171)$$

i.e.

$$S_t = F_{0,t} \cdot \exp\left(-\frac{1}{2}\int_0^t \sigma_F^2(s, t)ds + \int_0^t \sigma_F(s, t)dW_s\right)$$

$$= F_{0,t} \cdot \exp\left(I_t\right) \qquad (2.172)$$

with $I_t = -\frac{1}{2}\int_0^t \sigma_F^2(s, t)ds + \int_0^t \sigma_F(s, t)dW_s$. We can now write

$$dS_t = dF_{0,t} \cdot \exp\left(I_t\right) + F_{0,t} \cdot d\exp\left(I_t\right)$$

$$= dF_{0,t}\frac{S_t}{F_{0,t}} + F_{0,t}\exp\left(I_t\right) \cdot d[I_t]$$

from which we obtain

$$\frac{dS_t}{S_t} = \frac{dF_{0,t}}{F_{0,t}} + d[I_t]$$

$$= \frac{1}{F_{0,t}} \frac{\partial F_{0,t}}{\partial t} dt + d[I_t]$$

$$= \frac{\partial \ln F_{0,t}}{\partial t} dt + d[I_t].$$

It remains to calculate

$$d[I_t] = d\left(-\frac{1}{2} \int_0^t \sigma_F^2(s, t) ds + \int_0^t \sigma_F(s, t) dW_s \right)$$

$$= \left[-\int_0^t \sigma_F(s, t) \frac{\partial \sigma_F(s, t)}{\partial t} ds + \int_0^t \frac{\partial \sigma_F(s, t)}{\partial t} dW_s \right] dt + \sigma_F(t, t) dW_t$$

where the second line follows via differentiating under the integral sign. We therefore obtain (A.4) from Clewlow and Strickland (1999a), i.e.

$$\frac{dS_t}{S_t} = \left[\frac{\partial \ln F_{0,t}}{\partial t} - \int_0^t \sigma_F(s, t) \frac{\partial \sigma_F(s, t)}{\partial t} ds \right.$$

$$\left. + \int_0^t \frac{\partial \sigma_F(s, t)}{\partial t} dW_s \right] dt + \sigma_F(t, t) dW_t. \qquad (2.173)$$

It is shown in the original paper that (2.173), with $\sigma_F(t, T) = \sigma e^{-\kappa(T-t)}$, is equivalent to

$$\frac{dS_t}{S_t} = [\mu_t - \kappa \ln S_t] dt + \sigma dW_t \qquad (2.174a)$$

with

$$\mu_t = \frac{\partial \ln F_{0,t}}{\partial t} + \kappa \ln F_{0,t} + \frac{\sigma^2}{4} \left(1 - e^{-2\kappa t} \right). \qquad (2.174b)$$

Note that, as a result, the drift term in (2.174a) is obtained implicitly in terms of the initial forward curve.

Option pricing under this model is straightforward; the same equations (2.197) as for the Schwartz model are applicable, but where $F_{0,T}$ are obtained directly from the market and there is no need to calibrate a mean reversion level to the forwards.

The mean reversion rate κ and volatility σ can now easily be imbued with a term structure (i.e. κ_t and σ_t), the only computation required being the integral

$$\sigma_{0,T} = \sqrt{\int_0^T \sigma_t e^{-2\kappa_T(T-t)} dt}. \qquad (2.175)$$

2.10.2 Multi-Factor Models

Single factor models, while simple, are inadequate for several reasons. Firstly, they can only describe perfect correlation between non-coinciding forward contracts. As discussed in Chapter 5 of Eydeland and Wolyniec (2003), even a generic one-factor forward model of the form $dF_{t,T} = \sigma(t, T)F_{t,T} dW_t$ has $\rho(t, T_1, T_2) = 1$ describing the correlation between $\ln F_{t,T_1}$ and $\ln F_{t,T_2}$.

Secondarily, only a limited variety of volatility term structures can be captured, all of which decay to zero for increasingly long-dated forwards.

2.10.2.1 The Schwartz–Smith (2000) Two-Factor Model

In order to tackle some of these concerns, Schwartz and Smith (2000) introduced a two-factor commodities spot model, under which logspot is described as the sum of two factors

$$\ln S_t = \chi_t + \xi_t$$

where

$$d\chi_t = -\kappa \chi_t dt + \sigma_\chi dW_t^\chi \qquad (2.176a)$$

$$d\xi_t = \mu_\xi dt + \sigma_\xi dW_t^\xi \qquad (2.176b)$$

and $\langle dW_t^\chi, dW_t^\xi \rangle = \rho dt$.

The first factor χ_t is a short-term mean reverting factor analogous to the Schwartz (1997) one-factor model, as is particularly evident from comparing (2.176a) to (2.164), while the second factor ξ_t captures the long-term dynamics. While previously we had $X_t = A_t + \alpha_t$ with α_t being deterministic, now we have $X_t = \chi_t + \xi_t$ with ξ_t also being stochastic. This is a two-factor model, driven by two correlated Brownian motions W_t^χ and W_t^ξ.

From $X_t = \ln S_t = \chi_t + \xi_t$, by summation of the two stochastic differential components in (2.176) we have

$$
\begin{aligned}
dX_t &= (\mu_\xi - \kappa\chi_t)dt + \sigma_\chi dW_t^\chi + \sigma_\xi dW_t^\xi \\
&= (\mu_\xi - \kappa(X_t - \xi_t))dt + \sigma_\chi dW_t^\chi + \sigma_\xi dW_t^\xi \\
&= (\mu_\xi + \kappa\xi_t - \kappa X_t)dt + \sigma_\chi dW_t^\chi + \sigma_\xi dW_t^\xi.
\end{aligned} \tag{2.177}
$$

If we add a constant offset to ξ_t, making $\theta_t = \xi_t + \mu_\xi/\kappa$, then clearly $d\xi_t$ obeys the same SDE as (2.176b), i.e.

$$
d\theta_t = \mu_\xi dt + \sigma_\xi dW_t^\xi \tag{2.178}
$$

and we can write (2.177) as

$$
\begin{aligned}
dX_t &= (\mu_\xi + \kappa\xi_t - \kappa X_t)dt + \sigma_\chi dW_t^\chi + \sigma_\xi dW_t^\xi \\
&= \kappa(\theta_t - X_t)dt + \sigma_\chi dW_t^\chi + \sigma_\xi dW_t^\xi \\
&= \kappa(\theta_t - X_t)dt + \sigma_X dW_t^X
\end{aligned} \tag{2.179}
$$

where $W_t^X = \frac{1}{\sigma_X}[\sigma_\chi dW_t^\chi + \sigma_\xi dW_t^\xi]$. Consequently, the Schwartz–Smith two-factor model can be seen to be equivalent to a mean-reverting model, but where the mean reversion level is itself stochastic.

The original paper derives the following expressions for the first and second moments of χ_t and ξ_t:

$$
\mathbf{E}\left[\chi_t\right] = e^{-\kappa t}\chi_0 \tag{2.180a}
$$

$$
\mathbf{E}\left[\xi_t\right] = \xi_0 + \mu_\xi t \tag{2.180b}
$$

and

$$
\mathbf{Cov}\left[\chi_t, \xi_t\right] =
\begin{bmatrix}
\left(1 - e^{-2\kappa t}\right)\frac{\sigma_\chi^2}{2\kappa} & \left(1 - e^{-\kappa t}\right)\frac{\rho\sigma_\chi\sigma_\xi}{\kappa} \\
\left(1 - e^{-\kappa t}\right)\frac{\rho\sigma_\chi\sigma_\xi}{\kappa} & \sigma_\xi^2 t
\end{bmatrix} \tag{2.181}
$$

from which one can derive the result that X_T is normally distributed with

$$
\mathbf{E}\left[X_T\right] = \xi_0 + \mu_\xi T + e^{-\kappa T}\chi_0 \tag{2.182a}
$$

$$
\mathbf{Var}\left[X_T\right] = \left(1 - e^{-2\kappa T}\right)\frac{\sigma_\chi^2}{2\kappa} + \sigma_\xi^2 T + 2\left(1 - e^{-\kappa T}\right)\frac{\rho\sigma_\chi\sigma_\xi}{\kappa}. \tag{2.182b}
$$

Equation (2.152) can then be used to express the first and second moments of the lognormal distribution describing S_T. Note, however, that for pricing one needs to correct for the market price of risk. This can be done by introducing λ_χ and λ_ξ (market risk factors) and putting $\hat{\mu}_\chi = -\lambda_\chi$ and $\hat{\mu}_\xi = \mu_\xi - \lambda_\xi$, then writing

$$d\chi_t = \left(\hat{\mu}_\chi - \kappa\chi_t\right) dt + \sigma_\chi dW_t^{(\chi;d)} \qquad (2.183a)$$

$$d\xi_t = \hat{\mu}_\xi dt + \sigma_\xi dW_t^{(\xi;d)} \qquad (2.183b)$$

where we use $W_t^{(\chi;d)}$ and $W_t^{(\xi;d)}$ to denote Brownian motions under the domestic risk-neutral measure. Note that the drift adjustment only affects the first moment, i.e.

$$\mathbf{E}^d\left[X_T\right] = \xi_0 + \hat{\mu}_\xi T + e^{-\kappa T}\chi_0 + \frac{\hat{\mu}_\chi}{\kappa}(1 - e^{-\kappa T}) \qquad (2.184a)$$

$$\mathbf{Var}^d\left[X_T\right] = \left(1 - e^{-2\kappa T}\right)\frac{\sigma_\chi^2}{2\kappa} + \sigma_\xi^2 T + 2\left(1 - e^{-\kappa T}\right)\frac{\rho\sigma_\chi\sigma_\xi}{\kappa}. \qquad (2.184b)$$

We can obtain the result in (2.184a) using the familiar stochastic integrating factor technique. From (2.183a), write

$$d\chi_t + \kappa\chi_t dt = \hat{\mu}_\chi dt + \sigma_\chi dW_t^{(\chi;d)}.$$

By putting $\hat{\chi}_t = e^{\kappa t}\chi_t$ we have

$$d[\hat{\chi}_t] = d[e^{\kappa t}\chi_t] = e^{\kappa t}d\chi_t + \kappa e^{\kappa t}\chi_t dt = \hat{\mu}_\chi e^{\kappa t}dt + \sigma_\chi e^{\kappa t}dW_t^{(\chi;d)} \qquad (2.185)$$

Integrating (2.185) we have

$$\hat{\chi}_T = \hat{\chi}_0 + \hat{\mu}_\chi \int_0^T e^{\kappa t}dt + \sigma_\chi \int_0^T e^{\kappa t}dW_t^{(\chi;d)}$$

$$= \hat{\chi}_0 + \frac{\hat{\mu}_\chi}{\kappa}\left[e^{\kappa T} - 1\right] + \sigma_\chi \int_0^T e^{\kappa t}dW_t^{(\chi;d)}. \qquad (2.186)$$

Since the Itô integral has zero expectation, we have

$$\mathbf{E}^d\left[\hat{\chi}_T\right] = \hat{\chi}_0 + \frac{\hat{\mu}_\chi}{\kappa}\left[e^{\kappa T} - 1\right]$$

and, after multiplying by $e^{-\kappa T}$ (since $\chi_T = e^{-\kappa T}\hat{\chi}_T$) we obtain

$$\mathbf{E}^d\left[\chi_T\right] = \chi_0 e^{-\kappa T} + \frac{\hat{\mu}_\chi}{\kappa}\left[1 - e^{-\kappa T}\right]. \qquad (2.187)$$

Since $\mathbf{E}^d\left[\xi_T\right] = \xi_0 + \hat{\mu}_\xi T$ by straightforward integration of (2.183b), the result (2.184a) follows. We can therefore obtain the prices for forwards in the Schwartz–Smith (2000) two-factor model

$$F_{0,T} = \mathbf{E}^d\left[S_T\right] = \exp\left(\mathbf{E}^d\left[X_T\right] + \frac{1}{2}\mathbf{Var}^d\left[X_T\right]\right)$$

$$= \exp\left(\xi_0 + \chi_0 e^{-\kappa T} + \left(\mu_\xi - \lambda_\xi + \frac{1}{2}\sigma_\xi^2\right)T\right.$$

$$\left. + \frac{\rho\sigma_\chi\sigma_\xi - \lambda_\chi}{\kappa}\left(1 - e^{-\kappa T}\right) + \frac{\sigma_\chi^2}{4\kappa}\left(1 - e^{-2\kappa T}\right)\right). \qquad (2.188)$$

Finally, these values for $F_{0,T}$ can be used in the Black equation together with a volatility $\sigma_{0,T}$ obtained from (2.182b)

$$\sigma_{0,T}^2 = \left(1 - e^{-2\kappa T}\right)\frac{\sigma_\chi^2}{2\kappa} + \sigma_\xi^2 T + 2\left(1 - e^{-\kappa T}\right)\frac{\rho\sigma_\chi\sigma_\xi}{\kappa}. \qquad (2.189)$$

Further discussion of the Schwartz–Smith model can be found in the original paper, Example 5.1 in Eydeland and Wolyniec (2003), and in Section 3.2.3 of Burger, Graeber and Schindlmayr (2007).

2.10.2.2   The Burger–Graeber–Schindlmayr (2007) Two-Factor Model

As presented earlier in our discussion of the Clewlow–Strickland (1999) model, we can model spot processes or we can model forwards. An interesting two-factor model is presented in Burger, Graeber and Schindlmayr (2007), which takes the latter approach. In this model, we have

$$\frac{dF_{t,T}}{F_{t,T}} = e^{-\kappa(T-t)}\sigma_1 dW_t^{(1)} + \sigma_2 dW_t^{(2)} \qquad (2.190)$$

where $\langle dW_t^{(1)}, dW_t^{(2)}\rangle = \rho dt$. Squaring (2.190), we have

$$\frac{dF_{t,T}^2}{F_{t,T}^2} = \left(\sigma_1^2 e^{-2\kappa(T-t)} + 2\rho\sigma_1\sigma_2 e^{-\kappa(T-t)} + \sigma_2^2\right)dt. \qquad (2.191)$$

Simple application of Itô's lemma to $\ln F_{t,T} = f(F_{t,T})$ with $f(x) = \ln x$ gives

$$d\ln F_{t,T} = \frac{dF_{t,T}}{F_{t,T}} - \frac{1}{2}\frac{dF_{t,T}^2}{F_{t,T}^2}$$

$$= e^{-\kappa\tau}\sigma_1 dW_t^{(1)} + \sigma_2 dW_t^{(2)} - \frac{1}{2}\left(\sigma_1^2 e^{-2\kappa\tau} + 2\rho\sigma_1\sigma_2 e^{-\kappa\tau} + \sigma_2^2\right)dt$$

where $\tau = T - t$. We integrate this expression, obtaining

$$\ln F_{t,T} = \ln F_{0,T} - \frac{1}{2} \int_0^t \left(\sigma_1^2 e^{-2\kappa(T-s)} + 2\rho\sigma_1\sigma_2 e^{-\kappa T - s} + \sigma_2^2 \right) dt + \chi_t^T + \xi_t^T$$

where $\chi_t^T = \sigma_1 \int_0^t e^{-\kappa(T-s)} dW_s^{(1)} ds$ and $\xi_t^T = \sigma_2 \int_0^t dW_s^{(2)} ds$. With a little algebra, we obtain

$$\ln F_{t,T} = \ln F_{0,T} - \sigma_1^2 e^{-2\kappa T} \frac{e^{2\kappa t} - 1}{4\kappa} - \rho\sigma_1\sigma_2 e^{-\kappa T} \frac{e^{\kappa t} - 1}{\kappa}$$
$$- \frac{1}{2}\sigma_2^2 t + \chi_t^T + \xi_t^T.$$

In their work, it is shown that the spot price process imputed by this, i.e. with $S_t = F_{t,t}$, is consistent with a Schwartz–Smith type model, but with time dependent parameters, of the form

$$\frac{dS_t}{S_t} = \kappa(\alpha_t + \xi_t - \ln S_t)dt + \sigma_1 dW_t^{(1)} + \sigma_2 dW_t^{(2)}. \quad (2.192a)$$

Under this model, we have

$$\ln S_t = A_t + \chi_t + \xi_t \quad (2.193a)$$

where

$$A_t = \ln F_{0,T} - \left(\frac{\sigma_1^2}{4\kappa}(1 - e^{-2\kappa t}) + \frac{\rho\sigma_1\sigma_2}{\kappa} + \frac{1}{2}\sigma_2^2 t \right) \quad (2.193b)$$

$$d\chi_t = -\kappa\chi_t dt + \sigma_1 dW_t^{(1)} \quad (2.193c)$$

$$d\xi_t = \sigma_2 dW_t^{(2)}. \quad (2.193d)$$

Note the similarity of (2.193c) and (2.193d) to (2.176). Since forwards are directly presumed to be martingales under the risk-neutral measure, no adjustment to remove the market price of spot risk is required.

2.10.2.3 The Clewlow–Strickland (1999) Multi-Factor Model for Forwards

Clewlow and Strickland (1999b) extended their earlier work to cover a sequence of models to describe the stochastic evolution of the forward curve. While for the one-factor model we have $\frac{dF_{t,T}}{F_{t,T}} = \sigma_F(t, T)dW_t$, the multi-factor model is given by

$$\frac{dF_{t,T}}{F_{t,T}} = \sum_{i=1}^{n} \sigma_i(t, T)dW_t^{(i)} \tag{2.194}$$

where $\{W_t^{(1)}, \ldots, W_t^{(n)}\}$ are n independent Brownian motions.

This can be integrated in the same manner as the Clewlow and Strickland one-factor model

$$\ln F_{t,T} = \ln F_{0,T} + \sum_{i=1}^{n} \left[-\frac{1}{2} \int_0^t \sigma_i^2(s, T)ds + \int_0^t \sigma_i(s, T)dW_s \right]. \tag{2.195}$$

Note that the presence of the $\int_0^t \frac{\partial \sigma_F(s,t)}{\partial t} dW_s$ term in the drift means that this model is non-Markovian, i.e. it has a memory and the stochastic evolution of the spot process S_t is not purely determined by the value of the stochastic variables at time t. Taking exponentials of (2.195), we have

$$F_{t,T} = F_{0,T} \cdot \exp\left(\sum_{i=1}^{n} \left[-\frac{1}{2} \int_0^t \sigma_i^2(s, T)ds + \int_0^t \sigma_i(s, T)dW_s \right] \right) \tag{2.196}$$

from which it is apparent that $F_{t,T}$ is lognormally distributed. As a result, as stated in Clewlow and Strickland (1999b), European style options on forwards can easily be priced needing "only univariate integrations involving the volatility functions of the forward prices"

$$V_0^{C/P} = \omega e^{-r^d T}[F_{0,T}N(\omega d_1) - KN(\omega d_2)] \tag{2.197a}$$

with

$$d_{1,2} = \frac{\ln\left(F_{0,T}/K\right) \pm \frac{1}{2}\sigma_{0,T}^2 T}{\sigma_{0,T}\sqrt{T}} \tag{2.197b}$$

where

$$\sigma_{0,T}^2 = \frac{1}{T} \sum_{i=1}^{n} \left[\int_0^T \sigma_i^2(u, s)du \right]. \tag{2.197c}$$

2.10.3   Convenience Yield Models

As well as introducing extra stochastic factors to capture extra degrees of freedom in the volatility, it is certainly quite possible to introduce extra stochastic factors for other terms in the model, such as convenience yield.

2.10.3.1   The Gibson–Schwartz (1990) Two-Factor Model

The first work in this area was Gibson and Schwartz (1990), who introduced a two-factor model – the first factor being commodity spot, and the second factor being convenience yield δ_t

$$\frac{dS_t}{S_t} = (\mu_t - \delta_t)dt + \sigma^{(1)}dW_t^{(1)} \qquad (2.198a)$$

$$d\delta_t = \kappa(\alpha - \delta_t)dt + \sigma^{(2)}dW_t^{(2)} \qquad (2.198b)$$

with $\langle dW_t^{(1)}, dW_t^{(2)} \rangle = \rho dt$. The same model is presented as "Model 2" in Schwartz (1997). In this model, α is the long term convenience yield, $\sigma^{(1)}$ is the spot volatility and $\sigma^{(2)}$ is the volatility of the convenience yield. The κ term gives the speed of mean reversion and ρ allows chances in convenience yield to be correlated with movements in the spot process.

Upon transforming to the domestic risk-neutral measure, we have

$$\frac{dS_t}{S_t} = (r_t^d - \delta_t)dt + \sigma^{(1)}dW_t^{(1;d)} \qquad (2.199a)$$

$$d\delta_t = (\kappa(\alpha - \delta_t) - \lambda_\delta)dt + \sigma^{(2)}dW_t^{(2;d)}$$
$$= (\kappa(\hat{\alpha} - \delta_t))dt + \sigma^{(2)}dW_t^{(2;d)} \qquad (2.199b)$$

with $\hat{\alpha} = \alpha - \lambda_\delta/\kappa$, where λ_δ denotes the market price of convenience yield risk. Note that the market price per unit of convenience yield risk λ in Bjerksund (1991) is equal to $\lambda_\delta/\sigma^{(2)}$ in our notation. The Brownians $W_t^{(1;d)}$ and $W_t^{(2;d)}$ are now Brownian motions with respect to the (domestic) risk-neutral measure, such that $\langle dW_t^{(1;d)}, dW_t^{(2;d)} \rangle = \rho dt$.

As discussed in Schwartz (1997), as originally derived in Jamshidian and Fein (1990) and Bjerksund (1991), this can be solved to obtain the forward price

$$F_{0,T} = S_0 \cdot \exp\left(-\delta_0 \frac{1 - e^{-\kappa T}}{\kappa} + A(T)\right) \qquad (2.200a)$$

where

$$A_T = \left(r^d - \hat{\alpha} + \frac{[\sigma^{(2)}]^2}{2\kappa^2} - \frac{\rho\sigma^{(1)}\sigma^{(2)}}{\kappa} \right) T + \frac{1}{4}[\sigma^{(2)}]^2 \frac{1 - e^{-2\kappa T}}{\kappa^3}$$
$$+ \left(\hat{\alpha}\kappa + \rho\sigma^{(1)}\sigma^{(2)} - \frac{[\sigma^{(2)}]^2}{\kappa} \right) \frac{1 - e^{-\kappa T}}{\kappa^2}. \qquad (2.200b)$$

Upon changing to the risk-neutral measure and removing the market price of risk, we have

$$V_0^{S_T} = e^{-r^d T} \mathbf{E}^d \left[S_T \right]$$
$$= S_0 \exp \left(\hat{\mu} + \frac{1}{2}\hat{\sigma}^2 \right) \qquad (2.201)$$

where

$$\hat{\mu} = \left(-\frac{1}{2}[\sigma^{(1)}]^2 + \hat{\alpha} \right) T + \left(\hat{\alpha} - \delta_0 \right) \frac{1 - \theta}{\kappa} \qquad (2.202a)$$

$$\hat{\sigma} = \left[[\sigma^{(2)}]^2 - \frac{2\rho\sigma^{(1)}\sigma^{(2)}}{\kappa} + \frac{[\sigma^{(2)}]^2}{\kappa^2} \right] T \qquad (2.202b)$$
$$+ 2 \left(\frac{\rho\sigma^{(1)}\sigma^{(2)}}{\kappa^2} - \frac{[\sigma^{(2)}]^2}{\kappa^3} \right) (1 - \theta) + \frac{[\sigma^{(2)}]^2}{2\kappa^3}(1 - \theta^2)$$

with $\theta = \exp(-\kappa T)$. This can be used directly for European option pricing, following Bjerksund (1991) we have

$$V_0^C = V_0^{S_T} N(d_1) - K e^{-r^d T} N(d_2) \qquad (2.203)$$

where

$$d_{1;2} = \frac{\ln(V_0^{S_T}/K) + r^d T \pm \frac{1}{2}\hat{\sigma}^2}{\hat{\sigma}}. \qquad (2.204)$$

The convenience yield does not appear directly in (2.203), as it is already accounted for in computation of $V_0^{S_T}$ via $\hat{\mu}$.

Finally, and as a prelude to the next model, Cortazar and Schwartz (2003) noted that (2.198) can be simplified somewhat by defining the so-called "demeaned" convenience yield $y_t = \delta_t - \alpha$ (clearly $dy_t = d\delta_t$). With this, we transform (2.198b) as follows

$$dy_t = d\delta_t = \kappa(\alpha - \delta_t)dt + \sigma^{(2)}dW_t^{(2)}$$
$$= -\kappa y_t dt + \sigma^{(2)}dW_t^{(2)}. \qquad (2.205)$$

As for (2.198a), we introduce a "long-term" price return $v_t = \mu_t - \alpha$. Since both terms y_t and v_t are adjusted by the same constant factor, we have $v_t - y_t = \mu_t - \delta_t$, and therefore

$$\frac{dS_t}{S_t} = (\mu_t - \delta_t)dt + \sigma^{(1)}dW_t^{(1)}$$

$$= (v_t - y_t)dt + \sigma^{(1)}dW_t^{(1)}. \qquad (2.206)$$

Note that v_t, like μ_t, is deterministic.

2.10.3.2   The Schwartz (1997) Three-Factor Model

Schwartz (1997) also presents a three-factor model, basically an extension of the Gibson–Schwartz model with an additional Ornstein–Uhlenbeck process for the instantaneous (domestic) short rate, i.e. $dr_t^d = a(m - r_t^d)dt + \sigma^{(3)}dW_t^{(3)}$, meaning we have a system of SDEs:

$$\frac{dS_t}{S_t} = (r_t^d - \delta_t)dt + \sigma^{(1)}dW_t^{(1;d)} \qquad (2.207a)$$

$$d\delta_t = \kappa(\hat{\alpha} - \delta_t)dt + \sigma^{(2)}dW_t^{(2;d)} \qquad (2.207b)$$

$$dr_t^d = a(m - r_t^d)dt + \sigma^{(3)}dW_t^{(3;d)} \qquad (2.207c)$$

where $\langle dW_t^{(i;d)}, dW_t^{(j;d)} \rangle = \rho_{ij}dt$. Equation (2.207c) is nothing other than the Vasicek interest rate model. Typically a rates model will be calibrated separately to caplet and swaption volatilities. These parameters will be used in calibrating the three-factor model to the commodities market. This model and the next are discussed in the original papers – additionally, a good technical overview of both can be found in Hosseini (2007).

2.10.3.3   The Cortazar–Schwartz (2003) Three-Factor Model

The three-factor model of Cortazar and Schwartz (2003) is a very simple extension, in principle, to the Gibson–Schwartz model. We have the same dynamics (2.206) and (2.205) for spot and convenience yield respectively, but we allow v_t, the long-term price return, to be stochastic, and model it by (2.208c) below – the three SDEs being

$$\frac{dS_t}{S_t} = (v_t - y_t)dt + \sigma^{(1)}dW_t^{(1)} \tag{2.208a}$$

$$dy_t = -\kappa y_t dt + \sigma^{(2)}dW_t^{(2)} \tag{2.208b}$$

$$dv_t = a(\bar{v} - v_t)dt + \sigma^{(3)}dW_t^{(3)} \tag{2.208c}$$

where $\langle dW_t^{(i)}, dW_t^{(j)} \rangle = \rho_{ij}dt$. Note that, as before, the market price of long-term price return is adjusted to correct for the market price of risk. Futures prices can be computed under this model, we refer the reader to equation (32) in the original paper.

We now progress to a discussion of how the theory presented in this chapter can be applied to the various traded commodities markets. Note that while we have been careful to discriminate between forward and futures contracts in this chapter, we shall be working under the assumption of (2.1) henceforth, in line with typical market terminology where futures curves and forward curves are often regarded as synonymous.

3

Precious Metals

We start with precious metals, not because these are the area in commodity derivatives with the greatest trade volume (in fact oil takes that distinction), but because they are the simplest to introduce to readers who may have previously encountered either equity or foreign exchange (FX) derivatives. As such, these metals provide a natural introduction to commodities. In fact, until the collapse of the Bretton Woods agreement on 15 August 1971, all currencies were pegged to the US dollar, which in turn was convertible into gold at a fixed price of (approximately) $35 per (troy) ounce. Gold was basically a currency, as all currencies were linked to gold on the gold standard, a parity relationship which commenced with the British pound in 1717, thanks to a proclamation made by Isaac Newton in his role as Master of the Royal Mint.

While this is no longer true, gold, silver and the other precious metals (platinum, palladium and rhodium) still share many of the features of currencies. They are a durable store of value, and they can be used as commodity money.[1] Base metals such as copper might be used in coinage, but copper is an industrial metal first and foremost – see Chapter 4. Conversely, in addition to their role as investment vehicles, the precious metals all have their own industrial applications, as discussed in Section 3.3. However, the overall price levels of the precious metals is significantly higher than the base metals, as seen in Table 3.1 (prices as of 10 February 2012).

For starters, the quotation style appears exactly the same. In FX one sees currency indices expressed in ccy1ccy2 terms, e.g. EURUSD, which means the price of 1 Euro (EUR) in units of US dollars (USD). The precious metals have their own ISO codes, also tabulated in Table 3.1, where all the precious metals have spot prices quoted in units of currency per troy ounce, an imperial measure equal to 31.1034768 grams. For example, the commodity index XAUUSD refers to the US dollar price of one ounce of gold and XAGEUR refers to the price of one ounce of silver

---

[1] A commodity that is used as a medium of exchange, accounting unit and store of value, where the value is due to the commodity out of which it is made.

Table 3.1   The precious metals (with base metals and iron for comparison).

Metal	ISO	N_A	Price ($/oz)	Price ($/kg)	Mine production (pa)
Gold	XAU	79	$1,722.60	$56,990.41	2,810 T
Silver	XAG	47	$33.64	$1,081.55	22,889 T
Platinum	XPT	78	$1,657.00	$53,273.79	193 T
Palladium	XPD	46	$702.50	$22,585.90	202 T
Rhodium		45	$1,550.00	$49,833.66	18 T
Copper		29		$8.51	15 mio T
Aluminium		13		$2.21	34 mio T
Zinc		30		$2.09	11 mio T
Nickel		28		$20.98	1.3 mio T
Lead		82		$2.13	3.3 mio T
Tin		50		$25.33	140,000 T
Iron		26		$0.47	1,000 mio T

in Euros. The ISO code on the left identifies which of the precious metals we are dealing with (by analogy with FX, this is sometimes called the foreign currency) and the ISO code on the right is the domestic currency.

To be clear, where a metal has a price quote expressed as an ISO pair in the fashion of an FX rate, the left hand ISO code will invariably be the metal, or the metal currency, and the right hand ISO will be the money, the money currency or the numeraire currency.

Precious metals also obey T+2 spot settlement, which means that a precious metals transaction entered into today at a spot trade price of S_0 will involve the exchange of N_d units of domestic currency for N_f ounces of metal, where the two notionals are related by the spot rate S_0, i.e. $N_d = S_0 \cdot N_f$. This exchange occurs on the *spot date*, which is two good business days after today. The specific convention depends on where the trading occurs, generally London but with some trading in other centres such as Zurich, New York and Tokyo. Basically, the rule is to roll forward two good business days from today (excluding holidays in London and New York, and the other trading centres if appropriate) to obtain the spot date.

The market parameters for the precious metals can also be identified with those for the currency markets. We shall need yield curves, or their equivalents, and we shall need a volatility surface. Suppose we take a term structure model, of the form

$$dS_t = \mu_t^d S_t dt + \sigma_t S_t dW_t^d, \tag{3.1}$$

where both μ_t^d and σ_t are deterministic processes. By risk-neutrality, we require

$$\mu_t^d = r_t^d - r_t^f. \tag{3.2}$$

Remembering that domestic can be identified with the numeraire currency, r_t^d can be obtained from the relevant yield curve. But what of r_t^f? Does gold, for example, have an interest rate? In fact it does.

3.1   GOLD FORWARD AND GOLD LEASE RATES

As discussed in Cross (2000), Lonergan (2006) and Whaley (2006), major holders of precious metals, such as central banks, often try to extract extra value from their holdings by leasing them out. This serves an added benefit as it provides bullion banks with a natural way to hedge their risk exposure from forward purchases of gold from mining companies – having bought gold for forward delivery from a producer, they can lease an equivalent amount of gold from a central bank and sell it in the market, parking the proceeds in a money market account until taking delivery of the bullion from the miner at the forward date. The leasing used to be a relatively ad hoc exercise, as there was no market consensus for what these returns should be, until July 1989 when about a dozen market makers started contributing to the Reuters GOFO page, which quotes gold forward offered rates for periods from 1 month to 1 year (published daily at 11:00 London time). What this represents is the rate that is payable if one lends out gold and borrows US dollars for the period under consideration. The GOFO rate $G_{0,T}$ relates forward prices and spot prices of gold, but expressed as a multiple rather than the more usual additive forward points seen in FX

$$F_{t,T} = S_t \left(1 + G_{t,T} \right). \tag{3.3}$$

We can thereby determine the gold lease rate (also sometimes called the gold LIBOR rate, hence our notation) from

$$L_{0,T}^f = L_{0,T}^d - G_{0,T}. \tag{3.4}$$

In fact, due to bid/offer spreads, LBMA and LPPM (2008) suggests the following rule applying a 16-bp adjustment to calculate mid rates for the gold lease rate

$$L_{0,T}^f = L_{0,T}^d - (G_{0,T} + 0.0016) \tag{3.5}$$

Table 3.2 GOFO and SIFO rates for 1 February 2012.

	LIBOR	GOFO	SIFO	LIBOR-GOFO	LIBOR-SIFO
1M	0.264%	0.546%	0.432%	−0.282%	−0.168%
2M	0.393%	0.572%	0.410%	−0.180%	−0.018%
3M	0.537%	0.593%	0.370%	−0.056%	0.167%
6M	0.773%	0.613%	0.330%	0.159%	0.443%
12M	1.091%	0.638%	0.304%	0.453%	0.787%

Such rates are also published on Reuters, on page LGLR. A silver lease rate also exists, the Silver Forward Offered Rate (SIFO), but we will retain the $G_{0,T}$ notation to avoid confusion with spot S_t. Lease rates[2] for platinum, palladium and rhodium also exist, but are far less liquid.

Case Study 3.1

As of 1 February 2012, the price of gold was $S_0 = 1742.0$ ($/oz). In this example, suppose that Bank C (a central bank) agreed to lease one hundred ounces of gold to Bank B (a bullion bank). The GOFO rate grosses up the spot to a 1Y forward rate of $F_{t,T} = 1753.11$ ($/oz). On the spot date (two business days after today) Bank C delivers 100 ounces of gold to Bank B and is paid $174,200. One year later the swap is reversed and Bank B returns the 100 ounces of gold to Bank C in return for $175,311. In the meantime, however, Bank C has been able to invest the $174,200 at the 1Y LIBOR rate of 1.091%, which means that when the swap is reversed the cash in hand has gone from $174,200 to $176,100. Even after accounting for the $175,311 required to effectively repurchase the gold, Bank C has made $788.60 on this trade. On a US dollar principal of $174,200, that equates to a 0.453% return, which is precisely the gold lease rate defined in (3.4).

Note that the central Bank (Bank C) *pays* the GOFO rate but expects to earn the higher LIBOR rate, which more than compensates for paying GOFO.

We can therefore use the GOFO (or SIFO) rates, such as are shown in Table 3.2, in the place of $\bar{\mu}_T^d$ in the Black–Scholes term structure machinery of Chapter 2, i.e.

$$\bar{\mu}_T^d = \frac{1}{T} \int_0^T \mu_s^d \, ds \qquad (3.6)$$

---

[2] See www.kitco.com/charts and look for "Current Lease Rates".

with

$$\bar{\mu}_T^d = G_{0,T}.$$ (3.7)

If, therefore, we had a term structure of volatility σ_t and an effective volatility $\bar{\sigma}_T$ over the period of interest, which must obey

$$\bar{\sigma}_T = \sqrt{\frac{1}{T} \int_0^T \sigma_s^2 ds}$$ (3.8)

we can price options on gold by simply using the approaches of Chapter 2. For vanilla options, for example, we have

$$V_0 = \omega P^d(0, T) \left[F_{0,T} N(\omega d_1) - K N(\omega d_2) \right]$$ (3.9a)

with

$$d_{1,2} = \frac{\ln \left(F_{0,T}/K \right) \pm \frac{1}{2} \bar{\sigma}_T^2 T}{\bar{\sigma}_T \sqrt{T}}$$ (3.9b)

and $F_{0,T}$ given by (3.3).

3.2 VOLATILITY SURFACES FOR PRECIOUS METALS

Equation (3.9) is all well and good if we want to price precious metals options with a term structure of volatility, but we know that the Black–Scholes model is inadequate for pricing options with various strikes, due to the presence of the volatility smile. Given a particular time to expiry, what we shall need is a volatility smile $\sigma_X(K)$ which gives the volatility for each strike. A collection of these volatility smiles for the different liquid tenors comprises the volatility surface.

In this section, we show how the market volatility surface is specified, and what it means from a practitioner's point of view. The standard references to FX market conventions for volatility surfaces are Malz (1997), Beneder and Elkenbracht-Huizing (2003), Reiswich and Wystup (2009) and Clark (2011). All of these are directly applicable to precious metals, as the market for precious metals options is specified by the implied volatilities for European style options at a variety of different tenors, typically from one week out to two or maybe five years.

Like FX, precious and base metals options markets have volatilities parameterised by deltas, not absolute strikes, where the at-the-money strike is taken to be the delta-neutral straddle. One simplifying factor is that the deltas are always pips deltas, never premium adjusted deltas, as the option premium is always paid in the money currency, and never in units of metal.

Let us therefore introduce these deltas.

3.2.1 Pips Spot Delta

The pips spot delta is just the change in PV of the option, in numeraire currency terms, with respect to changes in spot S_t, expressed in money/metal terms – i.e. in money pips.

$$\Delta_{S;\,\text{pips}} = \lim_{\Delta S_0 \to 0} \frac{\Delta V_{d;\,\text{pips}}}{\Delta S_0} = \frac{\partial V_{d;\,\text{pips}}}{\partial S_0}$$

where $\Delta V_{d;\,\text{pips}} \equiv V_{d;\,\text{pips}}(S_0 + \Delta S_0) - V_{d;\,\text{pips}}(S_0)$. Consequently,

$$
\begin{aligned}
\Delta_{S;\,\text{pips}} &\equiv \frac{\partial V_{d;\,\text{pips}}}{\partial S_0} \\
&= \omega e^{-r^f T} N(\omega d_1) + \omega S_0 e^{-r^f T} \frac{\partial N(\omega d_1)}{\partial S_0} - \omega K e^{-r^d T} \frac{\partial N(\omega d_2)}{\partial S_0} \\
&= \omega e^{-r^f T} N(\omega d_1) + \frac{\omega^2}{\sigma S_0 \sqrt{T}} \left(S_0 e^{-r^f T} n(\omega d_1) - K e^{-r^d T} n(\omega d_2) \right) \\
&= \omega e^{-r^f T} N(\omega d_1).
\end{aligned}
\tag{3.10}
$$

Up to a factor of $e^{-r^f T}$, this is just the standard Black–Scholes delta.

3.2.2 Pips Forward Delta

The pips forward delta is the ratio of the change in future value (FV) – note this is the future and not present value! – of the option to the change in the relevant forward – both quoted in money/metal quote terms.

$$
\begin{aligned}
\Delta_{F;\,\text{pips}} &= \frac{\partial \mathbf{E}^d[V_T]}{\partial F_{0,T}} = e^{r^d T} \lim_{\Delta F_{0,T} \to 0} \frac{\Delta V_{d;\,\text{pips}}}{\Delta F_{0,T}} \\
&= \frac{e^{r^d T}}{\frac{\partial F_{0,T}}{\partial S}} \frac{\partial V_{d;\,\text{pips}}}{\partial S_0} = e^{r^f T} \Delta_{S;\,\text{pips}} \\
&= \omega N(\omega d_1).
\end{aligned}
\tag{3.11}
$$

Readers familiar with FX will note that there is no mention of percentage deltas or premium adjustment. The reason is simple – in the commodities markets, option premiums are always paid in the money currency, and there is therefore never any need to premium adjust. As for whether to use a spot delta or forward delta, similar rules apply as in FX except with a different cutoff – spot deltas are generally used out to and including 1M (one month), and forward deltas thereafter for longer dated option maturities. Note that this is not the same as FX, where the cutoff is at two *years*. In practice, the impact of using spot deltas for 1M and within is so small that forward deltas can be used throughout with little loss of precision.

3.2.3 Notation

Once the expiry time T is known, we know which delta is meant. Let Δ_Q be defined by choosing whichever of $\Delta_{S;\text{pips}}$ and $\Delta_{F;\text{pips}}$ is to be used.

For simplicity, let $V(\omega, K, \sigma)$ denote the Black–Scholes money/metal price for a call/put option ($\omega = \pm 1$ respectively) with strike K (the time to expiry T is assumed to be implicit), i.e. $V(\omega, K, \sigma) = V_{d;\text{pips}}$, and let $\Delta_Q(\omega, K, \sigma)$ denote the Δ_Q delta for a call/put ($\omega = \pm 1$ respectively), both using volatility σ.

We are now able to construct and interpret volatility surfaces for the precious metals. Let's start with a typical volatility surface for XAU-USD.

3.2.4 Market Volatility Surfaces

We are now in a position to be able to understand and construct the volatility surface for precious metals. Consider Figure 3.1, which shows a typical market volatility surface for XAUUSD.

Note the presence of the at-the-money volatilities (marked as ATM), and the risk-reversal (RR) and butterfly (BF) volatilities describing the skew and smile, for various tenors from one day to seven years in this screenshot. Our objective will be to describe these.

3.2.5 At-the-Money

As described elsewhere in the literature, there are two possibilities that are used in practice. The ATM strike can be either set to be the forward,

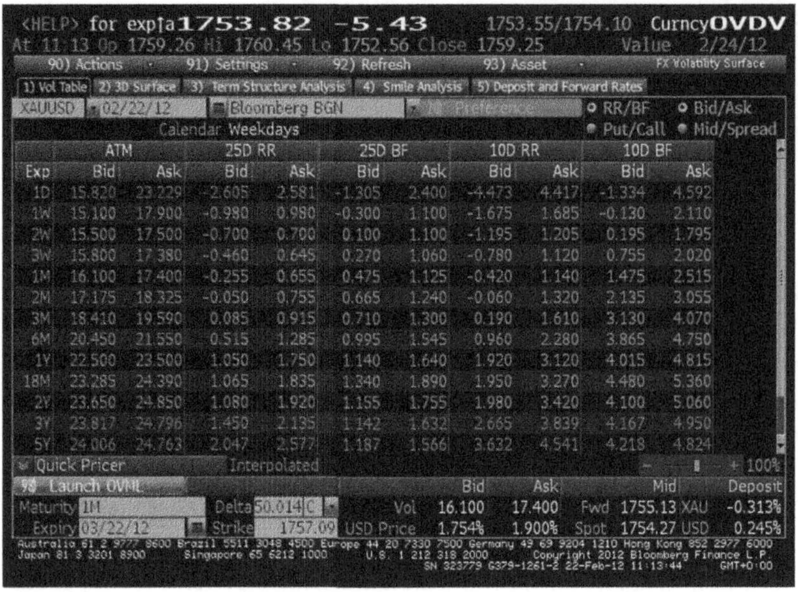

	ATM		25D RR		25D BF		10D RR		10D BF	
Exp	Bid	Ask	Bid	Ask	Bid	Ask	Bid	Ask	Bid	Ask
1D	15.820	23.229	-2.605	2.581	-1.305	2.400	-4.473	4.417	-1.334	4.592
1W	15.100	17.900	-0.980	0.980	-0.300	1.100	-1.675	1.685	-0.130	2.110
2W	15.500	17.500	-0.700	0.700	0.100	1.100	-1.195	1.205	0.195	1.795
3W	15.800	17.380	-0.460	0.645	0.270	1.060	-0.780	1.120	0.755	2.020
1M	16.100	17.400	-0.255	0.655	0.475	1.125	-0.420	1.140	1.475	2.515
2M	17.175	18.325	-0.050	0.755	0.665	1.240	-0.060	1.320	2.135	3.055
3M	18.410	19.590	0.085	0.915	0.710	1.300	0.190	1.610	3.130	4.070
6M	20.450	21.550	0.515	1.285	0.995	1.545	0.960	2.280	3.865	4.750
1Y	22.500	23.500	1.050	1.750	1.140	1.640	1.920	3.120	4.015	4.815
18M	23.285	24.390	1.065	1.835	1.340	1.890	1.950	3.270	4.480	5.360
2Y	23.650	24.850	1.080	1.920	1.155	1.755	1.980	3.420	4.100	5.060
3Y	23.817	24.796	1.450	2.135	1.142	1.632	2.665	3.839	4.167	4.950
5Y	24.006	24.763	2.047	2.577	1.187	1.566	3.632	4.541	4.218	4.824

Figure 3.1 Volatility surface for XAUUSD – © 2013 Bloomberg Finance L.P. All rights reserved. Used with permission.

or it can be set to be the delta-neutral straddle. For the ATMF convention, we have

$$K_{ATM} = K_{ATMF} \equiv F_{0,T}. \tag{3.12}$$

The other possibility is the delta-neutral straddle convention, where

$$\Delta_Q(+1, K_{DNS}, \sigma_{ATM}) + \Delta_Q(-1, K_{DNS}, \sigma_{ATM}) = 0. \tag{3.13}$$

Note that, as spot and forward deltas without premium adjustment differ only by the metal discount factor (obtained from the metals lease rate), it is irrelevant whether a spot or forward delta is used; either way, we have

$$K_{DNS} = F_{0,T} \exp\left(\frac{1}{2}\sigma^2 T\right) \tag{3.14}$$

Note that while the convention shown here is to use a spot delta, this is only applicable for 1M and shorter.

3.2.5.1   Example – XAUUSD 1Y

We see from Case Study 3.1 that the 1Y forward is 1753.11. From Figure 3.1, we see that the convention is "ATM DNS" – meaning delta-neutral straddle. We have an 1Y ATM implied volatility at mid (after taking the arithmetic average of the bid and the offer) of 28.585%. We therefore require for the 1Y volatility smile that $\sigma_X(K_{DNS}) = 0.28585$ with $K_{DNS} = F_T \exp(\frac{1}{2}\sigma^2 T) = 1753.11 * \exp(\frac{1}{2}[0.28585]^2 \cdot 1) = 1826.22$, i.e. $\sigma_X(1826.22) = 0.28585$.

3.2.6   Strangles and Risk Reversals

We now have a way to choose an at-the-money strike K_{ATM} and to mark an implied volatility there. What remains is to describe the volatility smile for strikes located either side of K_{ATM}. One way to achieve this is to introduce the concept of the market strangle instrument, which is a simple portfolio of an out-of-the-money put and an out-of-the-money call with strikes placed a similar distance away from the at-the-money strike in moneyness terms, and then to mark a single implied volatility for that instrument. Let's consider the 25-delta market strangle[3] first; other deltas follow similarly.

What is crucial is that the strikes for the calls and puts are both calculated using the Black–Scholes model with a single constant volatility of $\sigma_{ATM} + \sigma_{25-d-MS}$. The strikes obtained are known as the market strangle strikes $K_{25-d-P-MS}$ and $K_{25-d-C-MS}$.

We attempt to solve

$$\Delta_Q(-1, K_{25-d-P-MS}, \sigma_{ATM} + \sigma_{25-d-MS}) = -0.25$$
$$\Delta_Q(+1, K_{25-d-C-MS}, \sigma_{ATM} + \sigma_{25-d-MS}) = +0.25. \qquad (3.15)$$

Note that if the volatility smile is not symmetric, neither the call with strike $K_{25-d-C-MS}$ nor the put with strike $K_{25-d-P-MS}$ should be individually priced with volatility $\sigma_{ATM} + \sigma_{25-d-MS}$. However, the *aggregate* price obtained for the market strangle (long a call with strike $K_{25-d-C-MS}$ and long a put with strike $K_{25-d-P-MS}$) under the actual market volatility smile must be identical to the same aggregate price for the same market strangle instrument, under the assumption of a constant Black–Scholes volatility of $\sigma_{ATM} + \sigma_{25-d-MS}$.

---

[3] Sometimes called the single-vol strangle.

Mathematically, the required condition is

$$V_{25-d-MS} = V(-1, K_{25-d-P-MS}, \sigma_{ATM} + \sigma_{25-d-MS})$$
$$+ V(+1, K_{25-d-C-MS}, \sigma_{ATM} + \sigma_{25-d-MS}). \quad (3.16)$$

We now have two degrees of freedom to describe a volatility surface: σ_{ATM} fixes the level and $\sigma_{25-d-MS}$ measures the convexity. What about skew? In this case, we attempt to obtain a difference in volatility between the 25-delta call and the 25-delta put. Unlike the market strangle, we now need to use different volatilities for the two components and therefore need to suppose a volatility smile $\sigma_X(K)$ exists. Our task will be to choose a parameterisation for $\sigma_X(K)$ and then to choose parameters which fit the market volatility surface.

Firstly we have

$$\sigma_X(K_{ATM}) = \sigma_{ATM} \quad (3.17)$$
$$V_{25-d-MS} = V(-1, K_{25-d-P-MS}, \sigma_X(K_{25-d-P-MS}))$$
$$+ V(+1, K_{25-d-C-MS}, \sigma_X(K_{25-d-C-MS})) \quad (3.18)$$

and now, even though we have the market strangle strikes $K_{25-d-P-MS}$ and $K_{25-d-C-MS}$, we need to obtain the smile strangle strikes. This requires solution of

$$\Delta_Q(-1, K_{25-d-P}, \sigma_X(K_{25-d-P})) = -0.25 \quad (3.19a)$$

$$\Delta_Q(+1, K_{25-d-C}, \sigma_X(K_{25-d-C})) = +0.25. \quad (3.19b)$$

Now, with these strikes, we can obtain smile vols

$$\sigma_{25-d-P} = \sigma_X(K_{25-d-P}) \quad (3.20a)$$

$$\sigma_{25-d-C} = \sigma_X(K_{25-d-C}) \quad (3.20b)$$

and obtain the 25-delta risk reversal calculated from the difference, subject to a sign convention which indicates whether the risk reversal is defined as $\sigma_{25-d-C} - \sigma_{25-d-P}$ or $\sigma_{25-d-P} - \sigma_{25-d-C}$. We use $\phi_{RR} \in \{-1, +1\}$ to denote which is meant, writing

$$\sigma_{25-d-RR} = \phi_{RR} \cdot [\sigma_{25-d-C} - \sigma_{25-d-P}]. \quad (3.21)$$

The 10-delta market strangle and risk reversal are included similarly, with $\sigma_{10-d-MS}$ and $\sigma_{10-d-RR}$.

Of course, now that we have the entire smile $\sigma_X(K)$ (at least parametrically) and the smile strangle strikes K_{25-d-P} and K_{25-d-C}, we can obtain the smile strangle[4]

$$\sigma_{25-d-SS} = \frac{1}{2} \left[\sigma_{25-d-C} + \sigma_{25-d-P}\right] - \sigma_{ATM}. \quad (3.22)$$

If $\sigma_{25-d-RR} = 0$ then by (3.21) we have $\sigma_{25-d-C} = \sigma_{25-d-P}$ and therefore $\sigma_{25-d-SS} = \sigma_{25-d-C} - \sigma_{ATM} = \sigma_{25-d-P} - \sigma_{ATM}$. Consequently $\sigma_{25-d-MS} = \sigma_{25-d-SS}$ in the case where $\sigma_{25-d-RR} = 0$; but risk reversals almost never identically vanish. Consequently it is important to be careful with the distinction between market strangles and smile strangles.

The screenshot in Figure 3.1 shows smile strangles, which are easier to work with, but this may not always be the case, depending on the system one is working with.

The algorithm given in Section 3.7 of Clark (2011) can be used to determine a consistent smile interpolation $\sigma_X(K)$ which matches the ATM, strangles and risk reversals, i.e. satisfying

$$\sigma_X(K_{ATM}) = \sigma_{ATM} \quad (3.23)$$

$$V_{25-d-MS} = V(-1, K_{25-d-P-MS}, \sigma_X(K_{25-d-P-MS})) \quad (3.24)$$
$$+ V(+1, K_{25-d-C-MS}, \sigma_X(K_{25-d-C-MS}))$$

$$\sigma_{25-d-RR} = \phi_{RR} \cdot \left[\sigma_X(K_{25-d-C}) - \sigma_X(K_{25-d-P})\right] \quad (3.25)$$

where the strikes are determined as detailed above. When these three equations are satisfied, we have

$$\sigma_{25-d-SS} = \frac{1}{2} \left[\sigma_X(K_{25-d-C}) + \sigma_X(K_{25-d-P})\right] - \sigma_X(K_{ATM}). \quad (3.26)$$

3.2.6.1 Smile Strangle from Market Strangle – Algorithm

1. Decide on a parametric form $\sigma_X(K)$ for volatility.
2. Determine K_{ATM}, by using (3.12).
3. Use (3.15), together with σ_{ATM} and $\sigma_{25-d-MS}$ to determine $K_{25-d-P-MS}$ and $K_{25-d-C-MS}$.
4. Use (3.16) to determine $V_{\text{target}} = V_{25-d-MS}$.
5. Choose an initial guess for $\sigma_{25-d-SS}$, such as $\sigma_{25-d-SS} = \sigma_{25-d-MS}$.
6. Using σ_{ATM}, $\sigma_{25-d-SS}$ and $\sigma_{25-d-RR}$, find parameters for $\sigma_X(K)$ using a least squares optimiser which satisfies (3.23), (3.25) and (3.26), with

---

[4] This one is sometimes called the two-vol strangle, as it requires two vols on the smile.

smile strikes K_{25-d-C} and K_{25-d-P} given by $\sigma_X(K)$, i.e. satisfying (3.19).

7. Price up the market strangle with strikes $K_{25-d-P-MS}$ and $K_{25-d-C-MS}$ using the $\sigma_X(K)$ parameters obtained in Step 6. i.e. $V_{trial} = V_{25-d-MS}$ using (3.24).

8. If $V_{trial} \approx V_{target}$ then $\sigma_X(K)$ satisfies the smile conditions and the algorithm is complete. Otherwise, revise the guess for $\sigma_{25-d-SS}$ (downwards if $V_{trial} > V_{target}$ and upwards if $V_{trial} < V_{target}$) and repeat Steps 5 through to 7.

The optimisations detailed in Steps 5 to 8 are easily performed using a numerical optimiser, such as Levenberg–Marquardt (Press *et al.*, 2002). Suitable interpolation schemes for $\sigma_X(K)$ are also discussed further in Clark (2011).

3.2.6.2   Summary of Smile Conditions

In the case of a 3-point smile, parameterised by ATMs and 25-delta strangles and risk reversals, we have three strikes if the strangles are understood as smiles strangles, namely K_{25-d-P}, K_{ATM}, K_{25-d-C} and $K_{25-d-C-MS}$.

With these, we have

$$\sigma_{ATM} = \sigma_X(K_{ATM}) \tag{3.27a}$$

$$\sigma_{25-d-RR} = \phi_{RR} \cdot \left[\sigma_X(K_{25-d-C}) - \sigma_X(K_{25-d-P})\right] \tag{3.27b}$$

$$\sigma_{25-d-SS} = \frac{1}{2}\left[\sigma_X(K_{25-d-C}) + \sigma_X(K_{25-d-P})\right] - \sigma_X(K_{ATM}). \tag{3.27c}$$

If market strangles are specified, we have an extra two strikes $K_{25-d-P-MS}$ and $K_{25-d-C-MS}$, and the market strangle condition

$$V_{25-d-MS}(\sigma_{ATM} + \sigma_{25-d-MS}, \sigma_{ATM} + \sigma_{25-d-MS})$$
$$= V_{25-d-MS}(\sigma_X(K_{25-d-P-MS}), \sigma_X(K_{25-d-C-MS})) \tag{3.27d}$$

where

$$V_{25-d-MS}(\sigma_1, \sigma_2) = V(-1, K_{25-d-P-MS}, \sigma_1) + V(+1, K_{25-d-C-MS}, \sigma_2).$$

If 10-delta points are specified on the smile also, we merely adapt (3.27b) and either (3.27c) or (3.27d), with 10-delta strikes, imposing further constraints on our choice of $\sigma_X(K)$.

3.2.7   Temporal Interpolation

Having obtained a family of volatility smiles for the different tenors $\{\sigma_X(K)\}_{t_i}$, all that remains is to interpolate in time where necessary, e.g. if we are trying to price a 5M option, and we have a volatility surface specified at 3M and 6M. Let us suppose that implied volatilities σ_1 and σ_2 are known at times t_1 and t_2, and we wish to obtain the implied volatility at time t. A standard technique used is to assume that forward volatility is constant at equivalent points on the smile between t_1 and t_2, which gives the rule

$$[\sigma_{\text{imp}}(t)]^2 t = \sigma_1^2 t_1 + \left(\sigma_2^2 t_2 - \sigma_1^2 t_1\right) \frac{t - t_1}{t_2 - t_1}$$

$$= \frac{1}{t_2 - t_1} \left[\sigma_2^2 t_2 (t - t_1) + \sigma_1^2 t_1 (t_2 - t)\right]. \qquad (3.28)$$

This is perfectly fine for interpolating the ATM backbone, but what about the smile? One possibility is to choose a parametric form $\sigma_X(K)$ for the smile and then calibrate the parameters at times t_1 and t_2 and then to interpolate those parameters (perhaps linearly) for t between t_1 and t_2.

Another common technique is to use the method of the previous section to infer the smile in terms of the 10-delta put, 25-delta put, ATM straddle, 25-delta call and 10-delta call strikes at each tenor, obtaining an $n \times 5$ matrix, and then use (3.28) to obtain the smile at t by applying flat forward vol interpolation for each of the five rows corresponding to 10- and 25-delta calls and puts, and the ATM straddle.

3.3   SURVEY OF THE PRECIOUS METALS

An aside: we can see clearly in Table 3.1 that the precious metals are at *least* an order of magnitude more expensive than the base metals or iron. One reason for this is simple – they are rarer. Not only are they rarer, but unlike the base metals or iron, they do not corrode easily – a very attractive feature. A gold nugget would be an attractive find indeed even if for purely aesthetic value.

But why are these elements rarer? Note that all the atomic numbers for the precious metals are in excess of 26, the atomic number for iron. In fact, iron is the heaviest element that can be created through nuclear fusion in stars, and only the most massive stars are capable of fusing lighter elements into iron toward the end of their lifetimes. Such massive stars have a certain fate ahead of them – death by supernova, which smashes subatomic particles together with such force that elements both lighter and heavier than iron are produced. Including gold, platinum, etc. So, the precious metals are all stardust. Literally.

3.3.1 Gold

Gold hardly needs any introduction, being the valuable yellow metal known to all. It is chemically unreactive except when attacked with the most powerful acids, and thereby preserves its lustre for millenia, as evidenced by antiquities made of gold such as the Varna "Thracian horseman" antiquities and the Jiskairumoko necklace (dating to circa 5000 BC and 2000 BC respectively). Due to its durability, gold has historically been used for coinage, e.g. gold sovereigns in Victorian times.

While it has industrial applications, most notably in electronics, gold is first and foremost a store of value – either in the form of investment gold or in the form of jewellery. The division between investment and jewellery isn't as clear as it might seem at first, though. By *far* the greatest worldwide demand for gold, in the form of jewellery, comes from China and India – the latter in particular being influenced by customs involving dowries and ornate bridal jewellery (which can be seen as an investment). More specifically, gold is often seen as a natural hedge against inflation.

Lonergan (2006) compares the reserves that official bodies (such as central banks and multinational organisations such as the IMF) hold of some 32,000 tonnes of gold with the annual production of some 2,500 tonnes. We can estimate the amount of gold that has been extracted so far from underground sources[5] at about 155,000 tonnes, and therefore central banks in aggregate hold some 20% of all above ground gold. It is impossible to know just how much gold still exists in geological deposits, but a clue can be found in the reserves listed in the accounts of mining companies, which suggests some 50,000 tonnes (about half of which is estimated to be located in South Africa).

---

[5] Of course, we do not count bullion gold stored in underground vaults as being underground. An authority no less than Warren Buffett once said "Gold gets dug out of the ground in Africa, or someplace. Then we melt it down, dig another hole, bury it again and pay people to stand around guarding it".

3.3.1.1   Production

Gold production is in principle simple, though in practice complex and subject to many uncertainties and risks: find gold reserves, dig them up, and extract the metal (generally through cyanide extraction). Historically, in the gold rushes of the 19th and 20th centuries, vast reserves of gold were discovered in easily accessible surface placer deposits in California, Australia, the Klondike and in the vicinity of Johannesburg, the Witswatersrand (to where we can trace nearly half of the gold that has *ever* been extracted). Nowadays, of course, we have to dig deeper.

The mines are either open cut (such as the famous Super Pit near Kalgoorlie, Australia, effectively a 3.5 km by 1.5 km quarry) or underground (such as the world's largest gold mine, the Grasberg Mine in Papua Province, Indonesia). To give an idea of the production, these two produce about 28 and 58 tonnes of gold per year respectively. The economics of gold production make it quite viable, as Schofield (2007) states, to run open cut and underground mines with yields as low as 1 and 10 grams of gold per tonne respectively. The figures for the two mines listed above are around 1.50 g/T in 2008 for the Super Pit, and 30 g/T for the Grasberg Mine. The ore is partially refined on site into doré bars, which are up to 90% gold and which are transported elsewhere to be refined to bullion or jewellery grade purity. A fuller discussion of the geological aspects of gold mining can be found in Sections 4.4.4 and 5.2.1 of Arndt and Ganino (2012); for the principles involved in extraction we refer the reader to Yannopoulos (1991).

Some 2,800 tonnes of gold are obtained through production each year, a quantity which has somewhat plateaued in the early 21st century, but which has risen from about 1,000 tonnes per annum in 1980. Other sources of supply are official sales (meaning central banks and the IMF) amounting to 440 tonnes in 2011, and scrap recovery of 1,612 tonnes a year in 2011. The final factor influencing supply is producer hedging, where a miner leases gold from a central bank and sells it short in the market, confident that they can extract gold over the remaining period to meet their repayment obligations. Basically, this has the effect of bringing gold production forward several months to a year, though the amount in tonnes can be small. In aggregate, the total yearly supply of gold coming onto the market is about 4,800 tonnes per annum, as shown in Table 3.3.

Table 3.3   Supply of gold (2011).

	Supply	By country	By source
Primary (mining)			
China	368 T	13.1%	
Australia	281 T	10.0%	
USA	247 T	8.8%	
Russia	208 T	7.4%	
South Africa	197 T	7.0%	
Peru	157 T	5.6%	
Indonesia	124 T	4.4%	
Canada	115 T	4.1%	
Ghana	104 T	3.7%	
Uzbekistan	93 T	3.3%	
Other countries	916 T	32.6%	
Total mining	2,810 T	100%	57.7%
Hedging	12 T		0.2%
Official sector sales	440 T		9.0%
Secondary (recycling)	1,612 T		33.1%
Total	4,874 T		100%

3.3.1.2   Consumption

In 2010, according to the World Gold Council, the industrial applications of gold make up about 12% of the demand for the metal; investment (~40%) and jewellery (~48%) comprising the larger shares, as shown in Table 3.4.

In spite of increasing relative demand for gold as an investment vehicle, jewellery continues to provide the largest source of demand for gold, and together China and India make up over half of the global jewellery market for gold, as shown in Table 3.5. There may be seasonal components also, for example, the Diwali festival and Chinese New Year are often cited as key gold buying periods in Indian and Chinese markets

Table 3.4   Demand for gold (2011).

	Absolute demand	Relative demand
Investment	1,641 T	40%
Industrial	464 T	12%
Jewellery	1,963 T	48%
Total	4,068 T	100%

Table 3.5   Gold jewellery consumption in 2011 (leading countries).

	Absolute demand	Relative demand
India	745 T	38%
China	400 T	20%
USA	115 T	6%
Russia	75 T	4%

respectively. Gold has always been a popular metal for jewellery on account of its rarity, durability, colour and malleability.

Investment has experienced the greatest increase in demand since 2000. Of the 1,641 tonnes tabulated in Table 3.4 (for which we give a breakdown in Table 3.6 for the leading investment consumers), 1,487 tonnes were used in the production of gold bars and coins, whereas 154 tonnes were purchased by exchange traded funds (ETFs), a range of products that have become possible since they offer smaller investors the opportunity to gain exposure to gold prices without having to take physical delivery of the metal.

Technology makes up a final component of the demand for gold. Audiophiles will be familiar with the use of gold plated speaker cables and the like. Gold, silver and copper all have a high degree of electrical conductivity which makes them suitable for electronic applications but the latter two have a tendency to tarnish and corrode, whereas gold has an exceptional resistance to tarnishing and corrosion, which makes its use advantageous. The electronics sector alone accounts for some 300 tonnes of annual demand for gold, about 150 tonnes being from Japan and about 100 tonnes being from the USA. Another significant industry that uses gold is the dental industry (gold fillings and crowns), consuming about 60 tonnes a year. Other industrial applications make up the remaining 104 tonnes of demand.

Table 3.6   Gold investment consumption in 2011 (leading countries).

	Absolute demand	Relative demand
India	366 T	22%
China	259 T	16%
Germany	159 T	10%
Switzerland	116 T	7%
USA	80 T	5%
Turkey	80 T	5%

3.3.1.3 Purity and Grade

We are all familiar with the concept of purity of gold, as measured by carats. But what is 24 carat gold? Basically the equation is

$$K = 24 \frac{m_{Au}}{m_{Total}}$$

where the measure of purity relates the total mass of the gold m_{Au} to the total mass of the sample m_{Total}. So 9 carat gold is only 9/24 gold, i.e. 37.5% gold – the rest being mostly copper, silver and sometimes palladium or nickel (the more copper, the redder the colour of the gold alloy). We can also construct a decimal purity by leaving out the normalising factor of 24, obtaining

$$P = \frac{m_{Au}}{m_{Total}}$$

From this we see that so-called "24-carat" gold is actually always slightly under $P = 1$. There is no exact rule determining how pure a gold sample needs to be to be called "24-carat", except arguably $K > 23.5$. For this reason, and particularly for investment grade gold, the carat measure is too imprecise. Gold coins therefore are generally quoted with the purity in the decimal measure, e.g. Canadian maples with $P = 0.99999$ (since 2007), Australian nuggets with $P = 0.9999$, Chinese pandas with $P = 0.999$, krugerrands with $P = 0.917$, and sovereigns with $P = 0.9166$ (22 carat).

For bullion, the London Bullion Markets Association specifies, in the document "Good Delivery Rules for Gold and Silver Bars", that the purity of a Good Delivery bar must be 0.9995 (often written as 995.0, the scale is reasonably obvious) and that the gold content must be between 350 and 430 troy ounces (400 oz or thereabouts, i.e. 12.5 kg, is usual). Note that for gold, unlike the other precious metals, the purchaser only pays for the weight of the gold content of the bar – for silver, platinum and palladium, the purchaser pays for the weight of the entire bar, including the weight of the impurities.

3.3.1.4 LBMA Fixings

While gold trades continuously (weekends excepted) in the spot markets, the London Bullion Market Association (LBMA) confers to set a price twice a day, the London Gold Fixing, which has been in existence since 1919 – originally only once a day in the morning, with the afternoon

3pm fix introduced in 1968 to coincide with morning in North America. Nowadays, five members[6] of the LBMA confer by telephone at 10:30am and 3:00pm London time and publish a price on the LBMA site. Since much gold trading is over the counter (OTC), this merely has the effect of anchoring spot bullion prices around those levels twice a day. Gold bullion trades that settle via the LBMA are usually "loco London", meaning that settlement occurs two good London business days after the value date. Basically, holding a bullion account with an LBMA member is quite analogous to a dollar account with a New York bank, except with XAU or XAG as the value currency, not USD. As a result, while gold trades over the counter continuously around all timezones, the majority of settlement occurs via the LBMA.

3.3.2 Silver

While the gold standard is familiar, it is not so well known that for many centuries much of Western Europe was on a different standard, the silver standard. A clue can be found in the name "pound sterling" – tracing its origins back to the Anglo-Saxon pound (equivalent to 240 silver pennies) introduced by King Offa of Mercia in the 8th century AD. Sterling silver itself, as used in jewellery and silverware, is 92.5% Ag and 7.5% Cu (and other minor impurities). Silver is generally found in ores containing other metals, though it can be found in elemental form or in an alloy with gold. A graph available at http://goldinfo.net/silver-600.aspx shows the inflation adjusted price of silver and gold/silver ratio from 1344 to 2004, showing the effects of the exhaustion of European silver mines until silver reached an all time high in real terms in 1477, before the discovery of silver in the New World (initially South America). Indeed the gold/silver ratio was quite stable in the range between 10 and 20 until the early 1800s, before decoupling – the ratio is now around 50.

As tabulated in Table 3.7, top primary producers of silver in 2010 were Mexico (4,000 T), Peru (3,611 T), China (3,085 T) and Australia (1,863 T), contributing to a worldwide mining production of 735 million ounces, or 22,867 tonnes. Like gold, scrap contributes an important proportion of the supply of the metal.

---

[6] As of June 2008, Scotia-Mocatta, Barclays Capital, Deutsche Bank, HSBC Bank and Société Générale.

Table 3.7   Supply of silver (2011).

	Supply	By country	By source
Primary (mining)			
Mexico	4,000 T	17%	
Peru	3,611 T	16%	
China	3,085 T	13%	
Australia	1,863 T	8%	
Chile	1,275 T	6%	
Bolivia	1,275 T	6%	
United States	1,201 T	5%	
Poland	1,173 T	5%	
Russia	1,145 T	5%	
Argentina	641 T	3%	
Other countries	3,620 T	16%	
Total mining	22,889 T	100%	70%
Hedging	1,900 T		6%
Official sector sales	1,393 T		4%
Secondary (recycling)	6,687 T		20%
Total	32,870 T		100%

Table 3.8   Demand for silver (2011).

	Absolute demand	Relative demand
Industrial applications	15,160 T	46%
Net investment	5,536 T	17%
Jewellery	5,194 T	16%
Coins and medals	3,151 T	10%
Photography	2,261 T	7%
Silverware	1,565 T	5%
Total	32,870 T	100%

Sources of demand for silver include jewellery and silverware, optical applications, the dental industry, and analog photography,[7] the proportions of which are shown in Table 3.8.

Similarly to gold, the LBMA also publishes the London Silver Fixing, only once a day at 12:00 noon. In fact the silver fixing is historically the oldest, dating back to 1897. It plays a similar role in the markets to the gold fixing.

---

[7] A market very much in decline: 2,261 tonnes were used in 2011, down each and every year from a base of 6,628 tonnes in 2001.

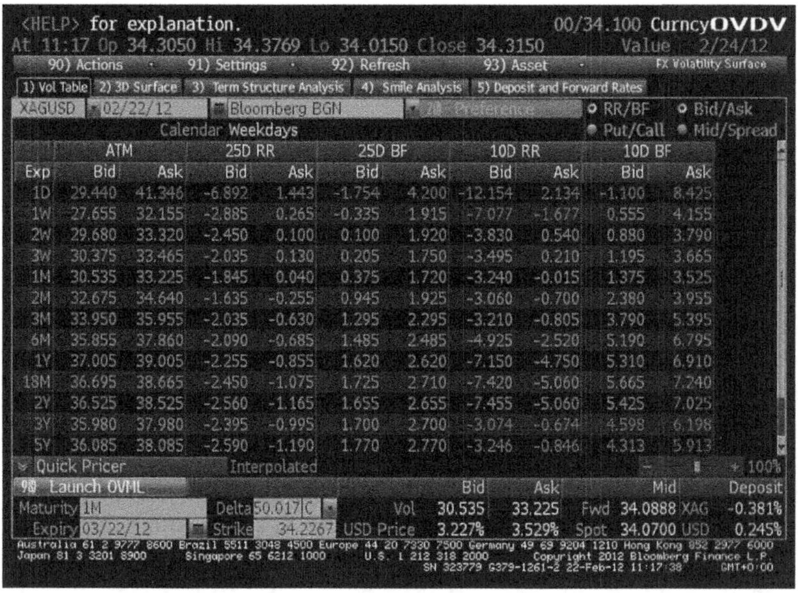

<HELP> for explanation. 00/34.100 CurncyOVDV
At 11:17 Op 34.3050 Hi 34.3769 Lo 34.0150 Close 34.3150 Value 2/24/12
90) Actions · 91) Settings · 92) Refresh 93) Asset · FX Volatility Surface
1) Vol Table 2) 3D Surface 3) Term Structure Analysis 4) Smile Analysis 5) Deposit and Forward Rates
XAGUSD 02/22/12 Bloomberg BGN Preference RR/BF Bid/Ask
Calendar Weekdays Put/Call Mid/Spread

	ATM		25D RR		25D BF		10D RR		10D BF	
Exp	Bid	Ask	Bid	Ask	Bid	Ask	Bid	Ask	Bid	Ask
1D	29.440	41.346	-6.892	1.443	-1.754	4.200	-12.154	2.134	-1.100	8.425
1W	27.655	32.155	-2.885	0.265	-0.335	1.915	-7.077	-1.677	0.555	4.155
2W	29.680	33.320	-2.450	0.100	0.100	1.920	-3.830	0.540	0.880	3.790
3W	30.375	33.465	-2.035	0.130	0.205	1.750	-3.495	0.210	1.195	3.665
1M	30.535	33.225	-1.845	0.040	0.375	1.720	-3.240	-0.015	1.375	3.525
2M	32.675	34.640	-1.635	-0.255	0.945	1.925	-3.060	-0.700	2.380	3.955
3M	33.950	35.955	-2.035	-0.630	1.295	2.295	-3.210	-0.805	3.790	5.395
6M	35.855	37.860	-2.090	-0.685	1.485	2.485	-4.925	-2.520	5.190	6.795
1Y	37.005	39.005	-2.255	-0.855	1.620	2.620	-7.150	-4.750	5.310	6.910
18M	36.695	38.665	-2.450	-1.075	1.725	2.710	-7.420	-5.060	5.665	7.240
2Y	36.525	38.525	-2.560	-1.165	1.655	2.655	-7.455	-5.060	5.425	7.025
3Y	35.980	37.980	-2.395	-0.995	1.700	2.700	-3.074	-0.674	4.598	6.198
5Y	36.085	38.085	-2.590	-1.190	1.770	2.770	-3.246	-0.846	4.313	5.913

Quick Pricer Interpolated 100%

98) Launch OVML					Bid	Ask		Mid		Deposit
Maturity	1M	Delta	50.017 C	Vol	30.535	33.225	Fwd	34.0888	XAG	-0.381%
Expiry	03/22/12	Strike	34.2267	USD Price	3.227%	3.529%	Spot	34.0700	USD	0.245%

Australia 61 2 9777 8600 Brazil 5511 3048 4500 Europe 44 20 7330 7500 Germany 49 69 9204 1210 Hong Kong 852 2977 6000
Japan 81 3 3201 8900 Singapore 65 6212 1000 U.S. 1 212 318 2000 Copyright 2012 Bloomberg Finance L.P.
SN 323779 G379-1261-2 22-Feb-12 11:17:38 GMT+0:00

Figure 3.2 Volatility surface for XAGUSD – © 2013 Bloomberg Finance L.P. All rights reserved. Used with permission.

Finally, it should be noted that silver is much more volatile than gold. Famously, the Hunt Brothers in the late 1970s/early 1980s attempted to corner the silver market and drove the spot price up from $11/oz to $50/oz in several months (it returned to $11/oz in another couple of months). While this is particularly noteworthy, silver has always been quite volatile, a fact reflected in the implied volatilities as seen in Figure 3.2.

3.3.3 Platinum

While the major precious metals are clearly gold and silver, there is an important class of metals in the so-called platinum group. The platinum group metals (PGMs) comprise platinum, palladium, rhodium, ruthenium, osmium, and iridium. From a markets point of view, the first two are the ones predominantly traded, while rhodium has had a surge of interest since the 1980s due to applications in catalytic converters. We shall only discuss those three metals further here; a survey of all the platinum group metals can be found in Chapter 9 of Gasparrini (1993), though it may be of interest that osmium was historically used for incandescent filaments, until replaced by tungsten,[8] and for making fountain pen nibs and phonograph record styluses because of its hardness. In more modern applications, ruthenium is used in the hard disk industry, and iridium is used in fabricating high purity single crystals (e.g. sapphire) which have applications in the fabrication of LED televisions.

Platinum, while known of and worked by Mesoamerican craftsmen for over a thousand years (Scott and Bray, 1980), was encountered by Spaniards in the middle of the 16th century in their search for silver.[9] The metal itself in elemental form was only discovered by the scientific community in the middle of the 18th century, in small quantities isolated from ore deposits from the Caribbean and South America. Until 1820, the only major known sources of platinum were in Brazil, Colombia and Saint Domingo, until platinum was discovered in the Ural mountains of Russia in 1822 with deposits about four times as productive as those in the Americas (those deposits being worked from 1824 onwards). Some other important other locations where platinum has been discovered are the Transvaal in South Africa (1923), Siberia (Noril'sk, 1935), Canada (Sudbury and other northern Ontario locations), the USA (Montana and Minnesota). The deposits in the Urals have been basically exhausted and now only contribute some 1% of Russia's platinum production today, a figure dwarfed by the Noril'sk area. However, for the world's largest reserves of the platinum group metals, we must turn to South Africa and the Bushveld Igneous Complex – the mines of the Merensky Reef especially, located within 200 km of Pretoria and Pietersburg, which currently produce about 75% of the world's platinum production (see Table 3.9) and 20% of the world's palladium production.

Platinum itself nowadays is most extensively used for automobile catalytic converters, an application that has grown in importance due to more stringent environmental standards (the actual amount of precious metal in a catalytic converter needs only be a gram or two). Declines in automobile production as a result of the economic downturn in the first decade of the 21st century and the Japanese earthquake crisis can be linked to declines in the spot price of platinum during that period.[10] Platinum is also used in jewellery, for investment, and other roles in

---

[8] Historical note – the OSRAM lighting manufacturer derived its name from OSmium-wolfRAM, wolfram being German for tungsten.

[9] Hence the name, from *platina*, meaning little silver.

[10] Another interesting ratio to follow is the platinum–gold ratio.

Table 3.9   Supply of platinum (2010).

	Supply	Within category	Overall
Primary (mining)			
South Africa	147,790 kg	77%	
Russia	25,100 kg	13%	
Zimbabwe	8,800 kg	5%	
Canada	3,900 kg	2%	
USA	3,450 kg	2%	
Colombia	998 kg	0.5%	
Other countries	2,500 kg	1.3%	
Total (mining)	192,500 kg	100%	77.1%
Secondary (recycling)			
Automobile scrap	33,700 kg	58.9%	
Electronics	300 kg	0.5%	
Jewellery	23,200 kg	40.6%	
Total (recycling)	57,200 kg	100%	22.9%
Total	249,700 kg		100%

industry where its catalytic and corrosion resistant properties make it effective.

The demand for platinum is tabulated in Table 3.10 and typical implied volatilities are shown in Figure 3.3.

Table 3.10   Demand for platinum (2010).

	Absolute demand	Relative demand
Automobile catalytic converters	112,700 kg	46%
Jewellery	75,950 kg	31%
Investment	19,600 kg	8%
Chemical sector	13,800 kg	6%
Glassmaking industry	10,700 kg	4%
Biomedical industry	7,930 kg	3%
Other	4,320 kg	2%
Total	245,000 kg	100%

3.3.4   Palladium

Palladium was discovered in 1802 by the chemist William Hyde Wollaston after treating platinum ore from South America with various strong reagents. He named it after the recently discovered asteroid Pallas. Palladium is notable for being perhaps the only element ever to be sold *before* the announcement of its scientific discovery – as discussed in

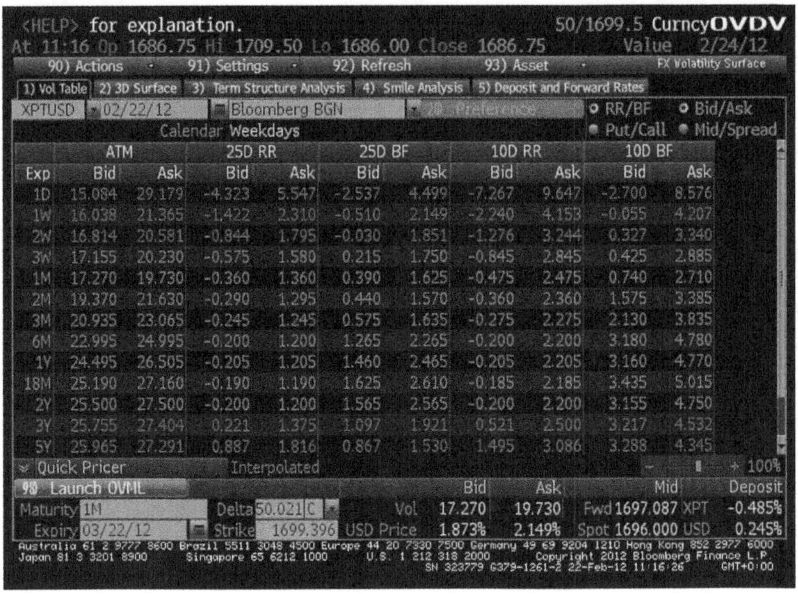

Figure 3.3 Volatility surface for XPTUSD – © 2013 Bloomberg Finance L.P. All rights reserved. Used with permission.

Griffiths (2003). While Wollaston's notebooks from 1802 give a record of his extraction of the metal, he suspected competitors to not be far behind and so, in order to establish the priority of their discovery, in April 1803 he distributed handbills offering samples of the metal "Palladium; or New Silver" for sale at 26 Gerrard Street, London, presumably intending that this provide a traceable historical record. The official announcement was only made in a paper he read to the Royal Society in July 1805. Like the other PGMs, it is currently produced mostly in South Africa and Russia.

Palladium also can be used as a catalyst and therefore has found considerable usage in automobile catalytic converters, particularly when it is cheaper than platinum or rhodium, as manufacturers prefer to substitute the cheapest suitable metal for this role. In fact, palladium was about the same price as platinum in 1999, rising to twice the price of platinum in 2000, but since then reverting to about half the price in early 2012. Palladium is also used in electronics – a 60% silver/40% palladium alloy provides a good balance between the high electrical

Table 3.11   Supply of palladium (2010).

	Supply	Within category	Overall
Primary (mining)			
Russia	84,700 kg	41.9%	
South Africa	82,200 kg	40.7%	
USA	11,600 kg	5.7%	
Zimbabwe	7,000 kg	3.5%	
Canada	6,700 kg	3.3%	
Other countries	9,800 kg	4.9%	
Total (mining)	202,000 kg	100%	77.9%
Secondary (recycling)			
Automobile scrap	41,200 kg	71.8%	
Electronics	13,700 kg	23.9%	
Jewellery	2,490 kg	4.3%	
Total (recycling)	57,390 kg	100%	22.1%
Total	259,390 kg		100%

conductivity of silver and the corrosion resistance of palladium. Palladium is also used in dental work, mostly in Japan, where a regulation requires that government-subsidised dental alloys must be at least 20% palladium, the so-called "kinpala" alloy, which is used in 90% of all Japanese dental treatment. The metal is also used in jewellery, both as an alloy component of white gold and in its pure form also.

The supply and demand for palladium are tabulated in Tables 3.11 and 3.12 respectively, and market implied volatilities are shown in Figure 3.4.

Table 3.12   Demand for palladium (2010).

	Absolute demand	Relative demand
Automobile catalytic converters	170,430 kg	57%
Electronics	44,850 kg	15%
Investment	32,890 kg	11%
Dental alloys	18,000 kg	6%
Chemical sector	12,300 kg	4%
Other (mostly jewellery)	20,530 kg	7%
Total	299,000 kg	100%

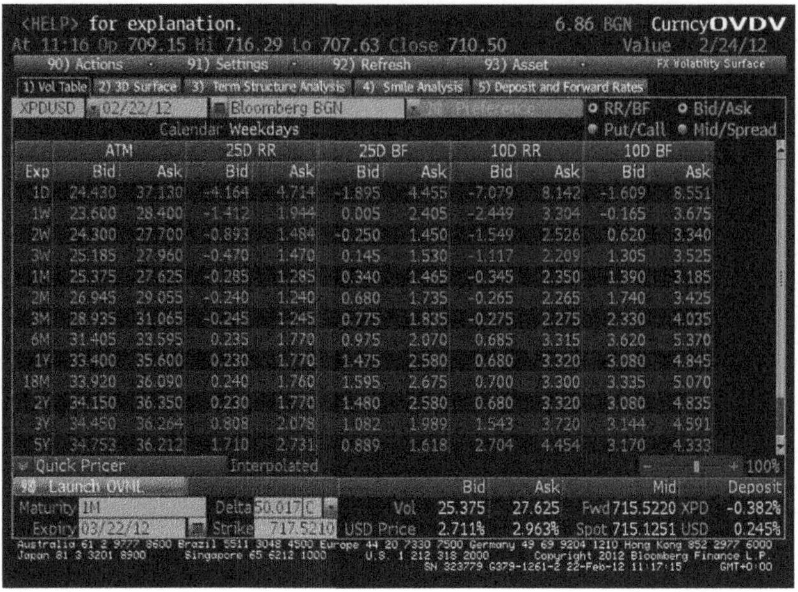

<HELP> for explanation. 6.86 BGN CurncyOVDV
At 11:16 Op 709.15 Hi 716.29 Lo 707.63 Close 710.50 Value 2/24/12
90) Actions · 91) Settings · 92) Refresh 93) Asset · FX Volatility Surface
1) Vol Table 2) 3D Surface 3) Term Structure Analysis 4) Smile Analysis 5) Deposit and Forward Rates
XPDUSD 02/22/12 Bloomberg BGN Preference RR/BF Bid/Ask
Calendar Weekdays Put/Call Mid/Spread

	ATM		25D RR		25D BF		10D RR		10D BF	
Exp	Bid	Ask	Bid	Ask	Bid	Ask	Bid	Ask	Bid	Ask
1D	24.430	37.130	-4.164	4.714	-1.895	4.455	-7.079	8.142	-1.609	8.551
1W	23.600	28.400	-1.412	1.944	0.005	2.405	-2.449	3.304	-0.165	3.675
2W	24.300	27.700	-0.893	1.484	-0.250	1.450	-1.549	2.526	0.620	3.340
3W	25.185	27.960	-0.470	1.470	0.145	1.530	-1.117	2.209	1.305	3.525
1M	25.375	27.625	-0.285	1.285	0.340	1.465	-0.345	2.350	1.390	3.185
2M	26.945	29.055	-0.240	1.240	0.680	1.735	-0.265	2.265	1.740	3.425
3M	28.935	31.065	-0.245	1.245	0.775	1.835	-0.275	2.275	2.330	4.035
6M	31.405	33.595	0.235	1.770	0.975	2.070	0.685	3.315	3.620	5.370
1Y	33.400	35.600	0.230	1.770	1.475	2.580	0.680	3.320	3.080	4.845
18M	33.920	36.090	0.240	1.760	1.595	2.675	0.700	3.300	3.335	5.070
2Y	34.150	36.350	0.230	1.770	1.480	2.580	0.680	3.320	3.080	4.835
3Y	34.450	36.264	0.808	2.078	1.082	1.989	1.543	3.720	3.144	4.591
5Y	34.753	36.212	1.710	2.731	0.889	1.618	2.704	4.454	3.170	4.333

Quick Pricer Interpolated 100%
Launch OVML Bid Ask Mid Deposit
Maturity 1M Delta 50.017 C Vol 25.375 27.625 Fwd 715.5220 XPD -0.382%
Expiry 03/22/12 Strike 717.5210 USD Price 2.711% 2.963% Spot 715.1251 USD 0.245%
Australia 61 2 9777 8600 Brazil 5511 3048 4500 Europe 44 20 7330 7500 Germany 49 69 9204 1210 Hong Kong 852 2977 6000
Japan 81 3 3201 8900 Singapore 65 6212 1000 U.S. 1 212 318 2000 Copyright 2012 Bloomberg Finance L.P.
SN 323779 G379-1261-2 22-Feb-12 11:17:15 GMT+0:00

Figure 3.4 Volatility surface for XPDUSD – © 2013 Bloomberg Finance L.P. All rights reserved. Used with permission.

3.3.5 Rhodium

Rhodium, another silvery platinum group metal also discovered by Wollaston in 1804, is also used in the production of catalytic converters, both in the chemical industry and in the automobile industry. It is also used for corrosion and heat resistant parts used in the manufacture of special

Table 3.13 Supply of rhodium (2010).

	Supply	Within category	Overall
Primary (mining)			
South Africa	20,000 kg	85.5%	
Russia	2,200 kg	9.4%	
Zimbabwe	750 kg	3.2%	
North America	370 kg	1.6%	
Other countries	80 kg	0.3%	
Total mining	23,400 kg	100%	76.2%
Secondary (recycling)	7,300 kg		23.8%
Total	30,700 kg		100%

Table 3.14   Demand for rhodium (2010).

	Absolute demand	Relative demand
Automobile industry	22,500 kg	82.7%
Chemical industry	2,110 kg	7.8%
Glassmaking	1,770 kg	6.5%
Electrical	124 kg	0.5%
Other	700 kg	2.5%
Total	27,200 kg	100%

substrate glass used in flat panel screens. The largest producer is South Africa, not surprisingly as rhodium is often found as a by-product of platinum mining.

The supply and demand for rhodium are tabulated in Tables 3.13 and 3.14 respectively.

Rhodium also has the distinction of being the precious metal with the highest ever all time price so far: $10,100/oz was reached on 19 June 2008 – though the price fell to under $1,000/oz by November that year.

4

Base Metals

Base metals, as a term, generally refers in the commodity markets to non-ferrous metals used primarily in industrial applications – typical examples,[1] as listed in Table 4.1, being copper, aluminium, zinc, nickel, lead and tin.

While gold and silver have been used by humans from the very early days in civilisation, when copper was known largely for ornamental purposes, one can trace the large-scale usage of copper back to the Chalcolithic period, or Copper Age, a subepoch at the beginning of the Bronze Age (3300 BC to 1200 BC). Bronze, of course, is an alloy of copper and tin,[2] while brass is an alloy of copper and zinc.[3]

We have seen already in Table 3.1 that the base metals are substantially cheaper than the precious metals. What this means, as discussed in Frankel (1997), is that the inventories of a certain value are voluminous and massive, and therefore prohibitively expensive to lease out for short periods to locations outside of a warehouse attached to an exchange. This is quite different to gold, which as we saw in Chapter 3 is very commonly leased out, e.g. by central bankers. The absence of the "stabilising effect of a lease rate market", as Frankel puts it, means that spot and forward prices are far more decoupled than for the precious metals. Between 1995 and 1996, for example, the correlation between cash (spot) prices and 15-month forward prices on the London Metal Exchange was as little as 65% for aluminium, though the correlation was as high as 97% for a period in 1993 when inventories were at historically high levels.

As a result, the first main difference we notice when we move from precious metals to base metals is that we encounter a commodity that is priced off a forward curve as opposed to a spot rate (the second main difference, which we will notice in Section 4.1, is an actively traded market in Asian options).

---

[1] A mnemonic to remember them by: "Crazy and zany nights like these".

[2] Such as UK 1p and 2p coins from before September 1992 which are a bronze alloy of 97% copper, 2.5% zinc, 0.5% tin – coins minted after this date are (with a few exceptions) copper plated steel.

[3] If the reader has a 10, 20 or 50 Euro cent coin in his or her pocket, that is a type of brass, the so-called "Nordic gold" which is 89% copper, 5% aluminium, 5% zinc and 1% tin.

Table 4.1   The base metals.

Metal	Atomic number
Copper	29
Aluminium	13
Zinc	30
Nickel	28
Lead	82
Tin	50

Table 4.2   Base metals traded on exchanges.

Metal	Maximum tenor for:		Price quote
	Futures	Options	
London Metal Exchange (LME)			
Copper	123 M	63 M	USD/tonne
Aluminium High Grade	123 M	63 M	USD/tonne
Aluminium Alloy	27 M	27 M	USD/tonne
NASAAC	27 M	27 M	USD/tonne
Zinc Special High Grade	63 M	63 M	USD/tonne
Nickel	63 M	63 M	USD/tonne
Lead	63 M	63 M	USD/tonne
Tin	15 M	15 M	USD/tonne
New York Mercantile Exchange (COMEX)			
Copper High Grade	60 M	24 M	US cents/lb

Futures contracts for base metals are primarily traded on the London Metal Exchange, as well as on some other exchanges.[4] We tabulate the contracts specific to base metals in Table 4.2.

Note there are three types of aluminium traded: high grade primary aluminium, the LME aluminium alloy, and NASAAC (the North American Special Aluminium Alloy Contract) – we describe these in Section 4.2.2.

The London Metal Exchange (Crowson and Markey, 2011) is the predominant exchange globally for metals trading and accounts for well over 90% of global trading in those base metals in which it maintains a

---

[4] An aluminium futures contract was traded on COMEX from December 1983 to February 1989 and from June 1999 to September 2009, but was unsuccessful on both attempts; similarly to the aluminium futures contract traded from April 1997 to October 2010 on the Tokyo Commodity Exchange. More successful is the COMEX copper futures contract, which was extended to 60 months in September 2010. Several base metals also trade on the Shanghai Futures Exchange, but these are not discussed here.

```
<HELP> for explanation.
```

Metal	Firm	Bid	Ask	Trade	Change	High	Low	Time
1) Prim Alum	LMES	1852.00	1855.00	1849.00y	-3.00	1866.75	1848.85	5/17
2) Alum Alloy	KERB	1780.00	1800.00	1790.00y	+10.00	--	--	5/17
3) NASAAC	LMES	1810.00	1840.00	1835.00y	+20.00	1839.85	1820.00	5/17
4) Copper	LMES	7308.25	7312.00	7305.00y	+25.00	7367.25	7234.00	5/17
5) Lead	LMES	2014.00	2016.00	2014.00y	+20.50	2018.50	1988.00	5/17
6) Nickel	LMES	14820.00	14849.00	14825.00y	-75.00	15000.00	14821.00	5/17
7) Tin	LMES	20910.00	20969.00	20975.00y	+20.00	21100.00	20816.00	5/17
8) Zinc	LMES	1839.25	1842.00	1840.00y	+7.50	1855.00	1830.00	5/17
9) Steel Billet	LMES	160.00	180.00	170.00y	--	--	--	5/17

Metal	Official Bid	Ask	Unofficial Bid	Ask	Warehouse Stock Stock	Change	Cash-3Mon Spread Bid	Ask
Prim Alum	10) 1863.00 y	1863.50 y	19) 1853.00 y	1854.00 y	28)5238500 y	+7575	39) -30.00	-28.00
Alum Alloy	11) 1780.00 y	1800.00 y	20) 1780.00 y	1790.00 y	29) 70260 y	--	38) --	--
NASAAC	12) 1835.00 y	1840.00 y	21) 1830.00 y	1840.00 y	30) 120780 y	-780	39) --	--
Copper	13) 7349.50 y	7350.00 y	22) 7300.00 y	7302.00 y	31) 629950 y	+5550	40) -31.00	-29.00
Lead	14) 2010.00 y	2010.50 y	23) 2000.00 y	2003.00 y	32) 240875 y	-2375	41) -7.75	--
Nickel	15)14900.00	14905.00 y	24)14840.00 y	14860.00 y	33) 177948 y	-828	42) -74.00	+73.00
Tin	16)20850.00	20855.00 y	25)20900.00 y	20950.00 y	34) 14075 y	-120	43) -55.00	-54.00
Zinc	17) 1843.00 y	1844.00 y	26) 1840.00 y	1841.00 y	35)1113875 y	-2100	44) --	--
Steel Billet	18) 160.00 y	180.00 y	27) 160.00 y	180.00 y	36) 76700 y	--	45) --	--

| 46) LMEX | 3129.9 y | 48) JPY | 102.51 y | 50) Gold | 1352.36 | 52) Platinum | 1448.25 | 54) 3M LIBO | 0.27310 |
| 47) EUR | 1.2873 y | 49) GBP | 1.5242 y | 51) Silver | 21.5685 | 53) Palladiu | 739.40 | 55) US 10Y | 1.923 |

Figure 4.1 Base Metals on the LME – © 2013 Bloomberg Finance L.P. All rights reserved. Used with permission.

presence. We show an overview of the base metals traded on the LME in Figure 4.1, largely to show representative price levels in the futures market. Even the least valuable of the base metals is over ten times the value of steel billet (ferrous).

While the LME proper dates back to 1877, the base metals market as a London institution dates back to the late 16th century. Trading in the metals was carried out in the Royal Exchange from its foundation in 1571, but due to both congestion and "rowdy manners", traders were forced to relocate to nearby coffeehouses in the City. One particular favourite of the metals trading community was the Jerusalem Coffee House on Exchange Alley, directly south of the Royal Exchange, near Cornhill. It is from these times that the tradition of ring trading originates, merchants originally drawing a circle in the sawdust on the floor and calling out for an assembly of interested buyers around the periphery of the circle by crying out "Change!".

With the Industrial Revolution, the UK and Europe in general became increasingly reliant on imports of metals, primarily copper and tin. At first, Cornwall was the major source for copper (at its peak around 1830, up to 30% of men in Cornwall were employed in copper mining,

Cornwall being the largest source of mined copper in the world) and especially after the 1866 copper price crash, tin – both immortalised in folk songs such as the following

> Come, all ye jolly Tinner boys, and listen to me
> I'll tell ee of a storie shall make ye for to see
> Consarning Boney Peartie, the schaames which he had maade
> To stop our tin and copper mines, and all our pilchard traade

In time, however, the English mines were exhausted to the point of being unprofitable when faced with competition from newly discovered sources of the metals from overseas, such as tin deposits in Malaya and copper from Chile. By a coincidence of geography, the 1869 opening of the Suez Canal meant that shipping times for tin from Malaya and copper from Chile were both in the vicinity of three months. At exactly the time when English mines were in decline, a viable market for forward delivery of copper and tin was therefore in the ascendancy. This led to a system of trading base metals for forward delivery, in a manner that still exists to this day on the LME. One obvious change, of course, is that all LME metal contracts are now denominated in US dollars, which the LME gradually switched to after the British pound was floated in July 1972.

4.1 FUTURES, OPTIONS AND TAPO CONTRACTS

In this section we introduce the various base metals contracts that trade on the London Metal Exchange.

4.1.1 Futures

Let us therefore introduce the maturity dates for futures contracts on the LME. The shortest dated one is the so-called cash or spot futures contract, which is two good London business days (not including holidays) from the trade date. Following the notation of Chapter 2, at time t the prompt date is denoted $\vec{T}(t)$ and is two good London business days hence.

A daily sequence of futures contracts exists for every good London business day out to three months, and then weekly (every Wednesday) for the next three months (months 4 to 6). After that the futures contracts revert to monthly, with futures dates on the third Wednesday from

Table 4.3   Maturity dates for base metals futures contracts on the LME.

	Copper Aluminium	Lead Nickel Zinc	NASAAC Aluminium alloy	Tin	
Cash/Spot	T+2	T+2	T+2	T+2	
0–3M	Daily	Daily	Daily	Daily	
4–6M	Weekly	Weekly	Weekly	Weekly	Every Wednesday
7–15M	Monthly	Monthly	Monthly	Monthly	3rd Wednesday
16–27M	Monthly	Monthly	Monthly	–	3rd Wednesday
28–63M	Monthly	Monthly	–	–	3rd Wednesday
64–123M	Monthly	–	–	–	3rd Wednesday

month 7 to month 15 for tin, month 27 for NASAAC and aluminium alloy, month 63 for lead, nickel and zinc, and month 123 for aluminium and copper. We summarise this in Table 4.3.

The most liquid futures contracts traded on the LME are for 3, 15 and (except tin, obviously) 27 months.

We illustrate with an example, as of Monday 20 May 2013, for tin futures on the LME. Note that Monday 27 May 2013 is an English bank holiday.

What we see in Table 4.4 is that on Monday 20 May 2013, the closest maturity date is the spot or cash contract, with delivery date Wednesday 22 May 2013. Three months from the 20th of May is Tuesday 20 August, so this is the final maturity date on which the daily sequence of futures contracts are offered. Weekly contracts are then offered on all Wednesdays[5] through six months counted forward from May (i.e. June, July, August, September, October and November) which have not already been included in the daily series. At this point, we then have monthly futures contracts offered on the third Wednesday of the subsequent nine months, i.e. 18 December 2013, 15 January 2014, and so on to 20 August 2014.

If the contract was on copper, zinc, or one of the other metals for which the futures contracts extend out beyond 15 months, we would continue with the additional 12, 48 or 108 maturity dates, straightfor- wardly applying the third Wednesday rule.

The choice of Wednesdays is no accident: they are particularly fortu- nate to deal with because all English public holidays – with the exception

---

[5] Adjustment of any Wednesdays which happen to coincide with Christmas Day, Boxing Day or New Years Day are handled according to the rules of the LME; Christmas Day is rolled back to the previous good business day, the others are rolled forward to the next good business day.

Table 4.4 Available maturity dates for tin futures on the LME as of Monday 20 May 2013.

	Mon	Tue	Wed	Thu	Fri
			22/5	23/5	24/5
		28/5	29/5	30/5	31/5
	3/6	4/6	5/6	6/6	7/6
	10/6	11/6	12/6	13/6	14/6
	17/6	18/6	19/6	20/6	21/6
	24/6	25/6	26/6	27/6	28/6
Daily	1/7	2/7	3/7	4/7	5/7
	8/7	9/7	10/7	11/7	12/7
	15/7	16/7	17/7	18/7	19/7
	22/7	23/7	24/7	25/7	26/7
	29/7	30/7	31/7	1/8	2/8
	5/8	6/8	7/8	8/8	9/8
	12/8	13/8	14/8	15/8	16/8
	19/8	20/8	21/8		
Weekly			28/8		
			4/9		
			11/9		
			18/9		
			25/9		
			2/10		
			9/10		
			16/10		
			23/10		
			30/10		
			6/11		
			13/11		
			20/11		
			27/11		
Monthly			18/12/13		
			15/1/14		
			19/2/14		
			19/3/14		
			16/4/14		
			21/5/14		
			18/6/14		
			16/7/14		
			20/8/14		

of Christmas, Boxing Day and New Years Day – land on either a Monday or a Friday. Further, Christmas Day, Boxing Day and New Years Day will never land on the third Wednesday of a month.[6] Generally,

---

[6] If they do land on a Wednesday, it would be the fourth, fourth and first Wednesday of the month respectively.

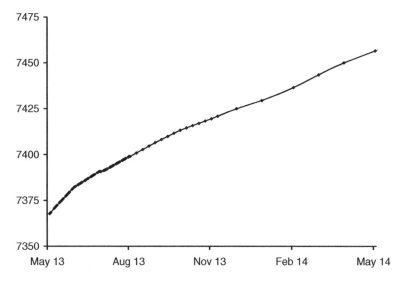

Figure 4.2   LME copper futures curve as of 21 May 2013.

maturity dates which happen to land on holidays are deferred to the subsequent business day, with some exceptions (see Rule 8.4.1 in the LME Rule Book).

Note that these contracts are technically forwards, not futures, as there is no margining requirement at the LME itself. Typically, LME members will require their customers to deposit margin on their behalf at the London Clearing House, but this is outside the scope of the LME itself.

Futures contracts on COMEX are subject to cash clearing and daily margining, though the only base metals contract we are likely to encounter traded on COMEX is copper.

The forward curve we see for base metals is therefore quite densely populated in the 0–3 month range as is apparent for the case of copper in Figure 4.2 (we only show forward prices out to one year, though the curve goes out to 2023, albeit with much less liquidity).

There are occasionally some mild seasonality effects in the base metals markets, such as increased demand in the summer for aluminium (beverage cans) and increased demand in the winter for lead (car batteries). Supply, however, is relatively constant year round, so the base metals are not particularly seasonal (Geman and Smith, 2013).

4.1.2 Options

Not surprisingly, not every futures contract has an option traded against it. The futures contracts which do have options available to trade against them are known as the monthly value dates, these being those futures with maturity dates on the third Wednesday of the month. I reserve capital letter notation for these, e.g. the "FEB13" contract will be understood to be the contract with maturity date on the third Wednesday of 2013 (for base metals). This notation will be useful for energy, where there is a particular futures contract specific to each calendar month.

These base metals options, while technically American style, are often treated as European style and assumed to be exercised on the exercise date, being the first Wednesday of the month (except on the rare occasion that this Wednesday is the New Years Day holiday, in which case the exercise date rolls back to 31 December, as seen in the example below). This is plausible as there is little reason to elect to exercise early, except in the case of negative interest rates or liquidity/credit concerns. Exercise is into the underlying futures contract, i.e. not cash settlement. Note that while high grade copper and primary aluminium have futures extending out to 123 months, options are only available on the first 63 futures in the monthly value date series. For the other metals, options exist on all those futures.

What this means is that, in contrast to FX and precious metals, we do not have a volatility surface defined by the implied volatilities at a set of tenors of constant maturity, e.g. 1M, 2M, 3M, etc. What we have instead is a set of actual exercise dates, and volatilities for European style options with expiries on those dates, for delayed physical settlement two weeks thereafter.

For LME options on copper, for example, as of 20 May 2013, we have the term structure of at-the-money volatilities as shown in Table 4.5. Note that the terminology for base metals can be somewhat ambiguous, ATM is sometimes used to denote at-the-money forward (this is a historical artifact from when base metals were quoted without a delta-based smile) and DN denotes delta-neutral (also referred to as 50 delta). For smile construction, we use delta-neutral strikes as the backbone of the smile and as smile construction for base metals follows the same market conventions as the precious metals, I use ATM and DN synonymously, reserving ATMF to denote the case when the strike is equal to the forward price.

We graph the ATM volatility curve for the six base metals (together with gold and platinum for comparison) in Figure 4.3. Note that the

Table 4.5   Dates for copper options on the LME as of Monday 20 May 2013.

Expiry	Delivery	Contract	σ_{DN}
Wed 05-Jun-13	Wed 19-Jun-13	JUN13	24.90%
Wed 03-Jul-13	Wed 17-Jul-13	JUL13	24.93%
Wed 07-Aug-13	Wed 21-Aug-13	AUG13	24.70%
Wed 04-Sep-13	Wed 18-Sep-13	SEP13	24.56%
Wed 02-Oct-13	Wed 16-Oct-13	OCT13	24.45%
Wed 06-Nov-13	Wed 20-Nov-13	NOV13	24.37%
Wed 04-Dec-13	Wed 18-Dec-13	DEC13	24.26%
Tue 31-Dec-13	Wed 15-Jan-14	JAN14	24.11%
Wed 05-Feb-14	Wed 19-Feb-14	FEB14	24.15%
Wed 05-Mar-14	Wed 19-Mar-14	MAR14	24.13%
Wed 02-Apr-14	Wed 16-Apr-14	APR14	24.07%
Wed 07-May-14	Wed 21-May-14	MAY14	24.02%
Wed 04-Jun-14	Wed 18-Jun-14	JUN14	23.99%
Wed 02-Jul-14	Wed 16-Jul-14	JUL14	23.92%
Wed 06-Aug-14	Wed 20-Aug-14	AUG14	23.89%
Wed 03-Sep-14	Wed 17-Sep-14	SEP14	23.88%
Wed 01-Oct-14	Wed 15-Oct-14	OCT14	23.83%
Wed 05-Nov-14	Wed 19-Nov-14	NOV14	23.81%
Wed 03-Dec-14	Wed 17-Dec-14	DEC14	23.80%
Wed 07-Jan-15	Wed 21-Jan-15	JAN15	23.69%
Wed 04-Feb-15	Wed 18-Feb-15	FEB15	23.68%

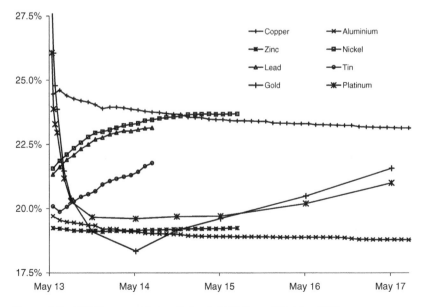

Figure 4.3   LME base metals implied vols [ATM] as of 21 May 2013.

Table 4.6(a)   LME aluminium implied volatility as of cob Tuesday 5 Feb 2013.

Expiry	Delivery	Contract	σ_{imp}
Wed 06-Feb-13	Wed 20-Feb-13	FEB13	18.65%
Wed 06-Mar-13	Wed 20-Mar-13	MAR13	18.37%
Wed 03-Apr-13	Wed 17-Apr-13	APR13	18.19%
Wed 01-May-13	Wed 15-May-13	MAY13	18.17%

volatility curve for copper displays the Samuelson effect for commodities, i.e. the implied volatility is higher in the short end and decays towards a long-term level of volatility. This is usually the case for energy, as we shall see in Chapter 5, but not for all precious metals (see gold). For base metals it is sometimes seen, such as for copper and aluminium in Figure 4.3, but not for nickel, lead and tin.

We therefore see that volatility surfaces for base metals are defined in terms of a delta based volatility surface, with 10- and 25-delta calls and puts and an at-the-money volatility defined as the 50-delta. This follows the same delta conventions as for precious metals, but with the option expiries being set to a fixed set of calendar dates in the future (first Wednesdays) rather than constant maturity (1M, 2M, 3M, etc.). This gives us our first chance to introduce the concept of the roll date.

At close of business on Tuesday 5 February 2013, the ATM volatility backbone for the first few options on LME primary aluminium was as shown in Table 4.6(a).

However, if we move forward a day to Wednesday 6 February 2013, the ATM volatility backbone (once again at close of business) is shown in Table 4.6(b).

Notice how the FEB13 implied volatility of 18.65% "rolls off" the curve as we move from Tuesday close of business volatility surfaces to Wednesday. This is known as the "roll". While we see the roll in the dates corresponding to traded options on base metals on the LME, we do not have to roll the maturity dates corresponding to the futures contracts on base metals, as the LME ensures that these are available daily out to

Table 4.6(b)   LME aluminium implied volatility as of cob Wednesday 6 Feb 2013.

Expiry	Delivery	Contract	σ_{imp}
Wed 06-Mar-13	Wed 20-Mar-13	MAR13	18.28%
Wed 03-Apr-13	Wed 17-Apr-13	APR13	18.14%
Wed 01-May-13	Wed 15-May-13	MAY13	18.13%
Wed 05-Jun-13	Wed 19-Jun-13	JUN13	18.09%

Table 4.7 LME base metals 3M implied volatility smiles on 21 May 2013.

Metal	$\sigma_{10\text{-d-P}}$	$\sigma_{25\text{-d-P}}$	σ_{DN}	$\sigma_{25\text{-d-C}}$	$\sigma_{10\text{-d-C}}$
Copper	29.35%	27.09%	24.40%	23.33%	23.48%
Aluminium	20.95%	20.07%	19.48%	19.86%	20.57%
Zinc	20.83%	19.89%	19.19%	19.70%	20.43%
Nickel	24.50%	23.26%	22.10%	22.59%	23.39%
Lead	23.62%	22.66%	21.90%	22.50%	23.27%
Tin	21.52%	20.66%	20.07%	21.03%	22.30%
Aluminium alloy	20.59%	19.66%	18.99%	19.29%	19.86%
NASAAC	19.73%	18.74%	18.10%	18.44%	19.00%

3M. For energy derivatives, however, both the futures and option dates experience the roll.

Volatility skews are generally quite symmetric for the base metals, with the notable exception of copper in recent times. We give some indicative 3M volatility smiles (i.e. the AUG13 contract) in Table 4.7 to show typical market behaviour.

Information on volatilities for base metals is easily available, e.g. from Bloomberg page LMIV ⟨GO⟩ and similar.

4.1.3 Traded Average Price Options

As well as American (which are, for all intents and purposes, European)[7] style options on the base metals on the LME, there are also Asian contracts traded on some metals.

TAPOs were introduced in February 1997 for trade on copper grade A and high grade primary aluminium, and were sufficiently popular that they were extended to the other base metals in September 2000.

They offer market participants the flexibility to hedge price exposure over a calendar month, using an arithmetic average rather than an individual fixing, a feature which is often desired by hedgers in the commodities markets. Copper producers, for example, quite often sell copper production at a price based on the monthly average, so the natural price hedge is an arithmetic Asian option, including the averaging feature. The question, of course, is what is the actual quantity that is being averaged. The TAPO contract is determined by averaging the spot or cash futures price over all good working days over a particular calendar

---

[7] The LME options are on LME futures, which are presumed to be driftless.

Table 4.8(a)   LME implied volatilities (ATM) for aluminium on Thursday 8 April 2010.

Expiry date	Futures date	Futures contract	σ_{ATM}
Wed 05-May-10	Wed 19-May-10	MAY10	22.26%
Wed 02-Jun-10	Wed 16-Jun-10	JUN10	23.12%
Wed 07-Jul-10	Wed 21-Jul-10	JUL10	23.27%
Wed 04-Aug-10	Wed 18-Aug-10	AUG10	23.51%

month, this average being known as the Monthly Average Settlement Price (MASP).

It is best to illustrate with an example. We attempt to sketch how an aluminium TAPO for the month of June 2010 would be valued. Consider the LME market on Thursday 8 April 2010. We have the implied volatilities as shown in Table 4.8(a). The futures market is shown in Table 4.8(b) together with interpolated volatilities.

Table 4.8(b)   LME futures curve for aluminium on Thursday 8 April 2010.

Date	Futures price	σ_{ATM}	Incl in MASP?
Mon 12-Apr-10	2322.44	22.26%	no
Tue 01-Jun-10	2341.20	22.66%	no
Wed 02-Jun-10	2341.54	22.69%	no
Thu 03-Jun-10	2341.88	22.72%	YES
Fri 04-Jun-10	2342.21	22.75%	YES
Mon 07-Jun-10	2343.22	22.84%	YES
Tue 08-Jun-10	2343.56	22.87%	YES
Wed 09-Jun-10	2343.89	22.91%	YES
Thu 10-Jun-10	2344.23	22.94%	YES
Fri 11-Jun-10	2344.57	22.97%	YES
Mon 14-Jun-10	2345.58	23.06%	YES
Tue 15-Jun-10	2345.91	23.09%	YES
Wed 16-Jun-10	2346.25	23.12%	YES
Thu 17-Jun-10	2346.52	23.12%	YES
Fri 18-Jun-10	2346.80	23.13%	YES
Mon 21-Jun-10	2347.62	23.14%	YES
Tue 22-Jun-10	2347.89	23.15%	YES
Wed 23-Jun-10	2348.17	23.15%	YES
Thu 24-Jun-10	2348.44	23.15%	YES
Fri 25-Jun-10	2348.71	23.16%	YES
Mon 28-Jun-10	2349.54	23.17%	YES
Tue 29-Jun-10	2349.81	23.18%	YES
Wed 30-Jun-10	2350.08	23.18%	YES
Thu 01-Jul-10	2350.36	23.18%	YES
Fri 02-Jul-10	2350.63	23.19%	YES

This can now be valued using the methods detailed in Section 2.7.4. Note that the futures dates required for TAPO valuation (i.e. the ones contributing to the MASP for June) are exactly those futures contracts which will in due course be the cash/spot contract on the 1st, 2nd, 3th . . . 29th and 30th of June – i.e. offset by two business days forward.

We therefore have the first moment from (2.127)

$$\mathbf{E}^d \left[A^{A,f}_{t_1,t_n} \right] = \frac{1}{n} \sum_{i=1}^{n} f_{0,\vec{T}(t_i)}$$

$$= \frac{1}{22} [2341.88 + 2342.21 + \cdots + 2350.63]$$

$$= 2346.63$$

which is the expectation of the Monthly Average Settlement Price (MASP) for June 2010, conditional on the futures curve as of 8 April 2010. The second moment is given by (2.128). This suffices to price an Asian option on LME base metals. Additionally, TAPOs can be priced under volatility skew by using volatilities interpolated on a two-dimensional strike by time matrix.

Unlike traded base metals options, TAPOs are cash settled two business days after the final fixing (i.e. on the second good business day of the subsequent month). Partially seasoned TAPOs can be traded up to the penultimate business day of the averaging month, i.e. with two or more indeterminate fixings.

4.2 COMMONLY TRADED BASE METALS

Excellent discussions of base metals and the practicalities of mines and mining valuation can be found in Rudenno (2009) and Lonergan (2006). While aluminium is the most important base metal in terms of industrial production, as shown in Table 4.9, copper is the most important for financial markets, being more sensitive to the economic cycle. Indeed it is sometimes known as Dr Copper (Amen, 2013) for its predictive powers.

Table 4.9 Base metal global production and reserves (~2009).

Metal	Production	Reserves (est.)
Copper	15.5 mio T	490 mio T
Aluminium	38 mio T	25 bio T
Zinc	10.5 mio T	180 mio T
Nickel	1.7 mio T	67 mio T
Lead	8 mio T	79 mio T
Tin	300,000 T	4.8 mio T

4.2.1 Copper

Copper is one of the few metals which naturally has a visible hue to it (along with gold, caesium and osmium), due to relativistic quantum mechanical effects in the atomic shell. It is the second most conductive metal (with respect both to heat and electrical conductivity) after silver, but is substantially cheaper and therefore often favoured for industrial applications.

Typically, copper occurs either in situ as native copper (often with gold and silver), or in copper sulphides (chalcopyrite and chalcocite), carbonates (malachite) or copper deposits. Copper ore is extracted and concentrated through a process such as froth flotation, where it is ground into a fine grade and mixed with air and reagents which preferentially attract the copper containing compounds. Basically, the copper ore sticks to the bubbles and can be collected from the surface, whereas the waste products are left behind. Very substantial increases can be achieved in this manner, from less than 1% copper in raw ore to 10–15% copper in concentrate is quite feasible. After this, the concentrate grade is sent to a smelter where it is roasted and smelted (heated and made to react with hot oxygenated air to convert the sulphides into oxides) and then eventually reduced to yield impure elemental copper. Finally, the elemental copper is purified by electrolysis (also known as electrowinning) to obtain a grade of copper of the necessary purity (BS EN 1978:1998), generally 99.9% purity, to be called high grade (Grade A) copper.

Major primary producers of copper are Chile, the United States ($\sim$60% Arizona, $\sim$40% others) and Peru. See Table 4.10 for a geographical breakdown. As well as primary production, copper is easily recycled in smelters.

The LME contract for high grade (Grade A) copper is for 25 tonnes of plate cathodes. A typical industrial copper cathode is a large copper

Table 4.10   Primary supply of copper (2009).

	Supply	By country
Chile	5,320 kT	35%
United States	1,310 kT	9%
Peru	1,260 kT	8%
China	960 kT	6%
Indonesia	950 kT	6%
Australia	900 kT	6%
Other countries	4,400 kT	29%
Total mining	15 mio T	100%

Table 4.11   Industrial usage breakdown of copper.

Category	Proportion
Electrical wires	60%
Roofing and plumbing	20%
Industrial machinery	15%
Alloying	5%

sheet about 1/4 to 3/4 of an inch thick, and from 100 to 350 pounds in weight. Once delivered, a copper cathode is melted in a shaft furnace and moulded into cylindrical ingots (often 40 cm in diameter, 10 m in length) which are cut into billets of a manageable length. These can be extruded into copper tubing and wiring, which are used in industry.

Major industrial applications of copper are in the electrical and electronics industries, construction, transport and consumer products, as shown in Table 4.11. A typical car contains 20 to 45 kg of copper, construction of an average house in the USA requires 200 kg of the metal. Within countries such as the United States, housing construction accounts for nearly half the demand for copper, so changes in building starts are of economic importance for the metal. Geographically, Asia is the main consumer of copper, as shown in Table 4.12, and China is the world's largest user of the metal on account of industrialisation, construction and demand both from domestic and export-driven industries. Changes in economic growth forecasts and housing construction are often reflected in price moves in the metal.

LME futures and options are traded on the LME, in contract sizes of 25 tonnes, following the market conventions described earlier in this chapter.

Copper futures contracts are also traded on COMEX – available futures contract months are the current and all 23 subsequent calendar months, together with March (H), May (K), July (N), September (U) and December (Z) futures contracts which fall within the next 60 months starting from today. The COMEX contract size is 25,000 pounds

Table 4.12   Geographical demand of copper (2010).

Category	Proportion
Asia	62%
Europe	22%
North America	10%
Other	6%

of copper and futures trading terminates on the third last business day of the delivery month, and the contract can be physically settled (via delivery of Grade 1 electrolytic copper cathodes, to ASTM grade B115-00) up to the last trading day of the delivery month. American style options are also traded on COMEX, with the expiry date being four business days from the end of the month (though if the expiry falls on a Friday or immediately before a COMEX holiday, it is moved back to the preceding business day).

4.2.2 Aluminium

Aluminium (or aluminum, in the USA and Canada, and sometimes colloquially referred to as "Ali" on the trading floor) is actually the most abundant metal by weight in the Earth's crust. However, it was only discovered in its elemental form in the 1820s and was for a while more expensive than gold on account of the difficulty in extracting it from aluminium containing bauxite ores. This changed with the invention of the Hall–Héroult electrolytic process, devised in 1886 by the two chemists Charles Martin Hall and Paul Héroult and taken very quickly to market by Hall, who opened a production plant in Pittsburgh[8] only two years later. From these beginnings, aluminium has grown to become the most produced base metal worldwide, with 44 million tonnes produced globally in 2012 (in terms of metal production, aluminium is second only to iron, of which 1.9 billion tonnes was produced globally in 2009).

Ground bauxite ore (less than 7 mm) is dissolved in aqueous caustic soda and the aluminium ore (alumina: chemical formula Al_2O_3) is extracted. Following this, the alumina is dissolved in molten cryolite (which lowers the melting point of alumina from $\sim$2,000 °C to slightly under 1,000 °C) and electrolytically separated, using carbon anodes, into aluminium metal and carbon dioxide. This is a fairly energy intensive operation, requiring six to eight kilowatts of electrical energy to produce each pound of aluminium. The cost and availability of electricity therefore plays a major role in the production of aluminium (for example, Iceland – an island country with no possibility of connecting to an electricity transmission network – basically exports its surplus renewable electricity in the form of refined aluminium).

---

[8] The Pittsburgh Reduction Company, which became the Aluminum Company of America in 1907, commonly abbreviated to Alcoa (only made official in 1999).

Table 4.13 Primary supply of aluminium (2011).

	Supply	By country
China	18 mio T	41%
Russia	4,000 kT	9%
Canada	2,970 kT	7%
United States	1,990 kT	5%
Australia	1,930 kT	4%
Other countries	15.2 mio T	34%
Total mining	44.1 mio T	100%

Aluminium, having atomic number 13, is very light for a metal, with a specific gravity[9] of 2.7 and consequently is heavily used in industry. Primary uses of aluminium are in manufacturing of transportation (motor vehicles,[10] bicycles, the aviation industry), consumer goods, construction and building, aluminium cans and kitchen foil.

The major producers of aluminium are, perhaps not surprisingly, the countries with the largest land masses, as can be expected from aluminium's crustal abundance. The leading producers are shown in Table 4.13; consumers in Table 4.14.

High grade aluminium contracts on the LME are for lots of 25 tonnes of high grade alumiunium (generally to 99.70% purity or higher, with no more than 0.20% iron and 0.10% silicon, or to an equivalent grade of purity such as may be specified by the LME in its rule book). The aluminium can be delivered in the form of ingots (12–26 kg), T-bars (no more than 675 kg) or sows (no more than 750 kg).

Aluminium alloy and NASAAC contracts, however, are for contract sizes of 20 tonnes.

4.2.3   Zinc

Zinc, a silvery-grey metal with atomic number 30, is most frequently found in nature as a zinc sulphide, often found in conjunction with lead and silver. The name comes from the German word "Zinke", meaning

---

[9] The lightest metal, lithium, has a specific gravity of 0.534 and therefore floats on water (with specific gravity of unity). The heaviest metal, osmium, has a specific gravity of 22.6. Neither is likely to be encountered in practice, unlike iron (7.85), copper (8.93), gold (19.3) and other common metals.

[10] Certainly responsible for growth in aluminium demand; cars in the USA have an aluminium content of 8.6% in 2009, up from 3% in the 1970s.

Table 4.14 Demand for aluminium (2012).

	Demand	By country
China	21.5 mio T	45%
Europe	8.1 mio T	17%
Other Asia/Oceania	7.6 mio T	16%
North America	6.2 mio T	13%
Japan	1.9 mio T	4%
Latin America	1.9 mio T	4%
Africa	0.5 mio T	1%
Total	47.7 mio T	100%

Table 4.15 Primary supply of zinc (2011).

	Supply	By country
China	3,500 kT	29%
Peru	1,520 kT	13%
Australia	1,450 kT	12%
India	750 kT	6%
United States	720 kT	6%
Canada	670 kT	6%
Other countries	3,390 kT	28%
Total mining	12 mio T	100%

tooth or prong, as zinc solidifies into jagged rough shapes (Schneider, 2012). The metal's extraction is performed similarly to that of copper, involving froth flotation, roasting and electrowinning.

The largest producers of zinc are China, Peru and Australia (see Table 4.15). Zinc is used in galvanisation, alloying and pigmentation. The predominant industrial use of zinc, comprising roughly half of the demand for the metal, is galvanisation. As steel and iron are prone to rust, it is commonplace to deposit a zinc coating onto industrial steel, zinc being more reactive and acting as a sacrificial anode. Alloys including zinc, such as brass, are used in automobiles, in electrical installations and in housing construction. Zinc is used in construction at a much later stage also, in paint – zinc oxide is a commonly used white paint pigment.

The human body contains more zinc by weight than the other metals discussed in this book, between two and four grams, where it plays the part of an essential trace element.[11]

---

[11] It can be found in oysters, lobster and red meat, if you need an excuse to indulge.

Table 4.16   Industrial usage breakdown of nickel.

Category	Proportion
Nickel steel	46%
Nonferrous alloying	34%
Electroplating	14%
Other	6%

Zinc contracts on the LME are for lots of 25 tonnes of special high grade zinc (99.995% purity or higher). It is delivered in the form of ingots of no more than 55 kg apiece, bundled together into parcels on pallets of no more then 1.5 tonnes each.

4.2.4   Nickel

Nickel, a silvery white metal, was first discovered in 1751 by Axel Cronstedt in Germany, originally as a red ore which appeared like a copper containing ore, but from which no copper could be extracted. The metal is generally found either as sulphides or laterites, for which refining techniques differ (sulphides are subjected to flotation, smelting and electrolysis, whereas laterites are directly smelted then electrolysed). Nickel was introduced into steel production in the late 19th century as a constituent of stainless steel, a role it continues to have to this day. Common types of stainless steel include 304-type or 18/8 which is 18% chromium and 8% nickel, and 18/10 stainless steel (18% chromium and 10% nickel) which is commonly used in domestic cutlery.[12]

So, while nickel is also used for electroplating and other minor uses, as described in Table 4.16, by far the primary use of nickel is as a constituent of various alloys, both ferrous (stainless steel) and non-ferrous (nickel brasses and bronzes, among others).

Locationally, the main reserves of nickel are in Australia and New Caledonia; however the major producers are as shown in Table 4.17.

Nickel is also used in fabrication of the 5 cent US coin with the same name, which contains 1.25 g of nickel and 3.75 g of copper (total weight 5 g), though in fact at the time this book was written, there were no longer any operational nickel mines in the United States itself. Given current metals prices, the melt value of the coin is sometimes above the

---
[12] Often stamped on the flatware, now you know what it means.

Table 4.17   Primary supply of nickel (2011).

	Supply	By country
Russia	280 kT	16%
Indonesia	230 kT	13%
Philippines	230 kT	13%
Canada	200 kT	11%
Australia	180 kT	10%
New Caledonia	140 kT	8%
Other countries	540 kT	30%
Total mining	1,800 kT	100%

face value of 5 cents. For this reason, melting or exporting nickels in significant volumes is illegal.

LME nickel contracts are for lots of 6 tonnes of refined primary nickel (99.80% purity or higher). It is delivered in the form of cathodes, pellets or briquettes either shipped as intact cathode sheets (no larger than 1 m × 1.3 m, with thickness between 2 mm and 15 mm) in bundles of no more than 1.6 tonnes, or cut into regular sizes and delivered in drums containing between 150 and 500 kg nickel.

4.2.5   Lead

One metal you do not want in your cutlery is lead. It has several useful properties, such as being resistant to corrosion and being soft and malleable, but it is a central nervous system toxin. So, while it was used in Roman times for plumbing,[13] with some 80,000 tones of lead produced annually for this purpose, lead pipes are no longer legal in much of the world, though some lead pipes and joints with lead-containing solders still exist in older houses.[14]

Lead, having atomic number 82, is one of the heavier[15] base metals encountered. Lead, while a heavy metal, is relatively abundant compared to other elements with similarly high atomic numbers as several isotopes of lead are the final stable endproducts after the radioactive decay of other elements, such as ^{238}U, ^{235}U and ^{232}Th. As a result, the abundances

---

[13] The industry taking its name from the Latin plumbum, for lead.

[14] This is why it is recommended to only use water from the cold water tap, as the hot water system is (a) more likely to have more soldered joints in situ, and (b) the heat is more likely to leach lead into the water from any pipes or joints containing lead.

[15] Liquid mercury has specific gravity of 13.6, so lead, with a specific gravity of 11.35, will float on it at room temperature. Best not to try this on the trading floor.

Table 4.18   Primary supply of lead (2010).

	Supply	By country
China	1,850 kT	45%
Australia	625 kT	15%
United States	369 kT	9%
Peru	262 kT	6%
Mexico	158 kT	4%
Other countries	876 kT	21%
Total mining	4,140 kT	100%

are greater than one would otherwise expect. It is typically found in nature in such ores as galena (lead sulphide), as well as lead carbonate and sulphate.

Lead production levels only reached the level of Roman times again in the 18th century, and with industrialisation and population growth, lead production is currently about one hundred times that of Roman times, at 9.8 million tonnes per year (2010). Approximately half of this is from recycled metal, with the remaining 4.3 million tonnes from primary mining. Table 4.18 shows the geographical breakdown of primary lead production, the discrepancy due to differing statistical sources.

The overwhelming primary use of lead these days is in lead-acid batteries in motor vehicles, with pigments/compounds coming a distant second (this includes glasses, glazes and stabilisers as well as pigments). Table 4.19 shows the typical uses of industrial lead. Lead, either in its pure elemental form or in an alloy, is used in bullets and lead shot as well as its former use for fishing sinkers (progressively being outlawed for environmental reasons). Lead was also once used as an anti-knock

Table 4.19   Industrial usage breakdown of lead.

Category	Proportion
Lead-acid batteries	79.2%
Cable sheathing	1.1%
Rolled and extruded products	4.9%
Shot/ammunition	1.7%
Alloying	2.1%
Pigments and other compounds	7.4%
Gasoline additives	0.1%
Other	3.5%

Table 4.20 Primary supply of tin (2011).

	Supply	By country
China	127 kT	42.4%
Indonesia	78 kT	25.9%
Peru	29 kT	9.7%
Bolivia	20 kT	6.8%
Brazil	10 kT	3.2%
Other countries	37 kT	12.0%
Total mining	301 kT	100%

fuel additive; this use has similarly almost disappeared (with the notable exception of leaded aviation fuel for small piston engine aircraft).

Contracts on the LME for lead are for lots of 25 tonnes of refined pig lead (99.970% purity or higher). It is delivered in the form of ingots (no more than 55 kg), bundled together into parcels of no greater than 1.5 tonnes.

4.2.6 Tin

The history of tin, like copper, dates back to the Bronze Age – hardly surprising, as bronze is an alloy of those two metals. Historically, bronze was produced with a small amount of tin (maybe 2%) but bronze in modern times is more typically 88% copper, 12% tin. Curiously, there are two[16] main allotropes of tin, the first and most common being β-tin (white tin) which is a metal, and α-tin (grey tin) which is a semiconductor more similar to silicon and germanium. Another frequently encountered alloy is pewter, which is comprised of 85% (or more) tin, the remaining composition being metals such as copper, antimony, lead (not found in modern pewter), and less commonly bismuth and silver.

Tin is primarily found in nature as casserite (SnO_2) ore. It is extracted by gravity concentration, then reduced in a furnace followed by electrolysis. Nowadays, it primarily used for solder (the melting point of pure tin being a comparatively low $\sim$232 °C). As much of the global electronics industry is in Asia, this localises demand for tin geographically to that region also.

Worldwide primary production for tin is shown in Table 4.20. It is worth noting that in the 1950s, the top four tin producers were Malaysia,

---

[16] Another two can be produced in the laboratory under conditions of high temperature and pressure.

Table 4.21   Industrial usage breakdown of tin (2011).

Category	Usage	Proportion
Solder	185.6 kT	52%
Tinplate	59.4 kT	17%
Chemicals	55.5 kT	15%
Alloying	17.5 kT	5%
Float glass	7.2 kT	2%
Other	34.3 kT	10%
Total	359.5 kT	100%

the UK, the Netherlands and the USA, in that order. Now, however, other producers such as Indonesia, China and Latin America are very much in the ascendancy.

Tin used to be used for electronics in 60/40 solder (60% tin and 40% lead) and for plumbing in 50/50 solder. However, as a result of the move away from lead solder (for previously discussed environmental reasons), lead-free solders[17] now make up over 50% of the demand for tin, as shown in Table 4.21. Other uses of tin are in tinplate (sheet steel electrolytically coated with a thin film of tin metal, such as in the canning industry), the chemical industry (used in organotin additives to prolong the lifetime of PVC plastics, also as a catalyst for other chemical reactions), alloying (brass and bronze), the production of float glass by the Pilkington process (float glass is floated on top of molten tin), and other miscellaneous applications.

Tin LME contracts are for lots of 5 tonnes of tin (99.85% purity or higher). It is delivered in the form of ingots (12–50 kg), bundled together into parcels of approximately 5 tonnes.

---

[17] Composition varies, and surprisingly many of these alloys have actually been patented – e.g. US Patent 5527628. A typical lead free solder contains 3–4% silver, 0–1% copper and the rest elemental tin. Antimony is sometimes used to reduce the amount of silver required, which makes the alloy cheaper.

5

Energy I – Crude Oil, Natural Gas and Coal

Fossil fuels such as crude oil, natural gas and coal have been known for thousands of years but have only been used for industrial purposes over the past couple of hundred years. In this chapter we treat all three together, describing their features and then discussing how they trade in the financial markets.

For most of history, crude oil was known as an oozy oily substance that seeped from the ground, of various grades from light oils through to thick tars and bitumens which have been discovered on stone tools used by Neanderthals (so the intelligent use of petroleum deposits actually predates our species). Oil has been in commercial use on an industrial scale since the middle of the 19th century, when oil wells were dug in Europe and North America, initially to provide oil for kerosene and oil lamps. Coal has a somewhat longer industrial history; used by Romans in blacksmithing (Freese, 2006) and certainly from the early days of the industrial revolution (e.g. James Watt's invention of the steam engine in 1781) to power steam engines and the like. Natural gas, being gaseous, was rather more mysterious. The smell of methane would have been apparent, but lightning strikes would on occasions ignite the gas and lead to the unusual spectacle of burning flames erupting from the rocks. There is conjecture that the eternal flame burning in the inner temple at the Oracle of Delphi was a result of natural gas emanating from Mount Parnassus, so in a sense the Olympic flame ceremony is a continuation of one of the earliest uses of natural gas by the ancient Greeks.

So, we have three fossil fuels: crude oil, natural gas and coal. A fossil fuel is a hydrocarbon mixture formed in geologically distant times when dead organisms (typically plants, algae or plankton) were buried under mud and sedimentary rocks and subjected to conditions of high heat and pressure. This doesn't happen immediately. The first stage is the formation of a kerogen, which is a dark coloured rock with a somewhat waxy consistency. Kerogen is dense, and typically contains a complex

Table 5.1   Types of kerogen.

Kerogen	Type I	Type II	Type III	Type IV
Biological source	Algae and plankton	Plants and animals	Plants	Organic debris
Geological source	Marine	Marine and terrestrial	Terrestrial	Various
Geochemistry	H-rich, O-poor	Medium in C, H and O	C-rich, H-poor	H-poor, C- & O-rich
H/C ratio	>1.25	<1.25	<1.0	<0.5
O/C ratio	<0.15	0.03–0.18	0.03–0.3	Various
Hydrocarbons formed	Liquid oil	Oil and natural gas	Coal and natural gas	None

mixture of organic chemical compounds containing carbon, hydrogen, oxygen, nitrogen, sulphur and phosphorous.

There are four types of kerogen, which we tabulate in Table 5.1. Of these, only the first three types end up becoming fossil fuels (different types) under the right conditions of geological compactification. The three different populations (Types I, II and III) are illustrated diagramatically in the Van Krevelen diagram (Figure 5.1).

Note that crude oil is generally produced in the marine environment (typically planktons and algaes in the seas and lakes) whereas natural gas and coal are more commonly produced as a result of the sedimentation of terrestrial material. Indeed, approximately half of all oil discovered since 1859 can be dated back to the Cenozoic Era – i.e. within the past 66 million years, after the demise of the dinosaurs (Downey, 2009).

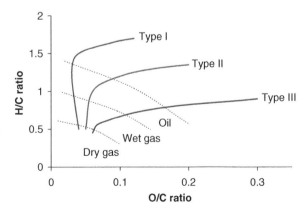

Figure 5.1   Van Krevelen diagrams for Kerogens: Types I, II and III.

In order for the dead organic material to be available as oil today, a sequence of events must have taken place: dead organic matter much have been present and formed into kerogen, the kerogen laden rock must have been buried at a sufficient depth for a suitable period of time, a suitable reservoir rock much have been present to collect the oil, and the deposit must have been located under a suitable cap rock to stop the hydrocarbons leaching to the surface and diffusing away between then and now. This explains why the majority of oil found today was deposited within the Cenozoic. Much of the oil produced in earlier geological epochs has simply had more time to diffuse to the Earth's surface and to be dispersed there.

Coal dates back to various historical epochs, such as the Carboniferous period (360 to 300 million years ago, just before the formation of the supercontinent Pangaea) when enormous tropical coal forests covered the land masses of Euramerica. This was not to last. The rainforests died away 305 million years ago in an event called the Carboniferous Rainforest Collapse, and the dead organic matter decayed in bogs to peat and, eventually, to the coal we find nowadays in the Appalachian region (coal reserves from more recent geological periods exist, such as the Russian deposits which date from the Permian and various other deposits dating from Triassic and Jurassic times).

From Table 5.1 above we see that oil is formed from hydrogen rich, oxygen poor kerogens, whereas coal is formed from carbon rich, hydrogen poor kerogen. This, along with the knowledge that coal, oil and natural gas are solid, liquid and gas respectively, gives us some clues about the chemical composition of these substances. Coal is particularly dense in carbon, typically over 80% carbon (the highest grade of coal, anthracite, being very similar to graphite) with the remaining components being mostly hydrogen and oxygen. Natural gas is comprised of around 82–95% methane (CH_4), 2.5–7.5% ethane (C_2H_6), and smaller proportions of other gaseous alkanes (propane and butane), with small amounts of carbon dioxide and nitrogen (Geman, 2005). Crude oil is a more complicated mixture of various liquid hydrocarbons, generally alkanes, cycloalkanes and aromatic compounds, ranging from naphtha with 5–11 carbon atoms all the way to residual fuel oils with 20–27 carbon atoms. Note that hydrocarbons that are solid at room temperature and pressure contain 25 or more carbon atoms per molecule, and bitumens contain 35 or more – which gives some indication of the molecular size of the constituent components of coal, since bituminous coal or black coal contains bitumen.

Having introduced the origins of the three major types of fossil fuels, we now go into more detail on each separately. Further detail on the petrochemistry and petroleum geology of oil, gas and coal can be found in Downey (2009), Freese (2006), Hantschel and Kauerauf (2010) and Bjorlykke (2010).

5.1 CRUDE OIL

We know from the introduction above that crude oil is a complex mixture of liquid hydrocarbons, generally formed from the organic decay of aquatic algaes and plankton. Our interest in it arises from its energy content. Crude oil typically contains around 42 megajoules of stored energy per kilogram. This is also expressed as the energy content of one tonne of crude oil, 41.868 gigajoules, which we call a tonne of oil equivalent (toe).

A frequently quoted statistic is that oil is the most traded commodity globally, but finding statistics at a global level across all commodities to back this up is difficult. While not going into too much detail, the UN Comtrade website lists various major commodities together with their global trade volumes for the year 2007, which we reproduce here in Table 5.2.

From this, we can see that around 40% of global commodity trade is in crude oil, around 20% is in refined oil products and around 10% is in natural gas. Notably, this list does not include coal or electricity, but it certainly gives an idea of the relative economic size of the various commodity markets.

Table 5.2   UN Comtrade global commodity trade volumes in US dollars (2007).

Category	Traded amount ($ billion)
Petroleum oils (crude)	$1,095
Petroleum oils (non-crude)	$495
Natural gas	$200
Copper	$158
Aluminium	$132.5
Gold	$87
Meat	$43
Wheat and similar grains	$32.9
Milk	$31.6
Cotton fabrics	$25.5
Sugars, molasses and honey	$25
Leather	$23
Coffee and coffee substitutes	$22

Table 5.3   Crude oil relative production by region (2005).

Region	Relative production
Middle East	31%
North America	13%
Latin America	13%
Asia/Pacific	12%
Africa	12%
Eastern Europe	12%
Western/Central Europe	6%

Source: Burger *et al.* (2007).

Table 5.4   Crude oil relative consumption by region (2005).

Region	Relative consumption
Asia/Pacific	30%
North America	28%
Western/Central Europe	20%
Latin America	8%
Middle East	7%
Eastern Europe	4%
Africa	3%

Source: Burger *et al.* (2007).

The total daily production of crude oil is in the vicinity of 85 million barrels a day (2012). The geographic breakdown is heavily skewed towards the Middle East (Burger *et al.*, 2007).

Note that the 12 OPEC countries,[1] including the six largest oil producing countries in the Middle East, are only responsible for around 30 million barrels a day production, about 40% of worldwide production, which we tabulate in Table 5.3. Nevertheless, the price signals provided by the OPEC cartel are still highly influential – the organisation meets twice a year to set target quotas for member countries, in an effort to stabilise oil prices and maintain a steady income to OPEC producers. It is also worth noting that the OPEC countries have current estimated reserves sufficient to maintain production for around 73 years, whereas for non-OPEC states the figure is closer to 13 years.

In contrast, consumption is dominated by Asia/Pacific, North America, and Western/Central Europe, due to the industrial economies in these regions, as shown in Table 5.4.

---

[1] Algeria, Angola, Ecuador, Iran, Iraq, Kuwait, Libya, Nigeria, Qatar, Saudi Arabia, UAE and Venezuela.

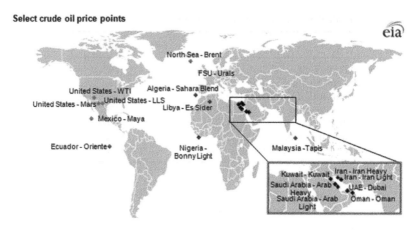

Figure 5.2   Crude oils – production regions. Source: US Energy Information Administration (July 2012).

From this we see that one characteristic of oil is that it is generally produced a long distance away from where it is consumed, some well known crude oil production regions are shown in Figure 5.2. Not only that, but crude oils produced in different locations are certainly differentiated from each other and trade at different price levels. In this section we discuss the various physical and locational factors affecting the various types of crude oil encountered.

The first is density. As the oils are comprised of a complex mix of hydrocarbons liquid at room temperature, the light oils are less dense, being composed of a greater proportion of small chain hydrocarbons than the heavy oils. The light crude oils are closer to transparent in colour, more fluid (i.e. less viscous) and tend to yield greater quantities of the more valuable refined products such as gasoline. The heavy crude oils contain a greater proportion of long chain hydrocarbons and are generally thicker and darker in composition. The standard measurement of density in the oil industry is the °API, which is defined as $141.5/SG - 131.5$, where SG is the specific gravity of the oil (generally less than unity). Since the specific gravity of water is unity, water has a density of 10 °API. The greater the density in excess of 10 °API, the lighter the crude (for example, an extra-light oil with a density of 50 °API will have a specific gravity of $SG = 0.78$, much lighter than water). We tabulate typical density classifications in Table 5.5.

The second is sulphur content, also known as sweetness or sourness, as shown in Table 5.6. As sulphur binds more easily to longer hydrocarbon

Table 5.5 Oil density classifications.

Density	API gravity
Extra-light	>50°
Light	40–50°
Intermediate	30–40°
Medium-heavy	25–30°
Heavy	10–25°
Extra-heavy	<10°

Table 5.6 Oil sulphur content classifications.

Density	%S by weight
Sour	>1.5%
Medium-sour	0.5–1.5%
Sweet	<0.5%

molecules, heavier crudes tend on average to be more sour than the lighter crudes. The sulphur in oil tends to be found as mercaptans and thiophenes, as well as hydrogen sulphide. It is undesirable for two reasons: firstly, the smells are unpalatable to consumers if found in refined oil products,[2] and secondly, the sulphur dioxide (SO_2) emissions are clearly higher from combustion of a sulphur rich fuel. Since sulphur dioxide is a strong pollutant, and a contributor to acid rain, it is removed from the crude oil in a refinery unit called a "sweetener". The added cost of this processing means that sour oils generally need to trade at a discount to sweet oils, to be competitive once these processing costs are taken into account. Density and sulphur content are shown together in Figure 5.3.

The most important, however, is location. The most commonly encountered oils by far are West Texas Intermediate (WTI) and Brent (BR). West Texas Intermediate trades on both the New York Metals Exchange (NYMEX) and the Intercontinental Exchange (ICE), whereas Brent trades predominantly on the Intercontinental Exchange (ICE). Other less frequently encountered crude oils are Dubai and Oman (or an average known as Dubai/Oman), Russian Urals, Malaysian Tapis, Nigerian Bonny Light, Mexican Maya and many others. We tabulate the futures prices for several of the more commonly traded futures in

---

[2] This is not a concern for natural gas, as natural gas actually has mercaptan added to it so that gas leaks can be detected. This is what the characteristic aroma of gas actually is.

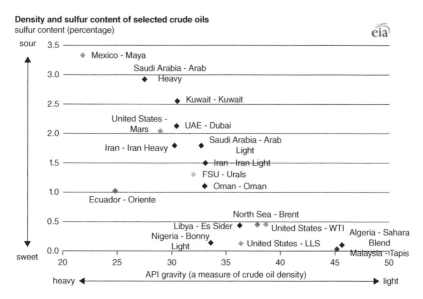

Figure 5.3   Crude oils – density and sulphur content. Source: US Energy Information Administration (July 2012).

Table 5.7, where we clearly see that Malaysian Tapis trades at a premium, on account of being lighter and sweeter than WTI or Brent. Conversely, WCC (Western Canadian Crude) trades at a significant discount, being a heavy oil.

Note that, like the base metals, the futures markets are dominant for the oil contracts. We have a sequence of futures for various calendar months, and the closest futures contract is known as the "prompt future" contract. In early June, typically all the prompt contracts are for the July contract, with the notable exception of Oman oil (for which the July contract ceases trading on the last business day of May). Now, *when* they roll off in June depends on the contract under consideration; we shall discuss the examples of WTI and Brent (the major crude oil contracts).

5.1.1   WTI

West Texas Intermediate (called WTI, and confusingly sometimes abbreviated to "TI" on trading floors) is a light sweet North American crude oil, with an density of 39.6 °API and an approximate sulphur content of 0.24%. It is traded for physical delivery to the transshipment point of Cushing, West Oklahoma, a small town (population 7,826 in the 2010 US census) roughly equidistant between Tulsa and Oklahoma

Table 5.7   Futures prices for various crude oils (4 June 2013).

	WTI	Brent	Oman	WTS	LLS	Mars	WCC	Dubai	Tapis
JUL13	92.60	101.79		92.85	101.80	97.22	74.36	98.28	104.67
AUG13	92.81	101.50	98.64	92.64	100.86	96.81	71.56	97.86	103.80
SEP13	92.90	101.06	98.26	92.42	99.84	96.37	70.21	97.52	103.24
OCT13	92.75	100.66	97.90	92.07	99.05	95.72	69.71	97.21	102.91
NOV13	92.43	100.31	97.57	91.63	98.29	95.07	69.20	96.95	102.51
DEC13	92.01	99.97	97.26	91.14	97.77	94.45	68.62	96.61	100.82
JAN14	91.56	99.66	96.97	90.67	97.27	93.98	68.16	96.33	101.66
FEB14	91.12	99.38	96.69	90.30	96.87	93.61	68.10	96.08	101.36
MAR14	90.72	99.09	96.43	89.79	96.53	93.25	68.04	95.85	101.08
APR14	90.35	98.81	96.15	89.53	96.35	92.99	67.87	95.64	100.71
MAY14	90.04	98.52	95.89	89.27	96.08	92.73	67.76	95.43	100.43
JUN14	89.81	98.23	95.62	88.98	95.88	92.47	67.64	95.22	100.16
JUL14	89.54	97.98	95.35	88.39	95.54	92.14	68.81	94.99	99.83
AUG14	89.24	97.71	95.08	88.08	95.22	91.83	68.99	94.79	99.50
SEP14	88.92	97.40	94.81	87.81	94.95	91.56	69.22	94.57	99.19
OCT14	88.63	97.08	94.54	87.55	94.66	91.31	68.22	94.33	98.88
NOV14	88.38	96.77	94.26	87.34	94.41	91.09	67.76	94.07	98.57
DEC14	88.17	96.45	94.00	86.94	94.01	90.74	67.16	93.79	98.32
JAN15	87.83	96.15	93.75	86.52	93.55	90.42	67.33	93.51	97.95
FEB15	87.53	95.91	93.50	86.28	93.26	90.18	67.34	93.25	97.70
MAR15	87.25	95.70	93.25	86.03	92.96	89.93	67.33	93.02	97.48
APR15	86.99	95.44	93.00	85.83	92.73	89.73	67.63	92.81	97.26
MAY15	86.79	95.22	92.79	85.62	92.49	89.53	67.92	92.60	97.04
JUN15	86.60	95.00	92.60	85.42	92.26	89.33	68.22	92.38	96.82
JUL15	86.38	94.77	92.40	85.22	92.01	89.12	68.51	92.16	96.59
AUG15	86.18	94.55	92.19	85.06	91.83	88.97	67.85	91.97	96.34
SEP15	86.01	94.31	92.00	84.94	91.69	88.85	67.24	91.79	96.12
OCT15	85.88	94.07	91.79	84.84	91.57	88.74	66.14	91.57	95.90
NOV15	85.76	93.85	91.54	84.75	91.46	88.66	65.81	91.38	95.70
DEC15	85.69	93.64	91.29	84.55	91.22	88.45	65.35	91.12	95.54

Source: Bloomberg.

City. The reason for its importance is location, location, location – West Oklahoma is centrally located within North America, almost directly north of Dallas, Texas, and is conveniently located for many pipelines connecting the Gulf Coast oilfields with consumers in the northern and eastern parts of the USA and Canada. We show this in Figure 5.4.

It is important to note (Carollo, 2012) that the North American pipelines are unidirectional, and the oil flow has historically[3] been from south to north. This means that excess inventory at Cushing, when it occurs, cannot easily be diverted southwards to Gulf Coast terminals for

---

[3] The direction of the Seaway crude pipeline was switched in 2012, however, to move oil from Cushing to Houston.

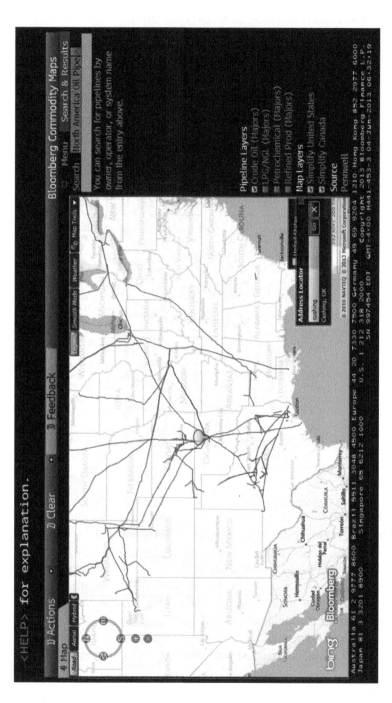

Figure 5.4 Location of Cushing, West Oklahoma, and crude oil pipelines in North America – © 2013 Bloomberg Finance L.P. All rights reserved. Used with permission.

export. This state of affairs was the case from 2011 to the date this book went to print, predominantly due to capacity constraints at Cushing, and is one of the reasons why WTI has been trading at a significant discount to Brent crude oil over that period.

Let us discuss the WTI futures market. As mentioned, WTI trades both on NYMEX and the ICE. The ticker code for WTI on NYMEX is "CL", standing for "Crude, Light". All twelve contract months, i.e. January (F), February (G), March (H), April (J), May (K), June (M), July (N), August (Q), September (U), October (V), November (X) and December (Z), are available for the current year and five subsequent years. For more distant years, out to nine years, only the June and December contracts are listed. Consequently, the JUL14 WTI contract has telequote code "CLN4", where the "CL" denotes crude light, the "N" is code for July, and "4" represents 2014. The "CLZ9" contract denotes December 2019.

WTI futures contracts on NYMEX are for physical delivery of 1,000 barrels, with a tick size of 1 cent. As crude oils are usually priced in US dollars per barrel,[4] this gives a tick value of $10 with a minimum price movement of one cent (which is typical). WTI contracts also trade on the ICE, but these are cash settled. One important difference is that the expiry dates for these two futures contracts differs by one business day. The NYMEX rule is that trading in a named contract month ceases on the 3rd business day prior to the 25th calendar day of the preceding month, whereas the ICE rule is that trading ceases at the close of business on the 4th business day prior to the 25th calendar day of the preceding month. This arises from the requirement that deliveries for a particular month must be notified by the 25th of the preceding month (Schofield, 2007).

In both cases, if the 25th calendar day of that month falls on a weekend or holiday, the first good business day beforehand takes its place in the above calculations. We tabulate these dates for all 12 monthly futures contracts for 2012 (the so-called Cal 12 strip) in Tables 5.8 and 5.9 respectively. A calendar strip is a portfolio of 12 futures or options; other structures with three or six futures/options exist, for example 1Q12, 2Q12, 3Q12, 4Q12, 1H12 and 2H12, corresponding to the four quarterly periods and the two half-yearly periods within calendar year 2012.

It is quite common for market participants to trade a calendar strip of futures or options, which provides exposure to the average price of oil over the course of a year (with monthly averaging).

---

[4] With a few exceptions, e.g. TOCOM.

Table 5.8   Cal 12 WTI-NYMEX strip of futures contracts.

Contract	Expiry date	Cash date	First notice	Delivery dates
JAN12	20-Dec-11	21-Dec-11	22-Dec-11	01-31 Jan-12
FEB12	20-Jan-12	23-Jan-12	24-Jan-12	01-29 Feb-12
MAR12	21-Feb-12	22-Feb-12	23-Feb-12	01-31 Mar-12
APR12	20-Mar-12	21-Mar-12	22-Mar-12	01-30 Apr-12
MAY12	20-Apr-12	23-Apr-12	24-Apr-12	01-31 May-12
JUN12	22-May-12	23-May-12	24-May-12	01-30 Jun-12
JUL12	20-Jun-12	21-Jun-12	22-Jun-12	01-31 Jul-12
AUG12	20-Jul-12	23-Jul-12	24-Jul-12	01-31 Aug-12
SEP12	21-Aug-12	22-Aug-12	23-Aug-12	01-30 Sep-12
OCT12	20-Sep-12	21-Sep-12	24-Sep-12	01-31 Oct-12
NOV12	22-Oct-12	23-Oct-12	24-Oct-12	01-30 Nov-12
DEC12	16-Nov-12	19-Nov-12	20-Nov-12	01-31 Dec-12

Table 5.9   Cal 12 WTI-ICE strip of futures contracts.

Commodity	Futures contract	Expiry date	Cash date
WTI-ICE	JAN12	19-Dec-11	20-Dec-11
WTI-ICE	FEB12	19-Jan-12	20-Jan-12
WTI-ICE	MAR12	17-Feb-12	21-Feb-12
WTI-ICE	APR12	19-Mar-12	20-Mar-12
WTI-ICE	MAY12	19-Apr-12	20-Apr-12
WTI-ICE	JUN12	21-May-12	22-May-12
WTI-ICE	JUL12	19-Jun-12	20-Jun-12
WTI-ICE	AUG12	19-Jul-12	20-Jul-12
WTI-ICE	SEP12	20-Aug-12	21-Aug-12
WTI-ICE	OCT12	19-Sep-12	20-Sep-12
WTI-ICE	NOV12	19-Oct-12	22-Oct-12
WTI-ICE	DEC12	15-Nov-12	16-Nov-12

We also include the "cash date" which I use to denote the date at which either the P/L in the margin account becomes available for physically settled derivatives, or the date at which cash settlement takes place for cash settled contracts. For exchange traded futures[5] and options it is generally the business day immediately after the expiry date (one should check the various exchange websites to be sure). For exchange traded swaps and most OTC products, it is generally five business days after the final fixing date. This is to allow enough time for systems and meters to be checked and for invoicing. This is particularly relevant for

---

[5] For futures, it is somewhat irrelevant for valuation since the margin earns interest and we therefore do not need to discount.

Table 5.10   Cal 12 WTI-NYMEX strip of options on futures.

Contract	Expiry date	Futures date	Cash date
JAN12	15-Dec-11	20-Dec-11	22-Dec-11
FEB12	17-Jan-12	20-Jan-12	24-Jan-12
MAR12	15-Feb-12	21-Feb-12	23-Feb-12
APR12	15-Mar-12	20-Mar-12	22-Mar-12
MAY12	17-Apr-12	20-Apr-12	24-Apr-12
JUN12	17-May-12	22-May-12	24-May-12
JUL12	15-Jun-12	20-Jun-12	22-Jun-12
AUG12	17-Jul-12	20-Jul-12	24-Jul-12
SEP12	16-Aug-12	21-Aug-12	23-Aug-12
OCT12	17-Sep-12	20-Sep-12	24-Sep-12
NOV12	17-Oct-12	22-Oct-12	24-Oct-12
DEC12	13-Nov-12	16-Nov-12	20-Nov-12

physically settled OTC trades, where the actual quantity delivered might be slightly different to the originally intended amount.[6]

Since WTI-NYMEX is physically settled, notification of intention to delivery can occur on any date from the first notice date onwards. A party who is short the futures contract can elect to deliver the oil on any of the acceptable delivery dates, and can notify the exchange (generally no less than two business days prior to delivery) of their intention (notification of delivery intent). The exchange will then find a counterparty with a long position and match the trades together, so any participants with a long futures position should close these out before the first notice date to avoid the risk of delivery (unless, of course, actual physical delivery is desired).

WTI-ICE, on the other hand, is cash settled, so the concepts of first and last notice and delivery dates are irrelevant. The dollar value of contract is financially determined on the expiry date, and cash settlement occurs the next business day.

Options on WTI futures are also traded on NYMEX, such as those in Table 5.10. These expire three business days before the expiry for the underlying futures contract.

5.1.2   Brent

Brent Crude is a European crude oil, containing about 0.37 per cent sulphur, which is what classifies the oil as "sweet". The density is 38.3 °API

---

[6] Ever intended to fill your car with $20 of fuel and accidentally pumped $20.03? Same idea.

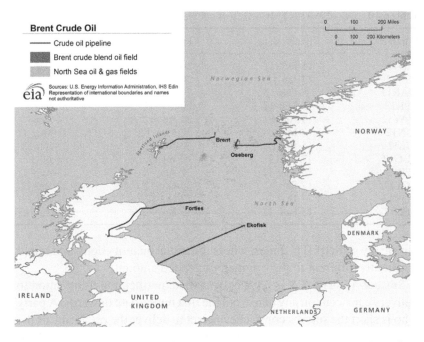

Figure 5.5   Location of Brent Oilfield in the North Sea. Source: US Energy Information Administration (May 2013).

and therefore Brent is a light sweet crude, not too dissimilar from WTI, except located on the other side of the Atlantic Ocean. It is named after the Brent oilfield some 180 km north-east off the Shetland Islands, Scotland (shown in Figure 5.5, together with the Forties, Oseberg and Ekofisk reserves also). In fact, the Brent oilfield was named after the Brent Goose, as Shell originally named all its North Sea oilfields after birds.[7] An important note is that what we call Brent is actually a blend of various deliverable oils from the North Sea oilfields. Pipelines connect the Brent and Ninian oilfields to the Sullom Voe shipping on the Shetland Islands, the Forties oilfield to the Hound Point terminal in the UK, the Oseberg oilfield to the Sture terminal in Norway, the Norwegian Ekofisk oilfield to the ConocoPhillips terminal at Teesside in the UK. The pipelines can be seen on Figure 5.5 also.

Note that the price for oil from the Brent oil stream is not the same as the price for Brent oil. This is because the Brent price is now taken as

---

[7] Auk, Brent, Cormorant, Dunlin, Eider, Fulmar . . .

a composite of the prices of Brent (including Ninian), Forties, Oseberg and Ekofisk oils (the first two in UK maritime territory, the third and fourth in Norwegian waters). The acronym BFOE is sometimes used. The various oils are not all of the same quality; Forties crude oil tends to have the highest sulphur content and the highest production, so it is generally the most likely to be delivered by sellers. Furthermore, actual production from the original Brent oilfields has declined from a peak of slightly over 400,000 barrels per day in the mid 1980s to practically zero now (due to exhaustion of the reserves), which is why the Brent blend was constructed, to keep the benchmark viable.

Originally, in the early 1980s, Brent traded purely on a spot market – the so-called Dated Brent market – and an informal physical forward market. We do need to describe the physical contracts first before discussing the ICE futures contracts, as the futures settle as contracts for differences and involve exercise into an underlying forward position. These are all described in the so-called SUKO 90 contract terms, which can be found detailed on the Shell UK webpage.[8] An understanding of the underlying physical market is definitely beneficial, though the Brent market is complicated and our treatment will necessarily be at a fairly basic level. A very good reference for further reading is Fattouh (2011).

Physical Brent oil is bought and sold with a three-day loading window (also known as the "laydays"). This is very different from the WTI market. Sellers of Brent need to give 25 days' notification[9] before the first day of the three-day loading window. This means that Brent oil for delivery in a loading window commencing 10 to 25 days ahead trades as Dated Brent, where the loading window has already been set. This is also known as a "wet" cargo. Since loading windows are three days long, this means the delivery could be anything from 10 to 28 days ahead.

Longer dated forward trades in physical Brent oil, however, are for delivery in a particular month but where the loading window has not yet been set. These are known as "paper" cargoes and this market is also known as the 25-day market. Generally these trade out to about 12 months. The dates for the loading window need to be nominated by the 5th of the preceding month, which means that the delivery schedule

---

[8] www.shell.com/global/products-services/solutions-for-businesses/shipping-trading/about-shell-trading.html

[9] This used to be a 15-day market until 2002, when Forties and Oseberg grades were added and it was extended to 21 days. Ekofisk was added in 2007 and the notification period was extended even further to a 25-day nomination period in 2012.

is planned by the 15th of the preceding month, at which point the Brent forwards convert into a Dated Brent market.

As the two markets are clearly coupled, Dated Brent is usually priced as a spread to a reference forward contract. Note that the physical contracts are in quite large size, a standard Dated Brent or Brent Forward contract being for 600,000 barrels.[10]

Six hundred thousand barrels of oil is a substantial cargo and the size of this position precludes trading by smaller market participants. As a result, there is a very liquid futures market with a much smaller contract size on the ICE. It is this futures market, and options on those futures, that comprises the largest market for commodity derivatives on Brent oil.

The contract size, like WTI, is 1,000 barrels and the price is in USD dollars per barrel (with a minimum price movement of 1 cent). The main differences are in the geography, the type of oil that is permissible for delivery (the contract is exchange for physical with an option to cash settle), and the specifics of the contract dates. Additionally, the contract settles as a EFP (exchange for physical) against the 25-day BFOE forward market. So, for example, a SEP14 ICE futures contract on Brent will settle by converting into a SEP14 Brent forward contract.

The ICE rule for Brent is that trading in a named contract month ceases on the first good business day immediately prior to the 15th calendar day before the first day of the contract month. Note this is 15 calendar days, not business days, before the contract month commences. The choice of 15 days is, however, somewhat of a historical artifact – when the Dated Brent notification period was 15 days (i.e. before 2002) then 15 calendar days from the last trading day for ICE futures would take us from the last trading day of the futures contract to the beginning of the contract month. Nowadays, the futures contracts expire 10 calendar days too late to obey this relationship; a new Brent NX futures contract[11] has been introduced which is in line with the 25-day BFOE forward market, but this has so far gained limited acceptance.

Trading in options on the futures contracts expires on the third good business day before the expiry of the underlying futures contract. We tabulate the dates for the 2012 futures in Table 5.11 and for options on futures in Table 5.12.

---

[10] Until recently, this used to be 500,000 barrels, a number which is still seen in the literature.
[11] "NX" for New Expiry.

Table 5.11 Cal 12 Brent–ICE strip of futures contracts.

Commodity	Futures contract	Expiry date	Cash date
BR–ICE	JAN12	15-Dec-11	16-Dec-11
BR–ICE	FEB12	16-Jan-12	17-Jan-12
BR–ICE	MAR12	14-Feb-12	15-Feb-12
BR–ICE	APR12	15-Mar-12	16-Mar-12
BR–ICE	MAY12	13-Apr-12	16-Apr-12
BR–ICE	JUN12	16-May-12	17-May-12
BR–ICE	JUL12	14-Jun-12	15-Jun-12
BR–ICE	AUG12	16-Jul-12	17-Jul-12
BR–ICE	SEP12	16-Aug-12	17-Aug-12
BR–ICE	OCT12	13-Sep-12	14-Sep-12
BR–ICE	NOV12	16-Oct-12	17-Oct-12
BR–ICE	DEC12	15-Nov-12	16-Nov-12

Being relatively simple products with only one fixing, oil futures and options are valued with respect to cash valuation one day after the expiry date (without discounting for futures; with discounting for options). While these trade individually, they are often assembled into strips of futures and options for a particular quarter, half-year, or entire year (calendar strip). This allows for monthly averaging. Many market participants, however, prefer to hedge their risk using daily averaging. For this reason commodity swaps (and Asian options and swaptions) are popular.

Oil swaps and other products with arithmetic averaging, however, are treated with a five business day cash settlement period after the final fixing. The question, of course, is what tradeable quote is being

Table 5.12 Cal 12 Brent–ICE strip of options on futures.

Commodity	Futures contract	Expiry date	Futures date	Cash date
BR–ICE	JAN12	12-Dec-11	15-Dec-11	16-Dec-11
BR–ICE	FEB12	11-Jan-12	16-Jan-12	17-Jan-12
BR–ICE	MAR12	09-Feb-12	14-Feb-12	15-Feb-12
BR–ICE	APR12	12-Mar-12	15-Mar-12	16-Mar-12
BR–ICE	MAY12	10-Apr-12	13-Apr-12	16-Apr-12
BR–ICE	JUN12	11-May-12	16-May-12	17-May-12
BR–ICE	JUL12	11-Jun-12	14-Jun-12	15-Jun-12
BR–ICE	AUG12	11-Jul-12	16-Jul-12	17-Jul-12
BR–ICE	SEP12	13-Aug-12	16-Aug-12	17-Aug-12
BR–ICE	OCT12	10-Sep-12	13-Sep-12	14-Sep-12
BR–ICE	NOV12	11-Oct-12	16-Oct-12	17-Oct-12
BR–ICE	DEC12	12-Nov-12	15-Nov-12	16-Nov-12

Table 5.13   Sample WTI futures contract prices on Monday 2 January 2012.

	Futures contract	Maturity date	$f_{0,T}$	$\sigma_{imp}(T)$
CL F2	JAN12	20-Dec-11	91.93	24.09%
CL G2	FEB12	20-Jan-12	91.90	23.97%
CL H2	MAR12	21-Feb-12	91.89	23.87%
CL J2	APR12	20-Mar-12	91.85	23.84%
CL K2	MAY12	20-Apr-12	91.89	23.76%
CL M2	JUN12	22-May-12	91.94	23.69%

averaged over the calendar month – the answer being that we construct the arithmetic average of the prompt contract over the calendar month, i.e. the futures price of the shortest dated futures contract. However, we already know that the futures contract for a particular month generally expires somewhere in the middle of the preceding month. This means that the monthly average will be an arithmetic average of two different futures contracts.

It is easiest to illustrate this with an actual example.

Case Study 5.1

Consider a WTI commodity swap over the month[12] of March 2012, i.e. a MAR12 swap. Suppose the futures curve is given as shown in Table 5.13 and let us suppose the value date is Monday 2-Jan-12.

WTI prices as a (1,0) commodity swap, i.e. the roll dates are included, but Brent prices as a (1,1) swap. I shall illustrate how both (1,0) and (1,1) swaps are priced using the futures curve above, with a strike of $K = 90$.

Basically we construct the schedule of fixing dates, and then take the arithmetic average, but interpreting the futures price on the roll date in one of two ways. For a (1,0) swap we include the prompt future on its roll date, for a (1,1) swap we do not. This is illustrated in Table 5.14, in the case where we have 22 fixing dates over all good business days in March 2012.

The settlement date for this commodity swap is five business days after Fri 30-Mar-12, i.e. on Mon 9-Apr-12 (as 6 April 2012 is a NYMEX holiday). Let us suppose an interest rate of 1%, in which case the

---

[12] I have chosen this month since it has no holidays. In general, holiday dates need to be excluded from the averaging dates.

Table 5.14   Case Study: swap pricing.

Date	F(1,0)	F(1,1)
Thu 1-Mar-12	91.85	91.85
Fri 2-Mar-12	91.85	91.85
Mon 5-Mar-12	91.85	91.85
Tue 6-Mar-12	91.85	91.85
Wed 7-Mar-12	91.85	91.85
Thu 8-Mar-12	91.85	91.85
Fri 9-Mar-12	91.85	91.85
Mon 12-Mar-12	91.85	91.85
Tue 13-Mar-12	91.85	91.85
Wed 14-Mar-12	91.85	91.85
Thu 15-Mar-12	91.85	91.85
Fri 16-Mar-12	91.85	91.85
Mon 19-Mar-12	91.85	91.85
Tue 20-Mar-12	**91.85**	**91.89**
Wed 21-Mar-12	91.89	91.89
Thu 22-Mar-12	91.89	91.89
Fri 23-Mar-12	91.89	91.89
Mon 26-Mar-12	91.89	91.89
Tue 27-Mar-12	91.89	91.89
Wed 28-Mar-12	91.89	91.89
Thu 29-Mar-12	91.89	91.89
Fri 30-Mar-12	91.89	91.89
$A^{A;f}_{0;\{t_1,t_n\}} = \frac{1}{N} \sum_i f_{0,\bar{T}(t_i)}$	91.864545	91.866364
$A^{A;f}_{0;\{t_1,t_n\}} - K$	1.864545	1.866364
$D^d_{0,T_{stl}}$	0.997319	0.997319
V_0	1.859546	1.8613593

discount factor from 2-Jan-12 to 9-Apr-12 is 0.997319 (assuming ACT/365 basis), i.e. with $T_{stl} = 0.268493$.

From this analysis we see that with $K = 90$, a (1,0) MAR12 swap PVs today to 1.859546 ($/bbl) whereas a (1,1) MAR12 swap PVs today to 1.8613593 ($/bbl). Note also that the MAR12 swap price is a linear combination of the futures prices for the APR12 and MAY12 futures contracts.

Note that we have a "swap price" K_{Swap} of 91.864545 and 91.866364 respectively for (1,0) and (1,1) type swap contracts. These contracts are therefore said to be valued at 1.859546 and 1.8613593 respectively, with crossing levels of 91.864545 and 91.866364. More typically, prices for commodity derivatives involving averages will often be quoted with a crossing number closer to a whole number, such as x92 (crossing of 92.00000), which means that the entire futures curve is artificially

Table 5.15   Case Study: Asian option pricing, with (1,0)-style averaging.

i	Date	t_i	$f_{0,\bar{T}(t_i)}$	$\sigma_{m(i)}$
1	Thu 1-Mar-12	0.162	91.85	23.84%
2	Fri 2-Mar-12	0.164	91.85	23.84%
3	Mon 5-Mar-12	0.173	91.85	23.84%
4	Tue 6-Mar-12	0.175	91.85	23.84%
5	Wed 7-Mar-12	0.178	91.85	23.84%
6	Thu 8-Mar-12	0.181	91.85	23.84%
7	Fri 9-Mar-12	0.184	91.85	23.84%
8	Mon 12-Mar-12	0.192	91.85	23.84%
9	Tue 13-Mar-12	0.195	91.85	23.84%
10	Wed 14-Mar-12	0.197	91.85	23.84%
11	Thu 15-Mar-12	0.200	91.85	23.84%
12	Fri 16-Mar-12	0.203	91.85	23.84%
13	Mon 19-Mar-12	0.211	91.85	23.84%
14	Tue 20-Mar-12	0.214	91.85	23.76%
15	Wed 21-Mar-12	0.216	91.89	23.76%
16	Thu 22-Mar-12	0.219	91.89	23.76%
17	Fri 23-Mar-12	0.222	91.89	23.76%
18	Mon 26-Mar-12	0.230	91.89	23.76%
19	Tue 27-Mar-12	0.233	91.89	23.76%
20	Wed 28-Mar-12	0.236	91.89	23.76%
21	Thu 29-Mar-12	0.238	91.89	23.76%
22	Fri 30-Mar-12	0.241	91.89	23.76%

bumped up by a constant offset until the arithmetic average $A^{A;f}_{0;\{t_1,t_n\}}$ equals the crossing level of 92. This is for ease of quotation, as the futures levels will move around intraday.

For other products which depend on an average, such as Asian options and swaptions, the same decision as to whether the (1,0) or (1,1) averaging style is used is required. The choice of which is to be used depends on the commodity and the exchange. An Asian option will generally be cash settled five business days after the final fixing date, whereas an energy swaption will generally have an expiry a few days before the first fixing date.

An Asian option with daily fixings over the course of March 2012 is priced in the manner shown in Table 5.15.

We follow the method of Section 2.7.4 and for simplicity we assume $\rho_{m(i),m(j)} = 1 \; \forall i,j$. We already have the first moment, i.e.

$$\mathbf{E}^d\left[A^{A;f}_{t_1,t_n}\right] = \frac{1}{N}\sum_i f_{0,\bar{T}(t_i)} = 91.864545 \tag{5.1}$$

The second moment is given by computation of (2.128), with the correlation term set to unity, i.e.

$$\mathbf{E}^d\left[[A^{A,f}_{t_1,t_n}]^2\right] = \frac{1}{N^2}\sum_{i,j=1}^{n} f_{0,\bar{T}(t_i)}f_{0,\bar{T}(t_j)}\exp\left(\sigma_{m(i)}\sigma_{m(j)}t_{\min(i,j)}\right)$$

$$= 8529.943575 \qquad\qquad (5.2)$$

We can now compute σ_A by use of (2.129), obtaining

$$\sigma_A = \sqrt{\frac{1}{t_n}\ln\left[\frac{\mathbf{E}^d\left[[A^{A,f}_{t_1,t_n}]^2\right]}{\left(\mathbf{E}^d\left[[A^{A,f}_{t_1,t_n}]\right]\right)^2}\right]}$$

$$= \sqrt{\frac{1}{0.241096}\left[\ln\left(\frac{8529.943575}{(91.864545)^2}\right)\right]}$$

$$= 0.210743$$

We can now price up a call option, with strike $K = 90$ and an initial asset value $f_{0,T^*} = 91.864545$, with time to expiry $T = 0.241096$, discount factor $D^d_{0,T_{stl}} = 0.997319$ and volatility of $\sigma_A = 0.210743$, obtaining

$$V_0 = df(0, T_{stl})[F_{0,T^*}N(\omega d_1) - KN(\omega d_2)]$$

$$= 4.745048$$

This Asian option is therefore valued at \$4.745048 (per bbl) with a crossing level of 91.864545.

Extending the pricing to handle the effect of decorrelation between adjacent futures contracts is trivial, given a suitable choice of $\rho_{m(i),m(j)}$. Pricing off a volatility smile can be handled by using $\sigma_{m(i)}(K)$, i.e. presuming that a volatility smile is given for each future. We shall discuss pricing with skew further in Section 5.1.4.

5.1.3 Calibration of WTI Volatility Term Structure

Let us suppose on Friday 4-Feb-11 that we are given an input set of market quotes in the following form

```
CL H1 91.5 355 375
CL J1 94 705 725
CL K1 96 955 985
CL M1 97 1185 1200
```

```
CL N1 98 1360 1380
CL Q1 98.5 1510 1535
CL U1 99 1660 1685
CL Z1 100 2005 2025

WTI q2 11 atm 97 540/560
WTI q3 11 atm 98.50 795/805
WTI q4 11 atm 99.50 955/975
WTI cal 12 atm 99.50 1190/1220
```

The first eight entries are price quotes for American straddles, whereas the last four entries are price quotes for Asian options.

What this means is that a strip of American straddles with the following parameters can be described in the following manner. Note that strike K and the bid and offer prices in Table 5.16 are all quoted in $/bbl, as is usual.

Table 5.16 WTI calibration inputs – straddles.

Code	Contract	Expiry date	Futures date	K	Bid	Offer
CL H1	MAR11	16-Feb-11	22-Feb-11	91.5	3.55	3.75
CL J1	APR11	17-Mar-11	22-Mar-11	94	7.05	7.25
CL K1	MAY11	14-Apr-11	19-Apr-11	96	9.55	9.85
CL M1	JUN11	17-May-11	20-May-11	97	11.85	12.00
CL N1	JUL11	16-Jun-11	21-Jun-11	98	13.60	13.80
CL Q1	AUG11	15-Jul-11	20-Jul-11	98.5	15.10	15.35
CL U1	SEP11	15-Aug-11	22-Aug-11	99	16.60	16.85
CL Z1	DEC11	15-Nov-11	18-Nov-11	100	20.05	20.25

Futures prices on the value date are given in Table 5.17. Approximating the prices of American straddles by European straddles, and solving

Table 5.17 Sample WTI futures contract prices and inferred volatilities on Friday 4 February 2011.

	Futures contract	Maturity date	$f_{0,T}$	$\sigma_{\mathrm{imp}}(T)$
CL H1	MAR11	22-Feb-11	92.23	27.35%
CL J1	APR11	22-Mar-11	94.33	28.35%
CL K1	MAY11	19-Apr-11	95.88	29.22%
CL M1	JUN11	20-May-11	96.80	29.36%
CL N1	JUL11	21-Jun-11	97.52	29.43%
CL Q1	AUG11	20-Jul-11	98.01	29.50%
CL U1	SEP11	22-Aug-11	98.35	29.50%
CL V1	OCT11	22-Sep-11	98.65	29.40%
CL X1	NOV11	22-Oct-11	98.95	29.30%
CL Z1	DEC11	18-Nov-11	99.26	29.20%

Table 5.18   WTI ATM calibration inputs – Asian options.

Asian option	Start date	Finish date	$f_{0,T}$	K	Bid	Offer
q2 11	1-Apr-11	30-Jun-11	97	97	5.40	5.60
q3 11	1-Jul-11	30-Sep-11	98.5	98.5	7.95	8.05
q4 11	3-Oct-11	30-Dec-11	99.5	99.5	9.55	9.75
Cal 12	3-Jan-12	31-Dec-12	99.5	99.5	11.90	12.20

for those implied volatilities that recover the market prices for these quoted instruments, we obtain the term structure of volatility shown in Table 5.17. Note that the volatilities for OCT11 and NOV11 futures contracts are interpolated.

Note that given the futures curve in Table 5.17, we can value swaps for q2 11, q3 11, q4 11, and cal 12 periods, obtaining 96.99, 98.45, 99.31 and 99.71 respectively for the strikes that make commodity swaps with these strikes costless to enter into.

Generally, what happens here is that quotes for Asian options, such as in Table 5.18, are published with strikes close to the swap values, rounded to the nearest half cent (per barrel). The prices are then quoted as atm prices for Asian options, assuming a crossing level equal to the strike (and therefore the prices for these instruments are quoted as if they are *exactly* at the money).

One thing to note is that since the futures curve is assumed flat, and assumed to be a constant equal to the strike, i.e. $f_{0,T} = F_{0,T} = K$, the Black price for the call and the put will be identical.

As we already have implied volatilities in the MAR11 to DEC11 contract range, we hope and expect to reprice the q2 11 and q3 11 Asian options. Note, however, that the q3 11 Asian option, being a composite of the prompt futures contracts observed over the period from 1-Jul-11 to 30-Sep-11, is sensitive to the volatilities of the AUG11, SEP11, OCT11 and NOV11 futures contracts, due to the rolls. Consequently, we lock down the volatilities obtained from the strangles, and allow the other volatilities to be modified, attempting to reprice the Asian options (assuming crossing level equal to the strike).

Doing so, we find that having $\sigma_{imp}(T)$ of 28.20% for JAN12 to JAN13 contracts, in conjunction with the volatilities given in Table 5.17, suffices to reprice the four Asian options to well within the bid/offer spread. However, the abrupt change in volatility between 29.20% for the DEC11 contract and 28.20% for the JAN12 contract is undesirable. We therefore attempt to fit a smoother volatility function in the range spanning JAN12 to JAN13 contracts, obtaining a form shown in Figure 5.6. Note that if

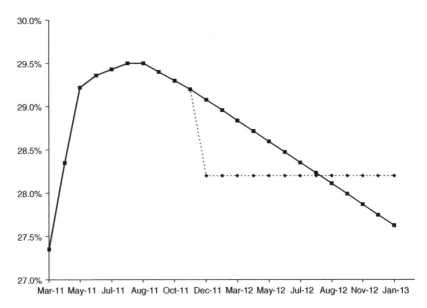

Figure 5.6 WTI ATM volatility term structure calibrated to straddles and Asian options.

Asian options are given for several calendar years out after the end of the straddles, we should be careful to avoid oscillatory behaviour in the calibrated shape for $\sigma_{imp}(T)$ – this can be handled by choosing suitably dampened splines or other similar techniques.

5.1.4   Calibration of WTI Volatility Skew

Up to this point, we have mostly neglected the impact of volatility smile, merely noting that it can be handled by using $\sigma_{imp}(K, T)$ depending on strike K as well as time T, rather than just $\sigma_{imp}(T)$. But how do we obtain such a volatility surface?

The calibration quotes shown above were specifically for at-the-money options, we show below a list of typical quotes that may be seen in the broker market for skew-sensitive options, corresponding to the information presented in Table 5.19.

```
WTI q2l1 125 call X97.00 37/47
WTI 2H11 125.00 Calls X 99.25 1.74/1.91
WTI 2h 11 80/120 fence X99.25 16/31 pp
WTI mar11-jun11 85/105 fence X96.00 43/55 cp
```

```
WTI April1-Dec11 110.00/130.00 C/S x96.50 2.35/2.47
WTI q4 11 125 call X99.75 229/238
WTI 1h 12 75/120 fence X100.25 7/22 cp
WTI Cal 12 90 puts x100.25 785/805
WTI Cal12 x100.25 80.00/120.00 Fence 0/6 pp
WTI APO Cal12 70.00/50.00 PS x100.75 2.20/2.30
WTI Cal12 75.00/120.00 Fence x100.00 1.08/1.22 cp
WTI Apr12-Sep12 135.00 Calls x100.25 2.60/2.80
WTI Cal13 85.00/115.00 Fence X 100.00 -5/+15 PP
```

Table 5.19 WTI skew calibration inputs – Asian options.

Asian option	Strategy	Start date	Finish date	$f_{0,T}$	Strike(s)	Bid	Offer
q2 11	call	1-Apr-11	30-Jun-11	97	125	0.37	0.47
2h 11	call	1-Jul-11	30-Dec-11	99.25	125	1.74	1.91
2h 11	fence	1-Jul-11	30-Dec-11	99.25	80,120	−0.31	−0.16
mar11-jun11	fence	1-Mar-11	30-Jun-11	96	85,105	0.43	0.55
apr11-dec11	call spread	1-Apr-11	30-Dec-11	96.50	110,130	2.35	2.47
q4 11	call	3-Oct-11	30-Dec-11	99.75	125	2.29	2.38
1h 12	fence	3-Jan-12	29-Jun-12	100.25	75,120	0.07	0.22
Cal 12	put	3-Jan-12	31-Dec-12	100.25	90	7.85	8.05
Cal 12	fence	3-Jan-12	31-Dec-12	100.25	80,120	−0.06	0.00
Cal 12	put spread	3-Jan-12	31-Dec-12	100.75	50,70	2.20	2.30
Cal 12	fence	3-Jan-12	31-Dec-12	100	75,120	1.08	1.22
apr12-sep12	call	2-Apr-12	28-Sep-12	100.25	135	2.60	2.80
Cal 13	fence	1-Jan-13	31-Dec-13	100	85,115	−0.15	0.05

The terminology for fences is slightly confusing and we shall explain it here, first by explaining a fence with a single expiry date. A long position in an asset which currently is trading at $F_{0,T}$ can be "fenced in" by shorting a fence, which is also known as a risk reversal in FX. A fence is a structure which is long a call with strike K_C and short a put with strike K_P, requiring that $K_P < F_{0,T} < K_C$. The combination of the long futures position and the fence is equivalent to a long futures position for futures prices between K_P and K_C, but with the downside floored at $K_P - F_{0,T}$ and capped at $K_C - F_{0,T}$.

The fences referred to here are with respect to Asian calls and Asian puts with strikes K_C and K_P respectively, rather than European or American calls and puts. Note also the terminology "cp" and "pp" which refer to "call positive" and "put positive" respectively – i.e. the price for a fence with "cp" is the price for an Asian call minus the price for an Asian put, whereas if it is quoted "pp" that means the quote is the price for an Asian put minus the price for an Asian call.

Call spreads and put spreads are easier. On occasion (not often), 1x2 call or put spreads are encountered – these just refer to call or put spreads where the notional for one strike is twice that of the other.

Generally, while we can obtain a good fit to the ATM instruments through a suitable ATM backbone, the skew instruments will be mis-priced using a volatility surface without smile. Various schemes for constructing volatility smiles are well known in the industry, for example, SABR (Hagan *et al.*, 2002) and polynomial in delta (Clark, 2011). Commodity energy smiles and skews, however, often tend to be more L-shaped than other asset classes, exhibiting linear behaviour in the wings as opposed to smoothly parabolic – and where the smile tapers off below a simple linear extrapolation well out in the wings. As a result, in this section we present a functional specification for the skew which gives a good fit to typical energy volatility skews and which can be easily calibrated to realistic markets.

The model is defined by seven parameters $\{c_0, c_1, c_2, l_1, l_2, l_3, k\}$ (per option maturity) which we attempt to use to fit the volatility smile for options on futures contracts with maturity T. The futures price is denoted $F_{0,T}$. Given a strike K we construct a moneyness

$$m = \frac{K}{F_{0,T}} - 1. \tag{5.3}$$

The form is basically a dampened quadratic in shifted moneyness. So, we define the shifted moneyness m' by

$$m' = m - k = \frac{K}{F_{0,T}} - 1 - k. \tag{5.4}$$

The implied volatility is then given by

$$\sigma_{\text{imp}}(K, T) = c_0 + c_1 m' + \frac{c_2(m')^2}{1 + [l_1 \mathbf{1}_{\{m'>0\}} - l_2 \mathbf{1}_{\{m'<0\}}]m' + l_3 \cdot (m')^2}. \tag{5.5}$$

The dampening terms l_1, l_2 and l_3 serve to provide the facility to tune the smile to capture local quadratic behaviour around the at-the-money strike, but with a degree of flattening for the wings. Note that if $l_1 = l_2 = l_3 = 0$, (5.5) reverts to purely a parabolic function of shifted moneyness. One can reduce this from seven parameters to six by setting $l_2 = l_1$, in which case the denominator of the third term in (5.5) becomes $1 + l_1|m'| + l_3 \cdot (m')^2$, and to five terms by setting $l_1 = l_2 = 0$.

Seven parameters allows for a fit to a five-point smile such as is typically used to mark FX volatility surfaces[13] (10-delta put, 25-delta put, at-the-money straddle, 25-delta call and 10-delta call) together with an extra two points to allow the degree of positive or negative convexity in the extrapolation to be suitably controlled.

Note, however, that c_0 can be directly inferred from σ_{ATMF}. For $K = K_{ATMF} = F_{0,T}$, $m = 0$ and therefore $m' = -k$. Substituting $m' = -k$ into (5.5) and using $\sigma_{imp}(K_{ATMF}, T) = \sigma_{ATMF}(T)$, we obtain

$$c_0 = \sigma_{ATMF}(T) + c_1 k - \frac{c_2 k^2}{1 - k[l_1 \mathbf{1}_{\{k<0\}} - l_2 \mathbf{1}_{\{k>0\}}] + l_3 k^2}. \quad (5.6)$$

This means that calibration of a volatility smile given a particular level for σ_{ATMF} – such as is given using the approach suggested in Section 5.1.3 – can proceed with one fewer degree of freedom in the skew parameters. A typical method involves varying the remaining parameters, i.e. $\{c_1, c_2, l_1, l_2, l_3, k\}$ (one for each option maturity) until the skew-sensitive instruments are all priced to within the bid/offer. Various approaches are taken, from quite manual processes (often spreadsheet based) requiring trader intervention, through to quite automated. Alternatively, if a volatility surface consisting of smiles parameterised by either moneyness or hard strike levels is given, then the decision variables $\{c_1, c_2, l_1, l_2, l_3, k\}$ can be solved for, using a nonlinear least squares minimisation engine such as Levenberg–Marquardt (Press et al., 2002) to obtain as good a fit to the prescribed market as possible using (5.5).

Figure 5.7 shows a typical volatility smile for WTI crude oil, as seen on Thursday 19-Aug-2010 for the DEC10 contract. Model parameters are given in Table 5.20.

Note that this volatility smile is not guaranteed to be arbitrage free, and standard checks should ideally be performed, for example checking that option prices have a monotonic dependency on the strike (call prices decreasing for increasing strike, put prices increasing).

5.1.5   Brent and Other Crude Markets

Quotes for Brent and other crude oils are less frequently encountered than for WTI, for example:

```
Brent K11 110.00 Call x102.50 2.10/2.12 (amer)
```

---

[13] See Clark (2011) or Reiswich and Wystup (2009) for further details.

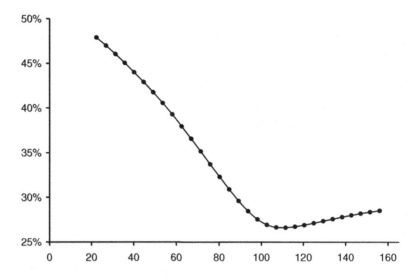

Figure 5.7   WTI volatility skew for DEC10 contract as of 19 August 2010.

As a result it is quite commonplace to fit derived volatility surfaces to Brent and other crude markets by reference to a "marker crude" such as WTI. Generally the same two-step procedure is followed: (i) the ATM structure is obtained, often by applying a simple spread in volatility terms to the ATM vols for WTI, and then (ii) a skew is fitted.

A sample set of volatility offsets is given in Table 5.21 below, as of late October 2010. As new Brent, Tapis or Dubai quotes become available, the spreads may need to be updated – the spreads here were marked during 3Q10 when Brent and Tapis were trading above WTI while Dubai was trading below. Generally, for crude oils which trade at

Table 5.20   Volatility skew model parameters for DEC10 WTI contract as of 19 August 2010.

T	0.252055
$f_{0,T}$	89.22
c_0	0.268419
c_1	−0.071669
c_2	0.745371
l_1	3.987475
l_2	0.863395
l_3	2.994692
k	0.162068

Table 5.21 ATM vols for other crudes marked by reference to WTI.

	WTI Swap vol	Brent/Tapis Diff	Brent/Tapis Swap vol	Dubai Diff	Dubai Swap vol
Nov10	29.48%	−0.85%	28.63%	−2.50%	26.98%
Dec10	30.02%	−0.80%	29.22%	−2.50%	27.52%
1q11	31.62%	−0.80%	30.82%	−1.75%	29.87%
2q11	32.13%	−0.60%	31.53%	−1.25%	30.88%
3q11	31.83%	−0.50%	31.33%	−0.75%	31.08%
4q11	30.98%	−0.40%	30.58%	−0.50%	30.48%
h112	29.42%	−0.35%	29.07%	−0.25%	29.17%
h212	27.65%	−0.35%	27.30%	0.00%	27.65%
h113	26.26%	−0.30%	25.96%	0.00%	26.26%
h213	25.26%	−0.30%	24.96%	0.00%	25.26%
h114	24.59%	−0.25%	24.34%	0.00%	24.59%
h214	24.12%	−0.20%	23.92%	0.00%	24.12%
h115	23.83%	−0.15%	23.68%	0.00%	23.83%
h215	23.63%	−0.10%	23.53%	0.00%	23.63%
h116	23.49%	0.00%	23.49%	0.00%	23.49%
h216	23.40%	0.00%	23.40%	0.00%	23.40%

price levels above WTI, the volatilities tend to be lower, as the volatilities are lognormal volatilities and in order to preserve a constant offset in arithmetic terms between the various crudes then the volatility for the commodity trading at the higher price level needs to be commensurately lower (see the note at the end of this section).

As for the volatility skew, given the paucity of skew-sensitive instruments in the other crude oils, this usually proceeds by taking the skew for WTI and applying it to the ATM vol backbone for the other crude oils, obtained as above. Note that the scaling can be one of two types, an arithmetic shift or a multiplicative shift, i.e. if the volatility smile $\sigma_{imp}(K_{WTI}, T)$ for WTI is given by (5.5) then we can define a volatility smile for the other crudes by setting a scale parameter $\lambda = \sigma_{ATMF;Crude}(T)/\sigma_{ATMF;WTI}(T)$ and then putting

$$\sigma_{imp}(K_{Crude}, T) = c_0' + c_1'm' + \frac{c_2'(m')^2}{1 + [l_1 \mathbf{1}_{\{m'>0\}} - l_2 \mathbf{1}_{\{m'<0\}}]m' + l_3 \cdot (m')^2}$$

where $c_i = \lambda c_i$ for $i = 0, 1, 2$ and $m' = \frac{K_{Crude}}{F_{0,T}} - 1 - k$ where $F_{0,T}$ refers to the forward price for the other crude contract (not WTI).

One point to note is that if two assets (e.g. WTI and Tapis) are trading at different price levels, e.g. $F_{0,T}^{(1)}$ and $F_{0,T}^{(2)}$ for WTI and the derived crude respectively, but driven by the same lognormal volatility σ (we can assume the two Brownians to be highly correlated), then an arithmetic move of $\sigma F_{0,T}^{(1)}$ in the first asset is likely to occur in conjunction with an arithmetic move of $\sigma F_{0,T}^{(2)}$ in the second asset. If we wish to choose an ATM scale factor such that the two assets move by the same amount in arithmetic terms, then we should choose σ_2 such that $\sigma_1 F_{0,T}^{(1)} = \sigma_2 F_{0,T}^{(2)}$, i.e. $\sigma_2 = \sigma_1 \cdot F_{0,T}^{(1)} / F_{0,T}^{(2)}$, which leads to a scale factor $\lambda = F_{0,T}^{(1)} / F_{0,T}^{(2)}$. This can be used to estimate these scaling factors for various maturities T, and thereby construct volatility spreads such as shown in Table 5.21.

5.1.6 A Note on Correlation

The pricing of Asian options and swaptions clearly depends on correlation. Rather than attempt to fit an entire correlation matrix, a useful parameterisation is given by the following

$$\rho_{ij} = \begin{cases} \alpha^{|i-j|} \times \beta^{N - \frac{i+j}{2}} & \text{if } i \neq j \\ 1 & \text{if } i = j \end{cases} \tag{5.7}$$

where ρ_{ij} is an $N \times N$ matrix.

Table 5.22 shows a 12×12 correlation matrix, using the form proposed in (5.7). One can see that it has a high degree of pairwise correlation, but with somewhat more decorrelation between adjacent contracts in the short end than adjacent contracts in the long end. This is typical for futures contracts and is exactly the sort of behaviour we intend to capture.

5.2 NATURAL GAS

Natural gas (or natgas), mostly methane, was originally a hazard encountered in coal mining. A flammable gas known as "fire damp" or "coalbed methane", this was particularly dangerous in the days when miners descended into the tunnels using lamps with naked flames. As a result it was feared and generally burnt off where possible.

While sometimes associated with coal, it is more commonly found together with oil (when it is known as "associated gas"). If no oil is found in conjunction with the gas, it is known as "non-associated gas". In the early days of the oil industry, natural gas was regarded as a superfluous by-product and burned off at the well head. Nowadays, however, it is extracted and sold for its energy content. Natural gas with a relatively high proportion of methane is known as "dry gas" whereas if there are

Table 5.22 Sample correlation matrix ($\alpha = 0.992$, $\beta = 0.994$ and $N = 36$).

1.0000	0.9313	0.9266	0.9219	0.9173	0.9127	0.9082	0.9036	0.8991	0.8946	0.8901	0.8856
0.9313	1.0000	0.9369	0.9322	0.9275	0.9229	0.9182	0.9136	0.9091	0.9045	0.9000	0.8955
0.9266	0.9369	1.0000	0.9425	0.9378	0.9331	0.9284	0.9238	0.9192	0.9145	0.9100	0.9054
0.9219	0.9322	0.9425	1.0000	0.9482	0.9435	0.9387	0.9340	0.9294	0.9247	0.9201	0.9155
0.9173	0.9275	0.9378	0.9482	1.0000	0.9539	0.9492	0.9444	0.9397	0.9350	0.9303	0.9256
0.9127	0.9229	0.9331	0.9435	0.9539	1.0000	0.9597	0.9549	0.9501	0.9453	0.9406	0.9359
0.9082	0.9182	0.9284	0.9387	0.9492	0.9597	1.0000	0.9655	0.9607	0.9558	0.9511	0.9463
0.9036	0.9136	0.9238	0.9340	0.9444	0.9549	0.9655	1.0000	0.9713	0.9665	0.9616	0.9568
0.8991	0.9091	0.9192	0.9294	0.9397	0.9501	0.9607	0.9713	1.0000	0.9772	0.9723	0.9674
0.8946	0.9045	0.9145	0.9247	0.9350	0.9453	0.9558	0.9665	0.9772	1.0000	0.9831	0.9782
0.8901	0.9000	0.9100	0.9201	0.9303	0.9406	0.9511	0.9616	0.9723	0.9831	1.0000	0.9890
0.8856	0.8955	0.9054	0.9155	0.9256	0.9359	0.9463	0.9568	0.9674	0.9782	0.9890	1.0000

substantial amounts of ethane, butane or propane[14] also, then the gas is known as "wet gas". Generally, wet gas is more likely to be associated gas, which makes sense on account of the heavier liquid hydrocarbons in proximity.

Once obtained from the ground, any water and impurities are removed in a natural gas processing plant – see Section 2.1 of Edwards (2010) for a discussion of the physical aspects of natural gas production. As the natural gas will be transported through pipelines at greater than atmospheric pressures, it is important that the NGLs be removed also (otherwise these will liquefy in situ in the pipeline).

Unlike oil or coal (liquids and solids respectively), measurement of natural gas is a little more involved. There are two main ways to measure commercial amounts of natural gas – one being volumetric and one being with respect to the energy content.

The usual volumetric measure, used in North America, is cubic feet (cf). This refers to the volume occupied by the gas at a temperature of 60 °F and an absolute pressure of 14.73 pounds per square inch (psi) (which is only slightly in excess of atmospheric pressure at sea level). Note that this is not standard temperature and pressure, which is 0 °C and an absolute pressure of 101.325 kPa (i.e. 14.696 psi). Clearly the units are usually scaled up to industrial size, e.g. Mcf (thousand cubic feet), MMcf (million cubic feet), Bcf (billion cubic feet), etc.

The energy content of a certain volume of natural gas does, however, vary depending on the chemical composition. As a result, it is quite commonplace to use the energy content as an alternate measure of the amount of natural gas to be bought or sold. The British thermal unit (Btu) is the amount of energy required to raise the temperature of one pound of water from 60 °F to 61 °F – this is equivalent to about 1055.056 joules. One million Btu is denoted 1 MMBtu and is equivalent to 1055.056 megajoules, while a common measure for consumer markets and some financial markets is the therm, which is 100,000 Btu (or 0.1 MMBtu).

A cubic foot of dry natural gas contains approximately 1 Btu of stored energy, so we can roughly equate 1 Mcf of natural gas to 1 MMBtu. The average energy contents (by volume) vary from year to year, and can be seen on the "Annual Energy Review" published by the EIA. Cubic

---

[14] These three being known as the natural gas liquids, or NGLs – being liquids at underground pressures but gaseous at standard temperature and pressure. Butane and propane are also found in conjunction with oil, see Chapter 6, and are usually turned into liquefied petroleum gas (LPG).

feet, as a measure, are generally used for indicative quotes, while actual trade confirmations are mostly with respect to energy content.

We quote an interesting statistic from Edwards (2010) – a gallon of gasoline contains 124,000 Btu of stored energy and only occupies about 0.14 cubic feet of space, whereas in uncompressed form the same energy equivalent of natural gas would take up about 100 cubic feet. If compressed to 250 atm the natural gas would still require 0.42 cubic feet – plus a heavy robust pressurised cylinder of the sort typically seen in scuba diving. From this we see the practical value of gasoline/petrol as an easily portable fuel, though one advantage natural gas has over gasoline/petrol and diesel is that it is a less polluting fuel. This, in conjunction with the readily available supply, means that natural gas is expected by many to gain greater market share in satisfying consumer demand for energy in future years.

As well as delivery by pipeline, natural gas can also be liquefied and converted to liquefied natural gas (LNG), requiring storage at very low temperatures, i.e. −161 °C. This is predominantly used for transportation via cryogenic LNG tankers via ocean shipping routes. For consumers, e.g. automobiles, compressed natural gas (CNG) is sometimes used, where the natgas is compressed but kept at ambient temperature, which means it still exists in gaseous form. Since CNG requires a greater volume for storage within the automobile compared to liquid fuels, vehicles powered by LNG have a shorter range and this fuel is therefore more suited to vehicles that operate in the urban environment where the environmental benefits are more directly apparent, e.g. taxicabs and urban buses. Neither CNG nor LNG should be confused with LPG.

Similarly to oil, natural gas contracts are traded in various geographical regions. Cash and financial aspects of natural gas markets are well described in Sturm (1997). The most liquid contract is the Henry Hub contract on the NYMEX for delivery of natural gas to the pipeline interconnector at Henry Hub, located near the town of Erath, Louisiana. Erath, like Cushing, is not a large city or town; in the 2010 census, the population of Erath was 2,114. We show its location in Figure 5.8 along with the natural gas pipeline network in North America.

Other North American natural gas contracts do certainly trade, such as KCBT Waha, NYMEX Permian and NGX AECO-C Alberta price (among others), but these are significantly less liquid and are generally priced by reference to NYMEX Henry Hub prices plus a basis. Natural gas contracts in other countries are treated similarly, though there are

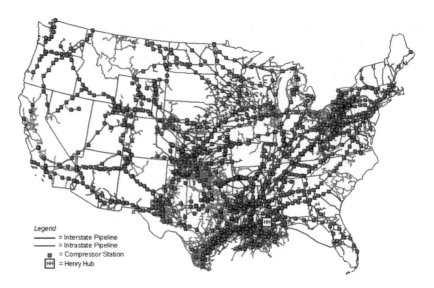

Figure 5.8   North American natgas pipelines and Henry Hub.

certainly distinguishing features – for example, North Sea natural gas is priced for delivery into or from the UK via the virtual National Balancing Point (NBP), whereas Zeebrugge natural gas is priced for physical delivery via Zee Beach in Belgium. Many other markets and delivery locations exist. For now we shall merely describe the most important natural gas contract, Henry Hub, with reference to both futures and options.

Henry Hub futures contracts on NYMEX are for physical delivery of natural gas containing 10,000 MMBtu of extractable energy, into the Henry Hub pipeline complex operated by Sabine Hub Services at Erath, Louisiana. The ticker code for Henry Hub natural gas on NYMEX is "NG", and all 12 contract months are available for the current year and the next 12 calendar years, i.e. for January (F), February (G), March (H), April (J), May (K), June (M), July (N), August (Q), September (U), October (V), November (X) and December (Z).

NG futures contracts on NYMEX are priced in US dollars per MMBtu, with a tick size of 0.1 cents per MMBtu, which corresponds to a tick value of $10.00.

A natgas futures contract also trades on the ICE, but is cash settled and is for a smaller contract size of 2500 MMBtu. Unlike WTI, the ICE futures contract has the same expiry date as the NYMEX contract.

Table 5.23   Cal 12 NG-NYMEX strip of futures contracts.

Contract	Expiry date	Cash date	Delivery dates
JAN12	28-Dec-11	29-Dec-11	01-31 Jan-12
FEB12	27-Jan-12	30-Jan-12	01-29 Feb-12
MAR12	27-Feb-12	28-Feb-12	01-31 Mar-12
APR12	28-Mar-12	29-Mar-12	01-30 Apr-12
MAY12	26-Apr-12	27-Apr-12	01-31 May-12
JUN12	29-May-12	30-May-12	01-30 Jun-12
JUL12	27-Jun-12	28-Jun-12	01-31 Jul-12
AUG12	27-Jul-12	30-Jul-12	01-31 Aug-12
SEP12	29-Aug-12	30-Aug-12	01-30 Sep-12
OCT12	26-Sep-12	27-Sep-12	01-31 Oct-12
NOV12	29-Oct-12	30-Oct-12	01-30 Nov-12
DEC12	28-Nov-12	29-Nov-12	01-31 Dec-12

The NYMEX rule is that trading in a named natural gas contract month ceases on the third business day prior to the first calendar day of the delivery month. What this means is that the final week of the month is generally the busiest time in the natgas markets, and has become known as "bid-week". We tabulate these dates for all 12 monthly futures contracts for 2012 in Table 5.23.

As energy prices are somewhat volatile, it is relatively common for a particular type of commodity swap to be traded for natural gas, the so-called "L3D" swap, which involves the purchase or sale of a certain amount of natural gas (measured in MMBtu) at a price determined by the arithmetic average over the last three days (L3D) that the futures contract is actually traded. So, for example, a L3D AUG12 swap would take the average of the AUG12 prices over the three dates Wed 25th, Thurs 26th and Fri 27th July rather than fixing against purely the 27-Jul-12 fixing. Note the difference with oil, where all the good business days of the month of August are used to sample the price of the prompt futures contract.

Unlike WTI oil, the delivery is scheduled for continuous delivery over the named contract month, i.e. for $10,000/N$ MMBtu per day delivered over the N calendar days of the delivery month, being 10,000 MMBtu in total.

Options on Henry Hub futures contracts trade on NYMEX, the expiry date being the business day before the futures contract expiry date.

One major difference between natural gas and oil is that futures contracts on natural gas display strong seasonality in much of the world, largely because natural gas is often used for heating. We show the price

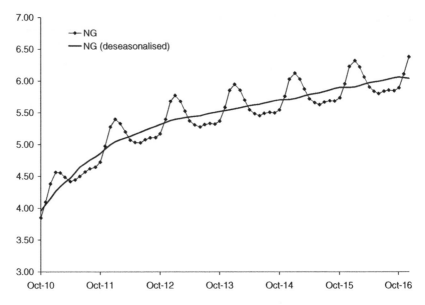

Figure 5.9 Natural gas futures curve as of 7 September 2010, demonstrating seasonality.

($/MMBtu) for Henry Hub natgas futures in Figure 5.9, noting the seasonal price peaks in the winter – generally highest for January contracts.

This is the first example of seasonality we have seen. It is a common technique in commodities to deseasonalise curves to remove predictable seasonal variation, Figure 5.9 also shows the deseasonalised forward curve, which we construct using the method below.

5.2.1 Deseasonalising Forward Curves

We start by constructing centred 12-month moving averages for the futures data in Figure 5.9, which extends from the OCT10 to the DEC16 futures contract. A centred 12-month moving average can be constructed by

$$\bar{F}_{0,T_i} = \frac{1}{12}\left[\frac{1}{2}F_{0,T_{i-6}} + F_{0,T_{i-5}} + \cdots + F_{0,T_{i+5}} + \frac{1}{2}F_{0,T_{i-6}}\right]. \quad (5.8)$$

This means that the moving average for JUL12, for example, is an average of all the futures prices from FEB11 to DEC11 (both with weights of 1/12), together with JAN11 and JAN12 futures prices (each with weight of 1/24). Since we need to work within an interior window

Table 5.24 Deseasonalising natural gas forward curves.

	2011	2012	2013	2014	2015	2016	$\bar{R}_i$	R'_i	ϕ_i
JAN		1.077	1.073	1.068	1.066	1.065	1.0697	0.9348	0.9347
FEB		1.055	1.051	1.048	1.047	1.046	1.0493	0.9530	0.9529
MAR		1.021	1.019	1.018	1.017	1.017	1.0184	0.9820	0.9819
APR	0.990	0.989	0.988	0.988	0.988	0.988	0.9884	1.0118	1.0117
MAY	0.979	0.975	0.974	0.974	0.974	0.975	0.9752	1.0254	1.0253
JUN	0.976	0.967	0.965	0.966	0.966	0.967	0.9679	1.0331	1.0330
JUL	0.976	0.970	0.969	0.970	0.971		0.9713	1.0295	1.0294
AUG	0.973	0.970	0.970	0.971	0.971		0.9710	1.0299	1.0298
SEP	0.965	0.966	0.965	0.967	0.968		0.9662	1.0350	1.0349
OCT	0.971	0.972	0.971	0.972	0.974		0.9721	1.0287	1.0285
NOV	1.011	1.011	1.008	1.007	1.009		1.0091	0.9910	0.9909
DEC	1.063	1.059	1.053	1.052	1.052		1.0558	0.9471	0.9470

excluding the first and last six months, we shall only be able to populate the centered 12m moving average from APR11 to JUN16.

Having obtained this, we take the ratio $R_{T_i} = \dfrac{\bar{F}_{0,T_i}}{F_{0,T_i}}$ and index by calendar month. Let us use $R_{i,j}$ to denote this ratio for the ith month and jth year, and we then use $\bar{R}_i$ to denote the arithmetic average of $R_{i,j}$ for those calendar years for which we have entries in the tableaux.

Define $R'_i = 1/\bar{R}_i$, i.e. the reciprocal, and finally we obtain the deseasonalising factors ϕ_i by normalising appropriately

$$\phi_i = \frac{R'_i}{\sum_{j=1}^{12} R'_j} \tag{5.9}$$

We tabulate the ratios $R_{i,j}$ together with the deseasonalising factors ϕ_i in Table 5.24.

These factors ϕ_i are used as multiplicative corrections, i.e. we just take $F_{0,T}$ and multiply it by whichever ϕ_i corresponds to that particular month for each T, thereby obtaining a deseasonalised futures curve such as shown in Figure 5.9. Other methods do exist, of course, this being just one of them.

While the forward curve exhibits clear seasonality, the prompt futures price – c.f. Figure 5.10 – does not look anywhere near as seasonal, as mentioned in Edwards (2010). Instead, the short-term behaviour which tends to drive the prompt futures price is more affected by shocks such as extreme weather events and energy spikes (such as were seen in 2008).

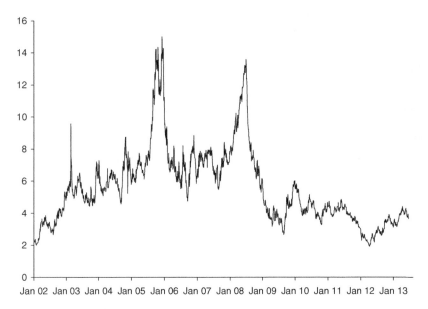

Figure 5.10   Natural gas – Henry Hub prompt futures prices.

Once an appropriate forward curve has been established, possibly employing techniques of deseasonalisation to interpolate missing or illiquid data and then reintroducing the seasonal factors, we need a volatility surface in order to price options on natural gas.

A typical market quote for natural gas is shown below:

```
q3 08 NG 12.55 call X-12 40/60
```

This means that a strip of 3Q2008 natural gas Asian call options (i.e. for July, August and September 2008) with a strike $K = 12.55$ and a crossing level of $12 (i.e. with the swap being costless to enter into with $K_{\text{Swap}} = 12$) has a bid of $0.40 and an offer of $0.60. Generally, the swap is calculated on the basis of L3D.

Similar methods to those for crude oil can be used to mark a natural gas volatility smile (or skew); we show in Figure 5.11 a typical volatility skew for the AUG08 natgas contract, as viewed from early June 2008.

5.3   COAL

A good overview of coal trading can be found in Croucher and Gillespie (2000). About 80% of all coal mined is used near to where it is extracted

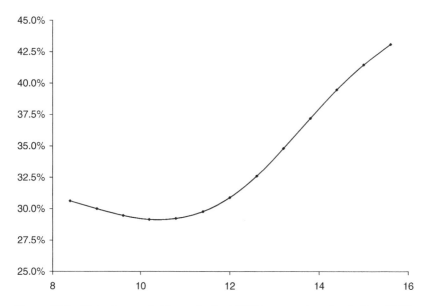

Figure 5.11   Natural gas volatility smile for AUG08 contract (as of early June 2008).

from the ground (Edwards, 2010) – primarily for electricity generation or steel production. Coal is, per energy unit, significantly cheaper than natural gas or crude oil. It is, however, heavier and more costly to transport, and more polluting than the other fossil fuels. As a result, coal is less important on the financial markets than the other energy commodities.

Nevertheless, there are three primary coal contracts which are traded, geographically based around the three busiest coal hubs: Rotterdam (Europe), Richards Bay (South Africa) and Newcastle (Australia).

API2 – for delivery to ARA (Amsterdam, Rotterdam, Antwerp), quoted cif (i.e. including cost, insurance and freight). Based on an Argus and McCloskey group index.

API4 – for shipment from Richards Bay, South Africa, quoted fob (free on board). Another Argus and McCloskey group index.

globalCOAL NEWC – for shipment from Newcastle, Australia, quoted fob. This is based on an index published by www.globalcoal.com – a coal trading platform. Note that the Argus and McCloskey group offer API5 and API6 coal indices for Newcastle trading also.

Approximately 90% of all coal trades are priced with reference to either API2 or API4 benchmarks. Note that the "API" stands for All Publications Index.

New contracts were being introduced at the time this book was in preparation. For example, a new API8 contract is available for delivery of coal to South China cfr (including cost and freight), and an API10 fob contract is available for shipments of coal from Puerto Bolivar, Colombia.

Coal prices are quoted in US dollars per metric tonne, for coal of either 5,500 or 6,000 kcal/kg. Most contracts are for notionals of 1,000 tonnes. However, as is typical for the commodities discussed in this chapter, no spot prices exist. API2 and API4 futures trade on the ICE, with expiry on the last Friday of the delivery month (except when the contract is for a quarter, season or calendar year as opposed to a month, in which case the expiry is on the last Friday of the first month in the delivery period). Global Coal Newcastle coal futures trade also, with expiry on the last Friday of the delivery month or on the last Friday in the delivery period (this being somewhat different to the ICE expiry rule).

While coal futures and options on futures exist, the bulk of the trade is in coal swaps and swaptions. One complicating feature is that, unlike most other commodity swaps, the fixings for coal swaps are weekly (on Fridays), with monthly settlement. There is a market for coal swaptions also.

Note that the expiry date for options and swaptions on coal is days before the first date of the underlying coal futures or swap contract (or the immediately preceding business day if that falls on a holiday). For example, the expiry date for the Cal 13 coal swaption is Friday 30 November 2012 since the first date for the Cal 13 coal swap is Tuesday 1 January 2013 (even though this is not actually a fixing date, since it is not a Friday), and 30 days before 1 January 2013 is Sunday 2 December 2012. Rolling backwards to the first good business day takes us to Friday 30 November 2012.

Fitting a volatility term structure for coal involves trying to back out a self-consistent term structure that recovers the prices for Asian options and swaptions.

A typical set of market quotes, dated as of 17 January 2011, is seen below.

```
Coal API2 Back Half 2011 $145.00 ASIAN calls 3.65-4.25
crossing 119.00. Monthly Settlement I see 28.9-30.8%
```

```
Coal API2 Cal 12 130.00 call 4.40-4.95...crossing
  115.00
Expiry 02/12/11 5pm London
I see 23.0-24.0%

Coal API2 Cal 13 105.00 put TRADES 6.80...crossing
  120.00
Expiry 30/11/12 5pm London
I see 21.4%
6.50-7.00 on the follow.
```

The broker quotes above are interpreted as prices for one Asian option (back half 2011) and two swaptions (Cal 12 and Cal 13 respectively). This can be interpreted as saying that an Asian call option on coal with strike $K = 145$ for the six months from July to December 2011 (assuming weekly fixings on Fridays) has a bid/offer price of \$3.65/\$4.25 (assuming the crossing level of \$119/tonne), which is consistent with a bid/offer volatility of 28.9/30.8%. For the swaption quotes, a call swaption (i.e. a commodity payer swaption) to enter into a Cal 12 swap on Friday 2 December 2011 with strike $K = 130$ is priced at \$4.40/\$4.95 (with crossing \$115/tonne), consistent with bid/offer volatility of 23.0/24.0%.

We can fit a relatively smooth term structure of volatility to reprice these instruments, though note that what we need to do is assume a flat futures curve in each of these three cases (where the futures prices is given by the crossing level, for each quote), but assuming the *same* volatility term structure.

Following this approach we can arrive at a smoothed form that suffices to reprice the broker quotes for coal Asians and swaptions, such as is illustrated in Figure 5.12. There is quite a lot of flexibility in choosing the exact shape of the volatility curve, generally one chooses to minimise oscillations and to fit a shape that looks more similar to typical commodity volatility surfaces (generally higher in the short end, with the Samuelson effect leading to lower volatilities for longer dated futures).

Coal volatilities are generally lower than oil or natural gas, largely because coal is much harder to transport (while easier to store) and the major consumers tend to be continuously operating power plants, the operators of whom tend to prefer long-term supply contracts. API2 tends to have the highest implied volatility, as API4 and the Newcastle contracts include insurance and freight, which stabilises the price to some extent.

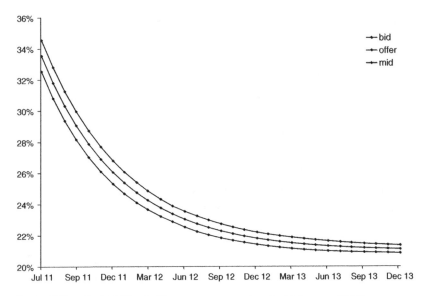

Figure 5.12   Coal API2 volatility term structure (as of mid-January 2011).

Some skew quotes for coal are available from time to time, but liquidity is limited. A sample skew quote is shown below, as of 9 December 2010.

```
Coal API2 Cal 13. Expiry 30/11/12 3pm London
90.00 put 2.60/3.75...crossing 115.00...19/22%
95.00 put 3.80/5.25...crossing 115.00...19/22.25%
100.00 put 4.85/6.85...crossing 115.00...18/22%
105.00 put 6.70/8.85...crossing 115.00...18/22%
140.00 call 5.15/6.75...crossing 115.00...20.35/23.20%
145.00 call 4.25/5.75...crossing 115.00...20.35/23.25%
150.00 call 4.00/5.25...crossing 115.00...21.45/24.00%
155.00 call 3.25/4.50...crossing 115.00...21.45/24%
```

Fitting more than an indicative skew shape to this is optimistic, and note that skew quotes such as this are by no means available each and every day in the broker markets. More commonly, call spreads are available, e.g.

```
Coal API2 Cal 12 120.00/140.00 c/s TRADES 5.55..
  crossing 118.50
Expiry 02/12/11 5pm London
I see +1.3% skew to the wing
```

This quote (also for 17 January 2011) indicates that the 140 strike is priced off an implied volatility 1.3% higher than the 120 strike. Considered in conjunction with the implied volatilities of 23.0/24.0 % for the 130 strike seen earlier, a coarse skew can be fitted.

As before, typical practice is to estimate skew factors (revising these estimates as and when new skew quotes become available) and then to use these factors to adjust the ATM volatility backbone for ITM and OTM options.

6

Energy II – Refined Products

Whereas coal and natural gas can be consumed directly, crude oil is a complex mixture of different hydrocarbons, and not generally used in its raw form.[1] The process of extracting different types of hydrocarbons of similar molecular weights is known as "cracking" and is how we arrive at the refined oil products that end users like, as all of us take for granted in our everyday lives, such as gasoline/petrol,[2] diesel, heating oil, jet fuel, etc. Many people wonder why the price of fuel at the pump doesn't rise (or fall!) in line with crude oil prices – the answer to this is that only about half of the retail price of a gallon of gasoline in the USA is directly linked to the cost of the crude oil required to make it; 20% comes from taxes, about 20% from the cost of the refining process and the remaining 10% or so comes from distribution and marketing. The proportion of taxes is certainly higher in various other countries.

While the financial market for crude oil completely dominates the market for refined oil products, some commentators[3] predict that futures and options on refined oil products will increase in importance between 2013 and 2018.

In this chapter, we describe the refined oil products that are typically extracted from crude oil, and relate these to the financial markets that exist on these products. We discuss what makes these behave differently from crude oil, and finally we mention the financial products that relate refined oil products to unrefined crude oil.

6.1 THE REFINERY BASKET

Oil refining is well discussed in Van Vactor (2010) and in Chapter 7 of Downey (2009), as well as Section 2.3 in Edwards (2010). The crude oil

---

[1] The primary exception being low sulphur crude oil, which is sometimes burnt in power stations in Japan, as mentioned in Schofield (2007).

[2] I shall use the term "gasoline" henceforth in this chapter, adopting the financial terminology of the NYMEX market.

[3] See "Oil trade shifts from crude to refined products" by Javier Blas, *Financial Times*, 15 May 2013.

brought as factory inputs to the refinery, known as the "feedstock", has any salts, residual water and impurities filtered and washed out in the desalting/dewatering stage. After this, the hydrocarbon mixture is distilled, by vapourisation at different temperatures, to separate it into light ends and heavy ends. Atmospheric distillation is used at first, where the crude oil is vapourised to a temperature of about 400 °C and allowed to circulate within a large tower called the atmospheric distillation unit (ADU), sometimes just called the "tower". The various constituents are collected in condensation trays at various heights, corresponding to different condensation points. The lightest products (e.g. butane, propane, ethane) rise to the top of the tower; medium weight hydrocarbons (such as gasoline and heating oil) condense somewhere halfway up, and the heavy products, such as residual fuel oil, either condense near the base of the tower or settle at the very bottom. The heavy residuals, not being easily vapourised at atmospheric pressure, are subjected to a second stage of distillation at lower than atmospheric pressure called vacuum distillation.

While the products from this first stage can be sold directly, in which case they are called the "straight-run" products, it is more common for a second conversion stage to be employed where various hydrocarbons are converted either to heavier or lighter hydrocarbons which can be sold for a higher price. Generally the most valuable refinery products are gasoline and the so-called "middle distillates" (jet fuel, kerosene, diesel and heating oil), so it is quite common for heavier petrochemicals to be "cracked" into lighter products, which ideally yields a greater proportion of middle distillates. This is done in cracking units under conditions of high pressure and temperature (often with a catalytic agent also). Petrochemicals can similarly be combined into heavier products (e.g. alkylation, wherein alkylate – a valuable high octane gasoline blend agent – is produced from lighter constituents), or the specific composition can be modified (e.g. catalytic reformation, isomerisation, or manufacture of ethyl additives such as MTBE).

At the final stage of the refinery is treatment and enhancement of the end products, to remove agents like sulphur (such as mercaptan and hydrogen sulphide) and nitrogen, and finally blending and finishing, arriving at the so-called "finished products".

Figure 6.1 shows a typical breakdown of the so-called "refinery barrel" showing approximate volumetric percentages of the refined oil products that can be extracted from a certain input quantity of crude oil.

The refinery basket composition in the USA is considerably higher in gasoline because of the extra processing capacity to break down the

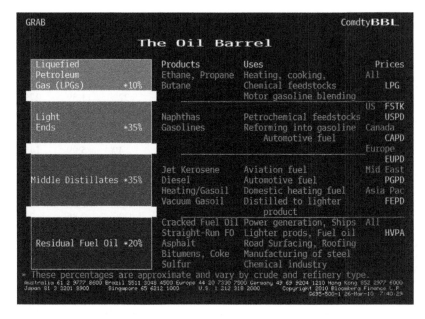

Figure 6.1   Refinery basket – © 2013 Bloomberg Finance L.P. All rights reserved. Used with permission.

heavy ends. The data in Table 6.1 is sourced from Downey (2009), which we categorise into petroleum gases, light ends, middle distillates, residual and other. One sees that the worldwide figures in Table 6.1 are broadly consistent with Figure 6.1.

Notably, more than 42 gallons of refined oil products can be obtained from one barrel, or 42 gallons, of crude oil. This is due to the phenomenon of refinery processing gain, where the refined products have greater volume (or equivalently, lower density) than the petrochemical inputs. This can be seen as a beneficial side-effect of cracking, where the dense heavy hydrocarbons are broken down into less dense lighter petrochemicals; an effect enhanced when a greater proportion of the heavy ends are cracked, such as seen in Table 6.1 for USA refinery production – compare the proportions of residual fuel oil #6 and motor vehicle gasoline.

6.2   GASOLINE

Gasoline is easily the most traded of the refined oil products. It makes up approximately half of the consumption of refined oil products in the

Table 6.1(a)   Refinery basket (per 42 gal barrel of crude oil).

		USA		World	
Refined product	Category	Gal	%yield	Gal	%yield
Motor gasoline blendstock	Light ends	19.66	44%	11.12	26%
Distillate fuel oil	Middle dist	10.04	22%	11.59	27%
Jet fuel	Middle dist	4.07	9%	2.46	6%
Petroleum coke	Residual	2.18	5%	1.72	4%
Still gas/refinery gas	Petroleum gases	1.85	4%	1.9	4%
Residual fuel oil (#6 fuel oil)	Residual	1.72	4%	5.99	14%
Liquefied refinery gas	Petroleum gases	1.68	4%	2.11	5%
Bitumen and road oil	Residual	1.34	3%	1.72	4%
Naphtha for feedstocks	Light ends	0.67	1.5%	1.29	3%
Other oils for feedstocks	Other	0.55	1.2%	1.08	3%
Lubricants	Residual	0.46	1.0%	0.86	2%
Special naphthas	Light ends	0.13	0.3%	0.13	0.3%
Kerosene	Middle dist	0.17	0.4%	1.03	2%
Aviation gasoline	Light ends	0.04	0.1%	0.03	0.1%
Waxes	Residual	0.04	0.1%	0.03	0.1%
Miscellaneous products	Other	0.17	0.4%	0.02	0.0%
Total		44.8	100%	43.1	100%

USA – slightly less than half if measured by blendstock, and slightly over half if measured by consumer motor gasoline, once other blending agents have been added.

The gasoline sold on financial markets such as NYMEX is a blendstock which needs to have an oxygenating product added to it to raise the octane number before it can be used in most internal combustion engines. This gasoline blendstock is denoted RBOB, standing for "Reformulated Gasoline Blendstock for Oxygenate Blending". The history of fuel additives is an interesting one – for many years, tetraethyl lead

Table 6.1(b)   Refinery basket (per 42 gal barrel of crude oil, by category).

	USA		World	
Category	Gal	%yield	Gal	%yield
Petroleum gases	3.53	8%	4.01	9%
Light ends	20.50	46%	12.57	29%
Middle distillates	14.28	32%	15.08	35%
Residual	5.74	13%	10.32	24%
Other	0.72	2%	1.10	3%
Total	44.8	100%	43.1	100%

(TEL) was used for this purpose, but when leaded petrol was banned for motor fuels,[4] methyl tertiary butyl ether (MTBE) was used in its place from 1979. Nowadays, concerns about soil contamination from MTBE contamination have led to its discontinuation as a fuel additive, fuel ethanol being used instead in concentrations of about 10%. The previous NYMEX gasoline contract, the HUA contract containing 2% MTBE, was therefore delisted after the January 2007 contract expired, and the RBOB contract is the standard gasoline contract now.

The NYMEX RBOB futures contract, with ticker code "RB", trades for all twelve calendar months (FGHJKMNQUVXZ) and is available for 36 consecutive months (as are options – American style – on all these futures).

RBOB futures contracts on NYMEX are for physical delivery of 42,000 gallons, with a tick size of 1 cent. Confusingly, gasoline futures have the same physical notional as WTI crude oil (42,000 gallons) but are generally priced in US cents[5] per gallon, not US dollars per barrel. The minimum price fluctuation is one hundredth of a cent, corresponding to a tick value of $4.20 per contract.

Trading on the futures contracts expires on the last business day of the month immediately preceding the named contract month, while the options expire three business days before the underlying futures.

Figure 6.2 shows a typical futures curve for RBOB gasoline, in which the seasonality is readily apparent. Gasoline for delivery in the months from April to September certainly trades at a premium to the months from October to March. The months from April to September cover the so-called US "driving season", when gasoline consumption for leisure travel is generally highest.

Prices in cents per gallon can be converted to a US dollar per barrel equivalent by multiplying by 0.42; for example, the prompt futures price for AUG13 RBOB gasoline in Figure 6.2 was 298.97 cents per gallon, which is equivalent to $125.56 per barrel.

As well as gasoline, we can also include naphtha in the light ends, this is somewhat closer to the middle distillates in molecular weight. It is generally used as a feedstock additive for producing high octane

---

[4] Aviation gasoline, or avgas, still remains as a leaded gasoline however, with a typical avgas blend such as 100LL containing approximately 0.5 grams of tetraethyl lead (TEL) per gallon of gasoline.

[5] Sometimes US dollars – be careful with quotation units.

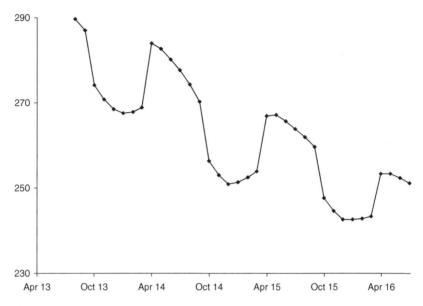

Figure 6.2 RBOB gasoline futures curve (as of 5 July 2013).

gasoline, but is also used as a fuel in its own right (white spirit, Coleman fuel, Shellite) and for other interesting purposes.[6]

6.3   HEATING OIL/GAS OIL

Middle distillates, such as heating oil (HO2, sometimes known as #2 fuel oil), were traded on NYMEX – though the middle distillates are more commonly known in the domestic market as diesel. Distillate is also known as gas oil when traded on the ICE. When sold as consumer diesel, however, there are stricter restrictions on the minimum pentane rating and sulphur content. So, in fact, about 80% of heating oil is actually sold in North America with diesel vehicle fuel being the final destination, the remainder being used for heating (residential and commercial). Because of this, high sulphur heating oil became less popular and in fact the HO2 contract changed in May 2013 to NY Harbor ultra-low sulphur diesel (ULSD) futures, primarily because this middle distillate contract with no renewable fuels or biodiesel content can be used as a marker for

---

[6] For example, fuel for fire spinning and fire juggling; *this* you do at your own risk, dear reader...

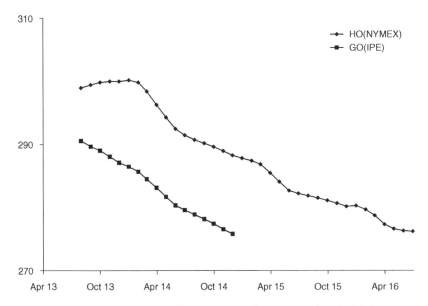

Figure 6.3   Heating oil and gas oil futures curves in ¢/gal (as of 5 July 2013).

both heating oil for the North Eastern region of North America, and for vehicular diesel. In line with many market providers we shall use the terminology "HO" to denote the new contract.

Similarly to RBOB on NYMEX, heating oil futures trade on NYMEX out for three years. The futures contracts expire on the last business day of the month immediately preceding the named contract month and American style options expire three business days before the underlying futures. The contract size is also for 42,000 gallons, with a tick size of 1 cent, and the price is quoted in US cents per gallon.

Figure 6.3 shows a typical futures curve for heating oil (NYMEX) and gas oil (ICE), showing some weak seasonality in the North American contract for extra demand around the northern hemisphere winter. Since diesel is used for transportation by industry all year round, the seasonality is much less than we saw previously for RBOB gasoline which has a strong leisure usage component.

Confusingly, gas oil traded on the ICE is priced in US dollars per tonne, as opposed to being priced volumetrically. The specification for gas oil is distillate of a density of 0.845 kg/litre at 15 °C. Since a barrel is 158.9873 litres, this means a barrel contains 134.344 kg of distillate, from which it is easily computed that approximately 7.45 barrels of gas oil are required to make up a metric tonne.

Table 6.2   Crack factors for $/T to
$/bbl conversion (approximate).

Product	CF
Propane	12.41
Butane	10.80
Naphtha	8.90
Gasoline	8.33
Jet fuel	8.00
Crude oil	7.33
Gas oil	7.45
Fuel oil	6.76

Van Woenzel (2012) refers to this conversion factor of 7.45 as the "crack factor", a ratio denoted CF which can be straightforwardly obtained from the density ρ by

$$CF = \frac{1000}{158.9873 \times \rho}. \qquad (6.1)$$

We tabulate this factor for a few refined products in Table 6.2, many of these conversion factors can be found in the NYMEX Rulebook,[7] published by the CME.

The price of gas oil ($/tonne) can therefore be converted into HO equivalent (cents per gallon) by multiplying by the conversion factor $100/(7.45 * 42) \approx 0.3200$. So, for example, the AUG13 gas oil contract shown in Table 6.6(b) trading at $908 per bbl is equivalent to 290.18¢/gal, as displayed in Figure 6.3. A further multiplication by 0.42 expresses this as $121.88 per bbl.

Gas oil futures on the ICE trade for all calendar months in the current and subsequent calendar year, and for January in the year thereafter. The expiry date is the second business day before the 14th of the named calendar month. Delivery is physical, via heating oil barge to Amsterdam/Rotterdam/Antwerp area (ARA) between the 16th and the final day of the contract month. A standard gas oil futures contract is for 100 tonnes, and with a minimum price fluctuation of 25¢ per tonne, this gives a tick value of $25.00 (per futures contract). American style options also trade on ICE, with the expiry being five business days before the underlying futures contract expires.

---

[7] www.cmegroup.com/rulebook/NYMEX

Jet fuel futures contracts trade for delivery in Singapore, priced in US dollars per barrel, which can be converted to cents per gallon by simply multiplying by $100/42 \approx 2.381$. Jet fuel generally trades at a fairly predictable spread to heating oil #2, reflecting its higher quality, but this is less apparent with the move from HO2 to ULSD as a benchmark for the middle distillates.

6.4 PETROLEUM GASES AND RESIDUAL FUEL OIL

The other sections of the refinery basket get much less attention. We discuss them briefly here.

A North American LPG (propane) contract trades on the Houston Mercantile Exchange for spot delivery of propane (FOB basis) to Lone Star's NGL storage facility at Mont Belvieu, Texas. Pricing is quoted in US dollars per gallon, and a historical time series is shown in Figure 6.4. At a current price of $0.863/gal, this equates to $36.25/bbl – much lower than gasoline or heating oil, partly because the energy density in volumetric terms is much less – and also because gasoline and heating oil tend to be the most valuable elements in the refinery basket in any case, reflecting their current ubiquity in the global industrial economy.

We tabulate these energy densities for the four most common refined oil products in Table 6.3, noticing that LPG (propane) has 20% less energy available on a volumetric basis than gasoline. Since LPG generally trades at a much greater discount than 20% to either gasoline or heating oil, LPG conversions have become popular with certain motorists who have a LPG supplier available nearby and who can justify the cost of conversion and the inconvenience of an additional fuel tank.

Butane, isobutane and ethane also trade on HMX. Options and other derivatives on NGLs/petroleum gases are very infrequently encountered.

Residual fuel oil (or "resid"), which comes from the heavy ends left over after the light ends have been extracted, also trades. Typical contracts are the Platts No. 6 Residual Fuel Oil 1% Sulphur, No. 6

Table 6.3 Energy densities (approximate) of refined oil products.

Product	kg/L	MJ/kg	MJ/L
LPG propane	0.54	46.10	26.00
Gasoline	0.75	43.50	32.18
Diesel	0.83	43.10	35.86
Fuel Oil #6	0.99	42.50	42.07

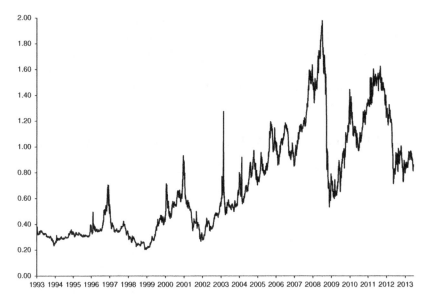

Figure 6.4 Propane (LPG) spot price history in $/gal (January 1993 to July 2013).

Table 6.4 Refined fuel oil grades (ASTM classification).

Product	Description
Fuel Oil No. 1	Light kerosene, also called stove oil.
Fuel Oil No. 2	Distillate heating oil (encountered in Section 6.3).
Fuel Oil No. 3	A low viscosity commercial heating oil. This grade no longer used.
Fuel Oil No. 4	Commercial heating oil.
Fuel Oil No. 5	Residual heating oil, needs pre-heating to 170–220 °F.
Fuel Oil No. 6	High viscosity residual heating oil, needs pre-heating to 220–260 °F.

Fuel Oil 3% Sulphur, Singapore – HSFO 180 cSt, Singapore – HSFO 380 cSt.[8] The No. 6 denotes the most viscous and heaviest grade of fuel oil, the sequence being tabulated for reference in Table 6.4.

Since fuel oil needs to be heated to temperatures greater than 100 °C/212 °F in order to achieve combustion, this fuel can only really be practicably used in power plants and to power large ships. Unfortunately, resid is also quite a polluting fuel, on account of its sulphur content. As a result, and not dissimilarly to coal, residual fuel oil is generally the cheapest oil available which is liquid at room temperature and pressure.

---

[8] The 180 or 380 cSt refers to the viscosity grade, as measured in centistokes.

Table 6.5 Residual fuel oils.

Identifier	Description	Mkt price	$/bbl
BUNKSI38	Bloomberg 380cSt Bunker Fuel Sing	$590/T	92.87
N6GF3.0	Bloomberg Gulf Coast 3% Sulphur No. 6 Fuel Oil	$90.88/bbl	90.88
N6SHS180	Bloomberg High Sulfur Residual Fuel Oil 180cSt Sing	$601.25/T	94.63
BUNKRD38	Bloomberg 380cSt Bunker Fuel Rotterdam	$591/T	93.02
NK1	3.5% (sulphur) Fuel Oil Swap Mediterranean	$586.09/T	92.25
NK6E4.0FB	Bloomberg High Sulphur Fuel Oil 3.5% FOB ARA	$590.50/T	92.94

Contracts on fuel oil are generally priced in US dollars per barrel in North America and in US dollars per tonne in Europe and Asia. Assuming a density of 0.99 kg/l, we can convert a price in $/t to a $/bbl price by multiplying by $158.9873 \times 0.99/1000 = 1/6.35 = 0.1574$. Some typical market prices for the residual fuel oils are tabulated in Table 6.5, where we see they trade at a discount to gasoline and heating oil, and indeed are less than the price of crude.

Gulf Coast No. 6 Fuel Oil 3.0% futures trade on NYMEX, though these are really more like swaps, since they are valued against the arithmetic average of the Platts Oilgram prices for Gulf Coast No. 6 Fuel Oil 3% Sulphur, as observed over the course of a calendar month considering only business days. These contracts cease trading on the last business day of the contract month. Average price options also trade on these futures on NYMEX, similarly expiring on the last business day of the contract month.

6.5 SEASONALITY AND VOLATILITY

From the discussions above, it is reasonably evident that the main refined oil product that displays seasonality is RBOB gasoline (with some seasonality apparent in the NYMEX heating oil contract, albeit to a lesser degree).

Volatilities can be obtained from various market providers, and/or calibrated to broker quotes seen in the market. A sample selection of broker quotes for refined oil products is shown below, which gives an idea of what may be seen. They are interpreted much the same way as the broker quotes for crudes seen earlier in Chapter 5.

```
HEAT : Q309 1.53 ATM Calls 2225 - 2425
HEAT : Q409 1.64 ATM Calls 2500 - 2700
```

```
HEAT : h209 1.94 ATM Calls 1400/1650
HEAT APO : Call0 2.05 ATM Calls 2650/2950
GAS OIL APO : Q111 737.00 ATM Calls 47.00/50.00
GAS OIL APO : 2H11 748.00 ATM Calls 76.00/80.00
GAS OIL APO : Q311 756.00 ATM Calls 74.25/78.25
JET NWE : Q111 701.00 ATM Calls 61.00/63.00
SING KERO : 1H11 80.00 Puts x92.40 360/405
Fuel 3.5% Q111 400.00/465.00 P/S x465.00 21.50/23.50
Fuel 3.5% 1H11 X490 ATM Call 34.5/37.5
FUEL 3.5% BG FOB ROTT : Call1 475.00 Puts x496.00
35.25/39.25
```

Tables 6.6(a) and 6.6(b) show typical levels of ATM volatility for some typical refined oil products. Note that the volatilities quoted for Singapore fuel oil are swap volatilities, others are for options on futures contracts. In general, implied volatilities for refined oils are sometimes slightly lower than those for the crude oil input (WTI for North American refined oil products, Brent for European, Tapis for Asian), though this is by no means always the case.

Table 6.6(a)   Term structure of futures and ATM volatilities for American refined oils vs WTI crude (as of 5 July 2013).

	NYMEX WTI		NYMEX RBOB		NYMEX HO	
	$F_{0,T}$	σ_{imp}	$F_{0,T}$	σ_{imp}	$F_{0,T}$	σ_{imp}
AUG13	103.22	24.37%	289.68	24.91%	298.97	22.34%
SEP13	103.05	24.29%	287.00	23.39%	299.46	21.29%
OCT13	101.80	23.33%	274.18	23.34%	299.85	20.61%
NOV13	100.45	22.86%	270.80	22.98%	300.01	20.00%
DEC13	99.11	22.49%	268.51	22.45%	300.00	19.44%
JAN14	97.84	22.22%	267.57	21.85%	300.19	19.32%
FEB14	96.74	21.88%	267.85	20.98%	299.84	18.94%
MAR14	95.83	21.49%	268.90	20.22%	298.41	18.84%
APR14	95.04	21.07%	283.98	18.49%	296.26	18.63%
MAY14	94.44	20.98%	282.68	18.09%	294.27	18.26%
JUN14	93.93	20.63%	280.18	18.09%	292.47	17.90%
JUL14	93.34	20.23%	277.68	18.09%	291.47	17.57%
AUG14	92.75	20.01%	274.33	18.09%	290.72	17.30%
SEP14	92.18	19.88%	270.28	18.09%	290.17	17.14%
OCT14	91.66	19.61%	256.38	18.09%	289.62	17.14%
NOV14	91.20	19.31%	253.03	18.09%	288.97	17.14%
DEC14	90.80	18.95%	250.93	18.09%	288.27	17.14%

Table 6.6(b)   Term structure of futures and ATM volatilities for European/Asian refined oils vs Brent crude (as of 5 July 2013).

	ICE BRENT		ICE GAS OIL		SING FO 380	
	$F_{0,T}$	σ_{imp}	$F_{0,T}$	σ_{imp}	$F_{0,T}$	σ_{imp}
AUG13	107.92	23.93%	908.00	19.21%	603.33	16.12%
SEP13	107.21	23.93%	905.25	19.09%	604.69	17.51%
OCT13	106.46	23.64%	903.25	18.78%	605.11	17.51%
NOV13	105.82	23.02%	900.25	18.54%	604.50	17.85%
DEC13	105.22	22.27%	897.25	18.39%	604.00	18.02%
JAN14	104.64	22.13%	895.25	17.97%	602.84	17.78%
FEB14	104.05	21.68%	892.75	17.76%	602.26	17.95%
MAR14	103.46	21.47%	889.00	17.42%	601.00	17.94%
APR14	102.92	21.25%	884.75	17.15%	599.74	17.38%
MAY14	102.40	21.05%	880.25	17.05%	598.48	17.42%
JUN14	101.85	20.60%	876.00	17.13%	596.55	17.48%
JUL14	101.37	20.27%	873.75	16.65%		
AUG14	100.87	20.09%	871.50	16.50%		
SEP14	100.33	19.74%	869.25	16.39%		
OCT14	99.79	19.58%	867.00	16.23%		
NOV14	99.31	19.26%	864.25	16.18%		
DEC14	98.84	19.07%	862.00	16.06%		

Skew factors are fitted similarly, though as so few skew-sensitive instruments exist it is often necessary to use skew factors from the crude oils to adjust the ATM volatilities to obtain an implied volatility smile for refined oils. We show a volatility skew from 2010 in Figure 6.5, demonstrating a typical shape for refined oil (though with a higher level of overall volatility than in 2013).

6.6   CRACK SPREAD OPTIONS

We have seen in this chapter that 42 gallons of crude oil can be turned into more than 42 gallons of refined products, and that many (not all) of these refined products trade at a premium to crude.

As a result, it is relatively common to trade a spread (either outright or as an option) which captures the arithmetic differential between the price of a refined product (or basket of refined products) and the price of the crude oil required to produce it.

The gasoline crack spread, for example, is the arithmetic difference between the price of 1 barrel of RBOB gasoline, and 1 barrel of WTI

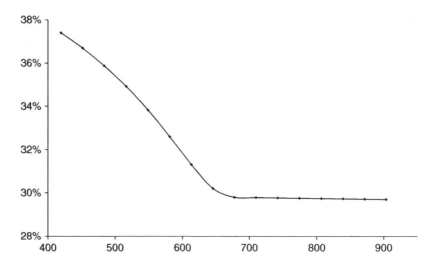

Figure 6.5   Heating oil skew for SEP10 contract (as of 19 August 2010).

crude oil. Since RBOB is quoted in cents per gallon, the gasoline crack
spread as measured in $/bbl is obtained by

$$V_{\text{RBOB crack}} = \frac{42}{100} V_{\text{RBOB}} - V_{\text{WTI}}. \tag{6.2}$$

Considering the market prices for the DEC13 contracts in Table 6.6,
we see WTI futures trading at $99.11/bbl and RBOB gasoline futures
trading at 268.51 ¢/gal. We thereby obtain the gasoline crack

$$V_{\text{RBOB crack}} = 0.42 \times 268.51 - 99.11 = 13.66 \quad (\$/bbl).$$

The heating oil crack follows similarly, with $V_{\text{HO}} = 300$ for the DEC13
contract:

$$V_{\text{HO crack}} = 0.42 \times 300 - 99.11 = 26.89 \quad (\$/bbl).$$

Note that crack spreads for other geographical regions need to have
the $/T prices for the refined products converted to $/bbl prices. For
example, if we construct a gas oil crack spread by taking the differential
between Gas Oil and Brent, we obtain

$$V_{\text{GO crack}} = 0.42 \times 897.25/7.44 - 105.22 = 15.38 \quad (\$/bbl).$$

One should be careful, however, as crack spreads are sometimes quoted
as the difference between the price of the crude oil minus the price of

the refined product (e.g. fuel oil barges fob Rotterdam minus ICE Brent, as traded on NYMEX) and sometimes quoted as the difference between the price of the refined product minus the price of the crude oil (e.g. NYMEX RBOB minus NYMEX WTI, see Chapter 559 in the NYMEX Rulebook). Generally the applicable sign convention can be inferred from context.

These two price differentials would only make economic sense if used to try to capture the refinery margin for an oil refinery that produced 100% gasoline, or 100% heating oil, from an input quantity of crude oil. We already know that this is unrealistic, given the composition of crude oil.

Since refineries produce a mixture of refined products, a more typical crack spread is the X:Y:Z crack spread. This is discussed in several works, e.g. Errara and Brown (2002), Downey (2009), Edwards (2010), Ripple (2011), and Madhumathi and Ranganatham (2012). I adopt the sign convention that assigns a negative weight to the crude and positive weights to the refined products (some authors adopt the opposite convention). In this case, the X:Y:Z crack spread is a position that is short X barrels of crude oil (reflecting the refinery's natural short position in its factory inputs) and long Y barrels of gasoline and long Z barrels of heating oil/gas oil/distillate (the refinery is clearly long the products it produces and can sell for a profit)

$$V_{\text{Crack spread}} = \frac{42}{100}\frac{y}{x}V_{\text{RBOB}} + \frac{42}{100}\frac{z}{x}V_{\text{HO}} - V_{\text{WTI}}. \quad (6.3)$$

A popular choice of weights in North America is the 3:2:1 crack spread, which is long 2 barrels of RBOB gasoline and 1 barrel of heating oil, and short 3 barrels of WTI crude, normalised to a reference notional of 1 barrel of crude. This choice of ratios is designed to replicate the refinery breakdown of North American refineries, which produce roughly twice as much gasoline as heating oil – see 44% and 22% in Table 6.1(a) – a refinery gasoline yield of 200% of distillate.

In this example, for a 3:2:1 DEC-13 crack spread with $V_{\text{RBOB}} = 268.51$ ¢/gal, $V_{\text{HO}} = 300$ ¢/gal and $V_{\text{WTI}} = \$99.11$/bbl, we would have

$$V_{\text{Crack spread}} = 0.42\left[\frac{2}{3}\times268.51 + \frac{1}{3}\times300\right] - 99.11 = 18.07 \quad (\$/\text{bbl}).$$

We also see from Table 6.1(a) and Table 6.7 that in much of the world, gasoline is not produced at the same high yield (relative to distillate) as in the USA. As a result, as mentioned in Ripple (2011), other ratios

Table 6.7 Refinery breakdown (Source: BP Statistical Review of World Energy, June 2013).

	North America	USA	So./Cent. Americas	Europe	FSU	Middle East	Africa	Asia Pacific	WORLD
Light ends	46%	48%	29%	21%	31%	23%	25%	31%	32%
Middle distillate	28%	29%	39%	52%	33%	33%	47%	35%	36%
Fuel oil	3%	2%	10%	8%	10%	23%	12%	12%	10%
Other	23%	21%	22%	19%	27%	22%	16%	21%	22%
L/M ratio	165%	164%	75%	40%	93%	69%	53%	89%	88%

such as the 5:3:2, 2:1:1 and 3:1:2 crack spread are popular which have the basket composition matched to refinery gasoline yields of 150, 100 and 50% of distillate.

The crack spread is also sometimes called the refinery margin, because it serves as a measure of the operating refinery margin, subject to prevailing prices in the market. It is possible for a refinery to "lock in" the value of a certain amount of future production by selling the crack spread forward – that way, if the market price of the refined products falls, then the short position in the crack spread becomes increasingly valuable. This hedges the risk, though it clearly is an imperfect hedge given the complexity of refinery production.

Clearly such a simple product as a crack spread neglects to take account of the other refinery products. Ripple (2011) describes a more complicated crack spread that includes fuel oil as well as gasoline and distillate in the basket of refined products, this is not so frequently encountered. Figure 6.6 shows how a more complex refinery margin basket can be constructed and priced.

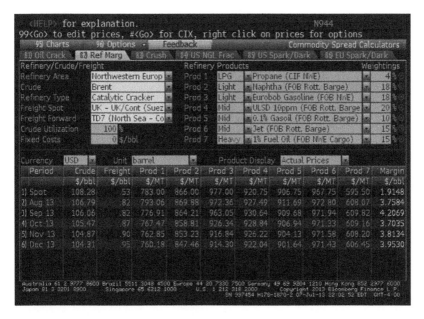

Figure 6.6   Refinery margin pricing screen (Bloomberg) – © 2013 Bloomberg Finance L.P. All rights reserved. Used with permission.

As well as crack spreads, options on the crack spread are traded, which are also known as refinery margin options. The purchase of options on this spread enables a refinery to hedge the risk against adverse moves in the profit. These can be valued using moment matching techniques such as described in Chapter 2. They are highly sensitive to the correlations between the various oil futures contracts, as well to the volatilities.

7

Power

Electricity is one of the more recent forms of energy available to power the industrial revolution. We already know that fossil fuels can be burnt to liberate the stored energy in the form of heat. Additionally, steam engines and internal combustion engines can harness the energy of fossil fuels via combustion and perform mechanical work – for example, pumping water, powering factories or powering motor vehicles, airplanes and ships.

There are, however, practical limits on how small an internal combustion engine can be made, largely due to the heat produced. Small steam engines are inefficient and are hard to maintain. Additionally, the fuel requirements place constraints on the physical location where such engines can be used. In contrast, electric motors are far more amenable to miniaturisation, and can be situated far more flexibly. For this reason, electric motors were often preferred in factories, such as those used for production of the Ford Model T car. Electric lighting is safer and less polluting than gas lighting, particularly in coal mines and factories where inflammable agents may be present.[1] Finally, electricity is an important factor in metallurgy, such as electroplating, electrowinning, and the extraction of aluminium.

In addition to its role in the so-called "Second Industrial Revolution", electricity is also crucial in its roles in telegraphy, telephone, radio and television, computers, the Internet, flight, space technology, medical applications, and so on.

Electricity is based on the principle that charged particles can be maintained at an electric potential (measured in volts), and this potential corresponds to the capacity (per unit charge) to do work. This is a meaningful representation of electric potential in both static electricity, in which case volts are measured as joules per coulomb, or in current electricity, in which case volts are measured as watts per ampere.[2]

---

[1] Not to mention buildings such as the Savoy Theatre in London, the first public building to be lit using electric lighting, and streets such as Electric Avenue, Brixton.

[2] Watts being joules per second; and amperes being coulombs per second.

Quantities of electrical energy in financial markets are usually denominated in megawatt-hours (MWh), for two reasons. One, a joule is one watt-second and this is too small for practical consideration; and secondly, electricity contracts are usually for delivery for a certain number of megawatts (MW) for a certain number of delivery hours (h), at pre-arranged times.

7.1   ELECTRICITY GENERATION

Electricity is typically generated in one of two ways, either using a steam turbine plant or using a gas turbine, though renewable sources such as hydroelectric turbines and wind turbines make up an increasingly important constituent. Over 80% of all electricity worldwide is generated using steam turbines (the proportion being closer to 90% in the USA). Good discussions of electricity generation can be found in Section 2.2 of Harris (2006) and in Section 2.2 of Edwards (2010). The principle of a steam turbine is that the superheated steam (obtained from combustion of fossil fuels, or nuclear) spins a rotary shaft, which operates an electric dynamo. In contrast, a gas turbine combusts a mixture of natural gas and air, the pressure from the reaction being used to drive a turbine directly. A combined cycle gas turbine (CCGT) uses the heat from the gas turbine to power a secondary steam turbine, a so-called heat recovery steam generator (HRSG), this lifts the efficiency of the power plant from around 40% to around 60%. It is commonplace for the turbine to be arranged in a sequence, starting with a high pressure turbine, then medium and lower pressure turbines further away from the source of steam or gas combustion. The remaining heat output can be used more efficiently as part of a combined heat and power (CHP) installation if the plant is physically located at a place where there is a need for heating. Obviously this demand is somewhat seasonal.

Power generators are categorised according to their load factor, a load factor of 100% meaning that it operates at maximum capacity (either as measured by megawatt hours or by actual number of hours). A power generator can be operated other than a mostly continuous basis (load factor over 70%), albeit with some variation in generation capacity, in which case it is known as baseload plant; on a reserve basis to supply extra power when needed at periods of high demand (load factor less than 15%) in which case it is known as peaking plant; or with a load factor between 15% and 70% when it is called mid-merit or cyclic generation. Some generator types are best suited to various modes of power production, e.g. nuclear plants and coal are usually baseload, while open cycle gas turbines are usually peaking plant. This reflects the ease with which gas combustion can be turned on and off, unlike coal or nuclear.

For gas powered generation, we can compute the amount of gas that is required to generate a certain amount of electrical power. This quantity is known as the heat rate.

$$HR = \frac{\text{Gas consumed [MMBtu]}}{\text{Power produced [MWh]}}. \tag{7.1}$$

Typical heat rates for gas fired power turbines are 7 to 10 MMBtu/MWh, with the more efficient CCGT turbines being closer to 7 MMBtu/MWh; coal fired turbines tend to be closer to 10 MMBtu/MWh. Clearly the lower the heat rate, the more efficient the plant. For gas, the theoretical maximum is 3.412 MMBtu per MWh, a figure not even remotely likely to be reached in practice.

We shall need the heat rate in calculating the spark spread and dark spread, which are the analogies in power generation of the crack spread in oil production. Much as unrefined oils are used to create refined oil products that are sold to end users, gas and coal are used to create electricity (also sold to end users).

Clearly, once electricity is generated, it need to be conveyed to consumers via a transmission line network. Figure 7.1 shows the major power transmission lines in North America.

There are various subtypes of transmission system operators in North America, such as Independent Systems Operators (ISOs) and Regional Transmission Organizations (RTOs). The RTOs are responsible for maintaining interstate and regional transmission networks, such as the PJM Interconnect, the Midwest ISO, the Southwest Power Pool and ISO New England (note that the second and fourth in this list are actually RTOs in spite of their names. In contrast, the ISOs generally are within a particular state (or small grouping of states), such as the California ISO, New York ISO, etc.

While there appears to be a dense network of transmission lines across North America, there are three main clusters: the so called Western Interconnection, the Eastern Interconnection and Texas Interconnection. They are, of course, linked.

In Europe, power transmission is similarly coordinated by the European Network of Transmission System Operators for Electricity

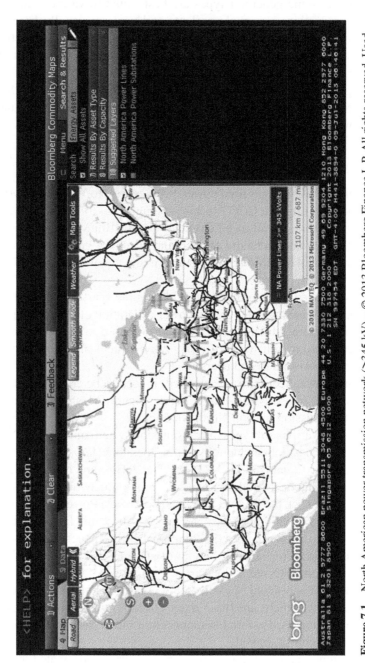

Figure 7.1 North American power transmission network (≥345 kV) – © 2013 Bloomberg Finance L.P. All rights reserved. Used with permission.

(ENTSO-E), which took control of Europe's power grids on 1 July 2009. A transmission system operator (TSO) is the electricity market's version of a pipeline operator for oil or gas, who is charged with maintaining the safety and reliability of the electricity transmission network used to conduct electricity from suppliers (power stations) to consumers.

7.2 NONSTORABILITY AND DECORRELATION

Electricity differs from fossil fuels in several ways. Firstly, one cannot physically locate current electricity – there is no meaningful way of requiring a certain amount of electricity to be delivered using incoterms such as cif or fob. As a result, electricity needs to be delivered into a transmission network, where it can be conveyed through high-tension cables to locations (often urban, not always) where end users can take advantage of the supply. Transmission networks are lossy over large distances and it is infeasible to route them across oceans, so electricity markets tend to be much more regional than other energy markets. Note that electricity is generally transmitted in three-phase power, using alternating current with three different power lines each 120° out of phase with the other two (Edwards, 2010).

Secondly, and closely related to this, electricity cannot easily be stored in inventories. While electric battery technology has improved considerably (as used in electric vehicles, laptop computers etc.), the cost of storing electricity on the scale of the quantities used in industrial transmission would be prohibitive.

What this means is that the various electricity markets, e.g. spot and forwards, trade in a much more decoupled manner than oil, gas and refined oil products. It makes no sense to attempt to buy electricity cheaply for one delivery period and to sell it expensively for a later delivery period if it cannot be stored. We shall introduce some typical spot and forward electricity products later in this chapter.

Since electricity networks need to have the supply and demand matched on a continual basis, transmission system operators have to match production schedules to the consumption patterns of consumers. These are unpredictable and highly seasonal – not only does electricity demand peak during the day and evening (with, conversely, minimal demand between midnight and dawn), but the demand increases as ambient temperatures move away from a comfortable level – generally around 65 °F or perhaps 18 °C – this we shall see in Chapter 9 in the context of weather derivatives.

7.2.1   Spot Markets

As a result, electricity trades for delivery in hourly slots, i.e. midnight to 1am, 1am to 2am, 2am to 3am, and so on until the 11 pm–midnight slot. As discussed in Section 1.4 of Burger *et al.* (2007) and in Section 4.2 of Edwards (2010), there are various electricity markets, all of which are auction markets. Discussion of the auction mechanisms employed in power markets is beyond the scope of this book, we refer the reader to Bunn (2004), Harris (2006) and Weron (2006) for discussion. Crucial in the extreme short term is the requirement to balance supply and demand at all points in the transmission network. This is known as the real-time market. More liquid, however, is the day-ahead market, where power producers agree delivery prices and schedules for each of the 24 hours in the forthcoming day.

The presence of the two-settlement system, as it is referred to in Benth and Koekebakker (2008), stabilises prices to some extent, but when the demand forecasts are out of line with predictions then extra supply may be called in. This requires the use of the real-time auction market. Real-time production is only feasible for power plants which are able to start at short notice, but has the potential to be more profitable – but riskier. Peaking plant is usually reserved to operate almost exclusively in the real-time market, whereas baseload power plants need to operate in the day-ahead market, as they cannot be called in at short notice. Mid-merit plants, on the other hand, can operate to some extent in both the real-time and day-ahead markets, which means their marginal costs of power production usually have the greatest influence on the price of electricity.

The dispatch stack is comprised of the various Load Serving Entities (LSEs) arranged in order of their price for electricity supply. Note that both LSEs from the day-ahead and the real-time markets are included.

The day-ahead market for Scandinavia is known as Elspot, whereas the real-time market is managed by each of the individual countries. In the UK, France and Germany, the day-ahead markets are known as the UK Power Exchange (UKPX), Powernext and EEX respectively. Further information can be found at the various web pages for these authorities. For Elspot, bids are required to be submitted by 12:00 CET, and these are fed into a computer algorithm which is capable of publishing hourly prices for the subsequent day by 12:45. This gives the afternoon to settle the trades and to arrange for physical delivery of electricity on the next calendar day, as agreed.

Day-ahead markets exist in North America as well, such as NEPOOL Mass Hub (New England), PJM (West Pennsylvania), ERCOT Houston, Indiana, Entergy Louisiana, Mid Columbia, SP 15 - EZ (Southern California), NP 15 (Northern California) Palo Verde and ERCOT SOUTH (Texas).

7.2.2   Futures and Forward Markets

A good introduction to electricity forwards and other typical financial products in the electricity markets can be found in Chapter 7 of Fiorenzani (2006), as well as Deng and Oren (2006). In Leoni (2013), a description of the German power market is given, detailing that it is possible to trade electricity forward for D+1 and D+2 (one and two days ahead), WE+1 and WE+2 (next and subsequent weekend), W+1 and W+1 (next and subsequent week), M+1 through to M+5 (five calendar months in sequence) Q+1 through to Q+5 (five seasons, in sequence) and CAL+1, CAL+2 and CAL+3 (three calendar years). Similar products exist on Nord Pool, for the Scandinavian market. This effectively sets up a sequence of electricity swaps which one can use to infer a price for the commodity. The method used is known as a "shaping methodology", where the longer traded products are used first, to infer the overall shape of the forward power curve, and then the finer granularity is added using the products that have a shorter duration over which power is supplied.

Baseload markets refer to those where the power is supplied over all 24 hours, whereas peakload markets refer to those where power is only supplied for a fraction of the day. Terminology varies from country to country, as discussed in Burger *et al.* (2007) – peakload on NYMEX is 7am to 11pm for Monday to Friday (generally not including holidays), whereas in France and Germany it is 8am to 8pm on Monday to Friday (irrespective of holidays). A commonly accepted convention for "on-peak" energy is from 6am to 10pm, whereas "off-peak" energy is the remaining hours from 10pm to 6am. One certainly needs to check the specifics for each market.

Depending on the term over which power is contracted to be delivered, the trade may be either a futures contract or a forward. For example, on Nord Pool, daily and weekly power contracts trade as futures (with margining), whereas monthly, quarterly and yearly contracts trade as forwards.

7.2.3   Options Markets

There exists a market in options on electricity, for example call and put options (European style) trade on Nord Pool where the expiry date is the third Thursday in the month before the relevant futures contract. In the USA, the vast majority of options are traded OTC, and no standardised rules for expiries exist. Note that what happens for options is that if exercised, the exercise decision applies to the delivery period (just as for futures and forwards, electricity is supplied over a time interval – possibly on-peak, off-peak, or round-the-clock). Exercise dates are generally a few days before the relevant period; some examples are given in Example 2.5 in Eydeland and Wolyniec (2003).

7.3   MODELLING SPIKES IN ELECTRICITY MARKETS

Figure 7.2 shows a time series of day-ahead electricity prices for the UK, from which we can see evidence of spikes, with subsequent rapid mean reversion back towards more regular levels.

It is reasonably clear from looking at Figure 7.2 that such a time series cannot be generated using a pure diffusive model. These spikes

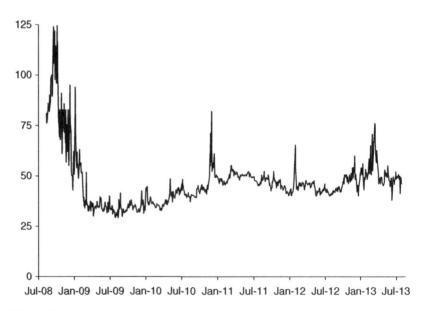

Figure 7.2   Day-ahead electricity prices (Generic Baseload UK).

are explained in Huisman (2009) as being due to either positive demand shocks or negative supply shocks (e.g. catastrophic equipment failure) causing auxiliary power plants with very high marginal costs of production needing to be brought into the real-time market.

Good reviews of modelling efforts in this direction can be found in Section 11.6 of Geman (2005), Chapter 4 of Huisman (2009), Chapter 6 in Fiorenzani (2006), and more recently Benth, Kholodnyi and Laurence (2014) – in particular the chapter by Carmona and Coulon (2014).

There are basically two modelling approaches which have found favour with practitioners and researchers for handling the spikes that are characteristic of electricity markets. The first are the so-called traditional *reduced-form* models, which presume stochastic asset price dynamics for electricity that capture typically observed market features (such as spikes). These can be handled in a number of ways; we shall discuss more below. The second are the *structural* models, as discussed in Pirrong (2012) and Carmona and Coulon (2014), which take advantage of the availability of supply and demand information in the merit graph (supply and demand curves for electricity) to attempt to model the fundamental sources of price movement impacting upon electricity markets.

To begin with, however, we introduce the Lucia and Schwartz (2002) one-factor model for logspot $\ln S_t$, presented in Section 3.2 of the original paper, which we can write as

$$dY_t = -\kappa Y_t dt + \sigma dW_t \qquad (7.2a)$$

$$\ln S_t = f(t) + Y_t \qquad (7.2b)$$

where $f(t)$ is deterministic and allows us to fit the seasonal component of the electricity forward curve, and Y_t is a pure stochastic component. An equivalent model for spot is presented too, with (7.2b) replaced by $S_t = f(t) + Y_t$.

Note that (7.2a) can also be written as

$$dE_t = \kappa(b(t) - \ln E_t)E_t dt + \sigma E_t dW_t \qquad (7.3)$$

with

$$b(t) = \frac{1}{\kappa}\left(f'(t) + \frac{1}{2}\sigma^2\right) + f(t) \qquad (7.4)$$

using the notation of Fiorenzani (2006) where E_t denotes the spot price of electricity (corresponding to the day-ahead price).

This is easily demonstrated. Put $X_t = \ln S_t$, i.e. $S_t = e^{X_t} = f(X_t)$ with $f(x) = e^x$. Since $f''(x) = f'(x) = f(x) = e^x$, by Itô's lemma we have

$$dS_t = f'(X_t)dX_t + \frac{1}{2}f''(X_t)dX_t^2$$

$$= e^{X_t}dX_t + \frac{1}{2}e^{X_t}dX_t^2$$

$$= S_t dX_t + \frac{1}{2}S_t dX_t^2. \tag{7.5}$$

Writing (7.2b) as $X_t = f(t) + Y_t$. we have $dX_t = f'(t)dt + dY_t$ and $dX_t^2 = dY_t^2$. We now write (7.5) as

$$\frac{dS_t}{S_t} = f'(t)dt + dY_t + \frac{1}{2}dY_t^2. \tag{7.6}$$

From (7.2a) we have $dY_t = -\kappa Y_t dt + \sigma dW_t$ and $dY_t^2 = \sigma^2 dt$, so

$$\frac{dS_t}{S_t} = f'(t)dt - \kappa Y_t dt + \sigma dW_t + \frac{1}{2}\sigma^2 dt$$

$$= \left[f'(t) - \kappa Y_t + \frac{1}{2}\sigma^2 \right] dt + \sigma dW_t$$

$$= \kappa \left[\frac{f'(t)}{\kappa} + \frac{\sigma^2}{2\kappa} - Y_t \right] dt + \sigma dW_t. \tag{7.7}$$

Finally, $Y_t = X_t - f(t) = \ln S_t - f(t)$, so (7.7) reduces to

$$\frac{dS_t}{S_t} = \kappa \left[\frac{f'(t)}{\kappa} + \frac{\sigma^2}{2\kappa} - \ln S_t + f(t) \right] dt + \sigma dW_t$$

from which we obtain

$$dS_t = \kappa \left[b(t) - \ln S_t \right] S_t dt + \sigma S_t dW_t \tag{7.8a}$$

with

$$b(t) = \frac{1}{\kappa} \left(f'(t) + \frac{1}{2}\sigma^2 \right) + f(t). \tag{7.8b}$$

There are, however, two primary shortcomings of this type of model. Firstly, as a one-factor model, changes in spot and all the forwards are perfectly correlated. Secondly, such a model has no ability to generate the spikes typically seen in electricity trading.

7.3.1   Reduced Form Models

There are, broadly, two different types of reduced form models. The first involves the use of a jump-diffusion model, following the original Merton jump-diffusion model (Merton, 1976), examples in commodity price modelling are presented in Johnson and Barz (1999), Deng (2000), Clewlow and Strickland (2000), Geman and Roncoroni (2006) and Kjaer (2008) for electricity and in Askari and Krichene (2008) in the context of oil. The second is a regime switching model, as described in Deng (2000), Huisman and Mahieu (2003), Mount, Ning and Cai (2006) and Huisman (2008). Both are discussed in Sections 9.1.12 and 9.1.13 of Harris (2006) respectively; good reviews comparing the two approaches can be found in Weron, Bierbrauer and Trück (2004), Borovkova and Permana (2006) and Bierbrauer *et al.* (2007).

7.3.1.1   Reduced Form Models – Jump-Diffusions

The typical formulation for jump-diffusion models for electricity prices is similar to (7.2), but with the pure stochastic component augmented with a Poisson process N_t with intensity λ

$$dY_t = -\kappa Y_t dt + \sigma dW_t + J_t dN_t \tag{7.9a}$$

$$\ln S_t = f(t) + Y_t. \tag{7.9b}$$

The jump distribution is described by a random variable J_t, which is frequently assumed to have a Gaussian distribution, e.g. $J_t \sim N(\mu_J, \sigma_J)$. Spikes can be modelled by presuming the jump distribution to be positive, however this means that the tendency of electricity prices to return to equilibrium levels within a short time period needs to be explained by mean reversion (with a relatively large value for κ). Calibration/parameter estimation is discussed in Cartea and Figueroa (2005) and in Chapter 4 of Eydeland and Wolyniec (2003).

The problem is that the strong mean reversion applied to the asset price after a jump will be overly high in other scenarios. In Kluge (2006) and Hambly, Howison and Kluge (2009), a variant of (7.9) is proposed where two different mean reversion rates are applied to regular and jump components of the dynamics, i.e.

$$dY_t^{(1)} = -\kappa_1 Y_t^{(1)} dt + \sigma dW_t \tag{7.10a}$$

$$dY_t^{(2)} = -\kappa_2 Y_{t-}^{(2)} dt + J_t dN_t \tag{7.10b}$$

$$\ln S_t = f(t) + Y_t^{(1)} + Y_t^{(2)}. \tag{7.10c}$$

The jump mean reversion rate κ_2 is taken to be 25–30 times larger than the purely diffusive mean reversion rate κ_1 in Hambly, Howison and Kluge (2009).

The same splitting of the stochastic component into two processes is followed in Villaplana (2003), where we have

$$dY_t^{(1)} = -\kappa_1 Y_t^{(1)} dt + \sigma_1 dW_t^{(1)} \qquad (7.11a)$$

$$dY_t^{(2)} = -\kappa_2 Y_{t-}^{(2)} dt + \sigma_2 dW_t^{(2)} + J_t dN_t \qquad (7.11b)$$

$$\ln S_t = f(t) + Y_t^{(1)} + Y_t^{(2)} \qquad (7.11c)$$

but noting that now there are two Brownian motions, which are presumed to be correlated, with $\langle dW_t^{(1)}, dW_t^{(2)} \rangle = \rho dt$.

One can certainly construct a model where negative jumps are possible as well as positive jumps. Geman and Roncoroni (2006) present a jump-diffusion model, which relies upon a jump process J_t which is a "marked point process", which is a mean reverting process with positive jumps. We have

$$d\ln S_t = \mu'(t) + \theta_1 \left[\mu_t - \ln(E_{t-}) \right] dt + \sigma dW_t + h(t_-) dJ_t \quad (7.12)$$

where $h(\cdot)$ is a sign function that gives the direction of the jumps, it can be chosen so that jumps are positive if electricity prices are below a threshold level U_t and negative if electricity prices are above U_t, i.e.

$$h(t_-) = \mathbf{1}_{\{E_t < U_t\}} - \mathbf{1}_{\{E_t > U_t\}}. \qquad (7.13)$$

A calibration scheme is proposed in the original paper which uses the Radon–Nikodym derivative and an elegant derivation of the log-likelihood function, but this is rather sensitive to practical implementation issues and filtering methods which need to be adopted, as discussed in Fiorenzani (2006).

Kjaer (2008) also proposes a model with jump-diffusive dynamics

$$dX_t = -\kappa X_t dt + dL_t, \qquad (7.14a)$$

$$\ln S_t = f(t) + X_t, \qquad (7.14b)$$

where L_t is a compensated jump diffusion. Note that if $dL_t = \sigma dW_t$ then this recovers the Lucia–Schwartz model quoted in (7.2) above. For most choices of jump distribution, the model fails to be analytically tractable, which prompts the choice of a two-sided exponential jump size distribution in the original paper. Finally, applications of the model to the pricing of swing options (see Section 7.4) are discussed.

Research in the area continues, being a fruitful area for model development. A good survey of up-to-date literature in the area in given in Section 1 of Janczura *et al.* (2013), which we refer the interested reader towards.

7.3.1.2   *Reduced Form Models – Regime Switching*

Regime switching models were originally presented in Hamilton (1989), where we assume there are a denumerable number of discrete states of the world, and the evolution of the asset price process is described by one of a number of pure stochastic processes – depending on which state is currently being occupied. For electricity these states could be, for example, a mean-reverting state (Regime 1) and a spike state (Regime 2).

As pointed out in Janczura and Weron (2012), there are two types of regime switching model. The first – the *parameter switching model* – is where a single process Y_t is given, but where there are several regimes which model parameters are be drawn from (an uncertain volatility model with a finite number of states is a good example of this). This can be described

$$dY_t = \mu_i(t, Y_t)dt + \sigma_i(t, Y_t)dW_t \tag{7.15}$$

where $\mu_i(t, Y_t)$ and $\sigma_i(t, Y_t)$ are specified separately for each of $i \in \{1, \ldots, L\}$. in an L-state parameter switching model. The second – the *independent regime model* – is discussed in de Jong (2006), where the notation is introduced for the stochastic component (denoted x_t in their work)

$$Y_t = Y_t^{(r_t)} \tag{7.16}$$

where $r_t \in \{1, \ldots, L\}$, for an L-state regime switching model, and separate processes are evolved with at least one being given by a mean reverting process of the following form

$$dY_t^{(i)} = \mu_i(t, Y_t^{(i)})dt + \sigma_i(t, Y_t^{(i)})dW_t^{(i)}, \tag{7.17}$$

other processes typically being independent discontinuous realisations of a random variable, e.g.

$$Y_t^{(i)} \sim F^{(i)}(y). \tag{7.18}$$

The models are usually constructed as discrete time models, where the times are presumed to occupy discrete states $\{t_i\}_{i \in S}$ for some index set S. Writing the diffusion for $Y_t^{(i)}$ in generalised form

$$dY_t^{(i)} = \mu_i(t, Y_t^{(i)})dt + \sigma_i(t, Y_t^{(i)})dW_t^{(i)} \qquad (7.19)$$

where $\mu_i(t, Y_t^{(i)})$ and $\sigma_i(t, Y_t^{(i)})$ denote the drift and diffusion terms respectively and $W_t^{(i)}$ denotes a standardised one-dimensional Brownian motion. If we consider a small time increment Δt then the Euler scheme can be written as

$$
\begin{aligned}
Y_{t+\Delta t}^{(i)} &= Y_t^{(i)} + \int_t^{t+\Delta t} dY_s^{(i)} \\
&= Y_t^{(i)} + \int_t^{t+\Delta t} \mu_i(s, Y_s^{(i)})ds + \int_t^{t+\Delta t} \sigma_i(s, Y_s^{(i)})dW_s^{(i)} \\
&\approx Y_t^{(i)} + \mu_i(t, Y_t^{(i)})\Delta t + \sigma_i(t, Y_t^{(i)})[W_{t+\Delta t}^{(i)} - W_t^{(i)}].
\end{aligned}
$$

Transition probabilities between the L states are described by a Markov chain transition matrix

$$\mathbf{P} = (p_{ij}) = \begin{pmatrix} p_{11} & \cdots & p_{1L} \\ \vdots & \ddots & \vdots \\ p_{L1} & \cdots & p_{LL} \end{pmatrix} \qquad (7.20)$$

where the matrix sums to unity along all rows $\sum_{j=1}^{L} p_{ij} = 1 \; \forall i \in \{1, L\}$. The analogous transition matrix for regime switching models in continuous time can easily be constructed by replacing p_{ij} by $\lambda_{ij}dt$.

We give some examples of regime switching models encountered in the literature.

Huisman and de Jong (2003) introduce a two-state regime switching model, where the first state is a regular mean-reverting stochastic process, i.e.

$$dY_t^{(1)} = \alpha(m - Y_t^{(1)})dt + \sigma dW_t,$$

and the second is given by a spike distribution

$$Y_t^{(2)} \sim N(\mu_S, \sigma_S).$$

A three-state regime switching model is given in Huisman and Mahieu (2003), where regime 1 corresponds to a "normal" mean-reverting state, regime 2 is a jump regime and regime 3 describes a state where the asset price process returns to the "normal" mean-reverting state from a post-jump state.[3] We have

$$dY_t^{(1)} = -\alpha_1 Y_t^{(1)} dt + \sigma_1 dW_t,$$

the second is given by a spike distribution

$$Y_t^{(2)} \sim N(\mu_S, \sigma_S)$$

and the third introduces a much higher mean reversion to bring the asset price process back from post-jump levels back towards a more usual equilibrium level

$$dY_t^{(1)} = -\alpha_3 Y_t^{(1)} dt + \sigma_3 dW_t.$$

A three-state regime switching model is also discussed in Andreasen and Dahlgren (2006), with $r_t = 1$ corresponding to a downwards spike, $r_t = 2$ corresponding to the usual mean-reverting commodity dynamics, and $r_t = 1$ corresponding to an upwards spike.

It can be clearly seen, as discussed by Kholodnyi (2001a, 2001b, 2006, 2008, 2014) that the regime switching approach naturally leads to non-Markovian dynamics for the asset price process Y_t, as the construction of the regime switching framework naturally allows transient spikes to be handled in a derivatives valuation framework.

For further reading, we recommend the reader investigate Section 6.1.3 of Fiorenzani (2006), Huisman (2009), and the recent review of Markov regime-switching models in Janczura and Weron (2014).

7.3.2 Structural Models

Electricity, not being in any way easily storable, is necessarily generated and consumed within a very short time horizon. The cost of production of electricity is highly correlated to the price for the fuel used for power generation, which we see is often natural gas. The demand for electricity shows a high degree of seasonality (being higher at peak periods) and increases as ambient temperatures rise or fall relative to a comfortable ambient level (typically around 65 °F or 18 °C) due to demand for cooling or heating respectively (more on this in Chapter 9). As a result, one can construct various models that attempt to model stochastic deformations in either supply and/or demand curves for electricity. Such models are known as structural models.

---

[3] Regimes are indexed differently here from those in the original paper.

The model of Barlow (2002) was an early application of the structural approach to electricity spot price modelling. In their paper, the supply and demand curves at time t for electricity as a function of price x are denoted $u_t(x)$ and $d_t(x)$ respectively. We assume $u_t(\cdot)$ to be monotonically increasing and $d_t(\cdot)$ to be monotonically decreasing, reflecting the increased propensity to supply an economic asset (and decreasing propensity to consume it) as prices increase.

Equilibrium spot electricity prices can be found by solving for the intersection of these two curves, i.e. S_t where

$$u_t(S_t) = d_t(S_t). \qquad (7.21)$$

Demand is presumed to be highly inelastic and therefore is modelled directly as a stochastic process D_t, whereas supply is modelled using a functional form that depends on the spot electricity price x

$$u_t(x) = g(x) = a_0 - b_0 x^\alpha \qquad (7.22a)$$
$$d_t(x) = D_t = a_1 - \sigma_1 Y_t \qquad (7.22b)$$

with $a_0, b_0 > 0$ and $\alpha < 0$. The quantity a_0 refers to the maximum amount of electricity that can be supplied (we presume $x > 0$), noting that $\lim_{x \to \infty} g(x) = a_0$. Unfortunately, $\lim_{x \to 0+} g(x) = -\infty$ and $g(x^*) = 0$ for $a_0 = b_0(x^*)^\alpha$, i.e. $x^* = (a_0/b_0)^{(1/\alpha)}$.

Solving for an equilibrium spot price S_t where supply and demand curves coincide, we obtain

$$u_t(S_t) = d_t(S_t). \qquad (7.23)$$

From (7.22a) we have $g(S_t) = d_t(S_t)$ and therefore $S_t = g^{-1}(D_t)$. The function $g(x)$ can easily be inverted: if $y = g(x)$ then

$$y = a_0 - b_0 x^\alpha$$
$$\Rightarrow b_0 x^\alpha = a_0 - y$$
$$\Rightarrow x = \left(\frac{a_0 - y}{b_0} \right)^{1/\alpha}, \qquad (7.24)$$

a relationship that holds for $y < a_0$ (while this can be extended to the domain $y \geq a_0$ for some values of α, we choose not to do so).

From (7.24) we obtain $x = f(y)$ with $f(y) = \left((a_0 - y)/b_0 \right)^{1/\alpha}$, thereby obtaining

$$S_t = g^{-1}(D_t) = f(D_t) = \left((a_0 - D_t)/b_0 \right)^{1/\alpha}. \qquad (7.25)$$

The caveat is that if demand D_t exceeds the maximum supply volume a_0 then the right hand side of (7.24) will be negative, with an infinite asymptote as $D_t \to a_0$. Barlow (2002) therefore sets a cap on spot prices where demand is equal to $a_0 - \epsilon_0 b_0$ for a suitable choice of ϵ_0, obtaining

$$
S_t = \begin{cases}
\left((a_0 - D_t)/b_0\right)^{1/\alpha}, & D_t < a_0 - \epsilon_0 b_0, \\
\epsilon_0^{1/\alpha}, & D_t \geq a_0 - \epsilon_0 b_0.
\end{cases}
\tag{7.26}
$$

Using the notation $X_t \sim OU(\lambda, a, \sigma)$ to denote an Ornstein–Uhlenbeck process following the stochastic process $dX_t = \lambda(a - X_t)dt + \sigma dW_t$, we have

$$
dD_t = \lambda(a_1 - D_t)dt + \sigma_1 dW_t
\tag{7.27}
$$

from which upon setting $D_t = a_1 - \sigma_1 Y_t$, i.e. $Y_t = (a_1 - D_t)/\sigma_1$, we have

$$
dY_t = -\lambda Y_t dt + dW_t.
\tag{7.28}
$$

We can therefore, in the region $D_t < a_0 - \epsilon_0 b_0$, i.e. where $Y_t > (a_1 - a_0 + b_0 \epsilon_0)/\sigma_1$, put

$$
\begin{aligned}
S_t &= \left(\frac{a_0}{b_0} - \frac{1}{b_0}D_t\right)^{1/\alpha} \\
&= \left(\frac{a_0}{b_0} - \frac{1}{b_0}(a_1 - \sigma_1 Y_t)\right)^{1/\alpha} \\
&= \left(\frac{a_0}{b_0} - \frac{a_1}{b_0} + \frac{\sigma_1}{b_0}Y_t\right)^{1/\alpha} \\
&= \left(1 + \alpha X_t\right)^{1/\alpha}
\end{aligned}
\tag{7.29}
$$

where

$$
1 + \alpha X_t = \frac{a_0}{b_0} - \frac{a_1}{b_0} + \frac{\sigma_1}{b_0}Y_t
$$

i.e.

$$
X_t = \frac{1}{\alpha}\left[\frac{a_0 - a_1 - b_0}{b_0} + \frac{\sigma_1}{b_0}Y_t\right]
\tag{7.30}
$$

and conversely,

$$Y_t = \frac{\alpha b_0}{\sigma_1} X_t - \frac{a_0 - a_1 - b_0}{\sigma_1}. \qquad (7.31)$$

Note that the condition $Y_t > (a_1 - a_0 + b_0 \epsilon_0)/\sigma_1$ is equivalent to $1 + \alpha X_t > \epsilon_0$, as can be shown directly from (7.31).

Barlow (2002) then puts $f_\alpha(x) = (1 + \alpha x)^{1/\alpha}$ with inverse $g_\alpha(x) = (x^\alpha - 1)/\alpha$. From (7.26) and (7.29) we then have

$$S_t = \begin{cases} f_\alpha(X_t), & 1 + \alpha X_t > \epsilon_0, \\ \epsilon_0^{1/\alpha}, & 1 + \alpha X_t \leq \epsilon_0 \end{cases} \qquad (7.32)$$

with

$$dX_t = \lambda(a - X_t)dt + \sigma dW_t \qquad (7.33)$$

where

$$a = \frac{a_0 - a_1 - b_0}{\alpha b_0}, \qquad (7.34a)$$

$$\sigma = \frac{\sigma_1}{\alpha b_0}, \qquad (7.34b)$$

as can be shown from (7.28) and (7.31) in the following manner. Firstly, from (7.31) we have

$$X_t = \frac{\sigma_1}{\alpha b_0} Y_t + \frac{1}{\alpha b_0}[a_0 - a_1 - b_0].$$

Then

$$\begin{aligned}
dX_t &= \frac{\sigma_1}{\alpha b_0} dY_t \\
&= \frac{\sigma_1}{\alpha b_0} \left[-\lambda Y_t dt + dW_t \right] \\
&= \frac{\sigma_1}{\alpha b_0} \left[-\lambda \left(\frac{\alpha b_0}{\sigma_1} X_t - \frac{a_0 - a_1 - b_0}{\sigma_1} \right) dt + dW_t \right] \\
&= -\lambda X_t dt + \frac{\lambda}{\alpha b_0}[a_0 - a_1 - b_0]dt + \frac{\sigma_1}{\alpha b_0} dW_t \\
&= \lambda \left(\frac{a_0 - a_1 - b_0}{\alpha b_0} - X_t \right) dt + \frac{\sigma_1}{\alpha b_0} dW_t \\
&= \lambda(a - X_t)dt + \sigma dW_t
\end{aligned}$$

with a and σ as given in (7.34). This model, referred to as a nonlinear Ornstein–Uhlenbeck model in Barlow (2002), is capable of generating spikes through purely diffusive dynamics (though being a one-factor model, it cannot capture any decorrelation between spot and futures prices). We refer the reader to the original paper for discussion of parameter estimation using maximum likelihood estimation techniques.

More realistic shapes for supply and demand curves can of course be modelled, for further discussion of structural models in electricity modelling we refer the reader to Eydeland and Wolyniec (2003) and Pirrong (2012).

7.4 SWING OPTIONS

In addition to electricity futures, forwards and options, there are a number of interesting products available on the power markets. One is the swing option, which also exists in natural gas markets. This is a volumetric option that allows the holder of the product to decide upon the volume of power (or other commodity) to receive, within limits generally set a certain distance either side of the initially agreed notional. Basically this means that a swing option is a financial derivative that permits multiple exercises, at various timepoints (though it is often the case that a swing option can only be exercised once a day at most).

Suppose the timepoints are given by $\{t_i\}_{i \in S}$ for some index set S. A strip of options would have value

$$V_i = N_i \omega_i \cdot (S_{t_i} - K)^+$$

at each of the exercise times, where ω_i is -1 for a put and $+1$ for a call.

A swing option allows some flexibility in the choice of the notionals N_i, each of which can be nominated at the time of exercise, subject to various rules:

1. The daily notional N_i must be between m and M.
2. The total notional $\sum_i N_i$ must be between A and B.
3. The total number of dates exercised $\sum_i \mathbf{1}_{\{N_i > 0\}}$ must be no less than $N_{\min}$ and no more than $N_{\max}$.

Note that the floor $N_{\min}$ on the number of exercise dates means it is possible that a swing option may need to be exercised when it is actually of negative value to the option holder. The path dependency of these products together with the volumetric feature makes them especially challenging to price, requiring techniques such as are typically used for pricing Bermudan products. We refer the reader to Kaminski, Gibner and Pinnamaneni (1999), Section 7.5.2 in Clewlow and Strickland (2000), Chapter 8 in Eydeland and Wolyniec (2003), Section 12.4 in Geman (2005), Section 7.3 of Fiorenzani (2006), Section 9.4 in Harris (2006), Hambly, Howison and Kluge (2009) and Kjaer (2008) for further discussions.

7.5 SPARK SPREAD OPTIONS

Spark spreads, also known as "tolling agreements", are discussed in Chapter 4.3 of Edwards (2010) and in Eydeland and Wolyniec (2003). These are effectively financial contracts that mirror the rental of a power plant from the owners, paying the differential between the price of electricity and the price of the fuel (e.g. natural gas) used to generate it. A spark spread option has payoff

$$V_T = P_{\text{electricity}} - HR \times P_{\text{fuel}} \tag{7.35}$$

where the heat rate HR is a measure of how much fuel is required to generate one unit (MW) of electricity. The heat rate is expressed in MW per barrel (of oil), Btu or therm (for natgas) or tonne (of coal), as appropriate.

A tolling agreement is basically a strip of spark spread options over a time interval (possibly with other exotic features). The same spread option methodology as for crack spread options is appropriate for these products; a case study of the pricing is presented in Section 9.3 of Benth and Koekebakker (2008).

Note that if the fuel is coal, rather than oil or gas, the product is known as a "dark spread" option – the terminology referring to the colour of coal, but just a spark spread option by another name.

8

Agricultural Derivatives

By now it is clear that most commodities come out of the ground itself, the commodities in Chapters 3 to 6 being mined directly, though electricity (Chapter 7) is generally (but not always) produced from fuel sources obtained through mining. However, mining is far from the only way to extract wealth from land. A second and equally established mode of production involves cultivating produce on the land itself, an economic sector which historically employed a great number of people in subsistence agriculture (and still does in much of the world).

In the modern world, however, industrialisation and mechanisation have greatly changed the way farming is carried out, a change in emphasis which has led to the development of financial markets around agriculture, including the use of futures and options. A general introduction to futures and options in the context of agriculture can be found in Bittman (2008), Bobin (1990) and Purcell and Koontz (1999). Agricultural commodities are also covered in Chapter 7 of Geman (2005) and Chapter 11 of Schofield (2007).

Not surprisingly given the reliance of agriculture on the seasons, seasonality is an important factor – we refer the reader to Sørensen (2002). Modelling efforts pertaining to agricultural commodities are covered in many papers, including Richter and Sørensen (2002), Koekebakker and Lien (2004), Geman and Nguyen (2005) and Schmitz, Wang and Kimn (2012), among others.

It should be noted that many of the productivity gains in farming are a result of advances in the use of chemically synthesised fertilisers since the latter part of the 19th century, many of which require fossil fuels for production. The major three macronutrients required in plant growth are nitrogen (N), phosphorus (P) and potassium (K), from where we get the NPK rating for various fertilisers. These each serve different functions: nitrogen promotes leaf growth, phosphorus serves to enhance the growth of roots and shoots, and potassium is crucial for flowering and fruiting. Typical fertilisers in each of these three categories are sulphate of ammonia, superphosphate and potash.

Nitrogen in particular has an interesting history to it. In the middle of the 19th century, nitrogen rich guano deposits were extracted from Latin America (Chile, especially) and shipped to Europe and the USA for use as fertiliser. However in 1908, a German chemist called Fritz Haber filed a patent on the industrial synthesis of ammonia, for which he obtained the 1918 Nobel Prize. The reaction is

$$N_2 + 3H_2 \rightarrow 2NH_3$$

and the fertiliser produced using this process was considerably less expensive than imports from Chile.

While nitrogen gas is plentiful in the atmosphere, hydrogen gas is not – the hydrogen in this reaction is generally derived from methane (i.e. industrial natural gas). This is where we establish our link between modern agriculture and fossil fuel energy. Indeed, about 3–5% of annual natural gas consumption worldwide is directly used in the manufacture of nitrogen fertilisers, in addition to that used in the operation of farm equipment, transporting goods to market and so on.

Clearly there are basically two types of agriculture: growing plants and growing animals (livestock). Within the category of plants, commodity futures and options markets only really have two major areas: grains and seeds, and the so-called softs (or "tropics"). We therefore follow the standard categorisation used in commodity markets and consider three different classes of agricultural commodities: (i) grains and seeds, (ii) softs and (iii) livestock.

8.1   GRAINS

The grains and the oilseeds are frequently grouped together for the purposes of commodity trading. We shall discuss each of these in turn. A very accessible nonmathematical discussion of the grain markets can be found in Kub (2012).

Grains, or cereals, are basically a type of edible grass. They are staples of the diet and are grown in much greater quantities than any other crop. Table 8.1 describes the annual production of various grains, from which it is clearly apparent (see Figure 8.1) that the yearly production of grain worldwide is dominated by three dominant grains – corn, rice and wheat – which make up almost 90% of worldwide production.

Cereals are annual crops, and generally only survive one harvest. Depending on their temperature sensitivity, there are cold season grains

Table 8.1   Global grain production – absolute (2010).

Cereal	Global production
Corn	844 mio T
Rice	672 mio T
Wheat	651 mio T
Barley	123 mio T
Sorghum	56 mio T
Millet	29 mio T
Oats	20 mio T
Triticale	13 mio T
Rye	12 mio T
Buckwheat	1.5 mio T
Fonio	0.5 mio T
Quinoa	0.1 mio T

such as wheat, rye, triticale, oats and barley and warm season grains such as rice and sorghum. The cold season grains can be categorised into winter and summer variants. The winter variants are planted in the autumn, germinate, and lie dormant over the winter and resume growth in spring, maturing in late spring or early summer (when they are harvested). Spring variants, however, are planted in early spring and harvested later that summer.

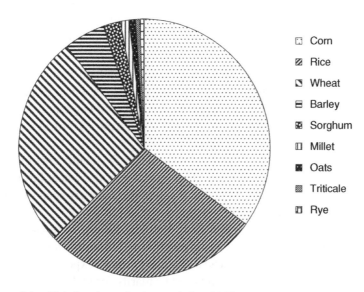

Figure 8.1   Global grain production – relative (2010).

Grains on North American exchanges are usually graded, with No. 1 being the highest grade (and trades at a premium), No. 2 being the usual specification and consequently trades at par, and No. 3 is an inferior grade which trades at a discount. Other inferior grades exist, No. 4 and No. 5, but are very infrequently encountered. Much information on US wheat grading can be found at www.wheatflourbook.org for those who are interested. Commodities come and commodities go – for example, on the CBOT, barley futures used to trade from 1885 to 1940 and rye futures from 1869 to 1970, but neither are currently traded on that exchange.

The major products traded on exchanges such as the CBOT are futures, options and calendar spread options, which we have previously encountered. Typical calendar spreads are between adjacent futures contracts, or between a differential of two contracts, each being either (i) the final contract in the first seven months of the year or (ii) the final contract in the final five months of the year. We can construct four examples: the Dec/July, the July/Dec, the Dec/Dec and the July/July wheat spread. For other agriculturals which do not trade a December contract (e.g. soybeans), the final contract in the final five months will differ.

8.1.1 Wheat

The cultivation of wheat dates back at least ten thousand years, to the Fertile Crescent and the Nile Delta in the Middle East. It is used to make flour (for bread, pasta, noodles, etc.) and can be fermented to make beer.

Wheat is cultivated on a greater proportion of land than any other vegetable crop. The total value of worldwide trade in wheat dwarfs any other crop, even though the tonnage of rice and corn is greater. A good, but dated, analysis of wheat can be found in Chapter 19 of Seidel and Ginsberg (1983).

There are various types of wheat, those that are frequently encountered are described in Table 8.2. About three-quarters of the wheat farmed in the USA is winter wheats. Note that many of these are grouped together for export designation under the label NAEGA No. 2.

The "red" wheats are brownish in colour (due to the presence of phenolic compounds in the bran layer) and are often bleached before being used, as a result white wheats tend to be more expensive.

Durum wheat is the hardest and used primarily for making pasta. The other hard wheats are used for bread-making, though are sometimes

Table 8.2 Common types of wheat.

Common wheat (global)	The most widely cultivated wheat.
Durum wheat (global)	The second most widely cultivated wheat.
Hard Red Spring (US)	Used for bread flour & hard baked goods. Traded at MGE.
Hard Red Winter (US)	Used for bread flour & hard baked goods. Traded at KCBOT.
Soft Red Winter (US)	Low-protein, used for baked goods. Traded on CBOT.
Hard White (US)	Used for breads and brewing.
Soft White (US)	Low protein, used for pie crusts and pastry.

blended with the softer wheats to make general purpose flour. Soft wheat is generally used for cake and other baked goods. Note that the hard wheats tend to have the higher vegetable protein content.

Let us examine the various types of wheat traded on the futures and option exchanges.

8.1.1.1 Chicago Wheat

As discussed in Chapter 1, modern futures exchanges developed in Chicago to enable agricultural trading to take place with less risk on the part of market participants. The various types of wheat contracts traded at the Chicago Board of Trade include No. 2 Soft Red Winter, No. 2 Hard Red Winter, No. 2 Dark Northern Spring and No. 2 Northern Spring (No. 1 grades can be delivered, and command a 3 cent per bushel premium). However the main wheat traded through the CBOT is Soft Red Winter wheat, which is a low grade wheat. It is often exported or used as animal feed, in addition to being used in cheaper breads and pizza doughs. Soft Red Winter wheat is cultivated in Tennessee, Arkansas, Missouri, Illinois, Indiana and Ohio (Geman, 2005).

The last trade date for the futures contracts is the business day prior to the 15th calendar day of the contract month, where the expiry months for wheat are March (H), May (K), July (N), September (U) and December (Z). The contract size is 5,000 bushels and the ticker symbol is "W". Settlement is physical and delivery is effected through registered warehouse receipts issued against stocks held in approved warehouses in either the Chicago Switching District or the Toledo OH Switching District (note that these districts refer to railroad yards). Ohio delivery is made at a discount to the contract price.

For CBOT grain options, the expiry date is determined to be the last Friday (or first good business day before the Friday, if Friday is a holiday) which precedes by at least two business days the final business day preceding the contract month. Standard options therefore expire around the end of February, April, June, August and November. There are option contracts which expire around the end of the other seven months of the year, these are called "serial" contracts and exercise into the prompt future contract.

8.1.1.2 *Kansas City Wheat*

Of the three major wheat types discussed in this chapter, this is the largest of the three crops. The wheat traded on the Kansas City Board of Trade is Hard Red Winter wheat, which accounts for 60–75% of the wheat grown in the USA, used primarily in breadmaking though about half is exported under the NAEGA No. 2 designation. It is grown in locations as diverse as Texas, Oklahoma, Colorado and Nebraska as well as Kansas.

Hard Red Winter wheat futures contracts are traded on the Kansas City Board of Trade for the usual delivery months for wheat: March (H), May (K), July (N), September (U) and December (Z), with contract size the standard 5,000 bushels. The last trading day is the business day preceding the 15th calendar day of the month.

In addition, options are traded on these futures, with the expiry date calculated the same way as for CBOT options on wheat.

8.1.1.3 *Minneapolis Wheat*

The Minneapolis Grain Exchange was formed as the Minneapolis Chamber of Commerce in 1881, and futures trading on Hard Red Spring wheat commenced only two years later in 1883. Hard Red Spring wheat is one of the varieties of wheat with the highest protein content, it is generally used for making better quality types of bread, as well as pizzas and bagels. On account of its high quality, it is not exported in any significant amount. The futures and options contracts are traded electronically on CME Globex, with the ticker symbol "MW".

Hard Red Spring wheat (US No. 2 Northern Spring Wheat, being 13.5% protein or higher) is traded on the Minneapolis Grain Exchange for the usual expiry months for wheat: March (H), May (K), July (N), September (U) and December (Z). The September contract is also called the "New Crop" contract. Like CBOT trading, the last trading date is the business day prior to the 15th calendar day of the contract month, Contract size is 5,000 bushels.

For options on Minneapolis wheat, the expiry date is determined to be the last Friday (or first good business day before the Friday, if Friday is a holiday) which precedes by at least two business days the final business day preceding the contract month.

8.1.2 Corn

Corn, also known as maize, originated in Mesoamerica where it was cultivated by the Aztecs and the Mayans, and has been used for human food since around 5,000 BC. After European exploration of the Americas, corn was brought back to Europe and has since made its way around much of the world, where it now holds the position of being the most produced grain crop in the world. About half the worldwide production is in the USA (centred heavily around the Midwest). Other notable corn producers include China, Brazil, Mexico, Argentina, India, Pakistan and France.

Corn is used more extensively than wheat in animal feeds, and it may be surprising to examine the consumption pattern of corn in the USA, see Table 8.3 and Figure 8.2. Only about 3% of corn is directly used in food consumption in the form of polenta, tacos, tortillas etc. (this 3% includes alcohol beverages such as bourbon whisky), and while another 8% of corn is used in the production of starches and sweeteners (e.g. high fructose corn syrup, or "HFCS") which are destined for human consumption, the vast majority of corn is either exported or used for bioethanol or animal feed.

Corn which is used for animal feed is sometimes called "dent corn", other competing grain products used for animal consumption are wheat, sorghum and soybean meal.

Table 8.3 Corn consumption – absolute (USA, 2008).

Livestock feed	5,250 mio Bu.
Ethanol production	3,650 mio Bu.
Exports	1,850 mio Bu.
Production of starch, corn oil, sweeteners	943 mio Bu.
Human consumption	327 mio Bu.

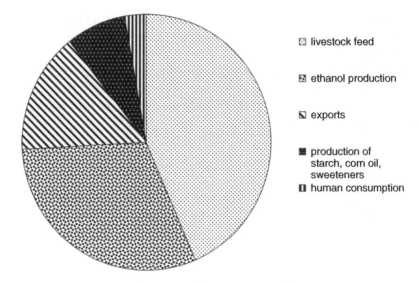

Figure 8.2   Corn consumption – relative (USA, 2008).

Corn futures are traded on the CBOT with the same expiry dates as wheat: March (H), May (K), July (N), September (U) and December (Z). Being a CBOT contract, the contract features are basically the same as for CBOT wheat, the futures maturity date is the last Friday (or first good business day before the Friday, if Friday is a holiday) which precedes by at least two business days the final business day preceding the contract month. The standard deliverable grade is No. 2 Yellow, though No. 1 Yellow and No. 3 Yellow may be delivered at a pre-arranged premium or discount respectively.

Corn options on CBOT also trade, the expiry date being the last Friday (or first good business day before the Friday, if Friday is a holiday) which precedes by at least two business days the final business day preceding the contract month.

8.1.3 Rice

Rice was the world's most produced grain crop as recently as the early 1960s, but since then wheat and corn production have overtaken it. Nevertheless, rice is still of great importance as the staple diet of billions of people on the planet. As much as one-fifth of all food calories consumed every year are estimated to come from rice. It has been grown for thousands of years, starting in East Asia, from where it was taken to Europe by the Moors to Spain and Portugal, and then subsequently taken to the Americas. While rice is most often used in its milled form, producing either brown or white rice depending on the degree of milling, it is also used to make rice noodles, rice flour and other food products.

Rough rice futures are traded on the CBOT with the ticker symbol[1] "RR" but with different contract months to wheat or corn: January (F), March (H), May (K), July (N), September (U) and November (X). The standard deliverable grade is No. 2 long grain rough rice and the contract size is 2,000 hundredweight (cwt). The calculation of the expiry date proceeds the same way though, the last Friday (or good business day if necessary) preceding by at least two business days the final business day before the contract month.

8.1.4 Oats

Oats are very much a hardy winter crop, a staple food of Scotland and grown predominantly in Russia and Canada. While used for human consumption, the main use of oats is livestock feed – horses especially are fond of oats.

Oat futures are traded on the CBOT with the same expiry dates as wheat and corn: March (H), May (K), July (N), September (U) and December (Z). The standard futures contracts are for No. 2 Heavy and No. 1, at par, with other grades trading at differentials determined by the exchange. The date calculation methodologies for oat futures and options is the same as for CBOT wheat, and the contract size is similarly 5,000 bushels.

8.1.5 Barley

Though no longer traded on the CBOT, futures contracts on barley are traded as Western barley (ticket code "AB") on the Winnipeg Commodity Exchange, with contract months March (H), May (K), July (N), October (V) and December (Z). The price is quoted in Canadian dollars per tonne, and the contract size is 20 tonnes. Barley is used for livestock feed, production of alcoholic beverages, and has a niche market in health foods.

---

[1] The letter "R" was used for rye, from 1869 to 1970.

8.2   OILSEEDS

Also frequently included in the same category are the oilseeds, such as soybeans and soybean products such as soybean oil and soybean meal (these three together make up the so-called "soybean complex") and canola.

8.2.1   Soybeans

Like rice, soybeans originated in China and spread to other parts of the world. Major producers of soya beans are the USA, Brazil and Argentina and, to a lesser extent, China and India.

Soybean oil makes up about half of all worldwide edible vegetable oil production. About 85% of soybean production worldwide is "crushed" into soybean meal and vegetable oil, with only about 6% used directly for human consumption (mostly in Asia).

Approximately 98% of the soybean meal produced, a huge proportion, is used as high protein animal feed (the remainder is used to make soy flour and soy proteins), and about 95% of the soybean oil is used as edible vegetable oil – the rest used in the manufacture of fatty acids, soaps and biodiesel. Soybean oil is also used as a feed in aquaculture.

8.2.1.1   Soybean Futures and Options

Soybean futures are traded on the CBOT under the ticker code "S" with expiry dates: January (F), March (H), May (K), July (N), August (Q), September (U) and November (X). The standard futures contract is for No. 2 Yellow, with grades No. 1 Yellow and No. 3 Yellow accepted at price differentials determined by the exchange. Delivery is via registered warehouse receipts against stocks lodged in the Chicago Switching District. Being a CBOT contract, the date calculation methodologies is the same as for CBOT wheat, the contract size is similarly 5,000 bushels, with prices quoted in dollars per bushel (a bushel of beans being equal to 60 pounds). The options contracts similarly obey the same date conventions as CBOT wheat.

8.2.1.2   Soybean Oil Futures and Options

Soybeans are crushed to extract the vegetable oil. It is traded on the CBOT in contracts of 60,000 pounds, which is equivalent to the contents of one standard tank car. Futures months traded are January (F), March (H), May (K), July (N), August (Q), September (U), October (V) and December (Z). The date calculations for futures and options are the same as for other CBOT agriculturals. Prices are quoted in dollars per pound.

8.2.1.3 Soybean Meal Futures and Options

Soybean meal is the residue left after soybeans are crushed to extract the oil. It is a yellowish coloured meal, commonly used as a filler in animal feeds. There is only one grade of soybean meal traded on the CBOT, with a minimum required protein content of 44%. Delivery is effected by production of a shipping certificate approved by either the CBOT or the Toledo, Ohio Switching District (at discount). The futures months traded are the same as soybean oil, i.e. January (F), March (H), May (K), July (N), August (Q), September (U), October (V) and December (Z), and the standard contract size is for lots of 100 short tons (each comprising 2,000 pounds), with prices quoted in dollars per short ton. Everything else, such as the date calculation rules for futures and options, is as standard for agriculturals on the CBOT.

8.2.1.4 Soybean Crush Options

Similarly to the refinery spread option, we can define a soybean crush spread that captures the price differential between refined products (soybean meal and soybean oil) and unrefined products (soybeans). We know that the two refined soybean products and unrefined soybeans are quoted in different terms, requiring normalisation. A typical bushel of soybeans weighs about 60 pounds and when crushed the typical result is 11 pounds of soybean oil, 44 pounds of soybean meal (~48% protein), 4 pounds of hulls and 1 pound of other waste. So we can extract approximately 11 pounds of soybean oil and 44 pounds (which is 0.022 short tons) of soybean meal from each bushel of soybeans that is taken to the crush.

The typical formula, as published on the relevant CME Group webpage, is

$$V_{crush} = 0.022 \times V_{meal} + 11 \times V_{oil} - V_{beans} \qquad (8.1)$$

where V_{meal} is denominated in dollars per ton, V_{oil} is in dollars per pound and V_{beans} is in dollars per bushel. Note that since the normalisation factor for V_{beans} in (8.1) is unity, the notional of the soybean crush spread is expressible in bushels of soybeans.

Soybean crush spreads and options are traded on the CBOT in contracts of 50,000 Bu. There are eight standard delivery months for the soybean crush spread: January (F), March (H), May (K), July (N), August (Q), September (U), October (V) and December (Z) – however, note from Section 8.2.1 that there are no V or Z contracts on soybeans. As a result the October and December soybean crush spreads are both referenced against the November (X) soybean futures contract. Note that a typical value for V_{crush} over the range 2000–2005 is around \$0.50 (per bushel).

8.2.2 Canola

Canola was derived from naturally occuring rapeseed oil at the University of Manitoba in the 1970s. The name is patriotic, being an acronym for **Can**adian **o**il, **l**ow **a**cid.

Futures contracts on canola are traded with ticket code "RS" on the Winnipeg Commodity Exchange, with contract months January (F), March (H), May (K), July (N) and November (X). Like Western barley, the price is quoted in Canadian dollars per tonne, and the contract size is 20 tonnes. The delivery is in the form of canola seed, which is crushed for the oil content.

8.3 SOFTS

The soft commodities, or "softs", mostly (but not solely) comprise agricultural products grown in tropical regions, such as the so-called "tropics" – commodities such as coffee, cocoa, cotton and sugar. However, the softs are sometimes taken to include other commodities such as orange juice, and forest products such as lumber and pulp.

In Chapter 1, we discussed the role of trade and commerce in commodity markets. Clearly, any agricultural good that can only be grown in the tropics but is heavily in demand in more temperate climates is going to need to be traded internationally. Economic historians can point to many examples, such as the Silk Road, the various East India Companies, trade with the West Indies and other historical examples.[2]

---

[2] Regrettably, much of this trade was in commodities produced through indentured slave labour – e.g. sugar, cotton, coffee. Thankfully we have moved on since those days. See www.sweethistory.org/about/transatlantic-slave-trade for a historical perspective.

8.3.1   Coffee

We start with coffee.[3] A stimulant, first used in Africa and the Middle East, this now constitutes one of the most traded commodities worldwide. Though there are about 80 types of coffee plant, only two major types of coffee bean are commonly encountered: the Arabica and the Robusta bean (other minor types such as liberica and dewevrei are of minuscule economic importance). Arabica is a longer straighter bean, whereas Robusta is more oval shaped.

The Arabica variety is a higher altitude coffee than Robusta, preferring an elevation of 600 to 2,500 metres in the subtropics. Robusta is a hardier variety, which can be grown from approximately 200 to 900 metres. Both Arabica and Robusta are grown worldwide, but their trading and consumption patterns differ. In fact Arabica constitutes about 80% of world production, and Robusta about 20%, as Arabica is generally felt to have superior taste – though Robusta is higher in caffeine at about 1.5–3.0% compared to the 1.0–1.5% in Arabica. Consequently, Arabica is predominantly used in coffee blends and single grade coffees, whereas Robusta is primarily used in instant coffee (and in small amounts in coffee blends, to provide *crema*).

The International Coffee Organization publishes export figures, which we have summarised in Tables 8.4 and 8.5. It can be seen that the largest producers are Brazil, Vietnam, Indonesia and Colombia. Vietnam, however, leads in Robusta production, possibly for geographical reasons. Of these countries, the only ones which generally have a sizable domestic market for coffee consumption are Brazil and Ethiopia, so about 75% of coffee is eventually destined for export.

Note that the countries that produce the Colombian Mild type are Colombia, Kenya and Tanzania – not what one might expect.

Coffee is generally priced in cents per pound. ICO Indicator prices are tabulated in Table 8.6, from which we see that Robusta generally trades at a 40–50% discount to Arabica (depending on which Arabica type is being considered: Colombian Milds, Other Milds or Brazilian Naturals).

This gives us the background we need to consider tradeable futures contracts on coffee, which are offered on three different exchanges – the ICE, NYMEX and LIFFE.

---

[3] No surprise to my friends and colleagues . . .

Table 8.4   Coffee export production (Mar 2012–Feb 2013, in units of 60 kg bags).

Type or country	Variety	Exports	Relative share
Colombian milds	A	8,723,085	8%
Other milds	A	26,986,179	24%
Brazilian naturals	A	31,249,910	28%
Robustas	R	46,608,620	41%
Brazil	A/R	28,666,228	25%
Vietnam	R	25,025,000	22%
Indonesia	R/A	10,944,621	10%
Colombia	A	7,525,367	7%
Honduras	A	5,514,259	5%
India	A/R	5,330,465	5%
Peru	A	4,015,740	4%
Guatemala	A	3,746,850	3%
Mexico	A	3,518,456	3%
Ethiopia	A	3,350,320	3%
Uganda	R/A	2,903,610	3%
Others		13,026,878	11%
Total		113,567,794	100%

Table 8.5   Relative coffee export production (2006).

Country & variety	Arabica	Robusta
Brazil Arabica	24%	
Colombia Arabica	11%	
Other Americas Arabica	18%	
Asia Pacific Arabica	3%	
Africa Arabica	6%	
Brazil Robusta		9%
Vietnam Robusta		12%
Indonesia Robusta		6%
Other Asia Pacific Robusta		5%
Africa Robusta		6%
Total	62%	38%

Table 8.6   ICO Indicator coffee prices (2012 daily weighted averages).

Category	Variety	Indicator price (¢/lb)
ICO Composite		156.34
Colombian milds	A	202.08
Other milds	A	186.47
Brazilian naturals	A	174.97
Robustas	R	102.82

8.3.1.1   Coffee – ICE

The ICE futures contracts on coffee are the world benchmark for coffee trading. Coffee futures on the benchmark Coffee "C" Arabica contract are traded on the ICE under the ticker code "KC" with expiry months March (H), May (K), July (N), September (U) and December (Z). The contract is on a notional of 37,500 pounds of Arabica beans of suitable grade ("C" grade). The maturity date, or the last notice date, is seven business days prior to the last business day of the delivery month.

Options exist on ICE coffee futures also. The last trading day for regular options is the second Friday of the calendar month before the futures contract month.

8.3.1.2   Coffee – NYMEX

The NYMEX coffee contract is similarly on a notional of 37,500 pounds and is financially settled, referenced against the underlying ICE coffee "C" contract. The traded futures months are therefore the same as ICE coffee futures. Trading ceases one day prior to the final day for the ICE contract. Options on NYMEX coffee futures are not currently offered, however.

8.3.1.3   Coffee – LIFFE

The LIFFE contract, in contrast to the other two, is on Robusta coffee. The contract is on 10 tonnes, on Class 1 Robusta coffee, with the price quoted in US dollars per tonne (noting that Arabica is generally quoted in U cents per pound, and a tonne is 2,204.62 pounds). Available futures months are January (F), March (H), May (K), July (N), September (U) and November (X). Options on LIFFE coffee futures are also traded, with expiry dates on the third Wednesday of the calendar month preceding the futures month. The options are American style.

8.3.2   Cotton

Cotton is a fibre obtained from the cotton plant, which can be spun to make a variety of fabrics. Leading producers of cotton are China, India, the United States, Pakistan and Brazil. It is traded on the ICE, the NYBOT and NYMEX, under separate ticker codes. About 64%

of cotton is used for apparel, 28% for home furnishings and 8% for industrial production.

8.3.2.1   Cotton – ICE

Cotton No. 2 futures contracts are traded on the ICE, with ticker code "CT". The cotton contract is on a notional of 50,000 pounds (priced in dollars per pound) and physically settled. The futures expire 17 business days from the end of the month, with traded contract months March (H), May (K), July (N), October (V) and December (Z). Delivery can be effected up to 12 business days from the end of the month. To give an idea of typical trading levels, over the 2012 calendar year the Cotton No. 2 contract traded approximately in a range between 70 cents and 1 dollar.

Cotton No. 2 options also exist, and expire on the last Friday preceding the first notice day for the underlying futures (five business days before the first business day of the month) by at least five business days.

8.3.2.2   Cotton – NYMEX

Cotton is traded on the NYMEX, under the separate ticker code "TT" – financially settled, and referenced against the underlying ICE coffee "C" contract. However, no cotton options trade on NYMEX.

8.3.3   Cocoa

Cocoa beans are obtained as fruits from the cocoa tree, and used to make cocoa powder and chocolate. Cocoa was originally cultivated in the Mesoamericas, where it was used as a trading currency on various occasions. Nowadays, cocoa is grown in various tropical countries, the leading producers of cocoa being the Ivory Coast, Ghana and Indonesia (about two thirds of worldwide cocoa production is in West Africa).

There are three main varieties of cocoa plant: Forastero, Criollo and Trinitario – where 95% of the world production is of the Forastero variety. The Criollo variant, however, is often regarded as producing the highest quality cocoa bean. Trinitario is somewhat of a hybrid between the other two types. One can draw parallels between Arabica coffee and Criollo cocoa, and between Robusta coffee and Forastero cocoa.

8.3.3.1   Cocoa – ICE

The futures contract size is 10 metric tons/tonnes (and therefore cocoa is priced in dollars per tonne – typical prices are around $2,000 per tonne though this will vary). Traded contract months are March (H), May (K), July (N), September (U) and December (Z), for physical settlement. The ticker code is "CC". The futures expire on the last notice day, which is 10 business days from the last business day of the contract month, though the first notice day is 10 business days before the *first* business day of the contract month.

   Cocoa options are also traded on ICE, which expire on the first Friday of the month before the underlying futures contract month.

8.3.3.2   Cocoa – NYMEX

Cocoa futures (not options) also trade on NYMEX, with telequote code "CJ", and cease trading on the day preceding the first notice day of the underlying ICE futures contract. In contrast to the ICE futures, NYMEX cocoa futures are financially settled.

8.3.3.3   Cocoa – LIFFE

Like Robusta coffee, cocoa is also traded in London – but with a price denominated in pounds sterling per tonne. The contract size is the same as cocoa on ICE or NYMEX, being 10 tonnes, and the same contract months are available: March (H), May (K), July (N), September (U) and December (Z). These futures expire on the last notice day, which is 11 business days immediately prior to the last business day of the contract month.

8.3.4   Sugar

Sugar is a sweet tasting carbohydrate disaccharide, chemically composed of sucrose ($C_{12}H_{22}O_{11}$). It is not to be confused with monosaccharides such as glucose and fructose (both $C_6H_{12}O_6$), which are the main constituents of high fructose corn syrup (HFCS). It is obtained either from sugar cane (grown in subtropical and tropical regions) or sugar beet (grown primarily in temperate regions of the USA and Europe). Most sugar traded in commodity markets, however, is raw sugar derived from sugar cane.

The five largest producers of sugar (2011) are Brazil, India, the European Union, China and Thailand.

The commodities contracts on sugar we shall be concerned with in this book are the Sugar #11 futures (and options thereon). The #11 is a synonym for free on board (fob), meaning that the price is quoted for delivery of the sugar to a loading port (typically in the Caribbean) including loading costs – but nothing else. One occasionally sees references to Sugar #14 and #16 contracts, these refer to sugar traded cif (i.e. with cost, insurance and freight) for delivery to U ports (New York, Baltimore, Galveston, New Orleans or Savannah). Sugar #14 has been delisted, and replaced by Sugar #16. We'll only consider Sugar #11 in this book.

8.3.4.1 Sugar – ICE

Futures contracts on Sugar #11 are traded on the ICE. These are contracts on raw cane sugar. The futures contract size is in units of 112,000 pounds (equivalent to 50 long tons). Sugar is therefore priced in dollars per pound, where typical prices for 2012 ranged between 19 and 25 cents per pound. Traded contract months are March (H), May (K), July (N) and October (V), for physical settlement [fob receiver's vessel]. The ticker code is "SB". The last trading day for the ICE futures contracts is the last business day before the contract month commences, and the notice day is the first business day of the contract month.

Options on sugar also trade, with contract months: January (F), March (H), May (K), July (N) and October (V) – the January option is an option on the March futures contract. Expiry is on the 15th day of the month preceding the contract month, modified following if the 15th is a weekend or holiday.

8.3.4.2 Sugar – NYMEX

Sugar futures (but not options) also trade on NYMEX, with telequote code "YO". These cease trading on the same day as the underlying ICE futures contract ceases trading. NYMEX sugar futures are financially settled.

8.3.5 Orange Juice

The four products considered above make up the most commonly traded of the "softs". The remaining two we shall consider, starting with orange juice, are less commonly encountered. We are mostly concerned with frozen concentrate orange juice (FCOJ), which was developed by the University of Florida's Citrus Research and Education Center in the late 1940s and patented in 1948.[4] It is a popular product – in the 1990s, about 80% of Florida's orange juice production ended up as frozen concentrate, though not for concentrate (NFC) juice is gaining market share. After pasteurisation, orange juice is evaporated until the concentrate is about 65% sugars by weight – also known as a Brix value of 65 degrees or 65 ° Bx. It is then lowered to a temperature of about −10 °C during the freezing process. At this point it can be shipped, and reconstituted at its final destination. Since fresh orange juice is about 12 °Bx, FCOJ is reconstituted to that level by mixing with suitable amounts of water and (some) fresh orange juice.

There are two grades of FCOJ: FCOJ-A (Grade "A") and FCOJ-B (Grade "B"), differentiated according to grading for colour, flavour and visible defects. Grade "A" is the only one which we shall encounter on traded commodity markets.

8.3.5.1   FCOJ – ICE

Futures contracts have been traded on frozen concentrate orange juice since 1966. The ICE FCOJ-A contract is in concentrated liquid shipments consisting of 15,000 pounds of orange juice solids (3% or less), where the orange juice in question must be of US Grade "A" and have a Brix value of not less than 62.5 °.

Allowed countries of origin are the US, Brazil, Costa Rica and Mexico, from which we can see that this contract is very specific to the Americas and the domestic market in the USA. In fact, the market is heavily dominated by two locations: São Paolo, Brazil, and Florida – not so much for agricultural reasons as because only these two geographical areas (so far) have the industrial processing facilities able to deal with large amounts of orange juice exports on this scale.

The ticker code, an easy one to remember for once, is "OJ". Contract months are January (F), March (H), May (K), July (N), September (U) and November (X). The final trading day for the futures is the 14th business day before the last trading day of the month. FCOJ-A options on futures also trade on the ICE, with expiry on the third Friday of the month preceding the futures contract month.

---

[4] US Patent Number 2,453,109.

8.3.6 Lumber

Lumber is one of the few commonly traded agricultural commodities that is not edible (the other obvious examples being pulp/paper and cotton). Also known as timber in the UK and Australia, lumber refers to wood and wood materials from trees. The unit of measure is the board-foot, which is the volume of a block of wood 1 foot square in area by one inch thick ($1' \times 1' \times 1''$). The random length lumber contract (launched on the CME in 1969) is for an assortment of random lengths of 2 inch by 4 inch lumber, in lengths from 8 to 20 feet in even number increments (i.e. 8, 10, 12, 14, 16, 18 and 20-foot lengths, with the 16-foot length being the most common). These $2'' \times 4''$ lengths are largely used for house construction, a typical North American house of 2,400 square feet requiring some 14,400 board-feet of softwood lumber.

The product code is "LB" and settlement is for physical delivery, with contract size 110,000 board-feet (110 MBF). Prices are quoted in US dollars per MBF. Available futures months are January (F), March (H), May (K), July (N), September (U) and November (X). The last day of trading is the business day prior to the 16th calendar day of the contract month.

Options contracts on random length lumber futures were introduced on the CME in May 1987. These are American style and expire on the last business day of the month preceding the futures contract month.

A useful site for lumber is www.randomlengths.com which provides various market reports.

8.4 PULP AND PAPER

Closely allied to the agricultural markets are the pulp and paper products. Like lumber, these are obtained from plant materials taken from de-barked trees. Table 8.7 shows where wood pulp is typically used.

Table 8.7 Usage of pulp.

Category	Proportion
Paper	55%
Towels/tissues	15%
Packaging	13%
Sanitary goods	9%
Other	8%

Futures and options on both softwood and hardwood pulp trade on the CME. The notional for the futures contracts is 20 metric tons (MT), and the price of pulp is quoted in US$/MT.

8.5   LIVESTOCK

No discussion of agricultural commodities would be complete without mention of contracts such as lean hogs and pork bellies. We can broadly and inexactly[5] categorise nonplant sources of food into that from three species: mammals, fish and birds (from which we get poultry and game). While chicken is an increasingly major source of food, there is no actively traded financial market in poultry or fish so we shall only consider meat. Broadly speaking, there are three major types of animal that are farmed for meat: cattle, pigs and sheep. However, there are really only organised commodity markets for the first two of these, so we shall discuss the specific commodity futures and options that trade on cattle (feeder and live), live hogs and pork bellies.

8.5.1   Feeder Cattle

The smaller type of cattle is known as "feeder cattle", presumably because they are sold to be fed in feedlots and fattened for the slaughter. These young animals, either steers (castrated males) or heifers (females), are between 650 and 849 pounds in weight. If the animals are less than a year old, they are known as feeder calves, otherwise (between 1 and 2 years of age) they are known as feeder yearlings.

Feeder Cattle futures are traded on the Chicago Mercantile Exchange, specifically for Medium and Large Frame #1 feeder steers and Medium and Large Frame #1–2 feeder steers, i.e. not heifers. The price is quoted in cents per pound, and the futures contract size is 50,000 pounds by weight of feeder cattle. The ticker symbol is "FC". Available contract months are January (F), March (H), April (J), May (K), August (Q), September (U), October (V) and November (X). The expiry date for the futures contract for all months except November is the last Thursday of the month which is not a holiday and for which the four preceding business days are good business days. For November, the rule is the latest Thursday in November prior to Thanksgiving holiday which is

---

[5] Readers with an interest in rattlesnake or crocodile meat will have to look elsewhere.

not a holiday and for which the four preceding business days are good business days.

Options on feeder cattle futures are also traded on the CME. These are American style and have the same expiry date as the underlying futures contract, but can be exercised any day up to expiry.

8.5.2   Live Cattle

Larger cattle are sold on the CME futures market as "live cattle," (also known as "slaughter cattle") where the contract is for delivery of 55% Choice, 45% Select, Yield Grade 3 live steers, where the yield grade (also known as the USDA Grade) refers to the cutability, or the ratio of lean red meat to fat. The typical weight of live cattle is 950–1,500 pounds, with the average being about 1,150 pounds. Cattle in age groups A and B (i.e. 9–30 and 30–42 months respectively) are graded, based on maturity and marbling (the amount of intramuscular fat) from highest to lowest

$$\text{Prime} \rightarrow \text{Choice} \rightarrow \text{Select} \rightarrow \text{Standard} \rightarrow \text{Utility}$$

Older cattle from 42 months onward are only eligible for Commercial, Utility and Cutter gradings, and are typically used in frozen or microwaveable ready meals, hamburgers and other processed food products. They are inadmissible for delivery under CME futures contracts.

Like feeder cattle, the price is quoted in cents per pound, but the futures contract size in this case is 40,000 pounds by weight. The ticker symbol is "LC" and the available contract months are February (G), April (J), June (M), August (Q), October (V) and December (Z). The expiry is the last good business day of the month, a much simpler rule than for feeder cattle.

CME options on live cattle are American style, and the regular contract months are the same as for the underlying futures contract, though there are serial options for the other six months of the year, each on the prompt contract. The expiry date for these options are generally the first Friday of the option contract month, adjusted to the preceding day (or first good business day beforehand) if the first Friday happens to be a holiday. Options which expire on the second and subsequent Friday in the month are known as "weekly" options or "weeklies".

Calendar spread options also trade on live cattle futures for spreads between the front contract month and either one, two or three months thereafter; details can be found on the CME website.

8.5.3 Lean Hogs

Unlike cattle, which are sold alive, pigs are sold after slaughter. Originally these were traded as the live hogs contract on the CME but in February 1997 these were replaced by the lean hogs contract, which trades with ticket code "LH" on the CME. This was the first contract for slaughtered livestock. The contract specifies "Hogs (barrows or gilts)", where a barrow is a castrated male pig and a gilt is a female pig that has never been pregnant. Generally it takes about six months for a hog to reach a marketable weight of 230–250 pounds (butcher hogs are generally 195 to 320 pounds in weight). Considered together with the gestational period of 114 days, since pig breeding starts in the spring, the slaughter season is in the fall. Production is centred around Iowa, Minnesota, Illinois, Indiana and Ohio and the meat from lean hogs is used for pork chops, ham and lunch meats.

The lean hog futures contract size is 40,000 pounds (20 short tons) of lean value hog carcasses, which are priced in cents per pound. Admissible contract months are February (G), April (J), May (K), June (M), July (N), August (Q), October (V), and December (Z) and the last trade is the 10th business day of the contract month. The contract is cash settled.

Lean hog options contracts (American style) also trade on the CME, with the same contract months and expiry date as the futures contracts. However, since they are American style they can be exercised early. Calendar spread options are also traded on lean hog futures for spreads between the front contract month and either one, two, three, four or five months thereafter.

8.5.4 Pork Bellies

In contrast to the entire lean hog carcass, pork bellies specifically are the source of meat used for making bacon. A particular contract for this used to trade on the CME in the so-called "belly pit", but was delisted on 18 July 2011 (having been traded since 1961, the first futures contract on frozen stored meat). We mention it here largely for historic interest, as it used to be quite emblematic[6] of the Chicago futures market, but in fact suffered diminishing trade volumes over the years (hence its discontinuation) as a result of a general move towards year round bacon consumption rather than during the summer "grilling season" (i.e. less

---

[6] For example the 1983 film "Trading Places" with Dan Ackroyd and Eddie Murphy.

Table 8.8   Milk classification.

Category	Typical products
Class I	Beverage milk
Class II	Soft dairy (yoghurt, cream, cottage cheese)
Class III	Cheeses (hard and cream cheese)
Class IV	Dry milk products/butter

price seasonality) and an increase in demand for fresh meat as opposed to frozen.

The pork belly futures contract size was 40,000 pounds (20 short tons) of frozen trimmed pork bellies (12–18 pounds in weight). Futures contract months were February (G), March (H), May (K), July (N) and August (Q), with the last trading day being the fourth last business day of the contract month.

8.5.5   Milk and Dairy

Futures and options (American style) on milk trade on the CME. The contract size is 200,000 pounds of Class III milk, and the price is quoted in US cents per hundredweight. All calendar months are available. Note that the four classes (I–IV) of milk correspond to the typical uses shown in Table 8.8.

9

Alternative Commodities

9.1 CARBON EMISSIONS TRADING

In recent years, the environmental impact of the petrochemical economy has become increasingly recognised. Regardless of one's personal thoughts about climate change, there is both evidence and opinion (McKibben, 2012) that greenhouse gas emissions are quite possibly linked to global warming. Even if this concern turns out to be overly cautious, it seems no bad idea to take some precautionary measures just in case, while preserving economic growth and maintaining living standards.

A greenhouse gas is one that absorbs and then re-radiates thermal infrared radiation. This effectively blankets the planet and, by reducing the heat dissipated into the upper reaches of the atmosphere, to maintain surface temperatures many degrees warmer than would otherwise be the case. Without the greenhouse effect, the Earth's temperature would be some 33 °C cooler than its current year-round planetary average of 14 °C. Conversely, with increased greenhouse gas concentrations comes the risk of global warming.

While there are many greenhouse gases such as water vapour, chlorofluorocarbons (CFCs), methane, nitrous oxide and ozone,[1] the one that currently attracts the most attention is carbon dioxide. Without meaning to sound too alarmist about things, if a planet gets sufficiently hot that all the oceans boil and turn into water vapour (a potent greenhouse gas) then this can lead to a runaway greenhouse effect. This extreme fate is most unlikely for the Earth for billions of years, but at some point probably certain, which will cause the future Earth to resemble today's Venus (an inhospitable place, with surface atmospheric pressures 92 times that of Earth and a surface temperature of 460 °C; feel free to imagine lakes of molten zinc and tin).

---

[1] Concern about ozone layer depletion is a separate but related issue. As well as CFCs being a greenhouse gas, they are also ozone-depleting substances and damage to the ozone layer increases the transmission of ultraviolet light (UV) to the Earth's surface, with risk of increased incidence of skin cancers and cataracts. This pertains to a different part of the electromagnetic spectrum than the greenhouse effect though: UV vs. infrared.

Carbon, however, is of particular concern as carbon dioxide is released as a result of fossil fuel combustion. The Keeling curve shows atmospheric CO_2 concentrations as measured at Mauna Loa Observatory, Hawaii, showing an steady increase from 320 ppm in the early 1960s to 400 ppm in mid 2013 (with a seasonal effect showing a peak in May and a trough in October).[2] Geological records show the CO_2 concentrations to have been quite steady at around 280 ppm for about ten thousand years before starting to increase at the beginning of the 19th century. It is impossible to prove this was a direct result of the Industrial Revolution and the large scale use of fossil fuels, but no other such straightforward explanations come easily to mind.

As a result, many governments and supra-governmental agencies have introduced measures (Kyoto Protocol, etc.) designed to create controls over the emission of carbon due to emitters' consumption of fossil fuels. Basically the problem is that current fossil fuel reserves were formed, over many millenia, from plant-based carbon that is now locked away in a petrochemical form that is inaccessible to the atmosphere, and when they are combusted this carbon is released back into the atmosphere very quickly indeed. The costs of fossil fuels are purely a composite of upstream and downstream activities such as exploration and production (E&P) and refining and marketing (R&M), and do not take into account the externalities such as carbon dioxide emission at the point of consumption.

Carbon trading and the Kyoto Protocol are discussed in Labre and Atkinson (2010), as well as Edward and Varilek (2000), Chapter 10 of Schofield (2007) and Section 13.2 of Geman (2005). The protocol agreed to in Kyoto involves 37 industrial countries agreeing to legally binding targets to reduce their carbon emissions in various phases, through the use of three so-called flexibility mechanisms: (i) emissions trading, (ii) clean-development mechanisms (CDMs) and (iii) joint implementation. The latter two primarily relate to emission reduction projects in developing and industrialised countries respectively, whereas the first is more relevant to commodities as a financial asset class.

The emissions trading framework involves the agreement to cap carbon emissions at a specific amount, measured in Assigned Amount

---

[2] The annual variation is due to the Northern hemisphere summer growth season removing CO_2 from the atmosphere via photosynthesis, the bulk of the Earth's landmass being in the Northern hemisphere.

Units (AAUs), which grant the holder the right to emit one tonne of carbon dioxide into the atmosphere. Where other greenhouse gases (e.g. methane) are subject to similar restrictions, these can be converted into an equivalent amount of carbon dioxide, and as a result an AAU is often understood as bestowing upon the holder the right to emit one tonne of carbon dioxide equivalent (tCO2e) of greenhouse gases. We still speak of the carbon markets, however.

The carbon emissions market is currently most developed in the EU, as a result of the European Union Emissions Trading Scheme (EU-ETS). Two particular types of carbon emissions trade on the ICE (formerly on the European Climate Exchange (ECX) which was acquired by the ICE in 2010), namely the EUA (European Union Allowance) and the CER (Certified Emission Reduction). The EUA involves a cap-and-trade philosophy to carbon emissions, and allowances within the cap levels can be traded on exchanges such as the ICE.

There is some measure of interchangeability between EUAs and CERs, as CERs can be submitted by carbon emitters to meet a small proportion (no more than 10%) of their emission allowance requirements, but the two trade as separate instruments. Details can be found on the ICE web page www.theice.com/emissions.jhtml where futures contracts on CER and EUA contracts are listed. Being EU based instruments, these contracts are priced in Euros per tonne of carbon dioxide.[3]

The CER reflects the cost of reducing carbon emissions[4] by one tonne in the industrialising world (e.g. China and India) while the EUA reflects the cost of reducing similar emissions specifically in Europe. Since China and India have a greater preponderance of production plants which are more amenable to being rebuilt with cleaner technology, whereas European industry is already operating at a lower overall level of greenhouse emissions, it is cheaper to reduce emissions by one tonne in the developing world than it is to reduce them in Europe. As a result, the CER price is invariably cheaper than the EUA price, which Figure 9.1 shows. The collapse in carbon prices is straightforwardly linked to the economic slowdown in Europe during the time interval shown.

Futures and options on futures are quoted on ICE (formerly ECX) for EUA and CER emissions. For both EUA and CER, futures are quoted for quarterly expiries (i.e. March, June, September and December) out

---

[3] Unlike most commodity prices, this is the price one pays to have the right to *dispose* of a certain amount of a commodity rather than the price paid to receive a certain amount.

[4] Or equivalent.

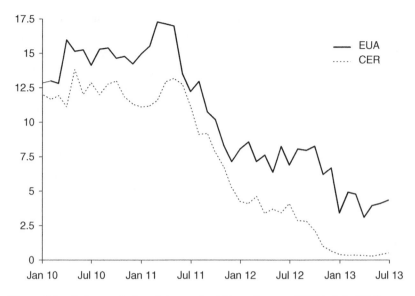

Figure 9.1   Carbon emissions futures price history (January 2010 to July 2013).

for several years and then solely for the December expiry for several years after that. The contract size is 1,000 tonnes. The expiration date for the CER future is generally the last Monday of the contract month, but if either that date or any of the four following dates are non-business days then the expiration date is set to the penultimate Monday of the contract month.

Options on EUR and CER futures are quoted, being European style. For both CER and EUA, options on futures are quoted for quarterly expiries (i.e. March, June, September and December) out for several months and then solely for the December expiry for several years thereafter. Note that the expiry of the option is three exchange business days before the expiry of the March/June/September/December futures contract, but all options are settled against the December futures contract. So, for example, the March 2015 option expires three business days before the March 2015 futures contract, but is an option on the December 2015 futures contract. Implied volatilities around the 30% mark with some smile convexity is usual, though implied volatilities of closer to 50% were seen in 2007 with little evidence of smile – see Figure 8.9 and 8.10 in Dorsman, Simpson and Westerman (2013), who argue this indicates the development of the emissions market in derivatives.

9.2   WEATHER DERIVATIVES

We noted in Chapter 7 that electricity is used for both heating and cooling, as both electric heating systems and air conditioners can be used to control the indoor temperature against adverse climate conditions outside. As a result, the demand for power tends to experience a convex dependency on temperature, where the minimum is generally somewhere around 65 °F or perhaps 18 °C; as shown in Dischel (1999), reprinted as Figure 13.13 in Geman (2005). We use T_{base} to denote whichever of 65 °F or 18 °C is meant as the reference base temperature, using the following rule

$$T_{base} = \begin{cases} 65 \,°\text{F}, & \text{for locations in the USA,} \\ 18 \,°\text{C}, & \text{all other locations.} \end{cases} \tag{9.1}$$

The temperature and weather in general are notoriously hard to predict. This creates an additional source of risk, which is clearly linked to power markets. Further, spikes in temperature (such as recent summer heatwaves) create similar spikes in demand for electricity to power air conditioners. As a result, market participants such as the Chicago Mercantile Exchange (CME) have introduced financial products which allow end users to hedge themselves against adverse moves in weather conditions. One of the first weather derivatives was a temperature linked power swap which transacted in August 1996 between Enron and Florida Power and Light (Clemmons, Kaminski and Hrgovcic, 1999) – a similar temperature related power swap also traded in July 1996 between Aquila Energy and Consolidated Edison Co. Since then, the market for these weather linked products has definitely expanded. We describe some of these products below.

As discussed in Broni-Mensah (2012) and Jewson and Brix (2005), a weather derivative is a financial contract that has a value at expiry contingent on an observable weather variable. Most commonly, the meteorological variable is linked to observed temperature, but as Benth and Benth (2012) point out, precipitation (either rainfall or snowfall) and windspeed derivatives are available also. We introduce all of these in this section.

9.2.1   Temperature Derivatives

Weather derivatives linked to temperature have been traded on the Chicago Mercantile Exchange since the 29th of September, 1999. Originally, contracts which were linked to Heating Degree Days (HDDs) and Cooling Degree Days (CDDs) traded for ten US cities. The coverage has grown, Alexandridis and Zapranis (2013) list in their Section 1.2.4 some 46 cities around the world on which weather derivatives trade, spanning the world from Toronto to London to Tokyo to Brisbane.

As described in Section 1.2.1 of Jewson and Brix (2005), a "degree day" is meant to act as a temperature-related proxy for the amount of power expected to be used for heating or cooling. Since we know (or assume) that heating and cooling is least likely to be needed for temperatures around T_{base}, a cooling degree day is defined to measure the number of degrees (in Fahrenheit or Celsius, as appropriate) that the daily average temperature exceeds the reference temperature of T_{base} (or zero, if the daily average temperature is less than T_{base}). A heating degree day, on the other hand, measures the number of degrees (in Fahrenheit or Celsius) that the daily average temperature is below the reference temperature of T_{base} (or zero, if above T_{base}). Mathematically, if T_i denotes the daily average temperature (in Fahrenheit or Celsius), which is often computed from the maximum and minimum temperatures on the day by $T_i^{\text{avg}} = (T_i^{\text{max}} + T_i^{\text{min}})/2$, then

$$\text{CDD}_i = (T_i^{\text{avg}} - T_{\text{base}})^+ \tag{9.2a}$$

$$\text{HDD}_i = (T_{\text{base}} - T_i^{\text{avg}})^+. \tag{9.2b}$$

Note that since T is denominated in degrees Fahrenheit in the USA and in Celsius in the rest of the world, a US degree day is different from one in other parts of the world.

It is standard to sum the number of HDD or CDD over a particular timeframe of interest, most usually a calendar month, and to use that as a measure against which a payout of a temperature-linked derivative can be linked, i.e.

$$\text{CDD} = \sum_{i=t_1}^{t_n} \text{CDD}_i \tag{9.3a}$$

$$\text{HDD} = \sum_{i=t_1}^{t_n} \text{HDD}_i. \tag{9.3b}$$

Other measures of temperature are used, most notably the cumulative average temperature (CAT), which is predominantly used for Europe in the summer months (the Pacific Rim Index is also linked to the cumulative average temperature). It is computed straightforwardly over n observation dates $\{t_1, \ldots, t_n\}$ as

$$\text{CAT} = \sum_{i=t_1}^{t_n} T_i^{\text{avg}}. \tag{9.4}$$

A final measure that is sometimes encountered is linked to the number of frost days, where a frost day is a weekday on which the temperature at 7am is below $-3.5\,°\text{C}$ or the temperature at 10am is below $-1.5\,°\text{C}$ or the temperatures at 7am and at 10am are both below $-0.5\,°\text{C}$, as introduced in Section 10.1 of Benth and Koekebakker (2008).

For further information on these interesting products, it is suggested to consult Section 6.2 and then the rest of Chapter 6 in Alexandridis and Zapranis (2013), together with references therein.

9.2.2   Windspeed Derivatives

One can see how windspeed derivatives could be useful for hedging production risk for offshore wind generation facilities – clearly, becalmed wind farms suffer a loss of production. Less obviously, construction companies may have to halt work in the event of high wind speeds (Jewson and Brix, 2005).

Wind-linked securities are discussed in Benth and Benth (2012), as well as Chapter 9 of Alexandridis and Zapranis (2013). One complicating factor is that the wind is a vector quantity – it has magnitude as well as direction. Nevertheless, the observed quantity is invariably taken to be some measure of average wind speed over a time interval of interest, the so-called DAWS (daily average wind speed), though alternative measures such as the Nordix windspeed index have been used in contracts traded on the US Future Exchange (however, no longer traded). Details can be found in the references above.

9.2.3   Precipitation Derivatives

Unlike windspeed derivatives, a market still exists on the CME for weather derivatives which are linked to observed rainfall and snowfall, see Chapter 10 in Alexandridis and Zapranis (2013) and Section 1.2.3 in Benth and Benth (2012). Modelling precipitation derivatives is a challenging task, as discussed in Carmona and Diko (2005).

9.2.3.1   Snowfall Futures and Options

The CME Snowfall Index is available for several US locations: Boston Logan, NYC Central Park, Chicago O'Hare, Minneapolis International Airport, Detroit International Airport, New York LaGuardia, Newark Airport, Baltimore Washington International Airport, Port Columbus International Airport and Colorado Springs Municipal Airport. Both futures and options on the CME Snowfall Index trade on the CME. One sees immediately that this product is useful for airlines who wish to hedge flight cancellation risk.

The snowfall is measured in inches, and the index is computed as the cumulative snowfall over a calendar month. The contract size is $500 (per inch of snow) and the contracts only trade for November through to April – the available contracts being futures, European options and binary options.

9.2.3.2   Rainfall Futures and Options

Similarly to snowfall derivatives, rainfall is measured in inches, and the CME Rainfall Index is computed as the cumulative rainfall over a calendar month. The contract size is $500 (per inch of rain) and contracts trade for March through to October.

The CME Rainfall Index is available for various US locations that are not the same as for the Snowfall Index, namely Chicago O'Hare International Airport, Dallas-Fort Worth International Airport, Des Moines International Airport, Detroit Metro Airport, Jacksonville International Airport, Kansas City International Airport, Los Angeles Downtown USC Campus, New York LaGuardia Airport, Portland International Airport and Raleigh/Durham International Airport.

Futures, European options and binary options on the rainfall index are available, just as for snowfall.

9.3   BANDWIDTH AND TELECOMMUNICATION TRADING

Some people speak of telecommunications as the "fourth utility", ranking somewhat behind water, gas and electricity. Most of us who move house certainly have experience in connecting to all four of these services. As a result, some people have spoken of creating a market in both water and bandwidth/telecommunications derivatives. Water, while an essential commodity, is perhaps too politically sensitive[5] to be amenable to financialisation.

There was, however, an active push towards bandwidth trading in the late 1990s/early 2000s, around the time of the dotcom Internet bubble. This is well discussed in Franks and Gee (2000) and Moore (2000). Bandwidth and telecommunications capacity in general can easily be accounted and charged for, as digital bandwidth is straightforwardly measured in kilobits/megabits/gigabits per second (Kbps/Mbps/Gbps). One of the most aggressive market participants was Enron, who initiated a bandwidth market in 1999 by proposing a standardised bandwidth product – the Digital Service 3 ("DS3"), which was traded by their Enron Broadband Services division. The DS3 is equivalent to a T3 Internet connection with throughput of 44.736 Mbps, and is capable of supporting 672 voice channels (or 672 DS0 channels). Note that the terminology and channel units in Europe differ from North America, with SL the preferred terminology[6] instead of DS. Pricing was in units of US cents per DSL mile, where a DSL mile is a commitment to provide a DS0 service over 1 mile, with costs tallied up per calendar month. A typical example, as given in Schwartz (2003), is for provision of an OC-12 (655Mbps) line from New York to Los Angeles at 0.4 cents per DSL mile, or $12,000 per month (2001 prices).

Unfortunately, however, the bandwidth trading business was disastrous for Enron. As discussed in Schwartz (2003), it was difficult to trade or even standardise bandwidth, largely because operational network billing systems were incapable of handling the switching between various carriers, and there was a glut in the telecommunications capacity due to overinvestment in the technology boom. This, combined with the larger financial problems that brought down Enron in December 2001, means that the bandwidth derivatives market is no longer in existence.

9.4   PLASTICS

As well as base metals, the LME also traded plastics contracts. These were originally launched on 27 May 2005, on polypropylene (PP) and linear low density polyethylene (LL). These contracts were not particularly successful, and were withdrawn with the final prompt date being

---

[5] Speculation on the soft commodities is sometimes regarded with suspicion, water would be even more contentious.

[6] See en.wikipedia.org/wiki/Digital_Signal_Designation

Table 9.1   Resin identification codes.

Code	Plastic	Typical uses
♵1♴	PET	Plastic soft drink bottles
♵2♴	HDPE	Plastic bottles, hard hats, 3D printer filament extrusion
♵3♴	PVC	White water/sewerage pipes (plumbing)
♵4♴	LDPE	Plastic bags and sheeting, squeezable bottles
♵5♴	PP	Automobile components, textiles, furniture, bottle tops
♵6♴	PS	Compact disc cases, food packaging, foam material for packing

29 April 2011. Plastics are still traded on various other exchanges, however, such as NYMEX, the Multi Commodity Exchange of India and the Dubai Gold and Commodities Exchange.

A good overview of plastics in the context of commodity markets can be found in Chapter 8 of Schofield (2007). The three most commonly produced industrial plastics are polypropylene (PP), polyethylene (PE) and polyvinyl chloride (PVC). Polyethylene exists in several variants such as high density polyethylene (HDPE) low density polyethylene (LDPE) and linear low density polyethylene (LL), the "linear" referring to the placement of the carbon atoms in the polymer chain. Polystyrene (PS) and polyethylene terephthalate (PET) are frequently used too.

Many of these plastics are recyclable. Table 9.1 shows the recycling codes together with typical industry uses for each of these plastics.

The PP and LL contracts used to be physically deliverable, with the contract being on 24.75 tonnes of the relevant plastic packed into 25kg bags and delivered on 18 pallets, with 55 bags per pallet, deliverable at the seller's choice of Houston, ARA or Singapore/Johor.

9.5   FREIGHT DERIVATIVES

In Chapter 1, we introduced commodities in the context of "Trade, Commerce and Commodities" discussing trade routes and transport. It seems appropriate to conclude the book with a discussion of financial instruments relating to that.

9.5.1   Shipping

We only consider maritime shipping, as the traded freight market is almost exclusively concerned with waterborne cargoes. The international shipping industry constitutes approximately 90% of global trade by volume.[7] The nature and structure of the shipping markets, with a particular emphasis on freight derivatives, are discussed in Kavussanos and Visvikis (2006, 2008, 2011) and Alizadeh and Nomikos (2009).

As discussed in Junge (2012), there are two main freight markets upon which freight derivatives trade: dry bulk and tankers. Dry bulk cargoes are mostly iron ore, coal and grain, the minor bulk cargoes (such as bauxite, alumina and phosphate rock) making up the balance, whereas the tankers carry crude oil and so-called clean[8] and dirty[9] refined oil products. A graph showing the breakdown can be found in Figure 1.4 of Kavussanos and Visvikis (2006), where it is shown that the split is about equal (in shipped tonnage) between dry bulk and tanker cargoes, each comprising about one third of seaborne trade. General (dry) cargo, which constitutes the remaining third, is shipped as a combination of containerised cargoes,[10] car carriers, roll-on-roll-off cargo and various other modes of transportable goods.

Shipping terminology is largely dominated by categorisation of the size of vessels, most importantly based on whether they are capable of traversing the major shipping canals, namely the Panama and Suez canal. A ship's size is generally expressed for maritime shipping purposes in deadweight tonnes (DWT), a measure which refers to the maximum weight (cargo plus fuel, ballast, crew and passengers and their supplies of food and water) the vessel can carry safely. The largest vessels which can be navigated through the Panama Canal are called "Panamax". Vessels which are too large for the Panama Canal but which can transit through the (larger) Suez Canal are called "Suezmax", and ships too large for either are known as "Capesize" for dry cargos and VLCCs or ULCCs for tankers, depending on the size.[11] Smaller vessels are known as handymax and handysize; the various size categorisations are tabulated in Table 9.2 for dry cargoes and tankers respectively.

---

[7] See "Global Shipping Contends with Oversupply Problems", Stratfor, 8 July 2013, http://www.stratfor.com/analysis/global-shipping-contends-oversupply-problems.

[8] Heavy fuel oil, asphalt, etc.

[9] Gasoline, jet fuel, diesel, kerosene, naphtha, etc.

[10] Container shipping was the fastest growing area within shipping markets in 2007, and very likely will continue to be so for a while.

[11] The largest of the supertankers at the time of writing this book, the TI class supertanker, has a deadweight tonnage of 441,000 DWT (380 m long, 68 m wide) and a capacity of 3.1 *million* barrels of crude oil. Compare this to the cruise ship "Allure of the Seas" (362 m long, 61 m wide, over 6,000 passengers) and the largest US aircraft carriers of the Nimitz class (332 m long, 77 m wide).

Table 9.2(a)   Cargo size categorisation: dry cargoes.

Class	Deadweight tonnage (DWT)
Capesize	100,000–180,000
Suezmax	80,000–100,000
Panamax	50,000–80,000
Handymax	25,000–50,000
Handysize	10,000–25,000

Table 9.2(b)   Cargo size categorisation: tankers.

Class	Deadweight tonnage (DWT)
ULCC	>320,000
VLCC	200,000–320,000
Suezmax	120,000–200,000
Aframax	75,000–120,000
Panamax	50,000–75,000
Handymax	25,000–50,000
Handysize	10,000–25,000

9.5.2   Pricing and the Baltic Freight Market

There are various types of shipping charter that can be entered into. The simplest is the voyage charter, where the shipowner undertakes to transport a specified amount of cargo from loading port to discharge port. In this case, the price of freight is expressed in US dollars per metric ton (MT). A so-called contract of affreightment (CoA) is an agreement to transport a certain (usually large) amount of cargo from a loading port/area to a destination port/region, in a number of shipments over a specified time window, and is similarly priced in USD/MT. In contrast, however, one can hire an entire vessel for a certain number of days under trip-charter (where the loading and discharge ports are nominated in advance), and time-charter and barebones charter contracts (where the operational control is in the hands of the chartering party). In these three cases, the pricing is in USD/days. For crude oil, however, a pricing mechanism has been in place since 1952 called "Worldscale" which provides a reference price against which various routes can be quoted, being anything from WS1 (1% of the Worldscale reference price) to WS1,000 (1,000% of the Worldscale reference price). Effectively, however, the price is still a USD/tonne price.

A freight index was published by the Baltic Exchange, London, from 1985. Since then the index has been modified into a number of different indices. Here we present three of the more commonly encountered indices.

The Baltic Capesize Index (BCI) is a composite of four trip charter routes (C8–C11) and six voyage routes, corresponding to various major trade routes. The composition is shown in Table 9.3, where indicative prices are taken from Junge (2012). Note that the four trip-charter components (C8–C11) are sometimes averaged to get a so-called four-time charter or 4TC price, this should not be confused[12] with the TC4 route from Singapore to Japan.

With regard to tankers, the Baltic Dirty Tanker Index (BDTI) is comprised of 18 shipping routes (TD1 to TD18) for crude oil and fuel oil, whereas the Baltic Clean Tanker Index (BCTI) is comprised of 10 shipping routes (TC1 to TC10) for unleaded gasoline, naphtha condensate and middle distillate. Alizadeh and Nomikos (2009) and Kavussanos and Visvikis (2006) provide a thorough description of all 18 shipping routes; we extract a selection of some of the more important routes from each of the two indices in Table 9.4, which serves to describe typical components that might be encountered in tanker freight.

9.5.3 Forward Freight Agreements and Options

The prices described above are calculated daily by the Baltic Exchange, which provides a price assessment based on prices provided by a panel of independent shipbrokers. None of these prices can be directly transacted, these indices merely track the market. Between 1985 and 2002 there was a market for a Baltic International Freight Futures Exchange contract (BIFFEX), which was a contract for differences linked to the Baltic Freight Index (one of the precursor indices, before it was separated into various indices). It was not particularly successful, largely because the prices of individual trade routes were only weakly correlated with the index, and was discontinued in April 2002.

As a result, forward freight agreements (FFAs), which are cash-settled contracts for differences referenced against individual components in one of the Baltic indices (or a suitably chosen basket), have become more popular. A thorough description and overview is in Chapter 5 of Alizadeh and Nomikos (2009). Basically, a FFA is a financial contract that allows a market participant to fix a price now to buy or sell any of the Baltic Exchange trade routes (or a basket thereof) against, at a

---

[12] This is the very last piece of confusing market notation/jargon for this book I promise you.

Table 9.3 Baltic Capesize Index.

Route	DWT	Cargo	Route	Weighting	Price (indic)
C2	160,000	Iron ore	Turabao (Brazil)–Rotterdam	10%	$11.006/MT
C3	150,000	Iron ore	Brazil–Beilun–Baoshan–Qingdao (China)	15%	$22.610/MT
C4	150,000	Coal	RB (South Africa)–Rotterdam	5%	$13.828/MT
C5	150,000	Iron ore	WA–Beilun–Baoshan–Qingdao (China)	15%	$10.883/MT
C7	150,000	Coal	Bolivar (Columbia)–Rotterdam	5%	$11.239/MT
C8	172,000	TC	Transatlantic (30–45 days; round trip)	10%	$34.167/day
C9	172,000	TC	Europe–China/Japan (~65 days; round trip)	5%	$49,380/day
C10	172,000	TC	China/Japan–Australia (30–40 days; round trip)	20%	$42.775/day
C11	172,000	TC	China/Japan–Europe (~65 days; round trip)	5%	$32,540/day
C12	150,000	Coal	Gladstone (Australia)–Rotterdam	10%	$19.152/MT

Table 9.4   Selection of routes (a subset) from the BCTI and BDTI.

Route	Size	Cargo	Route
TC2	Handysize	37,000 MT clean refined/RBOB	Rotterdam – New York
TC4	Panamax	30,000 MT clean refined/RBOB	Singapore – Chiba, Japan
TC5	Panamax	55,000 MT naphtha condensate	Ras Tanura (MEG) – Yokohama
TD1	VLCC	280,000 MT crude	Ras Tanura (MEG) – LOOP (Louisiana, USA)
TD3	VLCC	260,000 MT crude	Ras Tanura (MEG) – Chiba, Japan
TD5	Suezmax	130,000 MT crude	Bonny, Nigeria – Philadephia
TD7	Aframax	80,000 MT crude	Sullom Voe – Wilhelmshavem, Germany

fixed time in the future. Due to the bespoke nature of these trades, these are very much OTC products, though there is some movement towards allowing these to be cleared and margined on an exchange.

For some reason, FFAs and freight derivatives in general are much more popular on dry cargoes than tankers. Settlement rules are complex; for example, the floating rate is usually the average over the final seven trading days of the month for FFAs referenced against individual trade routes from either the BCI or the BPI, whereas for FFAs on tanker routes or the 4TC average, the floating rate is computed as an average over the entire month. Most FFAs are on the 4TC average or the BCI C4 or C7 route. From the FFAs, it is possible to construct a forward curve for freight shipment for each of the trade routes.

As well as cash-settled linear products that pay the arithmetic difference between a floating freight rate and a fixed strike (fixed earlier), it is of course possible to construct calls and puts on freight. This is capably discussed in Chapter 7 of Alizadeh and Nomikos (2009). Clearly, in this case, volatility plays a greater role, and this is particularly so given that freight volatilities are much higher than the typical 20–30% for many more commonly traded commodities – volatilities of 70–150% for the front month and 45–55% for the three-month forward freight rate are quite common (there is some evidence for reasonably symmetric volatility smiles, see Junge, 2012). Finally, the larger vessel categories tend to have greater volatilities, reflecting illiquidity due to the limited number of larger vessels.

Conversion Factors

1 tonne (T) = 1 metric ton (MT) = 1000 kg.

1 (oil) barrel (bbl) = 42 US gallons (158.9873 litres, 34.9723 Imperial gallons).

1 US gallon (gal) = 3.78541 litres.

1 pound (lb) = 453.592 grams – N.B. the avoirdupois pound is used in the US grain markets.

1 troy ounce (oz) = 31.1034768 grams (used for precious metals) – N.B. the avoirdupois ounce is never used in commodity markets.

1 US bushel (Bu) = 60 pounds (27.2155 kg) of wheat/soybeans, or 56 pounds (25.4012 kg) of corn.

1 short ton (ton) = 2000 lb $\sim$ 907.2 kg (used for soybean meal contracts).

1 long ton (ton) = 2240 lb $\sim$ 1016.05 kg (used for sugar contracts).

1 US hundredweight (cwt) = 100 lb $\sim$ 45.35923 kg (used for rough rice CBOT contracts).

1 British thermal unit (Btu) = 1055.056 joules.

1 board-foot (FBM) = 1 foot square in area by one inch thick (used for lumber contracts). Also 1 MBF = 1 thousand board-feet.

1 cf of natural gas = 1023 Btu (approx.) in energy content.

1 tonne of gas oil = 7.44 barrels.

1 dollar per barrel = 2.381 cents per gallon.

1 Wh (watt-hour) = 3600 joules.

Futures Contract Symbols

BY MONTH

F	January
G	February
H	March
J	April
K	May
M	June
N	July
Q	August
U	September
V	October
X	November
Z	December

BY COMMODITY – METALS

Symbol	Commodity	Exchange	Traded Months
GC	Gold	COMEX	GJMQVZ
HG/CP	Copper	COMEX	FGHJKMNQUVXZ then HKNUZ
PL	Platinum	NYMEX	FJNV
SI	Silver	COMEX	HKNUZ

BY COMMODITY – ENERGY

Symbol	Commodity	Exchange	Traded Months
CL	Crude Light (i.e. WTI)	NYMEX	FGHJKMNQUVXZ
HO	Heating Oil	NYMEX	FGHJKMNQUVXZ
HU/UR	Unleaded Gas	NYMEX	FGHJKMNQUVXZ
CO	Brent Crude	ICE	FGHJKMNQUVXZ
NG	Natural Gas (i.e. Henry Hub)	NYMEX	FGHJKMNQUVXZ
RB	RBOB Gasoline	NYMEX	FGHJKMNQUVXZ
QL	Central Appalachian Coal	NYMEX	FGHJKMNQUVXZ
QS	Gas Oil	ICE	FGHJKMNQUVXZ

BY COMMODITY – GRAINS AND OILSEEDS

Symbol	Commodity	Exchange	Traded Months
AB	Western Barley	WPG	HKNVZ
BO	Soybean Oil	CBOT	FHKNQUVZ
C	Corn	CBOT	HKNUZ
KW	Kansas City Wheat	KCBOT	HKNUZ
MW	Minneapolis Spring Wheat	MGE	HKNUZ
O	Oats	CBOT	HKNUZ
RR	Rough Rice	CBOT	FHKNUX
RS	Canola	WPG	FHKNX
S	Soybeans	CBOT	FHKNQUX
SM	Soybean Meal	CBOT	FHKNQUVZ
W	Wheat	CBOT	HKNUZ

BY COMMODITY – SOFTS

Symbol	Commodity	Exchange	Traded Months
CC	Cocoa	ICE	HKNUZ
CJ	Cocoa	NYMEX	HKNUZ
CT	Cotton No. 2	ICE/NYBOT	HKNVZ
TT	Cotton	NYMEX	HKNVZ
JO	Orange Juice	ICE	FHKNUX
KC	Coffee	ICE	HKNUZ
KT	Coffee	NYMEX	HKNUZ
RC	Coffee	LIFFE	FHKNUX
LB	Lumber	CME	FHKNUX
SB	Sugar #11	ICE	HKNV
YO	Sugar #11	NYMEX	HKNVZ

BY COMMODITY – LIVESTOCK

Symbol	Commodity	Exchange	Traded Months
DA	Milk Class III	CME	FGHJKMNQUVXZ
FC	Feeder Cattle	CME	FHJKQUVX
LC	Live Cattle	CME	GJMQVZ
LH	Lean Hogs	CME	GJKMNQVZ
PB	Pork Bellies	CME	GHKNQ

BY COMMODITY – EMISSIONS

Symbol	Commodity	Exchange	Traded Months
CER	CER emissions	ICE	HMUZ then Z
EUA	EUA emissions	ICE	HMUZ then Z

Glossary

AAU – Assigned amount unit. Emissions allowance under Kyoto Protocol that permits the holder to emit one tonne of carbon dioxide into the atmosphere.

Act of God – A natural disaster such as a flood, tornado, hurricane, earthquake etc.

Actuals – Trade in the actual physical commodity, as opposed to trade in futures contracts or other speculative contracts.

Aframax – Size categorisation for medium sized oil tankers, typically with capacity 75–120 kDWT which permits operation at most ports worldwide. The "AFRA" is an acronym for average freight rate assessment, not Africa.

American option – An option that can be exercised at any point during its lifetime, up to and including the expiration date.

API – American Petroleum Institute. Most commonly encountered with respect to API gravity.

API gravity – A measure of density of oil. Intermediate density is approx 30–39 °API, heavy is less than ~30 °, light is greater than ~40 °.

API2, API3, API4 – All Publications Index coal contracts, e.g. #2 (for delivery cif to ARA), #4 (for shipment fob from RB, South Africa), #5 and #6 (for shipment fob from Newcastle, Australia), #8 (for delivery cfr to South China), and #10 (for shipment fob from Puerto Bolivar, Colombia). N.B. Not to be confused with the "American Petroleum Institute" acronym in this glossary.

APO – Average price option. Also known as an Asian option.

ARA – Amsterdam, Rotterdam or Antwerp. Permissible locations for delivery of API2 coal contracts.

ASCI – Argus Sour Crude Index. A possible replacement for Brent.

Asian option – An option that, while it can only be exercised on the expiration date, depends on the average price for a tradeable commodity or asset over a portion of the lifetime of the option.

Asian volatility – An adjusted volatility which, when substituted into the Black-76 pricing formula for a European option, gives the price for an average rate option.

Associated gas – Natural gas found in conjunction with crude oil.

ASTM – American Society for Testing Materials. The official body in the USA which formulates standards for purity and prescribes methods for assaying and sampling.

ATK – Aviation turbine kerosene. A medium light fuel used in jet and turboprop airplane engines. Not to be confused with avgas.

Avgas – Aviation gasoline. A fuel used in airplane piston engines. Still mostly leaded. Not to be confused with ATK or jet fuel.

At-the money (ATM) – An option with a strike price equal to the current futures price (if a number of options are quoted then the one with the nearest strike price to the current futures price is regarded as the at-the-money instrument).

Avails – The availabilities of certain hydrocarbon types in a particular type or shipment of crude oil.

Back months – The various traded futures contracts with maturities subsequent to the front month.

Backwardation – Situation where the forward curve is higher in the short end and slopes downwards for forwards/futures with longer maturity.

Basis – The difference between the spot price and the futures price.

bbl – Barrel (generally of crude oil, terminology comes from "Standard Oil blue barrel"). Equivalent to 42 US gallons (158.9873 litres). Often used in multiplied form, e.g. Mbbl (1,000 bbl) or MMbbl (1 mio or 1 million bbl), with "M" from mille (Latin).

BCI – Baltic Capesize Index.

BCTI – Baltic Clean Tanker Index.

BDTI – Baltic Dirty Tanker Index.

Beans – Trader shorthand for soybeans.

BFOE – Brent–Forties–Oseberg–Ekofisk. Market of four North Sea light sweet crude oils, two from UK and two from Norway, each with a different geographical location and slightly different composition.

Bid-week – Final week of the month, when natural gas is predominantly traded for delivery in the subsequent month.

Billet – Medium sized intermediate rough metal casting with square or cylindrical cross-section.

B/L – Bill of lading. Document drawn up between a shipper and a carrier, detailing the shipment.

BLCO – Bonny Light Crude oil. A West African crude oil.

Blue months – Contract delivery months in contracts for delivery *two* years ahead (as seen from today). See also red months and green months.

Board-foot – Unit of measure for lumber, 1 foot square in area by one inch thick.

BOE – Barrel of oil equivalent. One oil barrel is approximately thermally equivalent to 5.8 MMBtu, or about 5,800 cubic feet of natural gas.

bpd – Barrels per day. Measure of oilfield production rate.

BPI – Baltic Panamax Index.

Brent – Crude oil blend from offshore Europe, produced among 20+ North Sea oilfields, delivered through Brent and Ninian pipelines and deliverable at Sullom Voe terminal, Shetland Islands, Scotland, UK. Prices are quoted fob Sullom Voe. Density of 38.3 °API and ~0.37% sulphur. Named after the Brent goose.

Btu – British thermal unit. Unit of energy required to raise the temperature of 1 pound of water by 1 degree Fahrenheit (from 60 °F to 61 °F) – equivalent to about 1,055.056 joules. Approximately equal to the energy obtained from burning a single wooden match. This measure is used for contracts of natural gas, and is often used in multiplied form, e.g. MBtu (1,000 Btu) or MMBtu (1 mio or 1 million Btu).

BTX – Benzene, toluene, xylene. A former octane booster, no longer used.

Bu – Bushel (US) which equates to 25.239 litres.

Bunker – Residual fuel oil (usually No. 6) used for large ships.

Capemax – Size categorisation for large dry cargo ships which are too large for operation through the Suez canal, and therefore need to travel around the Cape of Good Hope. Typically with capacity 100–180 kDWT.

CAPP – Central Applachian. A coal index traded on NYMEX (for shipment fob from central Appalachians.)

Cargo – (of sugar) 10,000 tonnes.

Carry-in – Surplus agricultural stocks from the previous year, which are brought to market in the subsequent year.

CAT – Cumulative average temperature.

CBM – Coal bed methane. See also CSG.

CBOT – Chicago Board of Trade. World's oldest futures and options exchange, now merged with CME.

CCGT – Combined cycle gas turbine.

CDD – Cooling degree day.

CDM – Clean development mechanism.

CER – Certified emission reduction (carbon emissions). European tradeable carbon contract based on Kyoto Protocol CDM.

Cetane number – A measure of ignitability for diesel, analogous to octane number for gasoline. Regular diesel has a cetane number of 40–45. Premium diesel has a cetane number of 45–50.

cf – Cubic feet. Measure of volume for US and Canadian natural gas – the amount of gas required to fill a volume of one cubic foot at 14.73 pounds per square inch absolute pressure at temperature of 60 °F. Often used in multiplied form, e.g. Mcf (1,000 cf), Bcf (10^9 cf).

CFD – Contract for difference.

c&f/cfr – Cost and freight. Means a commodity price is quoted *inclusive* of cost and international freight (but not insurance).

CFTC – Commodities Futures Trading Commission.

CHP – Combined Heat and Power.

cif – Cost, insurance and freight. Means a commodity price is quoted *inclusive* of cost, international freight and insurance.

CL – Ticker code for Crude Light on NYMEX. Synonymous with WTI.

CMA – Calendar month average. See Swap(1,0) and Swap(1,1).

CME – Chicago Mercantile Exchange.

CNG – Compressed natural gas. Primarily methane, delivered in a highly compressed but still gaseous form to power vehicles (usually urban vehicles such as taxicabs and urban buses).

CO – Ticker code for crude oil (meaning Brent oil) on Bloomberg.

CoA – Contract of affreightment. Contract to transport a certain (usually large) amount of cargo from a loading port/area to a destination port/region, in a number of shipments over a specified time window.

COB – California–Oregon Border, location for delivery of electricity as traded in NYMEX COB electricity futures contracts.

cob – Close of business.

COMEX – Commodity Exchange Division within the NYMEX Group that deals with metals.

Condensate – Lighter weight hydrocarbons, such as pentane and hexane, which are are liquid at standard temperature and pressure, and are extracted in conjunction with natural gas from condensate wells. Often very high in naphtha. See also NGLs.

Condy – Trader slang for "condensate".

Contango – Situation where forward curve is lower in the short end and increases for forwards/futures with longer maturity.

Crack spread – Differential between market price of a refined energy product (e.g. gasoline) or basket of refined energy products, and the price of the amount of crude oil required as input. Also called the refinery margin.

Cracking – Separating large hydrocarbon molecules (such as found in crude oil) into smaller lighter refined product hydrocarbons, either by thermal cracking or catalytic cracking.

CRB – Commodities Research Bureau – most commonly with respect to Thomson Reuters/Jefferies CRB index (commodity index).

Crop year – Twelve-month period from the first day of the month in which the harvesting of the crop begins to the calendar day before the beginning of the corresponding period in the subsequent calendar year.

Crossing – Arithmetic average of futures prices used in computation of a price for a commodity product depending on an average, such as an Asian option or a swaption. Often denoted x88 for a crossing level of 88. This just means that the price is quoted with reference to a particular assumed value for the average of the futures prices.

Crush spread – Differential between market price of the two refined soybean products (soybean meal and soybean oil) and the price of the soybeans required for their production, in the futures markets. Also known as "GPM" in the cash market.

CSG – Coal seam gas. Australian name for coal bed methane (q.v.).

CSO – Calendar spread option.

cSt – Centistoke. A measure of viscosity. Generally used in connection with fuel oil.

cwt – Hundredweight (US), equal to 100 lb. Sometimes known as short hundredweight, to differentiate it from the Imperial or long hundredweight (not used in this book). Unit of measure for rough rice.

DAM – Day-ahead market. Auction market for electricity for delivery of power one day ahead, in one of various timeslots (usually hourly).

Dark spread – (of coal) Differential between market price of electricity and the price of the amount of coal required to generate that amount of electricity. See also spark spread.

Dated Brent – Terminology for shipment of Brent Crude oil assigned a loading date at Sullom Voe.

DAWS – Daily average wind speed.

DDP – Delivered duty paid. Means a commodity price is quoted on a landed cost basis plus delivery to buyer's specified location.

Degree day – Deviation of one-day temperature from the benchmark of 65 °F (or 18 °C, depending on geographic region).

Delivery basis – Specified locations to which a commodity may be delivered (physically) to satisfy and thereby terminate the contract.

Demurrage – Amount paid as compensation for delays in loading or unloading cargo from a ship.

DME – Dubai Mercantile Exchange. Trading center for Oman Crude oil.

Downstream – Activities relating to crude oil after it is shipped as crude, i.e. refining and marketing. See R&M.

Driving season – Portion of the year in the USA from the Memorial Day weekend (late May) to the Labor Day holiday (early September) when demand for gasoline typically peaks, due to summer holidays and recreation.

DS0 – Digital standard "0". A measure of bandwidth, equivalent to one standard voice channel.

DSL mile – Digital standard line mile. A measure of bandwidth-distance. DS0 is usually taken as the benchmark, this being the provision of a standard voice channel over a distance of one mile.

Dubai Crude – Light sour crude oil blend from the Middle East. Density of 31 °API and ~2% sulphur.

DWT – Deadweight tonne. A measure of how much total weight (in tonnes) a ship can carry safely, being the sum of weights of cargo, fuel, ballast, crew, passengers, provisions (food and water), etc.

E&P – Exploration and production, aka "upstream" activities. Means locating and extracting crude oil and/or natural gas.

ECX – European Climate Exchange. Acquired by the ICE in 2010.

EEX – European Energy Exchange (Leipzig).

EFP – Exchange of futures for physical (as opposed to cash settlement).

EPEX – European Power Exchange.

ERCOT – Electric Reliability Council of Texas.

ERPA – Emission reduction purchase agreement. A carbon emissions contract.

ERU – Emissions reduction unit.

EU-ETS – European Union Emissions Trading Scheme.

EUA – European Union allowance (carbon emissions).

Expiry date – The date on which an option on an underlying spot or futures contract can be exercised (for an American or Bermudan option, the final date on which exercise is possible).

fas – Free alongside ship. Much like fob (free on board) except actual delivery of the cargo onto the ship is not required. Transfer takes effect quayside at the embarkation point.

FBM – Foot, board measure. Another term for board-foot used to measure wood volume for lumber contracts.

FCOJ – Frozen concentrate orange juice (FCOJ-A and FCOJ-B refer to US Grade A and B respectively).

Feed ratio – A ratio used to quantify the relationship of feeding costs to the value of livestock.

Fence – Option structure comprising a long position in a call with a short position in a put, with different strikes but the same expiry date. Also known as a risk reversal.

FFA – Forward freight agreement.

FGHJKMNQUVXZ – Ticker codes for the months Jan to Dec (inclusive).

fob – Free on board. Means a commodity price is quoted *exclusive* of any additional costs once delivered onto a shipping vessel. Transfer takes effect at the embarkation point.

Force majeure – A clause in a supply contract which allows either party to renege on their contractual obligations due to events outside their control, such as strikes or export delays.

Forward – OTC contract which fixes a price today for the commitment to buy (or sell) a commodity at a predetermined time in the future.

Frac spread – Difference between the price of refined natgas products (such as ethane, butane, iso-butane and propane) and natural gas. This is the gas industry equivalent of "crack spread".

Front month – The month of the traded futures contract with the closest maturity. Sometimes called spot month or nearby month. See also nearby month and prompt future.

Futures – Exchange traded contract which fixes a price today for the commitment to buy (or sell) a commodity at a predetermined time in the future, subject to margin and exchange rules.

Gallon – Generally means US gallon in commodities – i.e. 3.785411784 litres.

Gas oil – European terminology for the medium distillates produced during refining of crude oil. Used in production of diesel as well as in central heating and the chemical industry. See heating oil.

Gasoline spread – Differential between market price of unleaded gasoline and the price of the amount of crude oil required as input.

GBM – Geometric Brownian motion.

GIPSA – Grain Inspection, Packers and Stockyards Administration. A subsidiary of the USDA.

GOFO – Gold offered forward rate.

Gold lease rate – Implied leasing rate for gold.

GOR – Gas/oil ratio. A measure of the ratio between the amount of natural gas and oil produced from a well.

GPM – Gross processing margin (of soybeans). A measure of the price differential between the two refined soybean products (soybean meal and soybean oil) and the price of the soybeans required for their production, in the cash markets. Also known as "crush" in the futures markets.

Green months – Contract delivery months in contracts for delivery *three* years ahead (as seen from today). See also red months and blue months.

Grilling season – Another term for North American summer, more with reference to barbecues and meat consumption patterns. See also driving season.

HDD – Heating degree day.

HDPE – High density polyethylene (a plastic).

HDS – Hydrodesulfurisation. Chemical process used to remove sulphur from crude oil or natural gas, in a refinery unit called a "sweetener".

Heat rate – Conversion factor HR between amount of refined energy (e.g. resid or natgas) and electricity power output capacity. Usually expressed in MMBtu/MWh, so the *lower* the heat rate the more efficient the plant.

Heat spread – Differential between price of No. 2 heating oil and the price of the amount of crude oil required as input.

Heating oil No. 2 – North American terminology for the medium distillates produced during refining of crude oil. Used in production of diesel as well as in central heating and the chemical industry. See gas oil.

Heavy crude – Crude oil with a high proportion of heavy fractions (and therefore a low API gravity).

Henry Hub – Sabine Pipe Line Company's Henry Hub in Louisiana, location for physical delivery of natural gas futures as traded on NYMEX.

HFCS – High fructose corn syrup. A commonly used sweetener, often used in processed foods.

HMX – Houston Mercantile Exchange (where propane and other NGLs are traded).

HO – Heating oil. Distillate used for home/industrial heating. In USA, denoted as HO2 (heating oil No. 2).

HRSG – Heat recovery steam generator. Second stage of a CCGT power plant.

HRSW – Hard Red Spring wheat. Traded on the MGEX.

HSFO – High sulphur fuel oil (sulphur content greater than 1%).

HSS – Heavy grain, soya and sorghum. A term used in dry cargo shipping.

ICE – Intercontinental Exchange (prev IPE). ICE Europe is the primary exchange for Brent trading, also secondary trade in WTI.

IMM – International Monetary Market. An exchange in Chicago which offers futures contracts in financial futures and foreign currencies.

Incoterm – International commercial term, such as fob, cfr and cif.

Ingot – Intermediate rough metal casting (base metals) or synonym for bullion bar (precious metals).

Initial margin – The cash amount that is required to be posted with a futures exchange before a potential trader can engage in the desired futures trade.

IPCC – Intergovernmental Panel on Climate Change. Intergovernmental agency established by the UN in 1988, responsible for various reports and assessments which led to the Kyoto Protocol.

IPE – International Petroleum Exchange (now ICE), where Brent used to be traded.

IPP – Independent power producer.

ISO – Independent systems operator.

JET – Jet fuel, aka aviation fuel or jet-kero.

KCBOT – Kansas City Board of Trade.

kT – Kilotonne. One thousand tonnes.

kW – Kilowatt. One thousand watts, a measure of power (generally electrical).

L3D – Last three days. Sometimes used for pricing natural gas.

Landed cost – Means a commodity price is quoted *inclusive* of cif plus additional import duties at the port of delivery.

Lay/Can – Laydays/Cancellation. The window of time (earliest and latest day respectively) that a vessel can report to the loading port without being in breach of charter.

LCO – Ticker code for light crude oil (specifically meaning Brent oil) on Reuters and ICE.

LDC – Local distribution company (electricity).

LDPE – Low density polyethylene (a plastic). See also LL.

LHS – Left hand side (of a mathematical equation).

LIFFE – London International Financial Futures and Options Exchange (now part of the NYSE Euronext group).

Light crude – Crude oil with a high proportion of light fractions (and therefore a high API gravity).

LL – Linear low density polyethylene (a plastic). See also LDPE.

LLS – Louisiana Light Sweet – a North American crude oil.

LME – London Metal Exchange.

LMP – Locational marginal pricing. Used in electricity trading.

LNG – Liquefied natural gas. Natural gas that has been liquefied, requiring cooling to −161 °C at standard atmospheric pressure. Generally used for shipping in cryogenic sea tankers.

LOOP – Louisiana Oil Port.

LPG – Liquefied petroleum gas. A blend of propane and butane (composition varies).

LSE – Load serving entity (an electrical power plant which can be called in by the TSO when demand requires it).

LSFO – Low sulphur fuel oil (sulphur content less than 1%).

LVL – Laminated veneer lumber.

Maintenance margin – The level of margin funds that triggers a margin call if the account balance falls below the maintenance level.

Margin – Money held on account with an exchange to provide surety against default.

Margin call – The unfortunate event (for the holder of the position) when extra monies must be lodged with a brokerage as a result of disadvantageous movements in the trader's position.

Marker crude – A particularly heavily traded crude oil which is used to set reference price levels for other crude oils. WTI, Brent and Dubai are the main ones, in that order of precedence.

MASP – Monthly average selling price (for TAPOs on base metals).

Maturity date – The date on which a forward or futures contract becomes due for settlement or delivery.

MBF – 1,000 board foot. Unit for lumber.

MC – Mid-Columbia, a location for delivery of electricity as traded in MC electricity contracts.

MEG – Middle East Gulf.

Merc days – Trading days on which the NYMEX is open.

Metric ton – 1,000 kg (denoted as 1 MT). US terminology for tonne.

MGEX – Minneapolis Grain Exchange. Trading hub for spring wheats.

Mid-C – Mid-Columbia Hub. An electricity market in the north-west of the continental USA.

Middle distillates – Refined products such as jet fuel, kerosene, diesel and heating oil.

mio – Million.

MT – Metric ton, i.e. 1 tonne or 1000 kg.

MTBE – Methyl tertiary butyl ether. A gasoline additive, which is used instead of lead to raise the octane number of gasoline. Outlawed for this purpose in many jurisdictions, where fuel ethanol is used in its place.

MW – Megawatt. One million watts, a measure of electrical power, often used to measure energy in units of MWh (megawatt-hour). Sometimes (confusingly) appears as "MMW".

NAEGA – North American Export Grain Association.

NASAAC – North American special aluminium alloy contract. North American A380 .1 specification, i.e. 8–9.5% Si, 1% Fe, 3–4% Cu, 0.5% Mn, 0.1% Mg, 0.5% Ni, 2.9% Zn and 0.35% Sn

NBP – National balancing point. Virtual location for delivery of UK natural gas into the National Grid.

Nearby future – The traded futures contract with the closest expiry. See also front month and prompt future.

NERC – North American Electric Reliability Council. Established in 1968 to maintain reliable electrical transmission in North America. There are ten regional councils.

New crop – September grain contract (for HRSW).

NFC – Not for concentrate. Orange juice that does not end up in FCOJ form.

NG – Natural gas, aka natgas. Primarily methane, with other chemicals (e.g. other hydrocarbons, CO_2, N_2 and H_2S).

NGLs – Natural gas liquids. These refer to the hydrocarbons other than methane extracted from natural gas wells such as ethane, propane, butane and iso-butane and natural gasoline, generally referring to hydrocarbons which are liquid at underground pressures but gases at standard temperature and pressure. See also condensate.

NGX – Natural Gas Exchange, headquartered in Alberta.

NOCs – National oil companies (e.g. Saudi Aramco).

Numeraire – Unit of wealth (generally risk-free or nearly so) used to denominate the value of other potentially more risky goods such as commodities for purposes of comparison and exchange.

NWE – North-West Europe (common abbreviation).

NYBOT – New York Board of Trade.

NYMEX – New York Mercantile Exchange. Primary exchange for WTI.

Octane number – A measure of how much compression a liquid hydrocarbon fuel can withstand before spontaneously igniting, calibrated with reference to n-heptane, having an octane number of 0 and isooctane having an octane number of 100.

OECD – Organization for Economic Cooperation and Development.

OPEC – Organization of the Petroleum Exporting Countries.

Option – The right but not the obligation to enter into a financial contract, e.g. to buy or sell a commodity at a prespecified strike price.

OSB – Oriented strand board. Strands of thin wood adhered together, often used to replace plywood.

OTC – Over the counter. Denotes bilaterally negotiated contracts, tailored to specific customer requirements, as opposed to exchange traded (which are more standardised).

Oxygenate – Chemical additive, mixed with gasoline blendstock to increase the octane number by making more oxygen available to react with the carbon monoxide produced during combustion.

Panamax – Size categorisation for ship permitted to transit the Panama Canal, with various length/width/draft/height restrictions. Typically with capacity 65–80 kDWT but restricted to 52.5 kDWT during the actual canal transit.

Paper barrel – Barrel of crude oil for cash/financial settlement as opposed to physical, prior to being allocated a specific loading date. See also wet barrel.

PDE – Partial differential equation.

PE – Polyethylene (a plastic).

PET – Polyethylene terephthalate (a plastic).

Petroleum gases – Another term for NGLs, especially when extracted from oil wells rather than being found with associated gas.

PGM – Platinum group metals (ruthenium, rhodium, palladium, osmium, iridium and platinum).

Pit – Place where futures are traded on the floor of an open-outcry commodity exchange (US terminology). See ring.

PJM – Pennsylvania/New Jersey/Maryland, location for delivery of electricity as traded in NYMEX PJM electricity futures contracts.

PP – Polypropylene (a plastic).

ppm – Parts per million.

PPP – Pool purchase price. Used in UK electricity markets.

Prompt date – The date on which a forward or futures contract becomes due for settlement or delivery. I tend to use maturity date in this text, to avoid confusion with the prompt future.

Prompt future – The traded futures contract with the closest maturity. See also front month and nearby future.

PS – Polystyrene (a plastic).

PTFE – Polytetrafluoroethylene (a plastic). Commonly known as "teflon".

PV – (i) Present value. (ii) Palo Verde, Arizona. Location for delivery of electricity as traded in NYMEX PV electricity futures contracts.

PVC – Polyvinyl chloride (a plastic).

R&M – Refining and marketing, aka "downstream" activities. Involves conversion of crude oil and/or natural gas into end-user refined products.

RB – Richards Bay, KZN, South Africa. Largest export coal terminal in the world, 180km NE of Durban. See API4.

RBOB – US gasoline, as used for motor vehicles once an oxygenating product such as 10% fuel ethanol has been added (acronym for Reformulated Gasoline Blendstock for Oxygenate Blending).

REBCO – Russian export blend crude oil. Another name for Urals, quoted on NYMEX as RE.

RECs – Regional electricity companies.

Red months – Contract delivery months in the *subsequent* year (as seen from today). See also blue months and green months.

Resid – Residual fuel oil (mostly used for electricity generation).

RHS – Right hand side (of a mathematical equation).

Ring – Place where futures are traded on the floor of an open-outcry commodity exchange (UK terminology). See Pit.

R/L – Random length. Appears in connection with the random length lumber contract.

Roll date – The final day on which a prompt futures contract is traded (the next day, the shortest dated of the back month contracts becomes the new prompt futures contract).

ROTT – Rotterdam.

RTO – Regional Transmission Organization.

SDE – Stochastic differential equation.

Seasonality – Tendency of some commodities (notably refined energy products) to have repeated periodic highs and lows, as observed in the forward/futures markets, corresponding to somewhat predictable changes in demand over the course of a typical calendar year.

SECA – Sulphur emission control area. European maritime region where sulphur content on fuel oil used in shipping is controlled.

SIN/SING – Singapore.

Softs – Soft commodities, e.g. cocoa, cotton, orange juice, coffee, lumber and sugar.

Sour – (of oil) High in sulphur, i.e. > 1.5% by weight.

Spark spread – (Of oil or gas) differential between market price of electricity and the energy of oil/gas required to generate that amount of electricity. Generally oil spark spread denotes spread over resid, gas spark spread denotes spread over natgas. See also dark spread.

Spot month – The month of the traded futures contract with the closest maturity. Sometimes called Prompt month. See also Prompt future.

Spread – Either (i) a contract either to purchase one contract month and sell another contract month in the same commodity, or (ii) a long/short position to purchase and sell a basket of commodities (often as basket comprised only of two commodity assets) with the same maturity.

Suezmax – Size categorisation for large oil tankers, typically with capacity 120–200 kDWT, permitting operation through the Suez canal. Also used for dry cargoes, with capacity 80–100 kDWT.

Swap(1,0) – Commodity swap with prompt future rolled at the very *end* of the trading day.

Swap(1,1) – Commodity swap with prompt future rolled at the very *beginning* of the trading day.

Sweet – (of oil) Low in sulphur, i.e. < 0.5% by weight. N.B. the sulphur in oil is usually in the form of hydrogen sulphide or mercaptans.

Tapis – A light sweet crude oil produced off the east coast of peninsular Malaysia, used as crude oil benchmark in the Asia-Pacific region. Density of 45.2 °API and ~0.03% sulphur. A particularly expensive crude oil. The word "Tapis" means refine or process in Malay.

TAPO – Traded average price option. Term used for (arithmetic) average rate options on base metals, exchange traded on the LME.

TC – (i) Trip charter; (ii) Tanker, clean (both with respect to shipping).

TD – Tanker, dirty (shipping).

tCO2e – Tonne of carbon dioxide (CO_2) equivalent.

TEL – Tetraethyl lead. A lead containing additive used to boost the octane number of gasoline. Formerly used for automobile and aviation gasoline, now only used for the latter purpose in much of (but by no means all) the world.

Telequote codes – Futures contract symbols identifying the types of various traded commodities, e.g. "CL" for crude (light) oil.

TGE – Tokyo Grain Exchange.

TI – Informal market shorthand for WTI.

TOCOM – Tokyo Commodity Exchange.

Tonne – 1,000 kg (T). Also referred to as metric ton in the US.

toe – Tonne of oil equivalent. A measure of the energy content of one tonne of crude oil, generally taken to be 41.87 gigajoules (though of course it certainly varies depending on the particular chemical composition).

TSO – Transmission system operator. Agency in electricity markets who ensures the safety and reliability of the transmission network for conduction of electricity from suppliers (power stations) to consumers.

UKPX – UK Power Exchange.

ULCC – Ultra large crude carrier. The largest oil supertankers (over 320 kDWT).

ULSD – Ultra-low sulphur diesel. No more than 15 ppm sulphur.

Upstream – Activities relating to crude oil before it reaches the production terminal. See E&P.

Urals – A Russian blend of heavy crude oil from the Urals with light crude oil from Western Siberia. Density of 31.7 °API and ~1.35% sulphur. Sometimes referred to as REBCO (an acronym for "Russian export blend crude oil").

USDA – United States Department of Agriculture.

VLCC – Very large crude carrier. Large oil supertankers (200–320 kDWT).

Waha Hub – Valero pipeline Waha hub in West Texas, location for physical delivery of natural gas futures as traded on KCBOT.

WCC – Western Canadian Crude. A heavy crude oil.

Weeklies – Weekly options, which trade on the CME with expiries offset by one, two, three or four weeks from the standard option expiry dates.

Wet barrel – Barrel of crude oil for physical delivery, with allocated loading date. See also paper barrel.

Wheeling – Long-distance delivery of power from one region to another.

WPG – Winnipeg Commodity Exchange.

WS – Worldscale. A reference pricing mechanism for maritime shipping of crude oil.

WTI – West Texas Intermediate (synonymous with Texas Light Sweet Crude). North American crude oil contract primarily traded in futures and options markets on NYMEX. Physically deliverable to Cushing, Oklahoma. Prices are quoted fob Cushing. Density of 39.6 °API and ~0.24% sulphur.

WTS – West Texas Sour.

X-Grade – Synonym for No. 2 fuel oil.

References

Alexandridis, A. K. and Zapranis, A. D. (2013) *Weather Derivatives: Modeling and Pricing Weather-Related Risk*. Springer: New York.

Alizadeh, A. H. and Nomikos, N. K. (2009) *Shipping Derivatives and Risk Management*. Palgrave Macmillan: Basingstoke.

Amen, S. (2013) Dr Copper - The relationship between copper and other markets. *Thalesians Quant Strategy Notes* (30 September 2013). www.thalesians.com/finance/index.php/Quant_Strategy.

Andreasen, J. and Dahlgren, M. (2006) At the flick of a switch. *Energy Risk*, February: 71–75.

Angus, J. E. (1999) A note on pricing Asian derivatives with continuous geometric averaging. *Journal of Futures Markets*, 19(7): 845–858.

Arndt, N. and Ganino, C. (2012) *Metals and Society: An Introduction to Economic Geology*. Springer: Berlin.

Askari, H. and Krichene, N. (2008) Oil price dynamics (2002–2006). *Energy Economics*, 30: 2134–2153.

Barlow, M. T. (2002) A diffusion model for electricity prices. *Mathematical Finance*, 12(4), 287–298.

Barone-Adesi, G. and Whaley, R. E. (1987) Efficient analytic approximation of American option values. *Journal of Finance*, 42(June): 301–320.

Baxter, M. and Rennie, A. (1996) *Financial Calculus: An Introduction to Derivative Pricing*. Cambridge University Press: Cambridge.

Beneder, R. and Elkenbracht-Huizung, M. (2003) Foreign exchange options and the volatility smile. *Medium Econometrische Toepassingen* (Voorjaar), 11(2): 30–36.

Benth, F. E. and Benth, J. Š. (2012) *Modeling and Pricing in Financial Markets for Weather Derivatives*. World Scientific: Singapore.

Benth, F. E. and Koekebakker, S. (2008) Stochastic modeling of financial electricity contracts. *Energy Economics*, 30: 1116–1157.

Benth, F. E., Kholodnyi, V. A. and Laurence, P., ed. (2014) *Quantitative Energy Finance*. Springer: Berlin.

Bierbrauer, M., Menn, C., Rachev, S. T. and Trück, S. (2007) Spot and derivative pricing in the EEX power market. *Journal of Banking and Finance*, 31: 3462–3485.

Bingham, N. H. and Kiesel, R. (1998) *Risk-Neutral Valuation: Pricing and Hedging of Financial Derivatives*. Springer: London.

Bittman, J. B. (2008) *Trading and Hedging with Agricultural Futures and Options*. John Wiley & Sons: Hoboken, NJ.

Bjerksund, P. (1991) Contingent Claims Evaluation When the Convenience Yield is Stochastic: Analytical Results. Working paper, Norwegian School of Economics and Business Administration.

Bjerksund, P. and Stensland, G. (1993) Closed-form approximation of American options. *Scandinavian Journal of Management*, 9(Suppl.): S88–S99.

Bjerksund, P. and Stensland, G. (2002) Closed-Form Valuation of American Options. Discussion Paper 2002/09, NHH Bergen Norway. (Version: 21 October 2002). http://www.nhh.no/

Bjorlykke, K. (2010) *Petroleum Geoscience: From Sedimentary Environments to Rock Physics*. Springer: Berlin.

Black, F. (1976) The pricing of commodity contracts. *Journal of Financial Economics*, 3: 167–179.

Black, F. and Scholes, M. (1973) The pricing of options and corporate liabilities. *Journal of Political Economy*, 81(3): 637–659.

Bobin, C. A. (1990) *Agricultural Options: Trading, Risk Management and Hedging*. John Wiley & Sons: New York.

Borovkova, S. and Permana, F. J. (2006) Modelling electricity prices by the potential jump-diffusion. **In** Shiryaev, A. N., Grossinho, M. d-R., Oliveria, P. E. and Esquível, M. L., ed. (2006) *Stochastic Finance*. Springer: New York.

Briys, E., Bellalah, M., Mai, H. M. and de Varenne, F. (1998) *Options, Futures and Exotic Derivatives: Theory, Application and Practice*. John Wiley & Sons: Chichester.

Broni-Mensah, E. K. (2012) *Numerical Solution of Weather Derivatives and Other Incomplete Market Problems*. PhD thesis, University of Manchester.

Bunn, D. W., ed. (2004) *Modelling Prices in Competitive Electricity Markets*. Wiley: Chichester.

Burger, M., Graeber, B. and Schindlmayr, G. (2007) *Managing Energy Risk: An Integrated View on Power and Other Energy Markets*. Wiley: Chichester.

Carlton, D. W. (1984) Futures markets: Their purpose, their history, their growth, their successes and failures. *Journal of Futures Markets*, 4: 237–271.

Carmona, R. and Coulon, M. (2014) A Survey of Commodity Markets and Structural Models for Electricity Prices. **In** Benth, F. E., Kholodnyi, V. A. and Laurence, P., ed. (2014) *Quantitative Energy Finance*. Springer: Berlin.

Carmona, R. and Diko, P. (2005) Pricing precipitation based derivatives. *International Journal of Theoretical and Applied Finance*, 8(7): 959–988.

Carollo, S. (2012) *Understanding Oil Prices: A Guide to What Drives the Price of Oil in Today's Markets*. Wiley: Chichester.

Cartea, A. and Figueroa, M. (2005) Pricing in electricity markets: A mean reverting jump diffusion model with seasonality. *Applied Mathematical Finance*, 12(4): 313–335.

Carverhill, A. and Clewlow, L. (1990) Flexible convolution: Valuing average rate (Asian) Options. *RISK*, 4(3): 25–29.

CBOT (1989) *Commodity Trading Manual*, 7th edition. Chicago Board of Trade: Chicago.

Clark, E., Lesourd, J.-B. and Thiéblemont, R. (2001) *International Commodity Trading: Physical and Derivative Markets*. Wiley Trading: Chichester.

Clark, I. J. (2011) *Foreign Exchange Option Pricing: A Practitioner's Guide*. Wiley: Chichester.

Clemmons, L., Kaminski, V. and Hrgovcic, J. H. (1999) Weather Derivatives: Hedging Mother Nature. **In** Geman, H., ed. (1999) *Insurance and Weather Derivatives: From Exotic Options to Exotic Underlyings*. RISK Books: London.

Clewlow, L. and Strickland, C. (1999a) Valuing energy options in a one factor model fitted to forward prices. Working paper (April 1999).

Clewlow, L. and Strickland, C. (1999b) A multi-factor model for energy derivatives. Working paper (August 1999).

Clewlow, L. and Strickland, C. (2000) *Energy Derivatives: Pricing and Risk Management*. Lacima Group: Melbourne.

Collins, B. M. and Fabozzi, F. J. (1999) *Derivatives and Equity Portfolio Management*. FJF Associates: New Hope, Pennsylvania.

Cortazar, G. and Schwartz, E. S. (2003) Implementing a stochastic model for oil futures prices. *Energy Economics*, 25: 215–238.

Cox, J. C., Ingersoll, J. E. and Ross, S. (1981) The relation between forward prices and futures prices. *Journal of Financial Economics*, 9: 321–346.

Cross, J. (2000) *Gold Derivatives: The Market View*. The World Gold Council.

Croucher, L. and Gillespie, A. (2000) Coal Trading: The Core of Change. **In** Fusaro, P. C. and Wilcox, J. (eds) (2000) *Energy Derivatives: Trading Emerging Markets*. Energy Publishing Enterprises: New York.

Crowson, P. and Markey, C., ed. (2011) *Managing Metals Price Risk on the London Metal Exchange*, 4th edition. London Metals Exchange: London.

Curran, M. (1994) Valuing Asian and portfolio options by conditioning on the geometric mean price. *Management Science*, 40: 1705–1711.

Das, S. (2005) Commodity forwards and swaps. *Futures & Options World*, February.

de Jong, C. (2006) The nature of power spikes: A regime-switch approach. *Studies in Nonlinear Dynamics & Econometrics*, 10(3): Article 3.

Deng, S. J. (2000) Stochastic models of energy commodity prices and their applications: Mean-reversion with jumps and spikes. Technical report, University of California Energy Institute. Working Paper PWP-073 (February 2000).

Deng, S. J. and Oren, S. S. (2006) Electricity derivatives and risk management. *Energy*, 31: 940–953.

Dischel, R. (1999) A Weather Risk Management Choice: Hedging with Degree-day Derivatives. **In** Geman, H., ed. (1999) *Insurance and Weather Derivatives: From Exotic Options to Exotic Underlyings*. RISK Books: London.

Dorsman, A., Simpson, J. L. and Westerman, W., ed. (2013) *Energy Economics and Financial Markets*. Springer: Berlin.

Downey, M. (2009) *Oil 101*. Wooden Table Press.

Duffie, D. (1996) *Dynamic Asset Pricing Theory*, 2nd edition. Princeton University Press: Princeton, NJ.

Duffy, D. J. (2006) *Finite Difference Methods in Financial Engineering: A Partial Differential Equation Approach*. John Wiley & Sons: Chichester.

Edward, G. and Varilek, M. (2000) Emissions: Trading in Practice. **In** Fusaro, P. C. and Wilcox, J. (eds) (2000) *Energy Derivatives: Trading Emerging Markets*. Energy Publishing Enterprises: New York.

Edwards, D. (2010) *Energy Trading and Investing*. McGraw Hill: New York.

Errera, S. and Brown, S. L. (2002) *Fundamentals of Trading Energy Futures and Options, 2nd edition*. Pennwell Corporation: Tulsa, OK.

Eydeland, A. and Wolyniec, K. (2003) *Energy and Power Risk Management: New Developments in Modeling, Pricing and Hedging*. Wiley Finance: Hoboken, NJ.

Fattouh, B. (2011) An Anatomy of the Crude Oil Pricing System. Working Paper WPM 40, The Oxford Institute of Energy Studies.

Fiorenzani, S. (2006) *Quantitative Methods for Electricity Trading and Risk Management: Advanced Mathematical and Statistical Methods for Energy Finance*. Palgrave Macmillan: Basingstoke.

Flavell, R. R. (2009) *Swaps and Other Derivatives*, 2nd edition. Wiley: Chichester.

Flesaker, B. (1993) Arbitrage free pricing of interest rate futures and forward contracts. *The Journal of Futures Markets*, 13(1): 77–91.

Frankel, O. (1997) Special Issues in Valuing Metals Derivatives. In Jameson, R., ed. (1997) *Managing Metals Price Risk*. RISK Books: London.

Franks, L. S. and Gee, T. M. (2000) Bandwidth Trading – Developing a Market. In Fusaro, P. C. and Wilcox, J. (eds) (2000) *Energy Derivatives: Trading Emerging Markets*. Energy Publishing Enterprises: New York.

Freese, B. (2006) *Coal: A Human History*. Arrow: London.

Garman, M. B. and Kohlhagen, S. W. (1983) Foreign currency option values. *Journal of International Money and Finance*, 2: 231–237.

Gasparrini, C. (1993) *Gold and Other Precious Metals: From Ore to Market*. Springer-Verlag: Berlin.

Geman, H. (2005) *Commodities and Commodity Derivatives: Modeling and Pricing for Agriculturals, Metals and Energy*. Wiley Finance: Chichester.

Geman, H. and Nguyen, V. N. (2005) Soybean inventory and forward curve dynamics. *Management Science*, 51(7): 1076–1091.

Geman, H. and Roncoroni, A. (2006) Understanding the fine structure of electricity prices. *Journal of Business* 79(3): 1225–1261.

Geman, H. and Smith, W. (2013) Theory of storage, inventory and volatility in the LME base metals. *Resources Policy* 38(1): 18–28.

Gibson, R. and Schwartz, E. S. (1990) Stochastic convenience yield and the pricing of oil contingent claims. *Journal of Finance*, 45(3): 959–976.

Griffiths, W. P. (2003) Bicentenary of four platinum group metals. Part I – rhodium and palladium – events surrounding their discoveries. *Platinum Metals Review*, 47(4): 175–183.

Grigoriu, M. (2002) *Stochastic Calculus: Applications in Science and Engineering*. Birkhäuser: Boston.

Hagan, P. S., Kumar, D., Lesniewski, A. S. and Woodward, D. E. (2002) Managing smile risk. *Wilmott magazine*, July: 84–108.

Hambly, B., Howison, S. and Kluge, T. (2009) Modelling spikes and pricing swing options in electricity markets. *Quantitative Finance*, 9(8): 937–949.

Hamilton, J. D. (1989) A new approach to the economic analysis of nonstationary time series and the business cycle. *Econometrica*, 57: 357–384.

Hantschel, T. and Kauerauf, A. I. (2010) *Fundamentals of Basin and Petroleum Systems Modeling*. Springer: Berlin.

Harris, C. (2006) *Electricity Markets: Pricing, Structures and Economics*. Wiley Finance: Chichester.

Haug, E. (2007) *The Complete Guide to Option Pricing Formulas, 2nd edition*. McGraw-Hill: New York.

Hosseini, M. (2007) Stochastic modeling of oil futures prices, Uppsala University Department of Mathematics, Project Report 2007:1.

Huang, A. Y. (2007) *Commodity Basket Option/Swaption valuation: Geometric Conditioning and Moment Matching*, PG&E Internal Document.

Huisman, R. (2008) The influence of temperature on spike probability in day-ahead power markets. *Energy Economics*, 30: 2697–2704.

Huisman, R. (2009) *An Introduction to Models for the Energy Markets: The Thinking behind Econometric Techniques and Their Application*. RISK Books: London.

Huisman, R. and de Jong, C. (2003) Option pricing for power prices with spikes. *Energy Power Risk Management*, 7 (11): S12–S16.

Huisman, R. and Mahieu, R. (2003) Regime jumps in electricity prices. *Energy Economics*, 25: 425–434.

Hull, J. (2011) *Options, Futures and Other Derivatives*, 8th edition. Prentice Hall: Upper Saddle River, NJ.

Hull, J. and White, A. (1996) *Hull–White on Derivatives: A Compilation of Articles*. RISK Books: London.

Jamshidian, F. and Fein, M. (1990) Closed-Form Solutions For Oil Futures and European Options in the Gibson-Schwartz Model: A Note. Working Paper, Merrill Lynch Capital Markets.

Janczura, J., Trück, S., Weron, R. and Wolff, R. C. (2013) Identifying spikes and seasonal components in electricity spot price data: A guide to robust modeling. *Energy Economics*, 38: 96–110.

Janczura, J. and Weron, R. (2012) Efficient estimation of Markov regime-switching models: An application to electricity spot prices. *AStA – Advances in Statistical Analysis*, 96: 385–407.

Janczura, J. and Weron, R. (2014) Inference for Markov-regime Switching Models of Electricity Spot Prices. In Benth, F. E., Kholodnyi, V. A. and Laurence, P., ed. (2014) *Quantitative Energy Finance*. Springer: Berlin.

Jarrow, R. A. and Oldfield, G. S. (1981) Forward contracts and futures contracts. *Journal of Financial Economics*, 9: 373–382.

Järvinen, S. and Toivonen, H. (2004) Pricing European commodity swaptions. *Applied Economics Letters*, 11: 925–929.

Jewson, S. and Brix, A. (2005) *Weather Derivative Valuation: The Meteorological, Statistical, Financial and Mathematical Foundations*. Cambridge University Press: Cambridge.

Johnson, B. and Barz, G. (1999) Selecting Stochastic Processes for Modelling Electricity Prices. In Kaminski, V., ed. (2005) *Energy Modelling: Advances in the Management of Uncertainty*, 2nd edition. RISK Books: London.

Junge, A. (2012) Freight Derivatives – Navigating Exotic Opportunities. Presentation at Global Derivatives Trading and Risk Management 2012 conference, Barcelona.

Kaminski, V., Gibner, S. and Pinnamaneni, K. (1999) Energy Exotic Options. In Jameson, R. (1999) *Managing Energy Price Risk*, 2nd edition. RISK Books: London.

Kavussanos, M. G. and Visvikis, I. D. (2006) *Derivatives and Risk Management in Shipping*. RISK Books: London.

Kavussanos, M. G. and Visvikis, I. D. (2008) Freight Derivatives and Risk Management: A Review. In Geman, H., ed. (2008) *Risk Management in Commodity Markets: From Shipping to Agriculturals and Energy*. Wiley Finance: Chichester.

Kavussanos, M. G. and Visvikis, I. D. (2011) *Theory and Practice of Shipping Freight Derivatives*. RISK Books: London.

Kemna, A. and Vorst, A. (1990) A pricing method for options based on average asset values. *Journal of Banking and Finance*, 14: 113–129.

Kholodnyi, V. A. (2001a) A non-Markov method. *Energy Power and Risk Management Magazine*, March: 20–24.

Kholodnyi, V. A. (2001b) Analytical valuation in a mean-reverting world. *Energy Power and Risk Management Magazine*, August: 40–45.

Kholodnyi, V. A. (2006) Valuation and hedging of contingent claims on power with spikes: A non-Markovian approach. *Journal of Derivatives: Use, Trading and Regulation*, 11(4): 308–333.

Kholodnyi, V. A. (2008) The Non-Markovian Approach to the Valuation and Hedging of European Contingent Claims on Power with Spikes of Pareto Distributed Magnitude, 275–308. In Sivasundaram, S., ed. (2008) *Advances in Mathematical Problems in Engineering, Aerospace and Sciences*. Cambridge Scientific Publishers, Cambridge, UK.

Kholodnyi, V. A. (2014) Modelling Power Forward Prices for Positive and Negative Power Spot Prices with Upward and Downward Spikes in the Framework of the Non-Markovian Approach. **In** Benth, F. E., Kholodnyi, V. A. and Laurence, P., ed. (2014) *Quantitative Energy Finance*. Springer: Berlin.

Kirk, E. (1995) Correlation in Energy Markets. **In** Jameson, R., ed. (1995) *Managing Energy Price Risk*, 1st edition RISK Books: London.

Kjaer, M. (2008) Pricing of swing options in a mean reverting model with jumps. *Applied Mathematical Finance*, 15(5–6), 479–502.

Kluge, T. (2006) *Pricing Swing Options and Other Electricity Derivatives*. PhD thesis, Oxford University.

Koekebakker, S. and Lien, G. (2004) Volatility and price jumps in agricultural futures prices – evidence from wheat options. *American Journal of Agricultural Economics*, 86(4): 1018–1031.

Kub, E. (2012) *Mastering the Grain Markets: How Profits Are Really Made*. Kub Asset Advisory, Inc. (self published): Omaha, NE. www.masteringthegrainmarkets.com

Kwok, Y.-K. (1998) *Mathematical Models of Financial Derivatives*. Springer: Singapore.

Labre, M. and Atkinson, C. (2010) On the pricing of emission reduction purchase agreement contracts. *Journal of Energy Markets*, 3(2): 69–109.

Larsson, K. (2011) Pricing commodity swaptions in multifactor models. *Journal of Derivatives*, 12(2): 32–44.

LBMA and LPPM (2008) A Guide to the London Precious Metals Markets. London Bullion Market Association and the London Platinum and Palladium Market. http://www.lppm.com/OTCguide.pdf

Leoni, P. (2013) Energy Derivatives – From Financial Modeling to Physical Derivatives. Presentation at Global Derivatives Trading and Risk Management 2013 conference, Amsterdam.

Levy, E. (1992) Pricing European average rate currency options. *Journal of International Money and Finance*, 11: 474–491.

Levy, E. and Turnbull, S. (1992) Average Intelligence. *RISK*, 6(2): 5–9.

Lipton, A. (2001) *Mathematical Methods for Foreign Exchange: A Financial Engineer's Approach*. World Scientific: Singapore.

Lonergan, W. (2006) *The Valuation of Mining Assets*. Sydney University Press: Sydney.

Lucia, J. L. and Schwartz, E. S. (2002) Electricity prices and power derivatives: evidence from the Nordic power exchange. *Review of Derivatives Research*, 5: 5–50.

Ludkovski, M. and Carmona, R. (2004) Spot Convenience Yield Models for Energy Assets. AMS Mathematics of Finance (Yin, G. and Zhang, Y., ed.), Contemporary Mathematics, 351: 65–80. www.pstat.ucsb.edu/faculty/ludkovski/utahproc.pdf

Madhumathi, R. and Ranganatham, M. (2012) *Derivatives and Risk Management*. Dorling Kindersley (India): New Delhi.

Malz, A. (1997) Estimating the probability distribution of the future exchange rate from option prices. *Journal of Derivatives* (Winter): 20–36.

Margrabe, W. (1978) The value of an option to exchange one asset for another. *The Journal of Finance*, 33(1): 177–186.

McKibben, B. (2012) *The Global Warming Reader: A Century of Writing about Climate Change*. Penguin: London.

Merton, R. C. (1976) Option pricing when underlying stock returns are discontinuous. *Journal of Financial Economics*, 3: 125–144.

Moore, M. (2000) Bandwidth Trading – The New Commodity Gold Rush. **In** Fusaro, P. C. and Wilcox, J. (eds) (2000) *Energy Derivatives: Trading Emerging Markets*. Energy Publishing Enterprises: New York.

Mount, T. Y., Ning, Y. and Cai, X. (2006) Predicting price spikes in electricity markets using a regime-switching model with time-varying parameters. *Energy Economics*, 28: 62–80.

Musiela, M. and Rutkowski, M. (1997) *Martingale Methods in Financial Modelling*. Springer: Berlin.

Øksendal, B. (2010) *Stochastic Differential Equations: An Introduction with Applications, 6th edition*. Springer: Berlin.

Pelsser, A. (2000) *Efficient Methods for Valuing Interest Rate Derivatives*. Springer: London.

Pilipović, D. (1998) *Energy Risk*. McGraw Hill: New York.

Pilz, K. F. and Schlögl, E. (2013) A hybrid commodity and interest rate market model. *Quantitative Finance*, 13(4): 543–560.

Pindyck, R. S. (2001) The dynamics of commodity spot and futures markets: A primer. *The Energy Journal*, 22(3): 1–29.

Pirrong, C. (2012) *Commodity Price Dynamics: A Structural Approach*. Cambridge University Press: New York.

Piterbarg, V. V. and Renedo, M. A. (2006) Eurodollar futures convexity adjustments in stochastic volatility models. *Journal of Computational Finance*, 9(3): 71–94.

Press, W. H., Teukolsky, S. A., Vetterling, W. T. and Flannery, B. P. (2002) *Numerical Recipes in C++, 2nd edition*. Cambridge University Press: Cambridge.

Purcell, W. D. and Koontz, S. R. (1999) *Agricultural Futures and Options: Principles and Strategies*, 2nd edition. Prentice Hall: Upper Saddle River, NJ.

Reiswich, D. and Wystup, U. (2009) FX Volatility Smile Construction (Version: September 8 2009). http://www.mathfinance.com/wystup/papers/CPQF_Arbeits20.pdf

Richter, M. C. and Sørensen, C. (2002) Stochastic Volatility and Seasonality in Commodity Futures and Options: The Case of Soybeans. EFA 2002 Berlin Meetings Presented Paper. (Version: 27 February 2002). http://ssrn.com/abstract=301994

Riedhauser, C. (2005a) *Exact Swaption Pricing in a One-Factor Model*, PG&E Internal Document (Version: June 17, 2005).

Riedhauser, C. (2005b) *Energy Swaptions*, PG&E Internal Document (Version: July 5, 2005).

Ripple, R. D. (2011) International Energy Derivatives Markets. In Evans, J. and Hunt, L. C., ed. (2011) *International Handbook on the Economics of Energy*. Edward Elgar Publishing: Cheltenham.

Rubinstein, M. (1991) One for another. *RISK* (July-August): 30–32.

Rudenno, V. (2009) *The Mining Valuation Handbook: Australian Mining and Energy Valuation for Investors and Management*. Wiley-Blackwell: Brisbane.

Schmitz, A., Wang, Z. and Kimn, J. (2012) A Jump Diffusion Model for Agricultural Commodities with Bayesian Analysis. Proceedings of the NCCC-134 Conference on Applied Commodity Price Analysis, Forecasting, and Market Risk Management. St. Louis, MO. http://www.farmdoc.illinois.edu/nccc134

Schneider, L. (2012) An Introduction to Commodities Markets. EMLYON Lecture Notes.

Schofield, N. C. (2007) *Commodity Derivatives: Markets and Applications*. Wiley Finance: Chichester.

Schwartz, A. (2003) Enron's Missed Opportunity: Enron's Refusal to Build a Collaborative Market Turned Bandwidth Trading Into a Disaster. BRIE Working Paper 152. The Berkeley Roundtable on the International Economy: Berkeley.

Schwartz, E. (1997) The stochastic behavior of commodity prices: Implications for valuation and hedging. *Journal of Finance*, 52(3): 923–973.

Schwartz, E. and Smith, J. (2000) Short-term variations and long-term dynamics in commodity prices. *Management Science*, 46(7): 893–911.

Scott, D. A. and Bray, W. (1980) Ancient platinum technology in South America: Its use by the Indians in prehistoric times. *Platinum Metals Review*, 24(4): 147–157.

Seidel, A. B. and Ginsberg, P.M. (1983) *Commodities Trading: Foundation, Analysis and Operations*. Prentice-Hall: Englewood Cliffs, NJ.

Shreve, S. E. (2004) *Stochastic Calculus for Finance II: Continuous-Time Models*. Springer-Verlag: Heidelberg.

Sørensen, C. (2002) Modeling seasonality in agricultural commodity futures. *The Journal of Futures Markets*, 22(5): 393–426.

Sturm, F. J. (1997) *Trading Natural Gas: Cash Futures Options and Swaps*. Pennwell Publishing Co: Tulsa, OK.

Sundaram, R. K. (1997) Equivalent martingale measures and risk-neutral pricing: An expository note. *The Journal of Derivatives*, Fall: 85–98.

Sundaram, R. K. and Das, S. (2010) *Derivatives*. McGraw Hill: New York.

Tan, C. (2012) *Market Practice in Financial Modelling*. World Scientific: Singapore.

Tavella, D. and Randall, C. (2000) *Pricing Financial Instruments: The Finite Difference Method*. John Wiley & Sons: New York.

Turnbull, S. M. and Wakeman, L. M. (1991) A quick algorithm for pricing european average options. *Journal of Quantitative Analysis*, 26(3): 377–389.

Vaillant, N. (1995) Convexity adjustments between futures and forward rate using a martingale approach. Probability Tutorials. http://www.probability.net/convex.pdf

Van Vactor, S. (2010) *Introduction to the Global Oil and Gas Business*. Pennwell Publishing Co: Tulsa, OK.

Van Woenzel, S. (2012) *The Oil Traders' Word(s): Oil Trading Jargon*. Author House: Bloomington, IN.

Venkatramanam, A. and Alexander, C. (2011) Closed form approximations for spread options. *Applied Mathematical Finance*, 18(5): 1–26.

Villaplana, P. (2003) Pricing Power Derivatives: A Two-Factor Jump-Diffusion Approach. Universidad Carlos III de Madrid. Working Paper 03-18, Business Economics Series 05.

Weron, R. (2006) *Modeling and Forecasting Electricity Loads and Prices: A Statistical Approach*. Wiley: Chichester.

Weron, R., Bierbrauer, M. and Trück, S. (2004) Modeling electricity prices: jump diffusion and regime switching. *Physica A*, 33: 39–48.

West, G. (2009) Exotic Equity Options. Financial Modelling Agency (Version: 7 October 2009). http://www.finmod.co.za/exotics.pdf

Whaley, R. E. (2006) *Derivatives: Markets, Valuation and Risk Management*. Wiley Finance: Chichester.

Williams, J. C. (1986) *The Economic Function of Futures Markets*. Cambridge University Press: Cambridge.

Wilmott, P., Dewynne, J. and Howison, S. (1993) *Option Pricing: Mathematical Models and Computation*. Oxford Financial Press: Oxford.

Wilmott, P., Howison, S. and Dewynne, J. (1995) *The Mathematics of Financial Derivatives: A Student Introduction*. Cambridge University Press: Cambridge.

Yannopoulos, J. C. (1991) *The Extractive Metallurgy of Gold*. Van Nostrand Reinhold: New York.

Zhang, P. G. (1998) *Exotic Options: A Guide to Second Generation Options*, 2nd edition. World Scientific: Singapore.

Further Reading

Allen, C., Brearley, T., Clarke, A., Harman, J. and Berry, P. (1999) *Australia in the World Gold Market*. ABARE Research Report 99.8, Australian Bureau of Agricultural and Resource Economics: Canberra.

Amen, S. (2013) Golden Times? – Discussing gold in the context of rates and flows. *Thalesians Quant Strategy Notes* (24 September 2013). www.thalesians.com/finance/index.php/Quant_Strategy.

Andersen, L. (2010) Markov models for commodity futures: theory and practice. *Quantitative Finance*, 10(8): 831–854.

Arthur, H. B. (1971) *Commodity Futures as a Business Management Tool*. Graduate School of Business Administration, Harvard University: Boston.

Aravindhakshan, S. C. (2010) *Essays: Biofuel Feedstock Production Economics and Identifying Jumps and Systematic Risk in Futures*. PhD thesis, Oklahoma State University.

Baeva, T. (2011) On the Pricing and Sensitivity of Spread Options on Two Correlated Assets. (Version: 9 May 2011). http://ssrn.com/abstract=1836689

Bauwens, L., Hafner, C. and Pierret, D. (2011) Multivariate volatility modeling of electricity futures. SFB 629 Discussion paper 2011-063 (13 October 2011).

Benth, F. E., Benth, J. Š. and Koekebakker, S. (2008) *Stochastic Modelling of Electricity and Related Markets*. World Scientific: Singapore.

Benth, F. E., Kallsen, J. and Meyer-Brandis, T. (2007) A non-Gaussian Ornstein-Uhlenbeck process for electricity spot price modeling and derivatives pricing. *Applied Mathematical Finance*, 14 (2): 153–169.

Benth, F. E., Kiesel, R. and Nazarova, A. (2012) A critical empirical study of three electricity spot price models. *Energy Economics*, 34 (5): 1589–1616.

Benth, F. E., Lange, N. and Myklebust, T. Å (2012) Pricing and Hedging Quanto Options in Energy Markets. (Version: 30 October 2012). http://ssrn.com/abstract=2133935

Branger, N., Reichmann, O. and Wobben, M. (2010) Pricing electricity derivatives on an hourly basis. *Journal of Energy Markets*, 3(3): 51–89.

Brennan, M. J. and Schwartz, E. S. (1985) Evaluating natural resource investments. *Journal of Business*, 58(2): 135–157.

Brown, S. L. and Errera, S. (1987) *Fundamentals of Trading Energy Futures and Options*. Quorum Books: New York.

Carmona, R. and Durrlemann, V. (2003) Pricing and hedging spread options. *SIAM Review*, 45(4): 627–685.

Cavalla, N. (1993) *OTC Markets in Derivative Instruments*. Macmillan: Basingstoke.

Chance, D. (2003) Swaptions and options. *Journal of Risk*, online publication. www.risk.net/journal-of-risk/technical-paper/2161141/swaptions-options

Chance, D. and Rich, D. (1996) Asset swaps with Asian-style payoffs. *Journal of Derivatives*, 3: 64–77.

Christian, J. M. (2006) *Commodities Rising: The Reality Behind the Hype and How to Really Profit in the Commodities Market*. Wiley: Hoboken.

Clubley, S. (1998) *Trading in Oil Futures and Options*, 2nd edition. Woodhead Publishing Ltd: Cambridge.

Cortazar, G. and Schwartz, E. S. (1994) The valuation of commodity contingent claims. *Journal of Derivatives* (Summer): 27–39.

Crabbe, P. D. (1998) *Metals Trading Handbook: A Market Companion for Users of the London Metals Exchange*. Woodhead: Abington.

Cross, J. (1994) *New Frontiers in Gold: The Derivatives Revolution*. Rosendale Press: London.

Crosby, J. (2008a) A multi-factor jump-diffusion model for commodities. *Quantitative Finance*, 8: 181–200.

Crosby, J. (2008b) Pricing a class of exotic commodity options in a multi-factor jump-diffusion model. *Quantitative Finance*, 8: 471–483.

Dahl, C. A. (2004) *International Energy Markets: Understanding Pricing, Policies and Profits*. Pennwell Publishing Co: Tulsa, OK.

de Keyser, D. R., ed. (1979) *Guide to World Commodity Markets*. Kogan Page: London.

Duffie, D. (1989) *Futures Markets*. Prentice-Hall: Englewood Cliffs.

Ekstrand, C. (2011) *Financial Derivatives Modeling*. Springer: Berlin.

Evans, J. and Hunt, L. C., ed. (2011) *International Handbook on the Economics of Energy*. Edward Elgar Publishing: Cheltenham.

Eydeland, A. and Geman, H. (1999) Fundamentals of Electricity Derivatives. **In** Kaminski, V., ed. (2005) *Energy Modelling: Advances in the Management of Uncertainty*, 2nd edition. RISK Books: London.

Fiorenzani, S., Ravelli, S. and Edoli, E. (2012) *The Handbook of Energy Trading*. Wiley Finance: Chichester.

Fusaro, P. C. and Wilcox, J. (2000) *Energy Derivatives: Trading Emerging Markets*. Energy Publishing Enterprises: New York.

Fusaro, P. C. (2002) *Energy Convergence: The Beginning of the Multi-Commodity Market*. Wiley Finance: New York.

Garner, C. (2012) *A Trader's First Book on Commodities*, 2nd edition. FT Press: Upper Saddle River, NJ.

Geman, H., ed. (1999) *Insurance and Weather Derivatives: From Exotic Options to Exotic Underlyings*. RISK Books: London.

Geman, H., ed. (2008) *Risk Management in Commodity Markets: From Shipping to Agriculturals and Energy*. Wiley Finance: Chichester.

Gibson-Jarvie, R. (1976) *The London Metal Exchange: A Commodity Market*. Woodhead-Faulkner (in assoc. with Metallgesellschaft AG): Cambridge.

Green, A. (2011) *Commodity Derivatives: CISI Certificate Programme*, 4th edition. Chartered Institute for Securities and Investment: London.

Guvenen, O., Labys, W. C. and Lesourd, J.-B., ed. (1991) *International Commodity Market Models*. Chapman and Hall: London.

Higgs, H. and Worthington, A. C. (2008) Stochastic price modeling of high volatility, mean-reverting, spike-prone commodities: The Australian wholesale spot electricity market. *Energy Economics*, 30(6): 3172–3185.

Hilliard, J. E. and Reis, J. (1998) Valuation of commodity futures and options under stochastic convenience yields, interest rates, and jump-diffusions in the spot. *Journal of Financial and Quantitative Analysis*, 33(1): 61–86.

Hilliard, J. E. and Reis, J. (1999) Jump processes in commodity futures prices and options pricing. *American Journal of Agricultural Economics*, 81(2): 273–286.

Jameson, R. (1995) *Managing Energy Price Risk*, 1st edition. RISK Books: London.

Jameson, R. (1997) *Managing Metals Price Risk*. RISK Books: London.

Jameson, R. (1999) *Managing Energy Price Risk*, 2nd edition. RISK Books: London.

Janczura, J. (2013) Pricing electricity derivatives within a Markov regime-switching model: a risk premium approach. *Mathematical Methods of Operations Research*, August, online publication.

Järvinen, S. (2004) Essays on Pricing Commodity Derivatives, Helsinki School of Economics A-238. http://epub.lib.aalto.fi/pdf/diss/a238.pdf

Kaminski, V., ed. (2005) *Energy Modelling: Advances in the Management of Uncertainty*, 2nd edition. RISK Books: London.

Kaminski, V. (2013) *Energy Markets*. RISK Books: London.

Kao, T-C. and Lin, C-H. (2010) Setting margin levels in futures markets: an extreme value method. *Nonlinear Analysis: Real World Applications*, 11(3): 1704–1713.

Leppard, S. (2005) *Energy Risk Management: A Non-Technical Introduction to Energy Derivatives*. RISK Books: London.

Loferski, P. J. (2010) Platinum-Group Metals. **In** United States Geological Survey 2010 Minerals Yearbook. http://minerals.usgs.gov/minerals/pubs/commodity/platinum/myb1-010-plati.pdf

Mabro, R. E., ed. (2006) *Oil in the Twenty-First Century: Issues, Challenges and Opportunities*. Oxford University Press: Oxford.

Mastro, M. (2013) *Financial Derivative and Energy Market Valuation: Theory and Implementation in Matlab*. Wiley: Hoboken, NJ.

Miltersen, K. R. and Schwartz, E. S. (1998) Pricing of options on commodity futures with stochastic term structures of convenience yields and interest rates. *Journal of Financial and Quantitative Analysis*, 33(1): 33–59.

Parker, E. and Perzanowski, M. (2010) *Commodity Derivatives: Documenting and Understanding Commodity Derivative Products*. Globe Business Publishing Ltd.

Poitras, G. (2013) *Commodity Risk Management: Theory and Application*. Routledge: London.

Reuters (2000) *An Introduction to The Commodities, Energy & Transport Markets*. Wiley: Singapore.

Riedhauser, C. (2006) *The Kirk Approximation: Going Where No Option Has Gone Before*, PG&E Internal Document (Version: September 19, 2006).

Roncoroni, A., Fusai, G. and Cummins, M. (2014) *Handbook of Multi-Commodity Markets and Products: Structuring, Trading and Risk Management*. Wiley: Chichester.

Savaiko, B. C. (1991) *Trading in Soft Commodity Futures*. Woodhead-Faulkner: Cambridge.

Schaeffer, P. V. (2008) *Commodity Modeling and Pricing: Methods for Analyzing Resource Market Behavior*. Wiley Finance: Hoboken, NJ.

Scott, N., ed. (2003) *Agribusiness and Commodity Risk: Strategies and Management*. RISK Books: London.

Serletis, A. (2007) *Quantitative and Empirical Analysis of Energy Markets*. World Scientific: Singapore.

Shiryaev, A. N., Grossinho, M. R., Oliveira, P. E. and Esquível, M. L., ed. (2006) *Stochastic Finance*. Springer: New York.

Siegel, D. R. and Siegel, D. F. (1990) *Futures Markets*. The Dryden Press: Orlando, FL.

Stace, A. W. (2007) A moment matching approach to the valuation of a volume weighted average price option. *International Journal of Theoretical and Applied Finance*, 10(1): 95–110.

Tarring, T. (2009) *Metal Bulletin's Guide to the LME*, 7th edition. Metal Bulletin Ltd: London.

Thompson, M., ed. (2001) *Base Metals Handbook: The Definitive Reference Source to the Major Base Metals*. Cambridge: Woodhead.

Trolle, A. B. and Schwartz, E. S. (2009) Unspanned stochastic volatility and the pricing of commodity derivatives. *The Review of Financial Studies*, 22(11): 4423–4461.

Tudor, J. A. (1997) Exchange-Based Metals Markets. **In** Jameson, R., ed. (1997) *Managing Metals Price Risk*. RISK Books: London.

Vecer, J. (2011) *Stochastic Finance: A Numeraire Approach*. World Scientific: Boca Raton, FL.

Wallace, N. and Evans, J., ed. (1993) *International Commodity Markets: An Australian Perspective*. Australian Bureau of Agricultural and Resource Economics: Canberra.

Warwick-Ching, T. (1993) *The International Gold Trade*. Woodhead Publishing: Cambridge.

Watkins, C. and McAleer, M. (2006) Pricing of non-ferrous metals futures on the London Metal Exchange. *Applied Financial Economics*, 16(12): 853–880.

Wolff, R. (1991) *Wolff's Guide to the London Metal Exchange*, 4th edition. Metal Bulletin Books Ltd: Worcester Park, Surrey.

Yang, X.-S. (2013) *Mathematical Modeling with Multidisciplinary Applications*. Wiley: Hoboken.

Index

Printed and bound by CPI Group (UK) Ltd, Croydon, CR0 4YY

23/04/2025

14660944-0004